MW01598708

Indianapolis Motor Speedway
1928 – 1945
The Eddie Rickenbacker Era

DENNY MILLER

authorHOUSE®

AuthorHouse™
1663 Liberty Drive
Bloomington, IN 47403
www.authorhouse.com
Phone: 833-262-8899

© *2020 Denny Miller. All rights reserved.*

*No part of this book may be reproduced, stored in a retrieval system, or
transmitted by any means without the written permission of the author.*

Published by AuthorHouse 12/17/2020

ISBN: 978-1-7283-7279-2 (sc)
ISBN: 978-1-7283-7280-8 (hc)
ISBN: 978-1-6655-0144-6 (e)

Library of Congress Control Number: 2020918665

Print information available on the last page.

*Any people depicted in stock imagery provided by Getty Images are models,
and such images are being used for illustrative purposes only.
Certain stock imagery © Getty Images.*

This book is printed on acid-free paper.

*Because of the dynamic nature of the Internet, any web addresses or links contained in
this book may have changed since publication and may no longer be valid. The views
expressed in this work are solely those of the author and do not necessarily reflect the
views of the publisher, and the publisher hereby disclaims any responsibility for them.*

DEDICATION

Fr. Glenn O'Connor
INDIANAPOLIS 500
"THE PRIEST IN THE PITS"
July 6, 1952 - March 15, 2019

Foreword

It's a humbling feeling and a great honor when I'm introduced as one of the foremost historians of the Indianapolis 500. I'm glad to say for my entire life, Race Day at the Indianapolis Motor Speedway continues to have that magical feel as my childhood Christmas mornings did growing up in the small Indiana town of Boswell.

On the night before the 500 in May 2018, at St. Elmo's restaurant in downtown Indianapolis, I was joined by Buddy Urbanski, his son Dr. Mark Urbanski, my daughter Corinna Miller and Fr. Glenn O'Connor. The question was asked, "Now that you finished your "Eddie Sachs—The Clown Prince of Racing" book, what are you going to write next?" I knew, but I certainly wanted to keep it a secret. Father Glenn said, "I think a book on Eddie Rickenbacker and his ownership of the Speedway would be very popular." I could have leaped out of my chair in excitement because that was one of the two books I had in development. I tried to act nonchalant to the suggestion, but I was thrilled that a priest- with a direct pipeline to God, thought a book on Rickenbacker's IMS was as good as I thought it would be. So immediately the other project was back-burnered.

Until this project began, my greatest expertise was "The Hulman Era" from 1946 to the present. I certainly knew the main highlights during the time frame between 1928-1941, but the more research I delved into, the more exciting this project became. Two things stood out: 1) Just how great Wilbur Shaw was as a race driver and that there can be no "Mount Rushmore of Racing" conversation without this native Hoosier being one of the ones chiseled in the mountain. And if you happen to be passionate toward the Speedway, or just like it a lot, continue to give thanks to Wilbur for saving the Indianapolis Motor Speedway from becoming a residential development following World War II. 2) Both Rex Mays and Ted Horn could have easily captured one or more of the four races (1942 thru 1945) cancelled during World War II. After reading this book, hopefully the name Rex Mays goes to the top of the "Greatest Driver Not To Have Won The Indianapolis 500" list.

I'm blessed with the new friendships that have been forged as I worked toward completing this project. I made the decision not to use photographs from this time frame but instead to showcase the artwork of the acclaimed racing artist Hector Cademartori. High quality reproductions of his artwork used in this book will be available for those passionate Indy 500 fans.

This Eddie Rickenbacker Era book is first and foremost an in-depth look of his ownership of the Indianapolis Motor Speedway from 1927-1945 and not intended to be another biography of Rickenbacker's life. A list of books of Eddie's military life or his ordeal about being lost 23 days in the South Pacific, which I highly recommend reading, follows.

Throughout the book, I listed key dates and headlines in United States history, in politics, sports and entertainment, that is intended to serve as a point-of-reference timeline throughout the Eddie Rickenbacker Era. Don't cringe on certain typos—I purposely capitalize the "R" in Race in various places as my way of showing reverence to the Indianapolis 500. Other grammar and punctuation irregularities are my humorous middle finger to those former "composition 101" profs who used so much red ink correcting my themes.

Hopefully this will be regarded as one of the definitive sources on the history of the Indianapolis Motor Speedway from 1927-1945———"The Eddie Rickenbacker Era".

GODSPEED,
DENNY MILLER

RECOMMENDED READING ON EDDIE RICKENBACKER

"Ace of Aces: The Life of Captain Eddie Rickenbacker" by H. Paul Jeffers.

"Enduring Courage, Ace Pilot Eddie Rickenbacker and the Dawn of the Age of Speed" by John F. Ross.

"Rickenbacker: An Autobiography" by Edward V. Rickenbacker.

"Seven Came Through, Rickenbacker's Full Story" by Captain Edward V. Rickenbacker.

"Fighting the Flying Circus" by Eddie Rickenbacker.

"We Thought We Heard The Angels Sing" by James Whittaker.

"Eddie Rickenbacker" by Colonel Hans Christian Adamson.

"Eddie Rickenbacker: An American Hero in the Twentieth Century" by W. Davis Lewis.

RECOMMENDED READING ON HISTORY OF THE INDIANAPOLIS 500

"Official History of the Indianapolis 500" by Donald Davidson and Rick Shafer.

"Indy 500 Recaps—The Short Chute Edition" by Pat Kennedy.

"Blood and Smoke. A True Tale of Mystery, Mayhem and Birth of the Indy 500" by Charles Leerhsen.

"Indianapolis 500. A Century of Excitement" by Ralph Kramer.

"Russ Snowberger" by John Snowberger.

"Pole Position Rex Mays" by Bob Schilling.

"Indianapolis 500 Chronicles" by Rick Popely and L. Spencer Riggs.

"100 Years, 500 Miles" by The Indianapolis Star.

"Gentleman, Start Your Engines, The Rest of the Story" by Bob Gates.

"Indy 500: More Than A Race" by Tom Carnegie.

"Pacesetter: The Complete Story" by Jerry Fisher.

"Umbrella Mike: The True Story of the Chicago Gangster Behind the Indy 500" by Brock Yates.

"Harry McQuinn, 'King of the Midgets'" by Brad T. Tinkle.

"500 Miles To Go" by Al Bloemker.

"Indy: Racing Before the 500, The Untold Story of the Brickyard" by D. Bruce Scott.

"Eddie Sachs—The Clown Prince of Racing" by Denny Miller.

BECOMING A RACE CAR DRIVER

When Eddie Rickenbacker was 12 years old, his father was killed. To help support his mother and younger siblings, he quit school to get a small job. However, his dream was to get a job working in an automobile factory. He applied five times and each time he was turned down. So he took a chance and went directly to the owner, Lee Frayer, saying, "Your foreman won't hire me, but I'm going to work here anyway. I'll work free of charge. I'll do anything. I'll sweep out." With that, to the surprise of the owner, Eddie grabbed a broom and starting to sweep the floor. Frayer was impressed with his ambition and earnestness and hired him.

One break time, Lee Frayer noticed Rickenbacker was intently studying diagrams and charts while his other workers were playing cards. He stopped to inquire what he was reading and was impressed when Eddie said he was taking an engineering correspondence course. Discovering he was well like by everyone in the plant, Frayer would increase his job responsibilities from foreman to sales branch manager.

Lee Frayer was also a race driver and he took Eddie Rickenbacker under his wing. When Frayer raced in the prestigious 1906 Vanderbilt Cup race on Long Island, New York, Eddie joined him as his riding mechanic. From that point on, Eddie was hooked and chose to become a race driver himself. He immediately displayed talent behind the steering wheel. In 1910 he would win ten races and would serve as a relief driver for Frayer in the inaugural 1911 Indianapolis 500.

CARL FISHER

Few people could rival P. T. Barnum as a showman and a promoter than Carl Fisher. At an early age he would quickly become enamored with bicycle racing then move with equal passion to racing automobiles. Carl would be at the forefront as an owner of an automobile dealership for Stoddard-Dayton in Indianapolis. Called Crazy Carl by many Indy residents, he would constantly come up with clever, innovative ideas to promote his products. His most noted gimmick was when he flew a hot-air balloon across the Indianapolis sky with a Stoddard-Dayton automobile serving as a substitute for the balloon's basket. Prominently painted on the balloon was Stoddard-Dayton. The stunt worked and a photo of the feat made the front page the following day. What locals didn't know was that, in effort to save weight, the engine had been removed. Hidden several miles away was an identical vehicle, which Fisher would triumphantly drive back to his dealership.

Fisher was a strong advocate that what the fledgling auto industry needed was a large race track, up to five miles in distance, where they could test their products at high speed. Fisher dreamed of building such a facility and shared those ideas in the November 15, 1906 issue of Motor Age magazine. To the Editor, Carl would remark:

CARL FISHER——"I note with considerable interest that you are taking up individual opinions regarding the advisability of track racing on large tracks. As you are probably aware, a large track of 3 to 5 miles in distance, with a width of 100 to 150 feet, has been a hobby of mine for the past 3 years, and I have done a great deal of work toward a track of this kind. The proposed track at French Lick fell through, for the reason that enough level ground could not be secured for a track of sufficient size. After considerable time and investment and investigation, arrangements were made with our fair board in Indianapolis for the ground for a 3-mile track, but after a careful survey it was found impossible to put more than a 2-mile track on it."

Very few people understand what an immense difference there is between a mile track and a 3-mile track, and to do this it will be necessary to have a drawing to scale of 1, 3 and 5-mile tracks in order to convey properly to the average driver the respective sizes. I have been an interested spectator in most of the big track meets and road races in this country and France—including the Vanderbilt and Bennett—and it is my opinion that the only successful racing course, and the one which will ultimately find favor with both drivers and the public, will be a 3 or 5-mile circular course.

There is no question in my mind that track racing on mile tracks is doomed. The average horse track is narrow, has fences that are dangerous, and is always dusty or muddy, and with high speed cars, where wide skids are necessary, racing becomes so dangerous that frequently the fastest cars, from a slow start or other temporary delay, gets off in the rear without chances of ever gaining the front on account of continuous seas of dust and skidding cars ahead that would make it too dangerous to attempt to pass. This condition would not exist on a 3 or 5-mile track.

To the spectators there is very little enjoyment in seeing a 25 or 50-mile road race, where immense crowds throng the course and where only fleeting glimpses can be held of the cars as they come and go down the road. There is no accommodation for the public in a race of this kind, and the thousands of dollars spent in advertising and for special privilege that go to private individuals could well come into the purse of the management of a 3 or 5-mile track. The American manufacturers annually spend thousands of dollars in building high speed racing cars to compete with French cars and without possible chance of winning, and I think this is largely due to the fact that American drivers do not have a chance to thoroughly test their cars continuously at high speed for weak spots in construction, or to become entirely familiar with and have their car under perfect control at very high speeds.

There is no question in my mind that it takes weeks and months of practice handling a car at 75, 80 and 90 miles an hour to be able to properly gauge distances, numerous road conditions, and the response of the car to such conditions. It has been my experience that quite a number of racing cars, when tested over the best roads we had in this country, seemed to have wonderful speed. There was no accurate way to time then for any distance, and the best anybody could do was to guess at what the cars were doing.

It seems to me a 5-mile track, properly laid out, without fences to endanger drivers, with proper grandstands, supply stores for gasoline and oil, and other accommodations would net for one meet such as the Vanderbilt cup race a sufficient amount to pay half of the entire cost of the track. With the present record of 52 seconds on a mile track, I am confident a 3-mile track 100 feet wide will stand a speed of 100 miles an hour, and that a 5-mile track will stand a speed of 2 miles a minute.

In diagrams I have seen of a 5-mile track it is possible any point of the curve to see in a direct line 800 feet ahead, and a curve of this kind, when gradual and continuous, is not nearly so severe as some of the short, choppy curves at Ormond beach, where a speed of 2 miles a minute was made by a couple of the contestants in the meet in the South last winter.——C. G. Fisher.

FOUNDING FATHERS

Indianapolis's version of P. T. Barnum was Carl Fisher. He had a passion for bicycle racing so he opened his own bicycle shop. Carl was an active member in the Zig-Zag Cycling Club established August 8, 1890, by fellow cycle enthusiast Arthur Newby. It was Arthur and two partners, Charles Test and Edward Fletcher, who started the Indianapolis Chain and Stamping Company to manufacture bicycle chains. Newby would also construct a quarter-mile, high-banked board track where many of the top bicyclists, including Barney Oldfield, would compete on one of the fastest tracks in America. The Zig-Zag Club became the watering hole for prominent Indianapolis business leaders in the developing automotive industry.

Fisher would join in a business venture with fellow club member James Allison to form the Prest-O-Lite Company. It quickly became a highly successful enterprise in the manufacturing of the first truly effective headlight for automobiles. Compressed acetylene gas was compressed into a canister and ignited by a sparking switch. They were mounted to the running boards of the automobiles.

Arthur Newby would sell his company for a huge profit and then became an owner of the National Motor Car and Vehicle Corporation. Two other members, the flamboyant Frank Wheeler and Stoughton Fletcher, would agree to invest in Fisher's grand idea to build a supersized speedway where manufacturers could test their product on a 400-acre plot of land about 12 miles West of Indianapolis on Crawfordsville Road.

The five gentleman entered an agreement to go into a partnership to build a two and one-half mile race track made of crushed stone and tar. Frank Wheeler was a partner with George Schebler in the Wheeler-Schebler Carburetor Company, the leading manufacturer of carburetors in the United States. Stoughton Fletcher was a prominent banker in his family's prestigious bank. Each had agreed to invest $50,000 but at the last moment Fletcher would decline to proceed in the partnership because family members felt being an owner of a race track didn't conform to their conservative banking image. Newby would decide to reduce his investment to $25,000. Therefore, Fisher and Allison would split the cost of the $75,000 shortfall of funds from Fletcher and Newby, thus becoming senior partners.

The Indianapolis Motor Speedway Company was officially formed on March 20, 1909, and work began promptly in the construction of the race track. When it became apparent that the facility would not be completed in time for their hoped-for opening date on the 4th of July, Fisher decided to stage a hot air balloon race on June 5, 1909. Nine gas-filled balloons would participate including the balloon, "Indiana", which Carl Fisher and George Bumbaugh would fly. A crowd of nearly 4,000 paid up to $1 for grandstand seats. Thousands more elected not to pay an admission fee and watched the balloons ascend from outside the Speedway grounds.

Two days of motorcycle races were scheduled for Friday August 13 and Saturday August 14 but the riders were concerned that the track's abrasive surface would cause tire blowouts. They postponed the events to Saturday August 14 and Monday August 16 (racing was not permitted on Sundays). When riders came in from their initial trial, they were covered with a white-type powder. To correct this, oil was applied to the track surface which resulted in riders returning to the pits covered in oil. After conclusion of an "East-West" race, the remaining events were cancelled.

Stung by the negative input from the motorcycle racers, Carl Fisher quickly shrugged off the negative comments and enthusiastically looked forward to the scheduled three days of racing set for the Speedway August 19-21. All told 16 racers were scheduled, mainly consisting of four-lap events with a feature race each day—August 19 Prest-O-Lite Trophy 250-Mile Race, August 20 G & J

Trophy 100-Mile Race and August 21 Wheeler-Schebler Trophy 300-Mile Race.

AUGUST 19, 1909   FIRST AUTO RACE

Louis Schwitzer, driving a Stoddard-Dayton, won the first auto race ever held on the Indianapolis Motor Speedway before a crowd of 16,000. It was a two-lap (five mile) race for Stock 161-230 cubic inches. Fisher, a local dealer of the Stoddard-Dayton, couldn't imagine a better start for his race track. Louis Chevrolet in a Buick, "Billy" Bourque in a Knox and Ray Harroun in a Marmon also scored victories on the dusty track.

Bob Burman became the first driver to win a "distance" race as he captured the Prest-O-Lite Trophy Race in which Billy Bourque and his riding mechanic Harry Holcomb were killed. On lap 58, Bourque made a quick glance to his rear and in doing so lost control of his Knox and skidded into a ditch which was beside the track. His car flipped end-over-end, tossing out both driver and mechanic. Holcomb was killed instantly when his head struck a fence post. Bourque would survive just 15 minutes before succumbing to a crushed skull, several broken ribs, and a pierced right lung. Billy Bourque became the first driver fatality at the Indianapolis Motor Speedway.

AUGUST 20, 1909   LEWIS STRANG WINS FORD TROPHY RACE

Because of the dusty conditions from the day before, the entire track was oiled to hopefully correct the problem. Seven races were scheduled for the second day at the Speedway—five races ranging in distance between five and ten miles. Winners included Lewis Strang in a Buick, Len Zengel in a Chadwick, Charlie Merz twice in a National and his teammate Johnny Aiken also captured two wins. (Arthur Newby was a co-owner of National). Carl Wright, driving a Stoddard-Dayton, won a 50-Mile event and Lewis Strang would be victorious again in the feature race of the day, the 100-Mile Ford Trophy Race.

AUGUST 21, 1909

There were four events scheduled for the final day of races. Tom Kincade started the day off with a 15-mile victory in his National. Eddie Hearne, driving a Fiat, won a ten-mile race and legendary Barney Oldfield, in a Benz, won a 25-mile event. The three-day races concluded with the 300-mile Wheeler-Schebler Trophy Race. Frank Wheeler had commissioned a seven and one-half foot silver trophy to be crafted.

Tragedy would strike for the second time in two days when 21-year old Charlie Merz's #8 National blew a right front tire and crashed through the outer fence into a crowd of people. They had failed to heed police orders to move from that area. Claude Kellum, Merz's riding mechanic, was killed as well as two spectators— James West and Homer Jolliff. Merz's car tore out five feet of stone culvert railings and came to rest upside down by a muddy creek. Miraculously Charlie survived without injury in what appeared to be a fatal crash. He had the presence of mind to shut off the engine which prevented a possible huge fire. Merz, crawling from underneath his race car, was covered with mud. His first remarks were, "For God's sake tell my mother and father I'm all right."

Merz immediately he went to check the condition of his riding mechanic and upon seeing the mangled body of Kellum, Charlie began to weep inconsolably. While sobbing he told an Indianapolis Star reporter his account of the accident.

CHARLIE MERZ——"I remember my car hitting the fence, there was a blurred vision of men falling beneath us as we swept through the air. Then the rest came in an instant. The car turned over and I found myself under it on the other side of the creek. I knew enough to stop my motor. Had I not stopped it there might have been an explosion that would have cost many more lives and my own."

For Claude Kellum, it was a day of tragic irony. He had been the riding mechanic for Johnny Aiken's #8 National, who was a teammate of Charlie Merz. Originally Herbert Lyne was riding with Merz in the #10 National when it stopped on the backstretch. Lyne took off running as fast as he could across the track infield to his pit to get gasoline. He would faint when he reached Merz pit so Kellum eagerly offered to take Herbert's place in Charlie's car.

S.R. Stevens, the Referee of the race, would order the starter to stop the race after 235 miles with Leigh Lynch the leader. He would state,

S. R. STEVENS——"Owing to the physical condition of the contestants, who had been subjected to the strain of a three days' race meet under trying climatic conditions, I deem it to the best interest of the entrants and spectators to abandon the race, therefore, I rule no race and no rewards."

Carl Fisher and James Allison knew they were going to have to come up with an alternative track surface since their use of chipped stones and tar disintegrated as the race wore on. Several options for a new surface were studied and they concluded that bricks would provide the best option taking into account harsh Indiana winters. An order was placed with the Wabash

Clay Company of Veedersburg, Indiana, to provide the bricks. On September 18, the first shipment of bricks arrived at the Speedway and by December 10 the job was completed with approximately 3,200,000 bricks laid. It was the birth of the nickname the "Brickyard". Fisher decided to host just three races—Decoration Day, 4th of July and Labor Day in 1910.

DECORATION DAY WEEKEND

MAY 27, 1910   TOM KINCADE WINS PREST-O-LITE TROPHY

24 races were scheduled for three days of racing over May 27, 28 and Decoration Day, May 30. Eight races would be held on May 27 on the new two and a half mile brick track. Louis Chevrolet would become the first winner on the brick surface capturing a two-lap event in a Buick. Ray Harroun, driving his Marmon, and Johnny Aitken, in a National, won 10-mile races. Art Greiner won a pair of five mile races in his National. Tom Kincade was the day's big winner, first capturing a 5-mile preliminary race in his National, then winning the Prest-O-Lite Trophy 100 mile race.

MAY 28, 1910   RAY HARROUN WINS WHEELER-SCHEBLER TROPHY RACE

Four races were in store for the second day at the Speedway. Johnny Aiken won the opening 10-mile event, Barney Oldfield, in a Knox, captured a 5-mile race, Howdy Wilcox, piloting a National, scored a win in a 10-mile race and Ray Harroun took the 200 mile Wheeler-Schebler Trophy Race.

MAY 30, 1910   HARROUN WINS REMY GRAND BRASSARD RACE

Ten races were on tap on Decoration Day, May 30. This was a day of entirely sprint-type racing. Five 5-mile races, six 10-mile events and the 50-mile Remy Grand Brassard were on tap. Caleb Bragg in a Fiat would win the 10-mile opening race of the day and later a five-mile event. Louis Chevrolet, in a Buick, would follow as winner in another 10-lap contest. Joe Dawson, driving a National, and Ray Harroun, steering a Marmon, captured 10-mile jaunts. Barney Oldfield, in a Knox, would best the competition in both a 5-mile and 10-mile event. Johnny Aiken would also take the top spot in a 5-mile and 10-mile race. Jack Reed finally gave Carl Fisher something to cheer about by capturing a 5-mile race in a Stoddard-Dayton. In the 50-mile feature, Ray Harroun led the field to the checkered flag. The Trophy was sponsored by Frank Remy, whose company was a magneto manufacture. The "brassard" was a specially designed arm shield to be worn by the winner.

INDEPENDENCE DAY WEEKEND

JULY 1, 1910   BILLY PIERCE CAPTURES G & J TROPHY RACE

24 races were scheduled for the three-day event leading up to the Fourth of July. Nine races were scheduled for July 1, 1910. Winners on Day One were Mortimer, Louis Chevrolet, Joe Dawson, Johnny Aitken, Harry Grant, N.J. Sutcliff, Arthur Greiner, Eddie Hearne and Billy Pearce. Billy's won the 50-mile G & J Trophy race to conclude activities for the day.

JULY 2, 1910   JOE DAWSON WINS REMY GRAND BRASSARD RACE

Nine more races were again scheduled for Day Two with a 100-mile grand finale. Capturing the checkered flag were Mortimer Roberts, Louis Chevrolet, Joe Dawson, Johnny Aitken won twice, Harry Grant, George Robertson and Art Greiner. Joe Dawson, driving a Marmon, won the 100-mile Remy Grand Brassard.

JULY 4, 1910   DAWSON WINS THE COBE TROPHY

Six races were on tap for the 4th of July including a 200-miler for the Cobe Trophy, presented by Ira Cobe, president of the Chicago Automotive Club. Louis Chevrolet, Mortimer Roberts, Louis Heineman, Art Greiner and Eddie Hearne won the day's shorter races.

In the marquee event of the day, Joe Dawson would again drive his Marmon to victory lane.

JULY 6, 1910   TOM KINCADE KILLED TESTING AT THE SPEEDWAY

Promising 23-year old Tom Kincade was killed at the Indianapolis Motor Speedway while on a 50-mile test run. Kincade's National apparently got sideways, skidded through a ditch twenty feet outside the track, then crashed through a wooden fence. His head was crushed and his right arm and shoulder were broken. Tom and his teammate Johnny Aitken were testing for National. It was ten minutes before Aitken and Charlie Merz arrived at the accident scene. Kincade, thrown from the car into the wood fence, was partially pinned under his race car. Johnny Aitken and Tom Kincade were roommates and constant companions. They were nickname "The Indigo Twins."

LABOR DAY WEEKEND

SEPTEMBER 3, 1910   HOWDY WILCOX WINS REMY GRAND BRASSARD RACE

Nine races were run on September 3, 1910. Louis Edmunds, Eddie Hearne and Howdy Wilcox were victorious twice each, with Wilcox capturing the main event, the Remy Grand Brassard 100-miler. Also winning were Ray Harroun, Johnny Aitken and Walter Emmons.

SEPTEMBER 5, 1910   JOHNNY AITKEN WINS LABOR
DAY 200-MILER

Johnny Aitken won the day's feature 200-mile Labor Day race as well as a five-mile race. Also receiving the checkered flag in support races were Walter Emmons, Ralph DePalma, Lee Frayer, Ray Harroun, Howdy Wilcox, W. J. Barndollar and Eddie Hearne.

The Founding Fathers had seen a decline in attendance throughout the year and there was a bit of boredom amongst the fans with all the numerous short races. In a radical departure, the announced that they would run just one race in 1911 for 500 miles on Decoration Day May 30. The winner was guaranteed a whopping $12,000. They were gratified that their gamble paid off as 46 cars filed entries and 42 cars would qualify for the first International Sweepstakes 500-Mile Race.

Carl Fisher and James Allison, majority owners of the Indianapolis Motor Speedway, hosted the 500-Mile Race from 1911 to 1927. (No races were held in 1917 and 1918 due to World War I). During this 15 years, there would be numerous, high drama "story lines" that would quickly make the Indianapolis 500 the most important race world wide. When Eddie Rickenbacker purchased the track in the autumn of 1927, the Speedway was already steeped in traditions with thrilling highlights. Each Indianapolis 500 Race holds its own unique memories.

1911 INDIANAPOLIS 500

Carl Fisher's gamble that a mega, once-a-year spectacular offering the largest purse in racing, would attract fans in droves and an international field of entries. 46 cars submitted an official entries. To qualify for the race, a driver would have to achieve a 75 m.p.h. speed from a flying start over a quarter of a mile on the main straightaway. 42 cars would qualify for the race. The starting lineup was based on the date the Indianapolis Motor Speedway received their entry. The first application arrived on October 22, 1910 from the J.I. Case Thrashing Company of Racine, Wisconsin. They nominated Lewis Strang as driver. Being the first entrant meant Strang would be starting the Race on the Pole Position and carry #1 on his race car.

All entrants would carry a riding mechanic to alert his driver of approaching cars as well as other mechanical issues that may occur. The exception was the yellow #32 Marmon Wasp driven by the acknowledged 1910 National Champion Ray Harroun. Ray fancied himself more of an engineer and builder than race driver. He had retired from driving at the end of the 1910 season but was persuaded to drive in the 500 by the Marmon owners. Harroun reluctantly accepted with the provision that he could have a relief driver so he could take a mid-race rest. Cyrus Patschke was tabbed for that role.

The calculating Harroun figured the less weight of a riding mechanic would give him an advantage over the

500 mile haul. When his competitors got wind of his intention, they cried foul. Ray somewhat neutralized their complaints by mounting a 3-inch by 8-inch mirror mounted above his dashboard—quite possibly the first rear-view mirror to be used on a race car. Harroun also conducted several test runs at different speed and he discovered that he could obtain nearly twice the mileage out of his tires by driving at a 75 mile pace compared to 80 mph. He decided that he would drive a consistent 75 mile pace regardless what speeds his competition would be averaging during the race.

On Decoration Day, Tuesday May 30, 1911 over 80,000 fans were in attendance to see the first 500-Mile race, which was officially called the International 500-Mile Sweepstakes Race. Aerial bombs exploded at 10 a.m. signaling the start of the Race. Carl Fisher, driving a Stoddard-Dayton Pace Car (Fisher owned the local Stoddard-Dayton dealership), paced the field down to receive the red flag (the green flag did not become the flag to start the race until 1930). This quite possibly was the first rolling start in auto racing. The front row was comprised of #1 Lewis Strang, #2 Ralph De Palma, #3 Harry Endicott and #4 Johnny Aitken.

Johnny Aitken, driving a National, would go down in history as the first person to lead a lap in the Indianapolis 500. In fact, he led laps 1 to 4 before being passed by the wealthy Spencer Wishart in his Mercedes Grand Prix car. Fred Belcher would then charge to the lead for 4 circuits before he was passed by socialite David Bruce-Brown (his family was listed New York's "Fashionable 400"). He would hold the top spot for the next six laps until Ralph De Palma would overtake him in his #2 Simplex. However, Bruce-Brown would re-take the lead and remain atop the field for 81 laps during the first half of the Race.

On lap 13, Art Greiner, driving an Amplex, overturned and his riding mechanic Sam Dixon of Chicago was killed. Greiner would forever be known as the first race driver to finish last in the 500-Mile race.

As he theorized, tire wear and blowouts caused many of the front runners into the pits. Ralph Mulford, a Sunday school teacher, had the misfortune to blow a tire as he entered turn one. He had to take the agonizing, slow drive back to the pits for new rubber. And while this was unfolding, Ray Harroun maintained his steady 75 mph pace and eventually took the lead for his first time on lap 103. Ray would continue on top through lap 137 until Mulford wrestled the lead away for five laps from laps 138-142. It was short-lived as Harroun would lead the rest of the way minus five laps Ralph was on top from 177-181.

After 6 hours and 42 minutes, with an average 74.602 mph, Ray Harroun received the checkered flag from Fred Wagner with Ralph Mulford second, David Bruce-Brown third, Spencer Wishart fourth, Joe Dawson fifth and Ralph De Palma sixth. Lee Frayer, driving the #30

Columbus Buggy Company Special, finished 13th with relief help from Eddie Rickenbacker. Cyrus Patschke drove approximately 35 laps for Harroun during the mid-race but would not be credited as a co-winner.

A controversy would occur after the finish with Lozier team convinced their driver, Ralph Mulford, won the race. However, the genial Mulford refused to file an official protest and two days later Carl Fisher ordered the official timing and scoring records destroyed. Sportsmanlike, Ralph congratulated Harroun for his win but would always claim until the day he died on October 23, 1973 that he won the race.

Fisher and Allison's gamble to conduct just one race with a large purse paid off. They were thrilled over the large turnout and enthusiasm showed by race-goers and promptly announced they were doubling the prize money for next year's Race to $50,000. Ray Harroun, earning $27,550 for his victory, would again retire from driving. And Marmon, ecstatic over the publicity of winning the 500-Mile Race and the resulting increase in sales of their passenger cars, announced they would no longer compete in the 500-Mile Race.

JULY 20, 1911 LEWIS STRANG KILLED IN
         PASSENGER CAR

1911 Pole Setter Lewis Strang would die in freak passenger accident while he was driving a Case automobile carrying the technical committee during the

Wisconsin Automotive Association's annual endurance tour on July 20, 1911. Strang, manager of the Case Racing team of the J.I. Case Company of Racine, Wisconsin, was considered such a reckless driver that his passengers refused to continue to ride with him after their stop in La Crosse, Wisconsin. Fellow driver Joe Jagersberger, Lester Clark and J.W. Tufts took their places. Before Louis's departure he boasted he "would show them all the fast way into Milwaukee."

As he approached Blue River, Wisconsin, Lewis swerved to avoid a collision with a wagon. His automobile would crash down a 30-foot embankment. His three passengers jumped from the vehicle and were not injured. The 26-year old Strang was killed instantly. Just the previous week he had told friends, "I'll never be killed in a race. If I get it at all, it will be on the road."

Some expressed the opinion he was "courting death" and suicidal. Friends thought he was seeking death after domestic issues ended his marriage with the beautiful actress-wife Louise Alexander two years ago. He became noticeably more aggressive on the race track and reckless on the highways. William Pickens, the former manager of Strang, discounted the suicide motive stating, "It was not anything about a woman. It was just a case of a bad road and a bad arm." Strang had broken his arm and dislocated an ankle in a race in Kenosha, Wisconsin on June 18 when his car crashed through a fence. The passengers indicated that they attributed the accident to a sudden caving in of the roadway.

Nearby farmers assisted Joe Jagersberger in recovering the body. When it was apparent that he was deceased, Joe collapsed and sobbed continuously for several minutes. Jagersberger would say, "I can hardly realize that Lewis is dead. At Indianapolis, I was spilled out going eighty-five miles an hour and escaped without a scratch and here is poor Lewis killed in a reliability run in which he is not even a competitor." Lewis Strang was inducted into the Indianapolis Motor Speedway Hall of Fame in 1982.

Preston Hubbanks was the driver of the other vehicle. He gave his account of the accident. "My wife said there was a machine coming. The road at this point is exceedingly narrow, but I pulled over to the right side as far as precaution would permit. The machine came along-side of us, when suddenly the road began to give way under it and turned over the bank. It was all done in an instant and how the other three occupants ever got out of the machine is a mystery to me. The car was just creeping along at the time."

1912 INDIANAPOLIS 500

There was the "buzz" over the upcoming running of the second International 500-Mile Sweepstakes Race even though there was a considerable drop to 29 entries. 24 would qualify for the 500 by having to post a speed of 75 mph lap around the oval. Gil Anderson would start on the Pole flanked by rookie Len Zengel, Teddy Tetzlaff and Ralph De Palma. Rookie Eddie Rickenbacker would start 13th in the Firestone-Columbus Special.

Teddy Tetzlaff would grab the opening lead for the first two laps before being reeled in by Ralph DePalma, who would go on to dominate the Race like few ever in the history of the Indianapolis Motor Speedway. Ralph would have a 5 1/2 lap lead as he began his 197th of 200 laps when his powerful Mercedes started to slow down, his motor billowing smoke. His car would come to a complete stop in turn four with a broken connecting rod. De Palma and his riding mechanic Rupert Jeffkins emerged from the car and began pushing the heavy Mercedes toward the starting line to a thunderous applause from 75,000 race attendees. Many race fans were of the opinion he was on his final lap and just need to push their car past the start/finish line to get the checkered flag as the winner. In reality, it would have been the beginning of his final lap.

22-year of Joe Dawson of Indianapolis, driving a National, would eventually make up the laps in arrears, to win the race. He would officially be credited leading just two laps—laps 199 and 200. Don Herr had served as Dawson's relief driver for laps 108-144. Teddy Tetzlaff finished second, Hughie Hughes third and Charlie Merz fourth. De Palma would be credited with an 11th place finish, out after 198 laps. Eddie Rickenbacker would finish 21st dropping out of the Race with a broken intake valve on lap 43.

The handsome millionaire David Bruce-Brown's day ended early departing from the race after just 24 laps to finish 22nd of the 24-car starting field. He would now give total focus to the October Vanderbilt Cup race to be held on the new Wauwatosa road course outside of Milwaukee. David had been victorious in the 1910 and 1911 Vanderbilt Cup races held in Savannah, Georgia. If he could capture this year's race, he would take permanent possession of the prestigious Vanderbilt Cup trophy.

OCTOBER 1, 1912   DAVID BRUCE-BROWN KILLED

As David Bruce-Brown was driving his Fiat at 90 mph on a practice run, the fastest time posted of the day, his left rear tire blew out on a narrow section of the course. The wealthy, young New Yorker racer catapulted high in the air throwing both Bruce-Brown and his riding mechanic Tony Scudalari from their car and across the track, landing in a adjoining field. The semi-conscious Bruce-Brown suffered a fractured skull and a broken left leg. Surgeons at Trinity Hospital trephined both sides of his skull in a futile to save his life but he would die three hours later of a cerebral hemorrhage. Tony Scudalari's skull was crushed, his body severely lacerated and his right arm broken. He would die later in the week. David Bruce-Brown would be inducted into the Indianapolis Motor Speedway Hall of Fame in 1980.

1913 INDIANAPOLIS 500

90,000 race fans watched French driver Jules Goux, driving a Peugeot, win the 3rd annual International 500-Mile Race Sweepstakes in a most dominant win over the youthful millionaire Spencer Wishart. Caleb Bragg had started the race on the Pole Position. Under the guidance of pit manager Johnny Aitkin, Goux led a total of 138 laps in his maiden trip to the Speedway. A broken magneto strap on the 188th lap robbed Gil Anderson of second place in his Stutz car. Then Charlie Merz appeared to have second place all sewed up, until his car caught fire on the 199th lap. He would drive the final circuit with his car ablaze as his riding mechanic, Harry Martin, crawled out on the hood and attempted to extinguish the fire with his jacket. Youthful Wishart passed Merz to finish second. On June 26, 1913 Martin would be killed instantly during in a test run at the Speedway. He allegedly ignored the orders of his car owner, Harry Stutz, for Martin to slow down.

During the race Jules Goux and his riding mechanic, Emil Begin, consumed four 4/5 pints of champagne as they took turns to quench their thirst. Some of the sparkling wine served as a mouth wash to hydrate their parched throats. While celebrating his victory Goux would proclaim, "but for the wine, I would have never been able to drive this race!"

1914 INDIANAPOLIS 500

After last year when the rookie Frenchman Jules Goux won the race, rookie driver Rene Thomas made it two consecutive wins for French drivers as he drove his #16 Delage to victory over fellow rookie Arthur Duray. Eddie Rickenbacker started 23rd in the #42 Duesenberg and finished 10th. Because of the liberties Jules Goux and his riding mechanic took consuming four bottles of champagne during last year's race, a new rule for this year's race banned the consumption of all alcohol beverages while participating in the 500-Mile Race.

The Pole Position went to Jean Chassagne with Teddy Tetzlaff second and Howdy Wilcox third. Ralph De Palma withdrew from the race, very concerned about the severe vibrations he was experiencing while driving the car in practice. He was convinced the engine would not last for the entire distance. Ray Gilhooley was chosen to drive the car. Ray was allegedly fearless and had earned a negative reputation as an erratic driver on the track. Many of his competitors feared him because of his unpredictably. Gilhooley would crash on lap 42 and be credited with a 27th place finish. Attendance grew to 110,000 spectators.

AUGUST 22, 1914   SPENCER WISHART KILLED

On August 22, 1914, while leading the Elgin National Road Race at Elgin, Illinois, Spencer Wishart was killed when his Mercer race car somersaulted through a picket fence and crashed into a tree. He would die shortly afterwards. His riding mechanic Joe Jenter and five spectators were injured. Wishart had been recently married to Miss Louise McGowan of Indianapolis. His bride of two months was at his side at his time of death. Just before his passing, Spencer awoke and would say "Louise".

Wishart, the son of a New York millionaire, quit playing polo to become a race driver and quickly emerged as one of the finest racers in America. Spectators removed an old barn door to use it as a makeshift stretcher. They carried Spencer to an automobile and rushed him to a nearby emergency hospital.

1915 INDIANAPOLIS 500

This year the racing gods smiled on Ralph DePalma as he powered his #2 Mercedes to victory over rookie Dario Resta. Gil Anderson would come home in third place. Ralph would lead two times for 132 laps. Eddie Rickenbacker would start and finish 19th in the #23 Maxwell. In 1915, May 30 would fall on Sunday so Carl Fisher scheduled the race for Saturday May 29. However, the weather did not cooperate as heavy rains fell during the days leading up to Saturday. The grounds were flooded so the race was move back to Monday, May 31, in an effort to dry the infield. Attendance dropped to 60,000.

APRIL 8, 1915   BOB BURMAN KILLED

On April 8, 1916 Bob Burman, one of the most famous early era race cars drivers, was killed while competing in the third annual Corona, California road race. Riding in second place and charging hard after race leader Eddie O'Donnell, "Wild Bob" would lose control of his race car on his 97th lap. Bob's car would plow into an area of spectators killing W.H. Speer, a Corona policeman, and injuring fifteen race fans. Burman's riding mechanic, Eric Schroeder, was killed instantly. "Wild Bob" would be transported 12 miles from the race course's temporary medical tent to Riverside Hospital. He would succumb at 6:10 p.m. of a crushed skull, multiple fractures of his left leg and several cracked ribs. His wife was by his bedside at his moment of death. Bob Burman was inducted into the Indianapolis Motor Speedway Hall of Fame in 1954.

1916

Eddie Rickenbacker

Started 2nd. Led Laps 1-9

1916 INDIANAPOLIS 500

In what has been attributed to the war raging on the European continent, the 500-Mile Race was being reduced in its distance to 300 miles. Not actually true. Carl Fisher believed the shorter race would appeal to more fans. The starting time was moved from 10 a.m. to 1:30 p.m. Fisher would also schedule a September race, the Harvest Auto Classic, which would consist of three races of varying distances. Johnny Aiken returned to the cockpit after a four year absence and would start on the Pole. In the number two spot would be Eddie Rickenbacker in his #5 Maxwell with Gil Anderson third and Dario Resta starting fourth.

At the start of the race, Eddie Rickenbacker would jump to the lead and maintain the top position for the first nine laps. However, his #5 Maxwell would drop out of the race with steering issues before he could complete another lap. Johnny Aitken would then inherit the top spot for the next eight circuits. It would be on lap 18 that Dario Resta would take the lead and never be challenged from then on—leading 103 out of 120 laps. Wilbur D' Alene, driving in his first 500, finished second and Ralph Mulford would come home in third place. 21 race cars would start the race with seven owned by the Indianapolis Motor Speedway. Attendance was estimated at 83,000 fans.

SEPTEMBER 9, 1916   HARVEST CLASSIC

The Speedway's decision to reduce the Indianapolis 500 to 300 miles and to host the September 10 Harvest Classic did not excite the fans as they had hoped. Only 15,000 spectators attended the autumn event. Johnny Aitken would be victorious in all three races—besting Howdy Wilcox in the initial 20-mile race, edging Hughie Hughes in a close finish in a 50-mile race, then capturing the 100-mile championship race finale in dramatic fashion.

The main event was full of high drama as Aitken closely battled Eddie Rickenbacker for the entire race. In the waning stages of the race Johnny Aitken's Peugeot broke a steering arm. Just as he prepared to head to his pit, he noticed Rickenbacker's right rear wheel wobble. Eddie ignored his pit crew's order to stop and continued his fast pace. With two laps remaining, the wheel broke and the car's axle dropped onto the track causing his racer to spin into the wall. Both Rickenbacker and his riding mechanic were uninjured. Johnny elected to stay on the course to nurse his crippled car home ahead of the hard charging Hughes, who had moved from fourth to second.

DECEMBER 4, 1916   HUGHIE HUGHES STRUCK BY RACE CAR

On December 4, 1916, a bizarre accident took the life of the popular Hughie Hughes at Uniontown, Pennsylvania Speedway. The Englishman had escaped possible

32

serious injury when he deliberately steered his car into the outer fence to avoid a collision with a car that had spun in front of him. As he made his way back to the scorer's stand, to the thunderous applause for his bravery, he began to describe the cause of his crash to his car owner, Chicago millionaire J.C. Hoskins. As they were speaking, Frank Galvin's Premier, speeding at over 100 mph on the board race track, lost control and headed directly toward the press stand less than 20 feet away. Hughes spotted Galvin's racer heading in their direction and he grabbed Hoskins's wrist to alert him of the looming danger. J.C. would dive head first to the ground and his action saved his life. Hughie would be struck and was killed instantly. Both Galvin and his riding mechanic were also killed.

J.C. Hopkins, distraught over the loss of his friend, told the Uniontown, Pennsylvania Morning Herald how Hughes saved his life.

J.C. HOPKINS——"I had heard that Hughie had been killed and was so surprised and glad to see that the report was untrue and that he had escaped that I rushed up to congratulate him.

"I owe my life to Hughes. Standing near the press box with Richard Adams and Hughes, I was warmly grasping Hughes by the hand, when with a warning twitch of his wrist, I glanced up and around, as I was standing with my back toward the track and saw the car bearing down on us three. I threw myself flat upon the ground on my face and was struck by pieces of wreckage from the press stand. After it was all over I found myself 20 feet from the car. Hughes had been knocked 15 feet past me and was lying on the ground breathing his last. Had it not been for the timely twitch of from Hughes, I would have been a victim, as I was nearer the machine than he was."

Carl Fisher and James Allison decided for 1917 to return the race to its original distance of 500 miles but on March 23, 1917 Allison announced the 500-Mile Race had been cancelled because the United States was on the verge of war. He would state, "Sport has no right in the minds of Americas when their country needs their attention." He would offer the entire Indianapolis Motor Speedway's facilities to the government as an aeronautic station and offer to convert his factory from the manufacture of racing engine to making airplane motors.

OCTOBER 15, 1918   JOHNNY AITKEN DIES FROM
SPANISH INFLUENZA

The Spanish Influenza was ravaging America and Europe in 1917 and 1918. On October, October 15, 1918, 33-year old Johnny Aitken died of bronchial pneumonia contracted from Spanish Influenza in his home at 4033 College Avenue in Indianapolis. He still holds the record as the most winningest driver at the Speedway. Aitken, taken ill ten days prior, appeared to be recovering from the influenza before pneumonia set in. His condition worsened during the evening Monday October 14 and he would succumb early next morning.

An expert mechanic, Aitken was vice president of the Allison Experimental Company. In 1981, Johnny Aitken was inducted into the Indianapolis Motor Speedway Hall of Fame.

EDDIE RICKENBACKER'S MILITARY CITATIONS

America's Ace of Aces, Eddie Rickenbacker, would receive seven Distinguished Service Cross citations.

FIRST DISTINGUISHED SERVICE CROSS CITATION

The Distinguished Service Cross is presented to Edward Vernon Rickenbacker, Captain (Air Service), US Army, for extraordinary heroism in action near Montsec, France, April 29, 1918. Captain Rickenbacker attacked an enemy Albatross monoplane, and after a vigorous fight in which he followed his foe into German territory, he succeeded in shooting it down near Vigneulles-les-Hatton Chatel. General Orders NO. 32, W.D.,1919.

SECOND DISTINGUISHED SERVICE CROSS CITATION

The Distinguished Service Cross is presented to Edward Vernon Rickenbacker, Captain (Air Service), U.S. for extraordinary heroism in action over Richecourt, France, on May 17, 1918. Captain Rickenbacker attacked three Albatros enemy planes, shooting one down in the vicinity of Richecourt, France, and forcing the others to retreat over their own lines. General Orders No. 32, W.D., 1919.

THIRD DISTINGUISHED SERVICE CROSS CITATION

The Distinguished Service Cross is presented to Edward Vernon Rickenbacker, Captain (Air Service), US Army, for extraordinary heroism in action over St. Michael, France, on May 22, 1918. Captain Rickenbacker attacked three Albatros monoplanes 4,000 meters over St. Michael, France. He drove them back into German territory, separated one from the group, and shot it down near Flirey. General Orders No. 32, W.D. 1919.

FOURTH DISTINGUISHED SERVICE CROSS CITATION

The Distinguished Service Cross is presented to Edward Vernon Rickenbacker, Captain (Air Service), US Army, for extraordinary heroism in action over Boise Rate, France, on May 28, 1918. Captain Rickenbacker sighted a group of two battle planes and four monoplanes, German planes, which he at once attacked vigorously, shooting down one and dispersing the others. General Orders No. 32, W.D., 1919.

FIFTH DISTINGUISHED SERVICE CROSS CITATION

The Distinguished Service Cross is presented to Edward Vernon Rickenbacker, Captain (Air Service), US Army, for extraordinary heroism in action on May 30, 1918. 4,000 meters over Jaulny, France, Captain Rickenbacker attacked a group of five enemy planes. After a violent battle, he shot down one plane and drove the others away. General orders No. 32, W.D., 1919.

SIXTH DISTINGUISHED SERVICE CROSS CITATION

The Distinguished Service Cross is presented to Edward Vernon Rickenbacker, Captain (Air Service), US Army, for extraordinary heroism in action in the region of Villecy, France, September 14, 1918. Captain Rickenbacker attacked four Fokker enemy planes at an altitude of 3,000 meters. After a sharp and hot action, he succeeded in shooting one down in flames and dispersing the other three. General Orders No. 32, W.D., 1919.

SEVENTH DISTINGUISHED
SERVICE CROSS CITATION

The Distinguished Service Cross is presented to Edward Vernon Rickenbacker, Captain, (Air Service), US Army, for extraordinary heroism in action in the region of Bois-de-Wavrille, France, September 15, 1918. Captain Rickenbacker encountered six enemy planes, who were in the act of attacking four Spads, which were below them. Undeterred by their superior numbers, he unhesitatingly attacked them and succeeded in shooting one down in flames and completely breaking the formation of the others. General Orders No. 32, W.D., 1919.

1919 INDIANAPOLIS 500

World War I was over and fans were starved for action on the Brickyard as 120,000 were in attendance. The Race had a patriotic name—The 7th Liberty 500-Mile Sweepstakes. Eddie Rickenbacker, America's Ace of Aces, had retired as a race driver to pursue business interests that titans of industry and finance dangled at him. However, he would accept Carl Fisher's invitation to serve as this year's Honorary Referee. Rickenbacker was truly honored and cancelled a speaking engagement to be able to perform this duty.

EDDIE RICKENBACKER——"I deem it a great honor
to officiate as referee in

the Liberty Sweepstakes Race, because it is the first big race since the war, and because it is on a track that has been one of the crucibles in which the gasoline engine has been refined. The lessons learned on the bricks at Indianapolis had as much to do with perfecting of engines for the airplanes, motor cars and trucks that played such an important part of winning of the Great War. Although it has been two years since I engaged in competition my interests in the speed sport remains, and I welcome the opportunity to play even a small part in the greatest race of the year."

Aerial bombs exploded at every five minute interval signaling the start of the 500-Mile Race was growing near. Eddie Rickenbacker would be the passenger in the Packard Pace Car driven by J. G. Vincent, vice-president of engineering of the Packard Motor Car Company.

1914 Indianapolis 500 winner Rene Thomas would start the race from the Pole Position with Howdy Wilcox starting second and for the first time there would be 33 cars in the starting field. It came as no real surprise to the that Ralph DePalma would jump to the front from the get-go. Driving the #4 Packard, Ralph would lead the first 65 laps. Louis Chevrolet would assume the lead for nine laps before DePalma would re-take the Race lead through lap 102. From that point on Howdy Wilcox, driving a Peugeot, would take command and go on to lead the remainder of the Race—laps 103-200—in an Indianapolis Speedway Team race car. Eddie Hearne would finish second with 1913 Indy 500 winner Jules Goux, also in an IMS-owned Peugeot third. Ralph DePalma held the top spot for 93 of the first 102 laps before tire problems necessitated in lengthy pit stops. He would settle for a disappointing 6th place finish.

Two race drivers and a mechanic were killed during the Race. On lap 44 rookie Arthur Thurman, driving the re-built Duesenberg #18 Thurman Special, lost a wheel as he entered the NE turn. His car swerved into the inner retaining wall, then overturned three times. Tossed from his race car, he would die within ten minutes. Nicholas Molinaro, Thurman's riding mechanic, suffered a fractured skull but he would survive after long, painful recovery. Fellow drivers stated that Arthur had been lacking control of his car the last few laps. Before the start of the Race, Thurman had expressed to some close friends his fear about driving on such a big, fast track. Eddie Rickenbacker would comment on his accident.

EDDIE RICKENBACKER——"It was Thurman's first event on the Speedway and his initial appearance in so fast a field of starters. Arthur was doing his best to dog the leaders and the pace of experience was evidently too much for the courageous novice."

On lap 96, rookie Louis LeCocq's Roamer Special would turn over and catch fire when the gas tank burst in the SE turn. Horrified spectators watched as the car burned for five minutes as guards and spectators tried to extinguish the flames. Both LeCocq and his riding mechanic, wealthy Robert Bandini from Los Angeles, perished in the inferno. Both were pinned under their race car. Louis drove the Roamer which race driver Roscoe Sarles owned. Roscoe had been impressed with his driving skills on the West Coast and offered him his car after he was selected to drive #28 for Barney Oldfield. (Ironically Sarles would finish 33rd, dropping out after just 8 laps.)

1920 INDIANAPOLIS 500

There was great post-war enthusiasm from the crowd of over 120,000 who were in attendance to witness the first race of the new decade. Ralph DePalma would win the Pole Position under the new qualification requirement that ever car must complete a four-lap qualifying run. Joe Boyer would start second and Louis Chevrolet third. Only 23 cars would start the race.

Joe Boyer would lead the first eleven laps and control the first half of the race leading on four occasions for 93 laps. He regained the lead from Rene Thomas on lap 70 and held to top spot through lap 107. Again Rene surged back out front for the next five circuits before Ralph De Palma muscled his #2 Ballot Special to the lead. DePalma looked as if he would become the first two-time winner, leading by a two lap margin—out in front from laps 113 through 186, when his motor would catch fire. Ralph's car stalled on lap 187. Believing his Uncle's car had ran out of gas, his riding mechanic/ nephew, Pete DePaolo, would hop out and run back to the pits for a can of gasoline. To his amazement, DePalma was able to get his car rolling again.

Gaston Chevrolet, running a consistent race, now found himself atop the field. Joe Boyer's fine effort would end on lap 192 when he crashed and turned over on the backstretch as he tried to avoid a skidding competitor. Boyer and his riding mechanic were uninjured. Joe would finish out of the money in 12th position, but would collect $9500 in lap prize money. (The Speedway prize money was for the Top Ten finishers only). Gaston would run out of fuel on lap 197 but he was able to coast into his pit and take on just enough gasoline to complete the distance without surrendering the lead to Rene Thomas, now running second. Roscoe Sarles in the #5 Monroe Special would crash on lap 58 then later relieve Bennett Hill, only to crash again on his 115th circuit.

NOVEMBER 25, 1920   GASTON CHEVROLET & EDDIE
                      O'DONNELL KILLED

On Thanksgiving Day, November 25, 1920, Gaston Chevrolet and Eddie O'Donnell were killed on the Beverly Hills Speedway high-banked board track. On lap 162, Chevrolet was in an intense battle with O'Donnell with Gaston on the lower part of the track and Eddie on the high side. As Chevrolet rapidly approached Joe Thomas's race car, he moved slightly to his right to pass him. As he was doing that, O'Connell was moving slightly down from the top portion of the race track. Their cars tangled causing Chevrolet to shoot toward the top of the track tearing out over 50 feet of heavy timber guard rail. The cars then slid upside down toward the bottom of the race track. O'Connell's car rolled over twice, sliding downward, and would come to rest upside down at the base of the incline.

The 28-year old Gaston was killed almost instantly by a broken neck and O'Connell would die the next morning of a fractured skull as well as two broken arms. Eddie's riding mechanic, 26-year old Lyall Jolls, would die soon of a broken neck as well. He was engaged to be married to Miss May Esch, who would have the unpleasant task to inform Lyall's mother that her son had been killed. Chevrolet's riding mechanic, John Bresnahan, escaped with minor injuries. Gaston's wife, the former Miss Marguerite Bueron of Brooklyn, New York, was a spectator at the race. Gaston Chevrolet was inducted into the Indianapolis Motor Speedway Hall of Fame in 1964, 12 years after his brother Louis had been enshrined into the Hall of Fame in 1952.

The 33-year old O'Donnell's foray into racing began as a riding mechanic with Eddie Rickenbacker in the Duesenberg. When Rick left to join the Peugeot team, O'Donnell took over as driver and eventually team captain of the Duesenberg race team. On July 22, 1917, O'Donnell's arm was shattered in a crash at the Kansas City Speedway. Doctors had to re-break his arm several times on the operating table to set it properly. Roscoe Sarles, driving the #10 Duesenberg, was victorious in the race. With the escalating prices of Beverly Hills real estate, the Speedway was torn down in 1924.

MAY 27, 1921   FRANK WHEELER COMMITS SUICIDE

On May 27, 1921, Frank Wheeler, one of the four founders of the Indianapolis Motor Speedway, committed suicide at 7 a.m. Wheeler shot himself with a shotgun in a bathroom of his home at 147 West Riverside Drive,

Indianapolis. Frank had been despondent over the suicide of his close friend Seymour Avery on February 28 after a lengthy illness. Complications from an 18-year battle with diabetes added to his medical woes. The 57-year old Wheeler discharged his double barrel shotgun by pulling both triggers simultaneously, blowing away the left side of his head. Dr. D. L. Kahn, Frank's personal physician, presented his idea on Wheeler's suicide motive.

DR. D.L. KAHN   "Although his business and estate was in excellent condition, he was prone to worry over the business outlook until I believe that I am safe in saying that he was on the verge of a severe nervous breakdown."

Frank Wheeler was president of the Wheeler-Schebler Carburetor Company, one of the largest manufacturers of gasoline engine carburetors in the United States. Wheeler would often boast he lost and made two fortunes. Several years ago, he divested his shares of stock in the Indianapolis Motor Speedway, in part, to build the Minneapolis Speedway.

1921 INDIANAPOLIS 500

Tommy Milton, who raced with eyesight in only one eye, would win the 1921 Indianapolis 500 driving for Louis Chevrolet before a crowd that was estimated to be between 135,000 to 150,000. Roscoe Sarles made up for the embarrassment of crashing two different race cars in last year's 500-Mile Race and finished second two laps behind Milton. Rookie Percy Ford finished third. Ralph DePalma would capture back-to-back Pole Positions with Sarles starting second and Joe Boyer on the outside of row one. This would be the first year where they would start the race with cars three abreast. Harry C. Stutz would be the Pace Car driver for his H.C.S. 6 model.

Ralph DePalma dominated the first half of the race leading three times for 108 laps. Ralph's #4 Ballot Special would be sidelined with a broken connecting rod on lap 112. Tommy Milton took the lead on lap 111 and led the remainder of the race.

JULY 1921   RICKENBACKER MOTOR COMPANY

The Rickenbacker Motor Company was incorporated in July 1921. Barney Everitt decided to start another car company. He sought permission from Eddie Rickenbacker if he could name his new automobile after the American war hero. They would use Rickenbacker's squadron insignia "Hat in the Ring" as the car logo. Everitt would name Rickenbacker vice president and director of sales. Barney would also bring in a long-time business associate, Walter Flanders, to supervise the design of the automobile.

On January 1922, the first of the Rickenbacker touring cars, coupes and sedans made their debut at the New York Auto Show. Their plant was located on Michigan Avenue in Detroit with the initial goal to manufacture 200 cars per day. A new plant at 4815 Cabot Avenue in Detroit was built to up production to 500 cars a day. Problems started when Walter Flanders was injured on June 15, 1923, while he attempted to pass another vehicle en route to his home. He suffered a broken leg and internal injuries. Three days later he died of kidney failure. Rickenbacker and Everitt began to bicker on design features of the car to the point Eddie resigned from the company in September, 1926. With the namesake no longer associated with the company, the business would go into bankruptcy in February 1927.

1922 INDIANAPOLIS 500

There had been a growing feud between Tommy Milton and Jimmy Murphy. Milton's victory in last year's 500-Mile Race only intensified Murphy's obsession to win the race himself and upstage Tommy. And he would surpass Milton's 1921 accomplishments—first by capturing the Pole Position, then by winning the race in dominating fashion.

Eddie Rickenbacker was chosen by Carl Fisher to be the Starter for the 1922 Indianapolis 500 and an appreciative crowd welcomed back the former driver and military hero. 135,000 fans watched Barney Oldfield, driving the National Sextet Pace Car, lead a front row of Jimmy Murphy, rookie Harry Hartz and Ralph DePalma down for the start of the 500-Mile Race. Most people thought DePalma would jump off to an immediate lead as had been his customary way to attack the Race. But instead, Jimmy Murphy would lead from the start through lap 77. He surrendered the lead to a pair of rookies, Leon Duray on laps 75-76 and Harry Hartz laps 77-83.

Pete De Paolo took command for three laps before Harry Hartz showed his strength by moving to the lead on laps 87-121. Jimmy Murphy would take the lead and remain out front until receiving the checkered flag—making him the first driver to start on the Pole and win the race. Hartz, who had served as a riding mechanic for Eddie Hearne the past three years, would finish second, Hearne third and Ralph DePalma fourth. All told, Murphy would lead the race for a total of 153 laps.

SEPTEMBER 16, 1922   RICKENBACKER   WEDS ADELAIDE FROST DURANT

Soon after Adelaide Frost Durant's divorce was finalized from race driver/playboy Cliff Durant, she and Eddie Rickenbacker were wed on September 16, 1922, at the First Congressional Church at Sound Beach, Connecticut. Rev. L. W. Varney performed the ceremony. Rev. Jason Pfister of St. Paul's Church in Chicago was Eddie's best man. He had baptized him years before. Mrs. Rickenbacker wore a broach shaped with her new husband's "Hat in the Ring" insignia that was set with a diamond, ruby and sapphire.

Following the ceremony the Rickenbackers would board the White Star liner Majestic to sail to Europe for a three month honeymoon before they would return to their home in Detroit. Adelaide would say, "Our romance began on New Year's Eve at the Commodore hotel although I had known Captain Rickenbacker slightly in California ten years ago."

SEPTEMBER 17, 1922.   ROSCOE SARLES BURNT TO DEATH

The opening of the new 1-1/4 mile speedway in Kansas City was delayed from Saturday to Sunday due to rain. The inclement weather on Saturday didn't dampen the enthusiasm of the race-goers as excited fans returned to see the nation's best race drivers compete on what was promoted as a wickedly fast race track. It turned out to be a day of carnage as a pair of two-car smashups and a singular car accident marred the day's activities.

The 27-year old Roscoe Sarles's penchant for being involved in crashes on the track finally caught up with him. The Lafayette, Indiana, native and runner-up in the 1921 Indianapolis 500, Sarles was burnt to death as his race car tangled with Peter DePaolo's machine on the 110th lap. Roscoe's car sailed over the outer retaining wall and landed upside down. He was trapped upside down in the flaming wreckage. His riding mechanic,

Christopher Pickup, attempted to jump from the car but failed to do so. With his shirt ablaze, the bloodied mechanic tried, unsuccessfully, to extricate Sales from the flaming racer. It would take several minutes for firemen and policemen to remove Roscoe's body. Christopher Pickup was badly burned but would survive.

Many fans did not see the crash because that section of the race track was concealed by several mature trees that obscured the accident. However, they were very aware of the billowing black cloud of smoke that could be seen rising from the outside of the facility.

Originally Sarles was intending to be a spectator but when Cliff Durant's father ordered his son to fly to the East Coast after Saturday's rainout, Roscoe would drive Durant's #34 vehicle on this fateful day. Pete DePaolo suffered injuries and lacerations to his face and left arm. His riding mechanic Cotton Henning received painful cuts and bruises.

In full sight of the packed main grandstand, Eddie Hearne had a frightening crash as his car #1 somersaulted three times. Hearne and his riding mechanic, Ed Hefferman, were tossed high into the air and their bodies would land hard upon the race track. Hearne escaped badly bruised and Hefferman would break his right arm in what had the appearance of a fatal crackup.

Jimmy Murphy and Joe Thomas tangled in the SE part of the bowl. Murphy's car blew a tire and it kicked up a cloud of dust obscuring Thomas's vision. Unable to see Jimmy's car, Joe would plow into his racer. Murphy received a deep cut under his left eye.

1923 INDIANAPOLIS 500

The "one-upmanship" between Tommy Milton and Jimmy Murphy escalated even further in 1923 as Milton would become the first two-time winner of the 500-Mile Race. By the midway point of the Race, Milton's hands had developed painful blisters. Howdy Wilcox, whose car had dropped out of competition on lap 51 with a bad clutch, would relieve Tommy from lap 103 through 151. Milton would go to the Speedway medical tent to have his blistered hands treated. He also switched to a more comfortable pair of racing boots. It was a particularly exciting race during the first 250 miles with 28 lead changes. Harry Hartz, two laps in the arrears, finished second and Jimmy Murphy, slowed by lengthy pit stops, came home in third position. Five drivers would lead the race: Milton 13 times for 128 laps; Wilcox (for Milton) 1 time for 41 laps; Murphy 6 times for 11 laps; Wilcox 5 times for 10 laps; Hartz 1 time for 6 laps; and Cliff Durant 3 times for 4 laps.

Milton had won the Pole Position with an eye-popping new track record of 108.170 mph. Harry Hartz was second fastest and Dario Resta, the 1916 Indy 500 winner, would start on the outside of the front row. This marked Dario's first return to the Brickyard since his victory in 1916. Fred Duesenberg drove a Duesenberg Pace Car to lead the field of 24 cars down to the start. Eddie Rickenbacker was invited by Carl Fisher to be the Official Starter of the Race.

On lap 22, Tom Alley, driving relief for Earl Cooper, lost control of his #29 Durant Special as he attempted to pass two race cars on the SW turn. His car skidded into the wall and then shot across the track and crashed through a wooden fence gate on the SE corner. Alley's car would strike a group of young boys from Lafayette, Indiana, that were watching the race through a knot-hole. Alley's car directly hit 16-year-old Bert Shoup. The youth was unconscious when he was taken to the Speedway's infield medical center. Doctors determined he suffered a compound fracture of the skull at the base of the brain. Shoup was transported to Methodist Hospital where an emergency operation proved to be unsuccessful. His parents hurried to Indianapolis and were at his side when he died at 7:30 p.m. without ever regaining consciousness.

Charles Elliott and William Goetz suffered severe head and body lacerations but their conditions were listed as non-serious. Harold Gritten, who was sitting with his back turned when the car that Alley was driving struck the fence, was knocked 30 feet away into an adjacent corn field. Standing next to Gritten was Fay Layton whose right leg was run over by the Alley vehicle. They both suffered painful injuries. The group of eight

Lafayette boys ranged in age from 13 to 18. Tom Alley broke his left arm and received severe cuts to his head.

On June 11, 1923 Carl Fisher submitted his letter of resignation as president of the Indianapolis Motor Speedway. James Allison, who had purchased from Frank Wheeler his shares of ownership of the Speedway, was now the majority partner and he assumed the presidency. Arthur Newby now would become vice-president, Theodore E. "Pop" Myers, secretary-treasurer. Allison would comment about Fisher's resignation.

JAMES ALLISON——"Mr. Fisher now lives in Miami Beach, Florida, during the winter months and recently he bought property on Long Island, New York. He expects to live there during the remainder of the year. It would be quite impossible for him to devote the necessary time to Speedway interests that the president should."

Allison also stated the 500-Mile Race would run again next May 30, 1924. There had been talk that there might not be a race next year and the Speedway might be abandoned.

SEPTEMBER 4, 1923   HOWDY WILCOX KILLED

It was during the inaugural 200-mile race on the 1-1/4 mile high-banked board track at Altoona, Pennsylvania, where Howdy Wilcox would be killed. Race fans held their collective breaths at the alarming speeds these race cars reached. It was a breathtaking perfect day until the 117th lap when 1919 Indy winner Howdy Wilcox, running in second position, dove too low on the planking then and into the adjoining dirt surface. Howdy attempted to swerve his Duesenberg Special back onto the track but in doing so his wheels traveled through the oil-soaked boards at the edge of the track. Now out of control, his car whipped around before rolling over several times. His neck was broken and his chest crushed when his racer overturned. The 34-year old Wilcox would die soon after arriving at an emergency hospital. Eddie Hearne won the race and closed in on the AAA National Driving title.

Wilcox, an Indianapolis resident, was extremely popular and had been a participant in every 500-Mile Race ran since its inception in 1911. His wife had died nearly a year ago and Wilcox would live with his mother and his two children. (His son Howard Jr. would be instrumental in the creation of the highly successful Little 500 bicycle race at Indiana University. Watch the Oscar winning film "Breaking Away" to view what iconic this event has grown into.)

Howdy Wilcox's mother, Mrs. B.A. Warhinton of 2044 North Meridian, shared with an Indianapolis Star reporter her belief that her son had a premonition about this race.

MRS. WARHINTON——"He took his bags outside on the porch, then came back inside and took each of the children by the hand and kissed them both goodby, then turned to me and said, 'What would I ever do without you, mother?' But he acted so unusual Wednesday that I believe he thought he might never see us again.

"A neighbor told me that Howard had remarked recently that he had got so he felt 'funny' every time he put his foot in a racing car."

Howdy Wilcox was inducted into the Indianapolis Motor Speedway Hall of Fame in 1963.

1924 INDIANAPOLIS 500

1924 would be the first time that there would be co-winners of the Indianapolis 500. L.L. "Slim" Corum started next to last in the 22-car field and had worked his way through the field but could not match the pace being set by Earl Cooper and Jimmy Murphy. As Murphy headed the field on lap 111, Joe Boyer would replace Corum in the #15 Duesenberg Special. Jimmy would surrender the lead to Earl Cooper on lap 121 and Earl would stay atop the field through lap 176 when tire issues slowed his pace. The hard-charging Boyer took the lead and would go on to win the race, leading the remaining 24 circuits. Cooper would hold off Pole sitter Jimmy Murphy for second. Harry Hartz finished fourth.

Murphy had established a new track record in winning the Pole for his second time. He was joined in the front row by Harry Hartz and Tommy Milton. Surprising this trio was Joe Boyer, who charged to the front from his fourth starting spot to lead lap 1 before supercharger problems began to plague his #9 Duesenberg. Murphy took the lead for the next 40 laps. On the opening lap rookie Ernie Ansterburg crashed his #10 Duesenberg.

In a complicated "chess" move by Fred Duesenberg, he ordered Ansterburg to relieve Boyer in his ailing machine on lap 93, thus clearing the way for Boyer to be the relief driver for Corum's car 18 laps later. Slim would then replace Ansterburg in the original Boyer mount on lap 159. Thane Houser took the controls on lap 176 and promptly crashed. Tommy Milton would drive 110 laps but fuel tank problems would sideline him and he'd finish 21st out of 22 cars. Rookie Alfred Moss, a dentist from England, would finish in 16th position. He was the father of the great Stirling Moss, who many consider the greatest Formula One driver never to capture a F1 driving championship.

In a span of ten days in September, three Indianapolis 500 winners were killed. Coupled with Howdy Wilcox fatal crash last September 4, there was a growing belief that there was a "jinx" attached to winning the 500-Mile Race.

SEPTEMBER 2, 1924   JOE BOYER KILLED

The reigning Indianapolis 500 champion Joe Boyer died of injuries sustained the day before during the running of the 250-mile race at Altoona, Pennsylvania. Running in second position, Boyer was driving furiously trying to catch race leader Jimmy Murphy in the waning stages of the race. It was believed that his #9 Duesenberg Special blew a tire as he sped through the corner. His car smashed into the upper guard rail destroying about 30 feet of railing. The rear of his racer hung suspended over the top of the wooden bowl. Boyer's mangled legs were trapped underneath his race car and would lose a significant amount of blood.

A policeman, who was the first to run to Joe's aid, kept falling as he tried to climb the steep banking. Harry Hartz had to swerve his car to miss the officer. A rope was tied around Boyer's car and the outer wall to prevent it from rolling back down the track. Other rescuers ascended from outside the track to respond to Joe's needs.

Both of Boyer's legs were crushed. Doctors would amputate his left leg between the knee and ankle and his right leg between the knee and hip. He would receive two blood transfusions to save his life. Jean Marcenac, his mechanic and friend, donated his blood for the first transfusion.

The multimillionaire Joe Boyer would die the following morning at 12:25 a.m. He was the son of Joe Boyer Sr., chairman of the board of the Burroughs Adding Machine Company in Detroit. Boyer was enshrined into the Indianapolis Motor Speedway Hall of Fame in 1985.

SEPTEMBER 3, 1924   DARIO RESTA KILLED

Dario Resta married the sister of Spencer Wishart. When her brother was killed she developed a deep paranoia fear for her husband's safety. She would sit in the row farthest from the race track. She pleaded for him to quit driving. To her extreme joy, Dario announced his retirement from auto racing in April 1917. However, the lure of racing would pull him back to the driver's seat. Resta would qualify on the outside of the front row on his return to the Speedway in 1923. Mrs. Resta's fears returned even more so.

On September 3, 1924 Dario Resta went to the Brooklands race track in Surrey, England, to attempt to set a new land-speed record. Driving a Sunbeam race car, a tire was punctured when a belt on his car broke loose. Dario was killed instantly when the Sunbeam he was driving went out of control, crashed through an iron fence, plunged from the track and caught fire. His riding mechanic Bill Perkins was injured and hospitalized. (Because Perkins's injuries prevented him riding in the San Sebastian Grand Prix, Tom Barrett was selected as a substitute. Driver Kenelm Lee Guinness had a serious crash and Perkins was fatally injured.). Dario Resta was enshrined into the Indianapolis Motor Speedway Hall of Fame in 1954.

SEPTEMBER 15, 1924   JIMMY MURPHY KILLED

1922 Indianapolis 500 winner Jimmy Murphy had all but mathematically clinched the 1924 AAA National Driving Championship. Although not exceptional at racing on dirt tracks, to help a promoter friend, he accepted an invitation to compete in the Syracuse 150 at the New York Fairgrounds. Nearly two laps behind, Murphy was running second to Phil "Red" Shafer in the waning stages of the race. On the 138th lap his race car skidded, looped around three times before crashing through the inside wooden guardrail. Timber shot like projectiles and a large beam pierced the 30-year old Murphy's chest, impaling him. Unconscious, Murphy was rushed to St. Joseph Hospital where he was dead on arrival. The Milton/Murphy feud was tragically over. A distraught Tommy Milton would remain in Syracuse to settle Jimmy's affairs and arrange for the shipment of the wrecked race car back to Los Angeles. A despondent Bennett Hill announced his retirement as a driver because of the loss of his good friend. Jimmy Murphy was inducted into the Indianapolis Motor Speedway Hall of Fame in 1964.

1925 INDIANAPOLIS 500

This would mark the year where the winning car averaged over 100 mph. Peter DePaolo, nephew of Ralph DePalma, would average 101.127 mph edging out Dave Lewis, who was driving the first front-wheel-drive car in the 500-Mile Race before a crowd estimated as 150,000 race fans.

Leon Duray won the Pole with a speed average 113.196 m.p.h. Pete DePaolo would qualify in second position and Harry Hartz would start third. For luck, DePaolo tied the baby shoes of his young son Tommy to the front axle of his Duesenberg. Eddie Rickenbacker was chosen to be the Pace Car driver in one of his new Rickenbacker 8 automobiles. Immediately Pete started charging at the start of the race, leading the first 54 laps. Rookie Phil "Red" Shafer took the top spot on the next circuit and continue to lead for the following 13 laps before De Paolo wrestled back the lead of the race. DePaolo would lead large segments during the first half of the Race——laps 66-85 and laps 89-104.

Pete's hands were badly blistered and he would come in for relief by Norm Batten from laps 106 to 127. From laps 127 through 173, Dave Lewis began to dominate the second half of the race in his father-in-law's, Harry Miller's, the front-wheel drive racer. No other drivers dared to drive this revolutionary car in the race. Unfortunately for Lewis, he was overcome with extreme fatigue and was relieved by Bennett Hill, who brought the car home for a second place finish. Phil "Red" Shafer finished third.

The five-story Pagoda, originally built in 1913, burnt to the ground on Monday June 1, 1925. Pop Myers attributed to a cigarette butt apparently dropped by the last person leaving the structure. Myers estimated the loss of the press pagoda was $7,000.

1926 INDIANAPOLIS 500

Never in the previous 13 years since the inaugural running of the Indianapolis 500 in 1911, had the race ever been shortened by rain—until 1926. Rookie Frank Lockhart had a two lap lead over Harry Hartz when showers began falling after 380 miles. The race was run under caution until the 400-mile mark when rain started coming down hard and the race was red flagged. Hartz had been a serious contender to win before a lengthy pit stop effectively cost him a chance for victory. Rookie Cliff Woodbury finished 3rd, Fred Comer 4th and defending champion Pete De Paolo finished 5th.

Louis Chevrolet would lead the field of 28 cars down to the start in the Chrysler Imperial 80 Pace Car. Phil "Red" Shafer, starting in the fifth spot, grabbed the lead on the opening lap and held the top spot for 15 circuits before car #1 Dave Lewis, again driving a Miller front-drive racer, took command. Lewis would lead on two occasions for 43 laps in the early stages of the Race. Dave's car would drop out after 92 laps with a bad valve.

Also driving a Miller front-drive machine was Earl Cooper, who captured the Pole Position with a speed average of 111.7 mph. Cooper was flanked by Harry Hartz and Leon Duray. A few days before qualifications, Peter Kreis would be hospitalized with pneumonia. He was the driver/owner of car #15, a rear-drive Miller. Kreis would select the promising rookie dirt car driver from California, Frank Lockhart, to be his replacement. The 23-year old Lockhart had originally been slated to be a relief driver for Bennett Hill.

Lockhart instantly branded himself as a future star by posting a new 1-lap qualifying record of 115.488 mph on his initial lap but Frank would abort the run on lap two because of a tire failure. On his second qualification attempt, he would blow an engine. Down to his final qualifying attempt, Frank cautiously put his white-painted racer into the field and would start the race in 20th position in a field of 28 cars.

Frank Lockhart would first take the lead of the race on lap 60 and would be atop the field when rains first fell, stopping the race after 71 laps. After more than an hour delay, the race was resumed and Lockhart continued to lead for the duration, except for six circuits Hartz would head the pack from 101-106. All told Lockhart would lead 95 of the 160 laps. A crowd estimated between 135,000-140,000 were in attendance to see the rookie triumph.

MAY 20, 1927   CHARLES   LINDBERGH'S   FIRST TRANS-ATLANTIC FLIGHT

Prior to this date, Eddie Rickenbacker was the most famous aviator in the United States. 25-year-old Charles Lindbergh's trans-Atlantic flight in the Spirit of St. Louis on May 20, 1927, took the nation by storm. Lindbergh won the Orteig Prize for making his non-stop flight from New York to Paris. (Numerous acclaimed aviators had made unsuccessful attempts to accomplish this feat and several lives were lost.) By flying solo, Charles would need to stay awake at the controls for 30 hours in his single-engine aircraft. Choosing to jettison as much weight as possible for the flight, even flying without a radio and parachute, the daredevil would say, "What kind of man would live where there is no danger? I don't believe in taking foolish chances. But nothing can be accomplished by not taking a chance at all." Jimmy Stewart would portray Lucky Lindy in the 1957 Warner Bros film, "Spirit of St. Louis".

A meteoric racing career reached its zenith as Frank Lockhart became the first driver to ever qualify over 120 mph in winning the Pole Position, 1925 winner Pete DePaolo would start 2nd and Leon Duray 3rd. Right from the get-go, Lockhart jumped out front and led the first 81 laps. That would be a record for the most laps led consecutively from the start of the race. (Emerson Fittipaldi would break that mark in 1990 when he led the first 92 laps.). Dutch Baumann took the lead for the following nine laps before Lockhart steamrolled back to the top. However, Frank would be sidelined on lap 119 with a broken connecting rod, having made the Race a yawner up to that point leading 110 of 119 laps.

34-year old Norman Batten's #8 Miller caught fire as he was entering turn four. He stood up in the cockpit and heroically drove his blazing car down the main straightaway and past where all the race teams' gasoline tanks were positioned. It was a frightening scene before Batten could slow his car down enough to bail out of his racer. Norm was hailed as a hero for this concern for his fellow pit crewmen's safety. Batten would spend several months recovering from his serious burns.

Pete De Paolo's #3 Perfect Circle Miller would fall out early on lap 31 as his supercharger failed. Pete would get back in the Race as relief driver for Bob McDonough's #14 Cooper and take the lead from laps

120 to 149. A lengthy pit stop to change spark plugs ended his chances to return to Victory Lane but he would soldier home to a disappointing sixth place finish. With DePaolo out of contention, rookie George Souders, driving the light blue #32 Duesenberg owned by Hollywood Bill White, became the race leader on lap 150. Souders would drive on to victory without the aid of a relief driver. All other cars in the Top Ten would make at least one driver change. The 26-year old Souders hailed from Lafayette, Indiana, and had been an undergraduate student at Purdue University.

Babe Stapp, who had relieved rookie Benny Shoaff in the #24 Perfect Circle Duesenberg, was running in second position with two laps remaining. His car would come to a halt on lap 198 with drive gear issues. Earl Devore would then go on to finish in the runner-up spot eight laps behind Souders. Tony Gulotta was 3rd and rookie Wilbur Shaw, with relief help by fellow rookie Louis Meyer for 41 laps, finished 4th. Two-time winner Tommy Milton would compete in his last 500-Mile Race finishing in a disappointing 9th position.

In August 15, 1927, James Allison and Carl Fisher found a willing buyer to purchase the Indianapolis Motor Speedway. They had tried, without success, to sell the Speedway to Tommy Milton. In "500 Miles to Go" by Al Bloemker tells how Fisher tried to get Milton to purchase the Speedway.

CARL FISHER——"If you are sure you're through with racing as a driver, why don't you buy Speedway? Jim and I haven't had any fun out of operating the track since our fight with the legislature. So far, our only offer has come from a group which wants to use the land for a real estate development. Because we believe the 500-Mile Race should be continued, we'd rather sell the race track to you for $100,000 less than they offered and I'm sure you can get more than enough financial backing to swing the deal. It's a foolproof investment, because the property is increasing in value every year. How about it?"

Milton would decline indicating he had neither the knowledge or interest to own a race track.

TOMMY MILTON——"I don't know a single thing about the responsibilities of a promoter. But if the Speedway is no longer fun for you, I'm sure it will be an even bigger headache for me. I'd rather put what money I've been able to save into your Montauk Beach project."

Coming off the sting of the Rickenbacker Automotive Company going bankrupt, Eddie Rickenbacker was able to pull together several Detroit "silent" partners to fund a 6 1/2% first mortgage bond of $700,000 for the acquisition of the Speedway. T.E. "Pop" Myers would be named General Manager.

1927

Rickenbacker-Allison-Fisher

Carl Fisher & James Allison
sell Speedway to Eddie Rickenbacker
for $700,000.

1928

FEBRUARY 19, 1928   MALCOLM CAMPBELL SETS
                       LAND SPEED RECORD

A trio of drivers descended upon Daytona Beach in quest of breaking Major H.O.D. Segrave's world record. Captain Malcolm Campbell brought his Napier Blue Bird Special to the South Florida sands. Philadelphia businessman J.M. White had recently finished construction of the 36-cylinder Triplex Special. And 1926 Indianapolis 500 winner Frank Lockhart had convinced F. E. Moskovics, owner of the Stutz Car Company, to invest in the construction of the streamlined Stutz Blackhawk Special.

It was Campbell who pushed his 12-cylinder Blue Bird to a new record of 206.956 mph besting Henry Segrave's record by 3.16 miles an hour. Campbell would imply that he could go faster.

MALCOLM CAMPBELL——"I did not have my machine open up at anytime during the trial.

                    "When I entered the official mile stretch after taking the four mile start, my machine had not even started to pick up good, and it did not begin to pick up until I had covered half of the mile. Just before

I crossed the final wire, I glanced at my instruments and I was making 220 mph. My instruments are accurate and I knew all during the runs just what speed I was making."

Soon after Campbell's record run, Frank Lockhart brought out his Stutz Blackhawk Special for a trial run. His streamlined, cigar-shaped racer weighed less than 3,000 pounds and was powered by two eight-cylinder Miller marine motors, each capable of generating 400 horsepower. He had designed the car to minimize wind resistance. The former Indy 500 king practiced at a disappointing speed of 181 mph. After his trial run Frank decided to wait until the following day to try for the record because the track conditions were now unfavorable. There had been a hard rain shower earlier and visibility was poor due to low hanging clouds.

A high tide caused J.M. White not to make a preliminary trial and he decided to wait until the following day as well. However, the AAA stated that in order to make an official run for the record, White would have to install a reverse drive.

FEBRUARY 23, 1928   FRANK LOCKHART CRASHES INTO OCEAN

Surprisingly Lockhart gave into the relenting encouragement of cheering fans who had gathered to see him break Campbell's record. Against his better judgment, he elected to make his trial run on a wet beach.

As his speeding racer was about to enter the measured mile to begin his official time, his car, traveling northward at 225 mph, sharply careened to the right and hit an incoming wave. Lockhart's racer did a complete flip and landed 50 feet out in the ocean.

Rescue workers ran out into the ocean in a frantic attempt to save him. Only a miracle prevented Lockhart from drowning, as waves were breaking over his head with water up to his neck. Frank was semi-conscious but he had the where-with-all to say, "Tell my wife I'm alright."

A crew member rushed out into chest-deep water and tied a rope to the car's front axle and workers pulled the damaged race car back to shore. Mechanics needed use a blow torch and chisels to pry Lockhart from the cockpit where he was pinned. Mrs. Lockhart fainted when she saw her semi-conscious husband. Both Frank and she were rushed by ambulance to the local hospital.

Lockhart received a severe laceration on his face and a ragged gash which severed tendons on his left wrist. It was first thought he had suffered internal injuries and a broken arm, but tests proved to be false. He, also, was in a complete state of shock.

Later that evening, William F. Strums, Lockhart's personal representative, visited Frank in the hospital. He relayed the Lockhart's account of the accident to the media.

FRANK LOCKHART——"I was traveling down the beach at a terrific rate of speed when I glanced at my tachometer to learn how many revolutions the motor was making. I was turning over 6,500 at the time just a few seconds before the accident happened.

"I drove through a bright place in the atmosphere where the sun was shining, then all at once I ran into rain and the visibility was completely gone. I could not see. The next thing I knew was when I was in the ocean."

It was William F. Strums's belief that Lockhart, because of the sudden poor visibility, hit the brakes too hard which caused his car to swerve. He added that Lockhart "because of his superior sportsmanship, he answered the cries of the crowd for action." George Spindler, an Indianapolis Stutz dealer, further added that Lockhart attributed the accident due to running into a sudden rain squall and could not see.

Surprisingly the race car was not damaged that severely. In addition to dents in its body, the frame was bent with a noticeable sag in the middle of the chassis. Lockhart would tell F. E. Moskovics, owner of Stutz Car Company, about the crash.

FRANK LOCKHART——"I know that the car is fast as we calculated it was. The only bad break is that the Chamber of Commerce insisted that we try for the record before we were ready.

"I was feeling my way, wide open in the mist and started instinctively pulling the car higher on the beach, away from the ocean, when I struck soft sand. I know I was too high and pulled her down again—but too quickly. The next thing I know I was in the water."

Lockhart indicated he planned to rebuild the car and make another attempt at the world record.

He felt certain that the severed tendons in his wrist would not affect his ability to race in the 500-Mile Race.

Perturbed by AAA's not allowing his 36-cylinder Triplex to make an official run at the record because the car lacked a reverse gear, J.M. White selected fellow Philadelphian and East Coast dirt driver Ray Keech to make an unofficial run on the beach. Keech electrified the crowd with an "unofficial" 203.73 mph run. They vowed, like Lockhart, to return in April to attempt another pursuit.

MARCH 18, 1928   RICKENBACKER TO BUILD GOLF COURSE AT THE SPEEDWAY

In a way to create greater utilization of their facility, Eddie Rickenbacker announced that he was going to build a top notch 18-hole golf municipal golf course at the Speedway. Nine holes would be inside the massive Speedway infield and the other nine would be just outside the race track. Pop Myers would serve as general manager assisted by a club professional and maintenance experts. Indianapolis golf architect Will Diddle was employed to design one of the top golf courses in the state of Indiana. The targeted date for the grand opening is June 1, 1929. Rickenbacker stressed at the press conference, "To my mind golf has already reached the point where it can be termed 'the great national recreation.' It is no longer a rich man's game as it was a few years ago."

※ ※ ※

Tommy Milton had been working on a car for multi-millionaire Cliff Durant to drive in the 500-Mile Race. He would announce positively that he would not try for his third 500 victory next month. Bob McDonogh, a Milton protege, was signed to be a relief driver for Durant.

Bill White, the "Banana King of Hollywood", announced that George Souders would defend his 500 title in a new car. Known as one to exaggerate, he was braggadocious that from the lion's share of the winner's purse from last year's race, he now owned two race cars, two passenger cars, a truck and a new wife.

APRIL 25, 1928   LOCKHART KILLED AT DAYTONA

Attempting to better Ray Keech's world's land speed record of 207.55 mph set last Sunday, Frank Lockhart, 26, was fatally injured when his Stutz Blackhawk Special, traveling at 200 mph, hit a soft spot on the sand, causing his racer to hurtle 30 feet through the air. Lockhart was thrown out of his vehicle. Spectators, who rushed to rescue him, found the 1926 Indy 500 winner bleeding profusely about the head and mouth. Frank's breathing was labored as he was placed in the ambulance and died en route to the local hospital. Mrs. Lockhart, one of the first to reach her husband, rode with him in the ambulance. She would become hysterical when physicians pronounced him dead.

The car was virtually destroyed in the violent crash. It hurtled 120 feet in the air before landing sideways. It then bounded nearly 50 feet through the air, then rolled several times after hitting the beach. So forceful the accident was, the car drugged a 16 inch hole in the sand.

The beach had deteriorated to its worst condition since Frank arrived a week prior. The sand had a washboard appearance due to adverse winds of the past few days. On a prior attempt that morning, Lockhart's car hit one of the ridges the sand causing his car to nearly run again into the ocean.

At the request of the Daytona Beach mayor, flags were lowered to half-staff as his body lay in state Friday. Wilbur Shaw, who was at Daytona to attempt to break the record for a 4-cylinder cars, was among many civic officials and AAA personnel at the train depot to join in a solemn send-off. F. E. Moskovics, President of Stutz Motor Company, accompanied Lockhart's body and his widow from Daytona Beach to Indianapolis.

A bizarre story began to circulate that Moskovics, administrator of the Lockhart estate, would hold the racer's body until all debts had been settled. He would emphatically deny that rumor.

Mrs. Carrie Lockhart, Frank's mother, left California along with her other son Richard, but became too weak to continue the trip.

Dr. Lewis Brown, rector of St. Paul's Episcopal Church, conducted a brief service. Pall bearers were fellow 500 winners Pete DePaolo, George Souders and L.L. Corum along with Earl Cooper, Tony Gulotta and fellow Stutz driving team member Gil Anderson.

※ ※ ※

There was a buzz in the racing community that World Land Speed record holder Ray Keech was coming to Indianapolis to examine the track to determine if he would like to compete in the Indy 500. It was reported he would either drive the car that Lockhart was to race in the 500 or possibly drive a Duesenberg.

A snafu soon became apparent that the Lockhart estate could not legally race the car. Keech, who had become a good friend of Lockhart's during their Daytona Beach escapades, returned to Philadelphia to obtain funding to purchase the car from the Frank's estate. Tony Gulotta had been promised a ride in the second Lockhart racer prior to his death and was not affected.

MAY 6, 1928   RAY KEECH BUYS LOCKHART'S INDY CAR

F.E. Moskovics approved the sale of the Lockhart car #15 to Ray Keech with funding assistance from J.M.

White. In their short time together at Daytona Beach, Lockhart and Keech had developed a strong friendship. The speed demon announced the purchase and indicated he would give a percentage of his prize money to Mrs. Lockhart. Jean Marcenac, Lockhart's chief mechanic, agreed to remain with the car for Keech. This was the car that Frank had set a world's dirt track record for 100 miles last September 25 at Cleveland.

In what came as a pleasant surprise to his legion of Indy 500 fans, legendary 1915 Indianapolis winner Ralph DePalma announced his intent to compete in the upcoming race. DePalma had hoped to buy one of the Lockhart racing cars. Upon learning of the purchase by Keech, he then began conversations with Augie and Fred Duesenberg for one of their cars. Ralph outlined what criteria he would require to return to the Speedway.

RALPH DePALMA——"I want to drive a car in the 500-Mile Race provided I can get a car by May 15. The only thing I insist on is the car I drive carry the name of its maker. I don't want to drive car whose car name has been changed overnight. This has always been my policy and I don't care to change now."

DePalma had last raced in the 500 in 1925 when he finished seventh.

With the retirement of two-time winner Tommy Milton and the loss of Frank Lockhart, the highly popular DePalma would make up for the sting of their absence. Also Eddie Hearn, runner up in 1919, also decided to no longer compete in the 500 after finishing seventh last year. Harry Hartz's hopes to race in the 500-Mile Race were doused when physicians said he would require an additional operation because of his leg's failure to heal properly.

The euphoria of Ralph DePalma's return abruptly changed when Ralph reversed his decision and stated he would not drive in the race. He was offered and accepted an experimental engineering position with the Lancia Motors of America. He telegrammed the IMS management.

RALPH DePALMA——"After much debating and much consideration, the Lancia Motors of America, with whom I am now engaged in charge of experimental engineering, feels it advisable for me not to participate at Indianapolis this year."

MAY 13, 1928   DAVE LEWIS COMMITS SUICIDE

Dave Lewis shot and killed himself with a .38 automatic pistol in his mountain cabin in San Francisquito Canyon, 40-miles NE of Los Angeles, when a brush fire near his cabin got out of control. A sheriff deputy theorized that

Lewis, second place finisher in the 1925 Indianapolis 500, had been clearing brush around his cabin when a fire, which he had set, went out of control. It was the deputy's opinion that he became excited and went inside his cabin and shot himself. There were incorrect reports that the 46-year old Lewis had shot himself with a shotgun.

Lewis had divorced Helen Lewis, a radio singer in March 1927, and only two months ago married Laura F. Lewis. Upon being notified about her husband's death, Laura rushed to their mountain home. Dave was a brother-in-law of famed racing car builder Harry Miller. On May 23, he had planned to leave for Indianapolis to drive a new creation built by Miller.

Deputy Sheriff Purrier's report to the coroner stated that death was self-inflicted with a .38 automatic that belonged to Dave Lewis. The pistol laid near his hand. Lewis had also methodically arranged all his personal effects on a dresser. Details reported by Forest Ranger Peterson appeared to contradict the notion that Lewis had panicked over an out of control brush fire noting his body lay full length on a bed with a bullet through his head. Homicide detectives reported that the bullet passed through his head, striking a wall, then ricocheted to the other wall. The bullet was located near the bed.

Relatives disagreed with the investigators claim that Lewis took his own life. They demanded a complete study, convinced that Dave may have been slain by a robber who tried to cover up the murder by starting the nearby fire. Tom Gardiner, a nephew to Lewis, was overly critical of the report saying his Uncle Dave did not own a pistol. Also Lewis was excited about his recent marriage and the opportunity to drive Harry Miller's new creation in the 500-Mile Race. LA County coroner Frank Nance debunked that theory and listed suicide on the death certificate.

Fellow race driver and friend Cliff Durant refused to accept the findings. He showed a telegram that Lewis had sent to him last Saturday proposing a deal where they could partner together for the 500.

CLIFF DURANT——"If he wanted to commit suicide he wouldn't have chosen the gun route. If life was dulling for him, he could have let loose of the steering wheel of one of the fast racing cars he drove while rounding a dangerous curve, and he would have been in a suicidal position. No, I don't think anyone as game as Dave would ever commit suicide."

At first, Mrs. Lewis refused to believe the findings of the police but eventually, very begrudgingly, accepted the verdict. She had her husband's body shipped to Syracuse, New York, for burial.

Fire crews brought the blaze under control with minimal effort. Less than an acre was burned.

Lewis will be remembered as the first person to drive a front-wheel-drive race car at Indy in 1925. Harry Miller had brought the car to the Speedway but no driver had a desire to drive such a revolutionary design. In the 500, he was the race leader from lap 127 thru 173. At that point an exhausted Lewis came into the pits for a relief driver. Dave was so fatigued that he couldn't brake to a stop. He had to make an additional lap and was replaced by Bennett Hill. The time lost in the exchange of drivers dropped the car into second position. Pete DePaolo was victorious by a 58 second margin over the Lewis/Hill mount and became the first driver to average over 100 mph.

Norm Batten had driven 22 laps in relief for De Paolo. AAA and IMS officials refused to credit Batten as a co-winner citing precedent of the relief roles of Cyrus Patschke in 1911 for Ray Harroun, Don Herr for Joe Dawson in 1912 and Howdy Wilcox for Tommy Milton in 1923.

Phil "Red" Shafer offered Wilbur Shaw a ride in his new Miller Special for the 500. However, when a sponsorship fell through, Red put his car up for sale. Louis Meyer persuaded the youthful Alden Sampson II of Troy, Ohio, to purchase it for him, leaving Wilbur temporarily without a ride. Flush with cash from selling his Chrysler car agency in Dayton, Ohio, Sampson grabbed Shafer's offer of $6000 and purchased the car for Meyer. The 23-year old Meyer, who relieved Wilbur Shaw in 1927 for 41 laps, was technically classified as a rookie. Louis would start his gold and black #14 Miller Special in 13th position.

Tony Gulotta would enter the race as the sentimental favorite driving Ella Lockhart's car #8 Stutz Blackhawk Special. Impressed with Gulotta's third place finish in the 1927 race, Frank Lockhart had told Tony two months ago that he could drive his second car in the 500. Mrs. Lockhart honored her late husband's commitment.

The race car was officially entered by J.R. Bergamy, Frank's uncle. It was the car that the 1926 Indy 500 winner had set a world's record of 164.009 mph on the dry lake at Muroc, California, last spring and also the car that Frank had captured the Pole Position with for last year's Race. He would lead two times for 110 laps earning $11,900 in lap prize money before being sidelined on lap 120 with a broken connecting rod. Only rookie driver Dutch Baumann, who would lead nine laps, interrupted Frank's dominate pace.

Both Tony Gulotta's and Ray Keech's cars were equipped with Lockhart's patented intake manifold cooler. It was believed this added five mph to the car's speed.

Henry Koehler, who initially was reported killed in last year's crash on lap 49, recovered and was entered in the Elgin Piston Ring Special #29. Last year, while driving relief for Fred Lecklider, Koehler's car touched wheels with Cliff Bergere in turn one. His car turned over three times and tossed Henry out near the upper retaining wall. He would roll toward the inside portion of the track and was extremely fortunate not to be struck by approaching vehicles. The courageous effort by George Auch, who rushed onto the track and dragged him to safety, no doubt saved his life. Bergere's car passed under Koehler's racer while it was airborne. Koehler's face was crushed and his left eye was detached from its socket. Following his recovery, he spent the winter preparing the race car.

Fred Frame, a successful West Coast dirt track driver, was selected by Bill White to drive the car that George Souders drove to victory last year while Souders would pilot a Harry Miller racer that Eddie Hearne had driven to a seventh place finish for White.

Leon Duray signaled he would be the favorite to earn to the Pole Position for his second time after he hustled his black Miller Special around the bricks for a new, unofficial track record of 120.951 mph. Prior to taking to the track, Cliff Durant needled Leon.

CLIFF DURANT——"Leon, I'll give you 100 bucks if you break the track record!"

Durant was first to greet the burly Duray, whose real name was George Stewart, to lay a $100 bill in his hand.

On May 21, 1928 Ray Keech made his first appearance on the IMS course shaking down the now-named Simplex Piston Ring Special for seven laps at 105 mph. He instantly won the respect of his fellow drivers with the smooth way he drove the track and for displaying a humble demeanor. Prior to establishing the World's Land Speed record at Daytona Beach, Keech had been wheeling cars on dirt tracks on the East Coast for seven years. Fellow rookie Lou Moore, from Los Angeles, also made some impressive initial laps. And in an eyebrow raiser, Tommy Milton took out the front-wheel drive Detroit Special of Cliff Durant for a number of fast laps.

MAY 26, 1928   LEON DURAY WINS POLE

Leon Duray, driving a black Miller Special, captured his second Pole Position by besting both one and four-lap records in unusual fashion. On his initial qualification run, Duray established a new track record with a blistering speed of 124.018 mph. He quickly aborted the run when his right front tire's tread chunked off.

Next Cliff Woodbury of Chicago would break the four-lap qualification record of Frank Lockhart with an average speed of 120.417 mph in the #10 Boyle Valve Special front-wheel drive car. However, his record was short lived as Duray would return to the track and post a four-lap speed of 122.391 mph. Hollywood stuntman Cliff Bergere rounded out the front row with a speed of 119.956 mph.

Tony Gulotta thrilled the fans of the late Frank Lockhart with an average speed of 117.631 mph, fourth fastest in one of the Lockhart team cars. He would be joined in row two by Ralph Hepburn and Babe Stapp. Filling row three were Louis Schneider, Fred Comer and rookie Lou Moore.

World land speed record holder Ray Keech would qualify for his initial Indy in the recently purchased racer from the Lockhart estate with an average speed of 113.421 mph to earn a spot on the inside of row four. Defending champion George Souders would start 12th with a disappointing average of 111.444 mph.

Rookie Louis Meyer, in the car bought out from under Wilbur Shaw by Alden Sampson II, qualified at an average speed of 111.358 mph. Meyer was unfazed at the thought of having to start 13th. Perhaps the biggest ovation came when Norm Batten returned to the Speedway from his severe burns suffered in his heroic drive in last year's race. He would average 106.585 mph to earn a spot in the inside of row six.

Batten became a national hero when on his 24th lap, his car caught fire as he rounded turn four. Aware there were several tightly bunched cars trailing him and thinking of their safety, he climbed to the back of his flaming race car and in a hunched position, drove his car along the inside portion of the track. As his car slowed to a near stop just past the pits, he leaped from his mount onto the track, his clothing ablaze. City fireman rushed to extinguish his burning clothes and to spray his race car with chemicals.

Batten was rushed to the track's emergency hospital in serious condition with second degree burns over much of his body. Physicians feared that he inhaled gasoline fumes that could affect his lungs. He also sustained severe cuts and bruises as he sought to extract himself from the car. Norm would be transferred to Methodist Hospital. The Indianapolis Real Estate Board would present him with a gold watch for his bravery. He would also be awarded with a sportsmanship trophy by the Hoosier Motor Club. Batten would be transferred to a Dayton, Ohio, hospital for rehabilitation for several months.

MAY 26, 1928   DE PAOLO INJURED IN CRASH

In what looked like a certain fatal crash, Peter DePaolo was involved in a spectacular accident in the NE turn on his first lap of his qualifying run. DePaolo smashed into the inside retaining wall then rolled over three times, as his car bounded to the top of the race track. The car then slid back down the track.

The 1925 500 winner was thrown clear of his front-drive Flying Cloud Special. By the time track rescue personal arrived, a dazed DePaolo was standing and miraculously had escaped death with only severe cuts to his arms and bruises. He was rushed to Methodist Hospital for examination which showed no internal injuries or broken bones. Many railbirds described the accident as one of the most spectacular ever occurring at the Speedway. DePaolo indicated that the accident occurred because his steering froze as he was entering the turn.

Damage to DePaolo's Flying Cloud Special was extensive but thought to be repairable. The car was taken to the Chevrolet Brothers race shop on West 10th Street where chief mechanic Cotton Henning and crew labored around the clock to ready the car for another qualifying effort.

A search for a replacement driver commenced when DePaolo felt he was incapable of driving in the 500 due to his injuries. Cliff Durant was approached by the Red Cloud team to get his approval to release Bob McDonough from his contract to be the relief driver for Durant in the race. Another driver considered was Wilbur Shaw, whose stock was on the uptick following his fourth place finish in his rookie try in last year's Race. McDonough had experience driving a front-drive car whereas Shaw had never driven that type of car design.

On Sunday, Peter Kreis headed the list of five qualifiers in his #32 Marmon Special. Three promising rookies— Billy Arnold in a Boyle Special, Jimmy Gleason in a Duesenberg and Russ Snowberger, in another Marmon car, qualified impressively.

Many felt that Kreis, in an Earl Cooper prepared, Marmon factory car, could be the "dark horse" favorite to win the race. He had a thrilling second place duel with Leon Duray last year at Rockingham. Others felt had he not fallen victim to the flu in 1926, he might have won the race in his car that he reluctantly allowed eventual race winner Frank Lockhart to drive.

Rookie Russell "Buddy" Marr had qualified earlier on Pole Day for the middle of row five sandwiched between Louis Meyer and Fred Frame. The AAA required that relief drivers practice in the car they are assigned to before the Race. Near sunset, Chet Miller, practicing in Marr's car so he could serve as his relief driver in the race, crashed heavily. Chet sustained a broken arm and a lacerated right eye when the race car overturned. Miller was unconscious when taken to City Hospital. The car sustained extensive damage eliminating Marr's chance to compete.

Recognizing the name value of Eddie Rickenbacker, LaSalle Motors, a luxury line of automobiles manufactured by the Cadillac division, announced the hiring of the war hero as a consultant to their sales department. Always aggressively self-advancing in the business world, this was the foot in the door at General Motors that would eventually lead to much greater career accomplishments.

In a startling statement, Earl McGinnis, advertising manager of A.C. Spark Plug Company, announced that his company would be constructing a two-mile concrete Speedway, near their corporate headquarters in Flint, Michigan. They planned to conduct two races yearly including a 500 mile race.

MAY 30, 1928   TWO DUESENBERGS CRASH EARLY
ON RACE DAY MORNING

Early on Race Day morning teammates L.L. "Slim" Corum and Dutch Baumann crashed their Duesenbergs in separate incidents. They both had changed carburetors and took to the track to adjust them. While warming up, Corum's #17 skidded on the NE turn and crashed into the wall. He suffered slight facial cuts. Baumann hit the north wall while attempting to qualify and damaged his car too badly to start the race. Both accidents were blamed on the wet condition of the track.

A crowd of over 140,000 packed the Speedway despite the fact that race fans awoke to a gloomy, early morning sky. Soon thereafter, a heavy downpour occurred. Eddie Rickenbacker initially was fearful the rains would force him to postpone the race. However, the rain was short lived.

Wilbur Shaw was selected to replace Pete DePaolo in the #1 Flying Cloud Special. He had never driven a front-drive car but easily made the field with a 100.96 mph speed average. 29 cars would start the race. In flamboyant fashion, the 1925 500 winner arrived at the Speedway in an ambulance and was carried on a stretcher to a viewing location in the press pagoda.

MAY 30, 1928   ROOKIE   LOUIS   MEYER   WINS
                 INDIANAPOLIS 500

Rookie Louis Meyer won the 16th running of the Indianapolis 500 as late race leaders Tony Gulotta and rookie Jimmy Gleason experienced heart-breaking incidents. The 23-year old Meyer from Huntington Park, California, beat Louis Schneider in a Miller Special by 44 seconds. Schneider had relieved rookie Lou Moore after the 350 mile mark. Last year's winner George Souders was third, rookie Ray Keech fourth and in his glorious return, Norm Batten finished fifth. Babe Stapp was sixth and rookie Billy Arnold seventh. Fred Frame, driving Souder's winning mount from a year ago, finished eighth, Fred Comer was ninth and Gulotta recovered to finish in tenth.

Louis Schneider, a former Indianapolis motorcycle policeman, was in the hunt with the leaders early in the Race driving the #24 Armacost Miller Special moving as high as third after 200 miles. The car began losing horsepower and Louis would climb out of the car past the half-way mark. He would take over for Lou Moore, who was riding in fifth, and move into second place for the last 50 miles. Since Moore drove more than half the race, he would be officially be credited as runner up.

Leon Duray jumped to the lead on the opening lap with Tony Gulotta second and Babe Stapp third, six seconds behind. The trio stretched their lead to a full lap and a half at the 50-mile mark with Louis Schneider fourth, Jimmy Gleason fifth and Peter Kreis sixth. Rookie Russ Snowberger ducked into the pits on his opening lap and was the first to drop out of the race after four laps with a broken supercharger in his Marmon Special. Two laps later Cliff Bergere was out with a broken distributor shaft. On lap eight Cliff Woodbury, who had steadily been dropping back, made a two minute pitstop to change all eight spark plugs.

At 100 miles Leon Duray had increased his lead to 11 seconds over Tony Gulotta. Babe Stapp was an additional 15 seconds in arrears in third. Jimmy Gleason had advanced to fourth and Peter Kreis fifth with Louis Schneider dropping to sixth. Wilbur Shaw's ride in the unfamiliar Red Cloud Special ended when he was eliminated by the technical committee on lap 42. Cliff Woodbury, who from the get-go kept falling backwards from his number two starting point, dropped out on lap 55 with a broken timing gear.

After leading the first 54 laps of the race, Leon Duray lost his lead to Babe Stapp from laps 55-57 before retaking over the top stop for the next five circuits. On lap 63, a three minute pit stop was the beginning of the end for the hard charging Leon Duray, who would drop from the top ten. Defending champion George

Souders took the lead and would remain out front for the next 16 laps.

After 200 miles race leader Jimmy Gleason had a commanding 30 seconds over Babe Stapp. Louis Schneider was now third and Louis Meyer had moved from ninth to fourth followed by Lou Moore, George Souders, Tony Gulotta, Earl Devore and world land-speed record holder Ray Keech moving into the top ten for the first time.

Before the race reached the half-way point, Ray Keech's car developed a leaking gas line. Wilbur Shaw would drive in relief for Keech for a few laps, but Wilbur came in soon after suffering from gasoline burns to his right leg. Ray returned to the cockpit and soldiered the car home to a fourth place finish. Afterwards Keech had to go to the track hospital for treatment of gasoline burns from his foot up to his knee.

At the half-way mark, Jimmy Gleason held a close lead over Dutch Baumann, who had relieved Gulotta. Dutch advanced the car from seventh to second. Lou Moore was third, Souders fourth, Meyer fifth and Stapp had dropped to sixth. One hundred miles later, Gleason's car, now being driven by rookie Russ Snowberger, was still leading by five miles over Meyer (Russ would lead the race from laps 136-148). Gulotta was third, Souders fourth and Moore fifth.

Louis Schneider, who had briefly worked his own car up to second only to have horsepower issues slow his pace significantly, abandoned the car in disgust. Soon he would take over Lou Moore's car for the final 77 laps and advanced the car from fifth to second.

Shortly after the 400-mile mark, a shower occurred and the caution flag was displayed. Frank Lockhart fans remember how rain stopped the race in 1926 after 400 miles giving Lockhart the victory. They were hoping history would repeat itself for Tony Gulotta capturing the race in a team car of Frank's. The Pace Car came out to pick up the leader, slowing the entire field. However, as quickly as the rains developed, they stopped and soon they resumed the race on the 173rd lap.

Now just 50 miles until the finish, Gulotta maintained his narrow advantage over Jimmy Gleason with Meyer third. Tony had set the pace from laps 149-181. As his lead began to diminish, Gulotta began to gesture to his crew as he drove past his pit. Crew members interpreted this to mean he was running low on gasoline. When Tony pitted, in somewhat a surprise, Dutch Baumann jumped into the car again and took off, chasing the new Race leader Jimmy Gleason.

Baumann had no longer left the pits than Jimmy Gleason's car #39 came sputtering into the pits. Water was allegedly spilled on the magneto when refueling. Momentarily there was jubilation, the Stutz pits believing they had the Race in the bag. Then the unthinkable happened. Other race cars were flashing by the start/finish line but there was no Baumann. Dutch had brushed the SE wall but he was able to limp the car back to his pit. They were able to eventually resume the race only to finish a disappointing tenth place while leading 33 laps.

Gleason would officially be out of the race after completing 195 laps, finishing 15th. Jimmy had led on two occasions for 43 laps. Louis Meyer took the lead on lap 182 and held it to the finish. Louis Schneider sped Lou Moore's car from fifth to second in the late stages of the race. George Souders was 3rd, Ray Keech 4th and Norm Batten climaxed his monumental return to the Speedway with a fifth place finish. Tony Gulotta's car had develop a leaking gas tank but he managed to finish in tenth spot.

Earl Devore, who had advanced up to ninth at the 400 mile mark, skidded into the wall on the 158th lap. Able to continue, he made three more circuits until he was black flagged into the pits with a broken gas tank. Buddy Marr was able to serve as a relief driver for Ira Hall's #26 Duesenberg but unfortunately he would crash after five laps.

In Victory Lane, a shy Louis Meyer commented about his surprise victory to the throng of reporters and broadcasters.

LOUIS MEYER——"Boy, I'm happy! I give all the credit to Frank Elliott. He taught me what I know about race driving. I worked for him two years as a mechanic.

"I thought I would win after 160 laps. I had worked pretty well into the Race then, although I did not hope to overtake Jimmy Gleason or Tony Gulotta. I just sat tight and hoped for something to happen."

Following the ceremonies in Victory Lane, Louis Meyer was taken to the Speedway infield hospital for a bath and a rub down. Meyer became the third consecutive rookie to win the 500, succeeding Frank Lockhart in 1926 and George Souders in 1927. The defending champ could identify with what Meyers was experiencing as an unexpected rookie race winner.

GEORGE SOUDERS——"A good boy won it. I was going good myself until trouble put me back. But I was glad to see Louis win."

All told there were seven race leaders lead by Leon Duray with 59 laps, Jimmy Gleason 43 laps, Tony Gulotta 33 laps, Louis Meyer 19 laps, Babe Stapp 17 laps, George Souders 16 laps and Russ Snowberger (in Gleason's car) 13 laps.

Eddie Rickenbacker couldn't have been more pleased over his first race as the new owner of the Indianapolis Motor Speedway.

EDDIE RICKENBACKER——"There never has been a race here in which the results was so closely contested and in which the lead changed so often.

"The advantages were so limited that it was an ideal day of sport for the more than one hundred thousand racing fans. The management is extremely happy because of the absence of any serious crashes. The two crashes in the race did not seriously injure anybody which is a record.

"I regret, however, that it was necessary to stop the drivers a few minutes, as the slippery condition of the track following it was undoubtedly the only thing that prevented the establishment of a new track record. The old record would have been beaten by at least two miles an hour, if it had not been necessary to stop the cars temporarily. It was fortunate, however, that we were not forced to call off entirely before the full course had been driven."

It was Rickenbacker's belief that had it not been for inclement weather, there would have been over 175,000 fans in attendance.

Rickenbacker explained the unpopular decision of why Earl Devore was called into the pits and subsequently disqualified following his crash into the retaining wall.

EDDIE RICKNBACKER——"We called Devore to make a technical inspection of his machine and found that the gasoline tank had sprung a bad leak. If he had been allowed to go on, the car would have undoubtedly have caught fire and he might have burned to death. There was hissing and booing by the fans, many evidently did not understand the situation, but we felt that discretion in this case was better part of valor."

At the Victory banquet the following evening, Louis Meyer was presented a check totaling $28,250 from Pop Myers. He also received the A.L. Block trophy and a watch from the Perfect Circle Company. Leon Duray received the Prest-O-Lite silver brick for leading at 300 miles. And the massive, 7-1/2 foot silver Wheeler-Schebler trophy went to Tony Gulotta for leading at 400 miles. Peter DePaolo did not attend the banquet. He sent a message stating he was going to retire from racing.

The Omar Baking Company made a huge multi-colored cake that was topped by a miniature race car and driver for Louis Meyer. It weighed 75 pounds and it measured three feet long, two and a half wide and 16 inches high.

JULY 15, 1928   GEORGE SOUDERS CRITICALLY INJURED

George Souders was critically injured in the Knights Templar Sweepstakes 100-Mile dirt track race at Detroit. His car sideswiped the inner guard rail then catapulted into the infield throwing Souders from his mount during the first of his car's multiple flips. George was attempting to make up the distance he had lost to eventual race winner Howard Taylor after a lengthy pit stop. Initially, it was reported that Souders was not expected to recover.

A hospital spokesman listed his injuries as a skull fracture, fractured bones in both arms and multiple contusions. He was unconscious when taken to the hospital. Test to determine if he had sustained any internal injuries had to be postponed due to the severity of his condition.

Further x-rays revealed that Souders did not sustain a fractured skull but he remained unconscious.

Ruth Souders, George's wife, was in Columbus, Ohio where George had recently purchased an accessory store, when informed of her husband's accident. She and George's brother Charles left immediately for Highland Park General Hospital. Souders had recently married Miss Ruth Heeman in Fort Worth, Texas. They both were classmates at Lafayette Jefferson High School. Upon graduation, George enrolled in Purdue University, but gave up his college career to open Fourteenth Street garage in Lafayette. After catching the racing bug, he leased his garage and moved to the Southwest to begin his racing career. He had the good fortune to meet Bill White, the multi-millionaire sportsman, and began competing in White's race cars.

On July 1, Souders had purchased Gabriel Service in Columbus, Ohio which he renamed George Souders Service. He was contemplating retiring from racing.

Souders had fast time during qualifications and immediately jumped to the lead at the start of the race followed closely by Howard Taylor. However on lap 23, he was forced to make an unscheduled pit stop to refill the car's radiator. Returning to the track, George was nearly a lap behind Taylor. Driving on the ragged edge, he began to rapidly make up the distance on Taylor.

On lap 26, he struck the inner guard rail and was thrown clear of the car during its many flips. Rescue workers found Souders unconscious. Dr. D.D. Stone, head of the surgical staff, would state, "The racer has a fair chance of recovery. He showed slight improvement Monday morning and was beginning to rally in the afternoon."

Charles Souders corrected some erroneous reports stating his brother suffered a broken and badly bruised left arm, a cut over his left eye and a slight brain concussion. George would recover but never race at Indianapolis again.

Less than a month had passed when Howard Taylor was killed instantly at Kalamazoo, Michigan in an accident similar to the George Souders crash. Taylor, too, hit the inside guard rail and he flipped to his death in the track's infield.

AUGUST 3, 1928   JAMES ALLISON SUDDEN DEATH

On Sunday afternoon, July 29, 1928 James Allison wed his former secretary, Miss Lucille Mussett, at the home of Carl Fisher at Montauk Point, Long Island, New York. The following day he contracted a heavy cold. On Thursday, while returning by train to his Indianapolis mansion at Riverside Springs with his new bride, the 55-year old industrialist became seriously ill with bronchial pneumonia. His personal physician, Dr. John Cunningham, was present around the clock. After Allison lost consciousness, Dr. Cunningham notified family and close friends that his condition was grave. Death was surprising and swift as James would die at 6:50 p.m. Allison was never in the best of health having had a heart attack in March 1914 at the age of 41. Funeral services would be held at Roberts Park Methodist Church and burial in Crown Hill cemetery.

James Allison and Carl Fisher were partners in Prest-O-Lite Company and would sell it after World War I to Union Carbide Company. Shortly before the War, he established Allison Engineering Company and would be awarded numerous war contracts. Allison's became one of the foremost airplane engine builders. Allison owned Miami Ocean View Company, a real estate development corporation, and he had a winter mansion in Miami Beach on Star Island. James would build Allison Hospital on Allison Island, considered one of the finest hospitals in the South. He also built an aquarium on the shores of Biscayne Bay at Miami Beach.

Three days after her former husband's death and before the funeral rites, Mrs. Sara Cornelius Allison filed a $2,000,000 damage suit against Mrs. Lucille Mussett Allison, the bride of five days. Mrs. Sara Allison charged that the new wife "systematically and deliberately" sought over an eight-year period to win

James Allison's affections and to destroy their marriage after she became James secretary in 1920. The estate was valued from $3.5 to $6 million. Sara and Jim Allison were married on July 16, 1907, at Colorado Springs, Colorado. Allison would claim,

SARA ALLISON——"About 1919 or 1920, the defendant, a young woman of great attractiveness and personal charm, whose name was Lucille Mussett, became acquainted and associated with my husband, as secretary or stenographer to him. She had remained in such capacity or under the pretense and guise of such capacity with him down to the date of her marriage to him.

"Lucille Mussett designed and inaugurated a course of deliberate, systematic and continuous intimate conduct toward and relations with for the wicked purpose of ultimately bringing about a divorce between myself and my husband, to the end that the she might marry him."

Florida judge W. F. Blaton would rule in favor of the widow, stating Mr. Allison died leaving no will and that she is legally entitled to the entire estate estimated to with up to 6 million dollars.

"Where no will is left, the widow becomes the sole heir if there are no children. There were no children by Mr. Allison's first marriage." An eventual court challenge gave the majority of the estate to Allison's mother.

Nearly a month later George Souders remained a patient at Highland Park Hospital. A spokesman stated that although Souders remains unconscious most of the time, he now has intervals where he is semi-conscious.

SEPTEMBER 8, 1928   LOUIS SCHNEIDER SERIOUSLY
                       INJURED

While attempting to pass Carl Marchese for the lead, Louis Schneider was seriously injured when his race car skidded off the track and crashed through a wooden fence. His car proceeded to turn over three times and tumbled down a 25-foot embankment at the Minneapolis State Fair in St. Paul, Minnesota. Louis was tossed high in the air and he landed several yards away from his race car. It was initially reported that he may have sustained potentially fatal injuries— possible skull fracture, crushed chest and a brain concussion. He was rushed to Northern Pacific Hospital in St. Paul in serious condition.

Earlier in the day, while competing in the time trials, an exhaust pipe from his machine flew off and painfully burned Louis's arm. In what turned out as positive news, further tests revealed Schneider suffered no broken bones but instead painful lacerations. He remained in a semi-conscious state for a 60-hour period of time. Schneider would recover in time for the 1929 racing season.

Two years ago, Schneider quit the Indianapolis Police Department after he was reassigned from the motorcycle squad after one and a half years on the force. This past August 6, Louis's brother Albert was killed piloting an airplane near Shreveport, Louisiana. An aviator during World War I, Albert died spraying cotton crops with chemicals to kill insect pests.

Until Ray Keech set the world's land speed record, he was an obscure East coast dirt driver. However, following his fourth place finish in the Indianapolis 500, he went on to dominate the AAA circuit with a June 10 win in record time in a 100-Mile race at the Michigan State Fairgrounds in Detroit. Next came a July 4th victory at Salem, New Hampshire. On September 1, he won the 100-mile feature at the New York State Fairgrounds in Syracuse. Then he captured the September 16 race on the Atlantic City, New Jersey, board speedway.

OCTOBER 12, 1928   FRED COMER KILLED AT ROCKINGHAM SPEEDWAY

During a Columbus Day AAA race at Rockingham Speedway, in Salem, New Hampshire, Fred Comer was killed in a day marred by three spectacular accidents. Before the race it was decided that Comer would trade race cars with Cliff Woodbury, his Boyle Valve racing teammate. Fred, who served as a mechanic for millionaire sportsman/driver Cliff Durant from 1914 to 1923, was one of the back markers on lap 24. As his car came off the steep bank, a blown tire caused his car to skid off the track toward the infield, then began somersaulting against the infield guard rail. The car came to a halt upside down. Still breathing, he was placed in the track ambulance, but he succumbed due to a crushed chest before reaching the hospital. Mrs. Comer rushed from her grandstand seat in tears. She was restrained by a newspaperman who said he was alright as the ambulance had not rushed him to the hospital.

While rescue workers were tending to Comer, a four-car crackup occurred along the main grandstands packed with 30,000 spectators. On the 36th lap Jimmy Gleason struck the rail near the starter's stand. Gleason was thrown from the car and he skidded 50 yards in a prone position down the board track. Jimmy picked himself off the race track and frantically waved to avoid being run over. Ray Keech, bearing down on Gleason, took evasive action to dodge the stricken driver and swerved into the fence. His car grazed Gleason's car and overturned. Bob McDonough and Lou Moore crashed into each other while trying to avoid Keech's car. Moore's car overturned. A spectator rushed out on the track to assist Jimmy. Gleason was rushed to Clover Hill Hospital in Lawrence, New Hampshire, suffering from a fractured ankle and sprained wrist.

Keech, Moore and McDonough were shaken but not seriously hurt.

On lap 50, Dave Evans would also hit the wall in front of the grandstands and was thrown from his car. He picked himself up, walked a few feet and then collapsed. AAA officials hurriedly canceled the race "because of the accidents and condition of the track."

NOVEMBER 12, 1928   BATTEN & DEVORE LOST AT SEA

Norm Batten and Earl Devore were among the 111 causalities when the SS Vestris sank off the coast of Virginia Monday November 12, 1928. The SS Vestris, after leaving New York on November 10, ran into a severe storm the following day and developed a starboard list. The list became more severe as cargo shifted and water began pouring through. Captain William Cherry stubbornly refused to issue S.O.S. orders until 9:56 a.m. An incorrect latitude/longitude location, off by 37 miles, was transmitted. A second S.O. S. was sent at 11:04 a.m. Both Batten and Devore along with their wives were en route to Buenos Aires, Argentina, to compete in races during their "summer" season. Mrs. Batten and Mrs. Devore were rescued by ships after several hours in life boats on the open sea. More than 100 of the 339 passengers were believed to have drowned.

Norm Batten would die after an exhausting struggle to keep an overloaded lifeboat upright. Time after time the craft would capsize and each time several passengers were swept away. When her husband Norman died, Mrs. Marian Batten held her deceased spouse. After letting go of his body, she and Mrs. Teruke Inouye, wife of the military attache of the Japanese Embassy in Buenos Aires, clung onto Gerald Burton, a massive-sized crew member from Barbados. Mrs. Batten said,"He told us to stick to him and we'd be all right." Burton had been the last crew member to leave the engine room. He chose to stay in waist-high water to help keep steam in the boiler to provide power for the radio generators so the ship could continue to send S.O.S. signals.

Marian told The Standard Union of Brooklyn, New York, about her night of horror in a half-swamped lifeboat and seeing her husband dying in her arms. When the U.S.S. Wyoming arrived the lifeboat was again upside down with Mrs. Batten and three others clinging to it. They were transported to Portsmouth Naval Hospital by the rescue ship Wyoming.

MARIAN BATTEN——"Our lifeboat was overloaded until it was grotesque. It was utterly unable to cope with the seas that were running; in its condition it could have supported its passengers only if was perfectly calm. The waves poured over us and soon one, larger than the others, turned us over.

"Then we all had to struggle to get back in again. Six times the lifeboat turned over. Each time there'd be a smaller number climbing back in again. It was awful.

"My husband was with me all this time. But he became more and more exhausted as he was thrown from the boat, only to claw wearily at the gunwale again. And once again, when he was in the boat, he had to keep bailing with all his might. The last time I remember the boat going over I found myself in the water next to my husband. He was too tired to go through the struggle again. I held him up in my arms where he died. Two hours later I was rescued. Norman had all our money—$800 in cash—when he was swept out of my arms."

In 1927, Batten became a national hero when he drove his speeding race car down the main straightaway ablaze. He stayed with the burning car so as to avoid a potential serious wreck with his fellow drivers then brought his car to a stop just past pits. Receiving painful burns, he spent months in hospitals recovering.

What was even more horrifying, eye witnesses saw a shark swimming in the vicinity of their lifeboat where Earl Devore was holding on, then suddenly his body was pulled under the water. He did not re-emerge. Mrs. Devore took unnecessary criticism by bringing her dog, Speedway, aboard the lifeboat with a cruel implication that she save her dog and not her husband. She was quite bitter over Captain William Cherry's inaction and blamed him for so many passengers' loss of life. Ann Devore would tell reporters of the horror she experienced.

ANNE DEVORE——"Saturday the weather was fine. Sunday it was rough. There was a swaying and listing of the ship. On Monday morning my husband examined the register in the room and said: 'I have never been on a ship where there has been such a list. It looks to me like serious trouble.' We dressed quickly and with difficulty found an officer. He assured us that everything was all right and by noon everything would be fine and dandy. Then came the order to take to the life boats.

"I was in lifeboat # 8, with my husband and Mr. and Mrs. Norman K. Batten. Norman is an automobile driver. He and my husband were going to South America to do some racing. This boat had a hole in it and five minutes before it was lowered, this hole was patched with a piece of tin and some nails. Several of us called the captain and asked 'isn't it dangerous to send people out in a boat in this shape' and he turned around and walked away and said nothing.

"We had nothing else to do but take the boat. We got into it. As soon as we got into the water it began leaking. We were overcrowded. Water was filling the boat fast now. Life boat #1, with four Negro seaman in it, came by. We called to them to give us aid and take some of us out so that all might be saved. They drew near and my husband urged me to jump. I did so, then they pulled away from #8. A wave came in between us. When I saw #8 again it was capsized and everyone was in the water. I begged the men to go back and pick up my husband and my friends but they would not do it."

Mrs. Devore called them cowards. They yelled to her to sit down and shut up. She obeyed them. Ann would meet up with Marian Batten and they were taken to the Hotel Belmont. Both had lost all their belongings and neither had the funds to pay their bill.

NOVEMBER 28, 1928   SCHNEIDER SENTENCED FOR ASSULT & BATTERY

Former Indianapolis policeman, Louis Schneider, was sentenced to 30 days in jail and fined $50 by Municipal Judge Clifton R. Cameron on a charge of assault and battery of his wife. Mrs. Helen Schneider charged that her husband had recently struck her in the face while they were attending a dance near Clermont, about 11 miles west of Indianapolis. The case was appealed to Marion County Criminal Court where Schneider posted a $500 bond and was released.

1928

Leon Duray

Pole Position. Led 59 laps

1928

Louis Meyer
Winner
99.482 mph Average. Led 19 Laps

LOUIS MEYER WINNER 99.482 M.P.H.
AVERAGE LED 19 LAPS

FEBRUARY 21, 1929   SCHNEIDER CHARGES
                     DISMISSED

The assault and battery charges against Louis Schneider were dismissed in criminal court on the charge that he had beaten his wife. The court learned that the alleged offense occurred in Boone County instead of Marion County. Schneider was facing charges that could have caused him to miss the 500-Mile Race.

In an effort to attract more automobile manufacturers back into racing, Eddie Rickenbacker announced for the 1930 500-Mile Race that the supercharged 91-1/2-inch engine will be banned. They would return to the two-seat cars requiring a riding mechanic. Engines up to 366-cubic inch displacement would be permitted and the starting field would be increased from 33 to 42.

MAY 25, 1929   CLIFF WOODBURY WINS POLE
                POSITION

Cliff Woodbury reversed last year's qualifying results by putting his Boyle Valve Special on the Pole with a four-lap average of 120.599 mph. Leon Duray was second quick at 119.087 mph in his Packard Cable Special. Ralph Hepburn, Duray's teammate, rounded out the front row with an average qualifying speed of 116.543 mph. All three were front-drive creations.

Woodbury's Pole run was made shortly after a mid-afternoon rainstorm had shut down the track. Babe Stapp, Pete De Paolo and Ray Keech made up row two.

Besides the qualifying action, the crowd of 30,000 also got to see the film crew filming a scene for the new movie, "Speedway." Multiple shots were made in front of the pits. The film's stars, William Haines and Anita Page, were introduced to the crowd after a tour of the race track in the Pace Car.

Indianapolis was abuzz over the possibility that Charles Lindbergh and his new bride, Anne Morrow, planned to attend the Indianapolis 500. They left Englewood, New Jersey, after their wedding Monday evening for an undisclosed honeymoon. Indiana Governor Harry G. Leslie had invited the couple. Former heavyweight champion Jack Dempsey would also attend. Another person that security guards would be on the lookout for was the noted gatecrasher "One Eye" Connolly, who made it his quest to "crash" all major sporting events.

Because of a rule that barred women from being permitted in the pits, Eddie Rickenbacker circumvented the rule for Mrs. Norm Batten. He had his maintenance workers construct a special pit box atop a small building by the pits. Another female, M.A. Maude Yagle, owned the car that Ray Keech would drive.

Harry Beaumont, director for MGM's movie "Speedway" had four cameramen spread out over the track to film both race and crowd scenes. Actor William Haines, who was wearing his racing uniform that he wears in the movie, posed for photos with race officials including official starter Seth Klein.

A popular pre-race tradition was W.S. Marshall leading the world's largest musician parade down the main stretch. The 1,000 piece ensemble made it the "largest band in the universe."

At 10 o'clock, a starting bomb exploded signaling George Hunt, technical engineer for Studebaker Corporation, to start driving the Studebaker roadster Pace Car and to lead the field down for the start of the race. 160,000 race fans were in attendance.

For the second consecutive year Leon Duray lead the opening lap of the race by several car lengths and would maintain the lead for the first seven circuits. Cliff Woodbury, after a poor start, moved into second briefly but his race was short-lived. On lap 3, his car's right rear wheel gave way entering the NE turn. Woodbury's car skidded, turning around twice before backing into the NW wall. A youngster who had snuck into the track and was sitting atop the retaining wall escaped with only a huge scare. He was knocked down by the impact of Woodbury's car. Neither the youth nor Cliff were injured. However, Louis Neville, an assistant cameraman for MGM, was injured slightly when Woodbury machine glanced into his camera stand.

MAY 30, 1929   BILL SPENCE KILLED

On lap nine, rookie Bill Spence, a talented 22-year old driver from Los Angeles driving the #10 Duesenberg Special, skidded before hitting the retaining wall in the SE turn and turned over several times. Spence was thrown out of his car and he landed on his head in the middle of the track. His car continued to roll over several additional times before coming to a stop, upright. Unconscious and bleeding profusely from the mouth, Spence was picked up and rushed to the track emergency hospital, dying before his arrival of a fractured skull. This was Bill's first 500-Mile Race although he drove in relief for Billy Arnold last year. Spence's death was the first in the race since 1919.

A visibly shaken Fred Duesenberg commented on Bill Spence's fatal accident. "He was a nice boy and had lots of nerve. I think he was trying to make up for lost time when the accident occurred."

Upon learning of his good friend's death, an emotional Babe Stapp broke down and cried. Having had a great friendship with Spence for several years, Stapp declared he would never drive a race car again.

With a surprising burst of speed from his ninth place starting spot, Deacon Litz stormed to the front on lap eight. Driving the car that Louis Meyer was victorious in a year ago, Deacon continued to pace the race until the 57th lap when his car hit the north turn wall. He was uninjured. He earned $4,900 lap prize money. Lou Moore took the lead after Litz's accident and scooped up $2,300 prize money by leading through lap 80.

Several pre-race favorites dropped out of the race before the half-way mark. Ralph Hepburn departed on lap 15 with a broken steering arm. He would later relieve Leon Duray; Peter De Paolo, on lap 26, was sidelined with a broken steering gear; Babe Stapp's day ended on lap 44 with a broken universal joint. Carburetor issues eliminated Leon Duray on lap 65 and Tony Gulotta left the race after 91 laps with a broken supercharger.

Midway through the race, Billy Arnold was struck by a flying object which broke the glass in his goggles. Virtually blinded, Arnold tried to continue despite the intense pain. Two laps later he brought the #9 Boyle Valve Special into his pit but the exhausted driver had to be lifted from the seat by his pit crew. He was taken to the infield hospital and treated for cuts about the eye. Cliff Woodbury would take over as relief driver for his car.

Louis Meyer appeared to be headed for back-to-back victories, leading the race from laps 80-94. Fred Frame, driving for Earl Cooper's team, assumed the lead for 11 laps and then Ray Keech was atop the leaderboard for three laps. Meyer re-took the lead and demonstrated his car's muscle by leading from laps 109-157 and garnering $6,400 in lap prize money.

At 392 miles, Ray Keech re-took the lead from Louis Meyer, who was forced to the pits to replace a worn front tire. Louis lost six minutes and 45 seconds when his pit crew was unable to restart his motor. Because of this lengthy delay, Ray Keech took command and led the remainder of the race. Meyer would finally return and go on to finish second nearly six minutes behind Keech. Jimmy Gleason with relief from Ernie Triplett finished third and rookie Carl Marchese of Milwaukee finished fourth, a fine accomplishment considering he had hit the wall prior to qualifying.This would be Marchese's only time racing in the 500.

Ray Keech drove a two-pit stop race. On lap 21, a blown tire forced him to make an unscheduled stop. He would pit again for gasoline on the 109th lap. Upon entering Victory Lane, Keech's first request was for a cigarette, "Gimme a Tareyton!" After finishing his cigarette and wiping his face of the dirt and grease from the track he would say, "I'm happy, but awfully tired." Ray drove one of Frank Lockhart-built cars to victory. In a short time they became good friends. The two were quite different. Lockhart was slight of built and highly nervous. He was a very talented engineer who obsessed over every detail on his race cars. Whereas

Keech was heavy set and had little interest in the mechanical side of a race car.

The biggest disappointment happened to Lou Moore during the final stages of the Race. Earlier Moore had sought relief from Barney Kloepfer in his Majestic Racing Special. Kloepfer had been impressive in advancing the car up into second place, two laps ahead of third place Louis Meyer. After a brief rest, Moore was ready to resume his chase of Keech. As Kloepfer drove past the officials stand, his motor was clanking. A crew member signaled to Kloepfer to stop but Barney was confused and he failed to respond to the order. When Barney came into the pits on lap 198, it was apparent his motor's bearings were burnt out. Apparently Moore felt he had the mechanical expertise to coax two more laps out of the car. Most likely it was Moore's intention to finish the race as runner-up. Barney did pit on lap 198 and Moore got back into the car. Soon after leaving the pits, his motor stalled on the backstretch when the motor threw a connecting rod through the crankcase. This would cost the team the $10,000 second place prize. Because of time lost while making the driver exchange, it would have been highly unlikely Moore could have caught Keech.

Technical experts felt that the change in temperatures during the driver exchange may have been the culprit that would cause his connecting rod to freeze and that Kloepfer would have most likely would have completed the remaining two laps of the race had he been permitted.

It was the hottest day of the month with temperatures rising to 89 degrees during the late stages of the race.

Bill Spence's widow, Vivian, said her husband had left six weeks ago for Indianapolis with Babe Stapp. He had hoped to have success racing until next October so he could retire and build a new home in Los Angeles. Bill began racing at age 17 and progressed to where he was racing on the large tracks across America with a top second place finish last year in Detroit. At Ascot he was victorious in the Italian Helmet dash for ten consecutive weeks. He placed fifth in the AAA standings in 1928 and was also Pacific Coast Champion. His last victory was on Easter Sunday at Ascot. Spence, who would have been 23 on June 9, had been married for three years.

Babe Stapp, who emotionally announced his retirement from racing, reconsidered and plans to drive at Altoona. With a heavy heart he remembered his good friend Bill Spence.

BABE STAPP——"Well, it's all over for me now—I'm going home and hang up my goggles.

"Bill and I palled around together on the coast and what were my troubles, were Bill's. He was a regular guy and with him gone, the racing game can't hold much for me any more. I'm going back to the coast—back home to try and forget."

JUNE 15, 1929   RAY KEECH KILLED AT ALTOONA

17 days after his glorious triumph in the Indianapolis 500, Ray Keech was killed on the 121st lap of the 200-mile AAA Championship race on the high-banked Altoona, Pennsylvania, board track. Keech's car was hit by Cliff Woodbury's racer, tossing Ray onto the track where he landed near the guard rail. The stunned Indy 500 winner struggled to reach the guard rail to sit. While resting with his left leg stretched across a steel guard rail, he was struck by Dave Evans's racer and hurled several feet. He was instantly killed——his body was badly mangled with the left side of his face crushed. The impact severed his left leg. Ray's right leg remained barely intact with his torso. Keech's car would briefly catch fire but was quickly extinguished. However, a portion of the board race track was burned.

Woodbury's race car came to a stop upside down. Unconscious when track rescuers arrived, he was taken to Mercy Hospital. Initially, Cliff was listed in critical condition with a possible basal skull fracture and a fractured shoulder blade. However, X-rays proved negative. A hospital physician stated, "The X-ray picture showed no evidence of fracture of the right shoulder. There was a slight fracture of the left side of his head which will give him no trouble." Multiple teeth were knocked out and he received numerous splinters over his entire body. Soon after admission, he regained consciousness but he was unable to recall any details of the crash. He was not informed of Keech's death.

Sarah Keech was in sitting in a reserved section of the grandstands with other drivers' wives. She was unaware that her husband had been killed for some time. When she noticed other wives reporting to the starters' stand, she became alarmed and rushed there to get a status report. While there, the ambulance carrying the body of Keech drove past her. Just before the start of a race, Ray Keech always would receive a telegram from his wife. He was carrying the "last one" for good luck when he was killed.

The wire services reported that Cliff Woodbury's wife had been confined to her room at St. Ann's Hospital in Chicago after giving birth nine days ago. After being informed of her husband's crash, she kept in constant contact with doctors until finally assured he would survive.

Louis Meyer's and Ernie Triplett's cars were damaged after colliding with a piece of steel guard rail that had been sheared off and was now blocking a portion of the race track.

Harry Hartz who was serving as assistant referee for the race said track conditions were no way responsible for the accident. Val Haresnape, official starter and secretary of the Contest Board of the AAA, after a thorough investigation, released an official statement about the accident.

VAL HARESNAPE——"Bob Robinson, driving car #24, hit a small hole in the track, spun up to a point near the guard rail, then slid into the safety zone. Ray Keech, coming into the curve, apparently saw Robinson skid, tried to swerve to the right to avoid him and at the same time applied his brakes. He put them on too quickly and his car somersaulted, catapulting at least six feet into the air and completely passing over Cliff Bergere's car. Keech's car then crashed into the outer rail and then slid down across the track, to be hit broadside by Cliff Woodbury's car, and was knocked into the rail again. Keech was hurled clear by the impact.

"The Woodbury car toppled over and the right front wheel flew over the outside of the bowl. Woodbury was pinned under his car, unconscious. As the cars of Keech and Woodbury rolled into the safety zone, the weakened guard rail ripped from its fastenings and slid down across the track, completely blocking the path of oncoming cars.

"Dave Evans, #15, struck Keech, the latter having his leg across the rail making an effort to rise. He was struck by the Evans car and killed. The Evans car was not wrecked.

"Jimmy Gleason was the first driver to cross the barrier safely. He drove toward the bottom of the track, saw people grouped about Keech's burning car, then drove toward the rim of the track and bounced safely across the looped rail. His course was followed by Deacon Litz and Fred Winnai.

"Ernie Triplett, too late to avoid the rail, drove straight through it. As he hit the far side of the loop, his car spun and the left front wheel was torn off. His car came to rest in the safety zone and he left it, seeking his wife to inform her of his safety.

"Lou Meyer, next to hit the looped rail, was thrown into a spin and landed in the safety zone, where, narrowly missing Robinson's car, Meyer crashed into the inner rail but escaped unhurt.

"The examination of Robinson's car proved conclusively that he did not hit the upper rail, as had been reported. Robinson did not cause the wreck and Cliff Bergere was not wrecked and did not collide with any other car. The bowl was in better condition than any other time in recent years. Harry Hartz, assistant referee and veteran driver, upheld this claim, asserting that the condition of the track was in no way responsible for the accident."

The hole which Bob Robinson hit was a minor one, not enough to be a threat to the driver's safety. Robinson's red car swung into the safety zone before Keech crashed. And the crowd started to applaud Bob's skillful driving, thinking the danger had passed, before they saw Keech's car skid toward the outer rail.

Keech was married and had a five year old son, Ray Jr. His fatality occurred less than 200 yards from where Joe Boyer was killed in 1924.

JULY 5, 1929   CLIFF WOODBURY RETIRES

After being discharged from Mercy Hospital July 5, Cliff Woodbury announced his retirement from auto racing.

CLIFF WOODBURY——"I've had a number of warnings and I'm through with the racing game as a driver, but I will retain connection with automobiles in the promotional field."

AUGUST 17, 1929   CARL MARCHESE CRITICAL AFTER SPRINGFIELD CRASH

Carl Marchese, fourth place finisher in the 500, was critically injured when his car locked wheels with Wilson Pingry at Springfield, Illinois. Marchese sustained a crushed chest and severe lacerations over his body. Pingry suffered a fractured skull.

Leslie Wright, attempting to avoid the crashed cars, swerved and skidded through a wire fence. His car overturned and plowed into a parked passenger automobile. 62-year old William Wayne, who was standing in the pathway of the errant racer, was struck and he would die that evening. Marchese would recover but never race at Indianapolis again. Later in life he would assist promoting Champ Car races with his brother Tom at the Milwaukee Mile.

SEPTEMBER 21, 1929   JIMMY GLEASON INJURED AT MINEOLA, NY

Jimmy Gleason was critically hurt in a crash at Mineola, New York, fairgrounds. Gleason was driving a car owned by Maude Yagle of Philadelphia, owner of Ray Keech's winning Indianapolis car. After touching wheels with Billy Arnold, his car overturned. Jimmy was hurled from his cockpit and through a fence. He suffered a fractured skull, a broken jaw and all of his front teeth were knocked out. Viewing the race from a private box in the grandstand, Mrs. Yagle collapsed when told of Gleason's potentially fatal injuries.

The report that Gleason was near death proved erroneous. During his stay in Nassau County Hospital, he indicated he intended to return to driving race cars as soon as he was able. A policeman saved Gleason's life by dragging him from the race track and out of the pathway of fast approaching race cars.

OCTOBER 29, 1929   BLACK   TUESDAY——WALL STREET   STOCK   MARKET CRASH

October 29, 1929, is known as "Black Tuesday." On that day the Wall Street Stock Market crashed as the market lost eleven percent in very heavy trading. It was the stock market crash that triggered the beginning of the Great Depression in America. Most fortuitous was it for Eddie Rickenbacker that he changed the rules on engines allowing the more cost effective stock block motors to compete in next year's 500.

1929

Cliff Woodbury
Pole Position.
Finished last. Crash on lap 3

1929

Ray Keech

Winner. 97.585 mph Average
Led 46 Laps

1930

Big changes were in store for the 1930 Indianapolis 500. Eddie Rickenbacker mandated that riding mechanics would be required. Superchargers were banned for the two-seaters. And the number of starting positions for the race would be increased from 33 to 40 starters.

When the official entry list was released by the Speedway, there was excitement that 1915 500 winner Ralph DePalma would drive as a part of a two-car team entered by his nephew Peter DePaolo. No top driver had driven a two-seater before in the 500-Mile Race. DePalma's experience in driving alongside a riding mechanic would somewhat neutralize the fact he hadn't driven in the 500-Mile Race since 1925 when he finished seventh. However, the euphoria of his return was squelched when Ralph had to decline the ride because of a business arrangement that he could only drive race cars with a supercharger bearing his name.

DePaolo then selected the tall, lean, dynamic local dirt track star Bill Cummings. Just 23 years old, "Wild Bill" had been electrifying crowds throughout the midwest since he had started racing five years ago.

Harry Hartz designed and built a new front-wheel drive two-seat race car. It would be powered by a 151-inch Miller engine. Still feeling the effects of his Rockingham crash in 1927, his choice to drive his car was Ralph Hepburn. However after a couple of test runs, Hep was not pleased with the car's handling performance and suggested to Hartz what to do to correct this. Instead of making the changes Ralph wanted, Hartz decided he'd qualify the car himself on Pole Day despite being away from the cockpit for 2-1/2 years. However, Harry felt there was more speed in the car than he had been able to reach.

On a daily basis, youthful Billy Arnold would stroll by the Hartz garage and each time he'd compliment Harry about his car—"Gee, Mr. Hartz, that's certainly a beautiful car." Then fate stepped in for Billy, who did not have a ride for the race. After aborting his very solid qualifying run, Hartz spotted Arnold standing near by his pit. "You've been admiring this car for several days, Billy, how would you like to take a ride in it?"

Billy Arnold jumped at the opportunity and in no time was running speeds faster than any posted speed for the month. Upon his return to the pits, Hartz inquired.

HARRY HARTZ——"How does it feel, Billy?"

BILLY ARNOLD——"Perfect. I wouldn't want a single nut or bolt changed."

To Hepburn's chagrin, Hartz surprised Billy stating,

HARRY HARTZ——"Help us push it up to the starting line and I'll give you a chance to set it on the Pole."

Arnold, who had attended the University of Illinois school of mechanical engineering in 1920-21 and 1921-22, was thrilled to have a chance to display his ability after just mediocre success in the single seat, supercharged cars—having finished seventh in 1928 and eighth last May. Misfortune cost Billy a possible third place finish in last year's race when a sharp piece of flying debris hit his goggles, shattering the glass and severely cut his eye necessitating him to make an unscheduled pit stop for relief.

In company with his riding mechanic Spider Matlock, Billy Arnold rewarded Harry Hartz's confidence in him by putting his eight cylinder front-drive on the Pole averaging 113.268 mph. Before Arnold's Pole run, Harry Hartz attempted his return to Indy after a two and a half year absence. Hartz turned a lap of 110.429 mph before terminating the run believing the car had much more speed than he had registered. He then turned the mount over to Billy Arnold. The switch to Arnold, a protege of Cliff Woodbury, surprised many of his fellow drivers who knew the fiery obsession Hartz had to win the 500. Harry indicated he would be available as a relief driver.

Louis Meyer, who had arrived at the track just two days prior, was second fastest in his 16-cylinder Sampson Special with a four lap average of 111.290 mph. His car owner, Alden Sampson, rode with him on his qualifying run. And rookie William "Shorty" Cantlon rounded out the front row in a four-cylinder Miller-Schofield Special at 109.810. Louis Schneider, Chet Gardner and Ernie

Triplett would start in row two on a day which saw 19 cars qualify.

The much-anticipated arrival of two Maseratis finally materialized. Italian standout Baconin Borzacchini was able to take to the track shortly before dusk but didn't attempt a qualifying run. Although he had only competed on European road courses, many felt he could come in and dominate like the French teams did pre-World War I. Baconin would qualify in 28th position but would have a short race day dropping out after 25 laps with ignition failure in his only run in the Indy 500. He was among 19 rookies to start the race highlighted by Shorty Cantlon, Bill Cummings and Chet Miller.

While driving Bill Cummings's car to the Speedway, Peter DePaolo was fortunate to escape death when he had to abruptly swerve the car into a ditch to avoid a collision with a train, barely missing the locomotive by inches.

May 30, 193   BILLY ARNOLD DOMINATES IN 500 WIN

In what would be the most dominant victory in Indianapolis 500 history, Billy Arnold led every lap with the exception of the first two circuits in which Louis Meyer held the top spot. He finished three laps ahead of the 5'4" Shorty Cantlon. (Herman Schurch drove in relief for Cantlon in Bill White's four-cylinder car from laps 97 thru 151). Driving the Bowes Seal Fast Special, Louis Schneider finished third in a car he built. Arnold would make only one pit stop for gasoline, oil and both front tires on lap 111. Billy told the fans over the public address,

BILLY ARNOLD——"I felt sure I would win. I knew I had the car to win this time and I could pushed it even harder. I really believe I could have been in front every lap, but I didn't want to use the car too hard when it was still cold. I never gave the car all it had."

Later that evening, Arnold discovered that someone had stolen his Chrysler roadster parked in the 1500 block of Illinois Street in downtown Indianapolis. A benevolent Arnold informed the investigating officer, "Tell the guy to come around to my room and I'll give him certificate of title."

Arnold, by leading all but two laps of the race, was awarded the largest prize money in Speedway history—$52,150. Now one of the most eligible bachelors in America, he was also given temporary possession of the Prest-O-Lite brick as leader at 300 miles and the Wheeler-Schebler trophy for being leader at 400 miles. L. Strauss Company presented the winner with a marble bench and bird bath from Europe. The following morning a jubilant Arnold was joined by Harry Hartz and Spider Matlock at the Fletcher Savings and Trust Company. It took Billy over an hour to endorse 160 lap prize checks earned by leading 198 of 200 laps.

Peter DePaolo was an early visitor to the pits and he turned his car over to Fred Roberts. DePaolo complained his car was too hard for him to handle. A six-car crackup occurred on lap 22 when Fred Roberts spun in the NE turn and he was hit by #8 Babe Stapp. Deacon Litz, following closely, hit Stapp. Johnny Seymour, in an attempt to miss both of them, hit car #8 Stapp, tearing off his car's left front wheel, before striking the wall. Marion Trexler, in car #45, hard on the brakes, was unable to stop and plowed head-on into Roberts's car #5. Seeing the melee ahead, Lou Moore, hit his brakes hard causing him to hit the outside wall. In what looked like a nasty accident, only Litz's wrist was broken and Seymour suffered minor injuries in the crash.

After persistently pestering his older brother, Cy Marshall agreed to allow his younger sibling Paul to ride along as his mechanic in the #36 Duesenberg. On lap 29, the 28-year old rookie driver suddenly swerved toward the wall on the NE turn. His car made hard contact against the 30-inch concrete barrier then bounced over the top of the wall. As the car tumbled 25-feet to the ground, Cy Marshall was thrown clear of the car. He suffered a fractured skull, fractured jaw and numerous bruises. Both Marshall's were taken to the infield emergency hospital. As he lay on the operating table, Cy Marshall begged the doctors to "fix Paul up first."

Paul Marshall sustained an even more serious skull fractured. For more than an hour physicians worked feverishly to save his life. Near death, he was revived briefly when adrenaline was injected into his heart. Both Dr. William Doeppers, superintendent of City Hospital and Dr. Horace Allen, surgeon at the Speedway, worked on Paul for an hour to save his life, before he succumbed.

Unaware that his brother had just died, Cy Marshall inquired on Paul's condition.

CY MARSHALL——"Did you get Paul fixed up?"

DR. H.R. ALLEN——"Sure, he's coming along fine."

Surprised by Arnold's race dominance, two-time winner Tommy Milton walked down to Billy's pit and consulted with car owner Harry Hartz.

TOMMY MILTON——"He is safely ahead now. Don't let him try to race any of those fellows who are chasing him."

Hartz agreed with Milton and stated he had signaled for him to slow down but Arnold failed toyed his orders.

Louis Meyer's quest for a second victory was hindered by the numerous times spent in the pits. He initially came in on lap 22 for four minutes and 30 seconds to fix a broken throttle connection. He lost another three minutes and 50 seconds on lap 103 to replace a tire and get gas and oil. He persisted to place fourth. Bill

Cummings had an impressive run finishing fifth. He was relieved by Fred Winnai from laps 117 to 147.

JUNE 3, 1930   MAC KENZIE'S RIDING MECHANIC KILLED AT DETROIT

Promising newcomer George (Doc) MacKenzie was seriously injured and his riding mechanic William Berry was killed when their race car crashed through a fence at the Detroit State Fair. Their machine somersaulted down the incline, pinning both beneath their race car. Berry would die at 3:45 p.m. from head injuries at Highland Park General Hospital. MacKenzie, who was unconscious until Sunday evening, suffered a lengthy laceration of the scalp, abrasions throughout his body and contusions. In a sad irony, just prior to the start of a 25 mile race, a torrential downpour turned the track into a quagmire and the remaining events were postponed.

JUNE 13, 1930   SIR HENRY SEGRAVE DIES TRYING TO SET RECORD ON WATER

Having owned the world's land-speed, Sir Henry Segrave set his sight on capturing a world speed record on water. His quest turned tragic when he died driving Miss England II. Segrave crashed just after he had completed his record-setting run of 98.76 mph at Windermere Westmorland, England.

Sir Henry, who had been recently knighted, was unconscious as his boat Miss England II sank following a crash. He would briefly regain consciousness and ask about the condition of his crew. There was a quick relapse and he died soon afterwards from an acute lung hemorrhage. His chief engineer, Victor Halliwell, was also killed when the boat rolled over him. Sir Henry was the first person to break the 200 mile barrier (203.79 mph) on March 29, 1927, at Daytona Beach, Florida.

JULY 27, 1930   BOB   ROBINSON   KILLED   AT WOODBRIDGE, NJ

Bob Robinson, 32, was killed instantly at the high-banked, half-mile board track at Woodbridge Speedway, Woodbridge, New Jersey. His car crashed through a guard rail and plummeted 35 feet to his death. His wife and three-year-old son watched the tragedy from the grandstands. The popular Robinson had attempted to pass Rick Decker on the 16th lap. Decker, who had driven in the 1929 & 1930 Indy 500s, described the accident.

RICK DECKER——"The right front tire of my car blew out, and I pulled up high on the track. I expected Robinson to pass under me but he too pulled high and went by me and through the guard rail."

AUGUST 16, 1930   "WILD BILL" ALBERTSON KILLED
AT MIDDLETON, NY

"Wild Bill" Albertson, popular East coast dirt track driver, met instant death before 16,000 spectators at Middleton Speedway, Middleton, New York. Albertson had told his pit crew he was going to try and establish a world half-mile dirt track speed record. His wife was among the spectators who witnessed his car upsetting and hurling him into a rail. His brake apparently locked and his car rolled over three times. Wild Bill was catapulted 60 feet through the air. Albertson's head was crushed.

He had been in numerous serious-looking accidents the past few years. Recently Bill told friends that he knew that he "had it coming" if he continued racing. His wife would always travel with him to his races. Last Labor Day he was seriously injured at Flemington Speedway and he blamed her for his wreck since she had not traveled with him to that race.

In 1927, Bill Albertson was scheduled to be a relief driver at the Indianapolis 500 but the untimely death of his mother-in-law forced him to cancel his plans. The following year, Wild Bill purchased a 1923 Miller for $12,000. Although the car had completed in three 500-Mile Races, Albertson felt confident he'd fulfills dream of racing at Indianapolis.

His quest suffered a setback when his car crashed through a fence at Langhorne the previous October. Due to his slow recovery from his injury, he ask Frank Farmer to drive his car in the 500. Albertson would be chief mechanic and would drive in relief from laps 119 to 134. The car would drop out on lap 140.

AUGUST 18, 1930   DUTCH BAUMANN DIES OF INJURIES

On Monday evening, August 18, Charles (Dutch) Baumann died due to injuries he sustained at the Kankakee, Illinois, Interstate Fairgrounds on the previous Saturday. Dutch had been in critical condition in St. Mary's Hospital from injuries received when he was pierced in his chest and right arm by a piece of wooden guard rail when his car crashed through a fence. Dutch never regained consciousness. The Indianapolis resident had been racing for eight years. Baumann was survived by his wife Beulah and their four year old son, Charles Jr.

Bryan Saulpaugh also crashed through the fence close to the spot where Baumann wrecked. He suffered a broken shoulder and arm.

SEPTEMBER 27,   1930 BOBBY JONES WINS GOLF'S GRAND SLAM

In what was considered a near-impossible feat to accomplish, Bobby Jones captured the British Amateur, the British Open, the U.S. Open, then completed the "slam" by winning the U.S. Amateur championship. Eddie Rickenbacker was anxious to have the new king of golf play at his Speedway golf course.

Although Billy Arnold had the most dominating win of any driver at Indianapolis, there were several, most notably Deacon Litz, that felt it was Hartz's race car and not Arnold that won the race. The needling continued to where a match race was proposed before the feature event at Altoona October 11. Cliff Woodbury, now fully recovered from his crash with Ray Keech last June, was named as Arnold's pit manager. The former Indy Pole winner voiced strong praise for Arnold's racing ability.

CLIFF WOODBURY——"I'm mighty glad that Billy is going back to Altoona to square some unfair things said against him by Litz. Every since I teamed up with Billy, I always said he had the stuff and I won't sit back and let anyone say he won a "fluke" victory—for there are no "flukes" among fellows like Arnold. And if there is anyone who doubts my word, I'll place my last nickel on Arnold—yes, and my garage too."

Billy Arnold was victorious over Deacon Litz in the best-of-three, ten mile, match race. The first two heats were neck-and-neck, with each driver swapping the lead almost every lap. Arnold won the first heat, Deacon the second. In the rubber match, Arnold captured the race by nearly a half-lap.

NOVEMBER 7, 1930   CONGRESSIONAL MEDAL OF HONOR

In what many Americans believed was long overdue, the nation bestowed on Eddie Rickenbacker the Congressional Medal of Honor for conspicuous gallantry in war. In a ceremony at Bolling Field, Washington D.C., President Herbert Hoover placed the Congressional medal on the World War I Ace of Aces.

PRESIDENT HOOVER——"Captain Rickenbacker, in the name of the Congress of the United States, I take great pleasure in awarding you the Congressional Medal of Honor, our country's highest decoration for conspicuous gallantry and intrepidity above and beyond the call of duty in action.

"At a stage in the development of aviation when the flying of airplanes was a much more hazardous undertaking than it is today, you were achieving victories which made you the universally recognized Ace of Aces of the American forces. Your record is an outstanding one for skill and bravery, and is a source of pride to your comrades and your countrymen.

"I hope that your gratification in receiving this medal of honor will be as keen as mine in bestowing it. May you wear it during many years of happiness and continued usefulness to your country."

Rickenbacker remarked after accepting the award.

EDDIE RICKENBACKER——"I should be ungrateful if I failed to recognize this great honor as true tribute to my comrades in arms— soldiers and sailors—living and dead. In peace and war, they have contributed their share.

"They have perpetuated the traditions and high ideas of these United States—in the air—as they have on land and sea."

To salute their compatriot, the 94th Pursuit Squadron, the First Observation Squadron and the 20th Bombardment Squadron staged an aerial demonstration.

Although Rickenbacker was credited with 26 air victories only one was cited in the Medal of Honor Citation.

MEDAL OF HONOR CITATION

The President of the United States of America, in the name of Congress, takes pleasure in presenting the Medal of Honor to First Lieutenant Air Service Edward Vernon Rickenbacker, United States Army Air Service, for conspicuous gallantry and intrepidity above and beyond the call of duty while serving as Pilot, 94th Aero Squadron, 1st Pursuit Group, Air Force, A.E.F., in action against enemy near Billy, France 25 September 1918. While on a voluntary patrol over the lines, First Lieutenant Rickenbacker attacked seven enemy planes (five type Fokkers, protecting two type Halberstadt). Disregarding the odds against him, he dived on them and shot one of the Fokkers out of control. He then attacked one of the Halberstadts and sent it down also.

General Billy Mitchell commented how Rickenbacker impressed him as a flyer.

GENERAL MITCHELL——"He learned to fly in three weeks. He worked at it constantly and distinguished himself particularly in the upkeep of his engine, airplane and armament."

1930

Billy Arnold
Pole Position & Winner
100.448 mph Average. Led 198 Laps

1930

Shorty Cantlon
2nd Place. Rookie

1931

MARCH 31, 1931   NOTRE DAME FOOTBALL COACH
KNUTE ROCKNE KILLED

Football fans in Indiana and throughout the nation were shocked and saddened to learn of the death of legendary Notre Dame football coach Knute Rockne in a plane crash over Kansas. His Fighting Irish teams had won National Championships in 1924, 1929 and 1930. During his 13 years as head coach, Rockne coached his teams to 105 victories, 12 losses and 5 ties.

On his deathbed George Gipp, ND's first All-American, told Rockne, "I've got to go, Rock. It's all right. I'm not afraid. Some time, Rock, when the teams up against it, when things are going wrong and the breaks are beating the boys, tell them to go in there with all they've got and win just one for the Gipper." Playing the powerful Army, Rockne told his team at halftime Gipp's, "Win one for the Gipper" story, and the inspired Irish went on to beat the powerful Cadets 12-6.

His 1924 team featured the "Four Horsemen" backfield of Don Miller, Jim Crowley, Elmer Layden and Harry Stuhldreher. Warner Bros. made the 1940 film, Knute Rockne, All American starring Pat O'Brien as Rockne and Ronald Reagan as George Gipp. Knute Rockne was a spokesperson for the South Bend—headquartered Studebaker Corporation and a fan of the Indianapolis 500.

�֎ ✖ ✖

As a result of the most dominant victory in the history of the Indianapolis 500, the perception of Billy Arnold changed from being a mediocre "field-filler" to one of the greatest champions ever—in a similar vein of Ralph DePalma and Frank Lockhart. His meteoric rise was chronicled in numerous publications and by the broadcast media, the bashful Arnold downplayed his overnight success.

BILLY ARNOLD——"I'm not the boy champion they talk about. I may look like a kid but I'm not. I'm 26. And I'm not a rookie wonder either. I've been driving for nine years, since 1922. Nine years of driving, but I'm not giving up. Nope.

"Not as long as I live.

"I got my first chance to drive in a 25-mile dirt track affair at Elkhart, Indiana, on Labor Day, 1922. In those days, they drew for position and had a standing start. I was lucky. I drew the pole position. I got out in front of the rest and drove all over the track, from side to side. I rambled around so much the older drivers were afraid to pass me. They hung back and I won."

Arnold had been fortunate to have never been hurt but one time.

BILLY ARNOLD——"Maybe I had what you might call a close call several years ago at Altoona's board track. I like boards better than brick. They're smoother.

"But sometimes pieces fly off—a plank—and you have no time to dodge.

"I was moseying along at a pretty fair clip when a board flew up and struck me on the head. I was knocked out. Three laps later I came to. I drove those three laps without knowing it. Instinct, maybe. I don't know, only that I was still in the race when I woke up."

Like 1927 500 winner George Souders enrolled in Purdue University, Arnold attended the University of Illinois for two years.

BILLY ARNOLD——"Several years ago, I managed to squeeze in a college engineering course in my time. I'm fitted for an engineering job—if I need one. But this is my real job, right here. I'm a race driver, that's all. This is my game. I love it.

"I'll stick to it. I don't even want to be out of it. I'm in this game for the money I've been able to win. It's the best job I know I can do."

MAY 23, 1931   RUSS SNOWBERGER WINS POLE POSITION

Russ Snowberger, driving his own Studebaker stock block powered racer, the Russell "8", surprised the crowd with a qualifying average of 112.796 mph to post the fastest time of the early day qualifiers. Most railbirds felt the Pole battle would be decided by defending champ Billy Arnold, Louis Meyer or Bill Cummings.

Surprisingly Billy Arnold was struggling to find the qualifying speed that would earn his second consecutive Pole Position. For the days leading up to the time trials, Arnold was several miles off of his times from a year ago. At 7:08 p.m. he took to the track—eight minutes after the official closing time—AAA officials relented to the crowds insistence that the defending champion be allowed to make a qualification attempt. And he didn't disappoint, averaging 113.848 mph to appear to capture the top spot. In a surprising development, AAA officials disallowed Billy Arnold's qualifying run which was the day's fastest speed. Arnold's car failed to pass a mandatory, post-qualifying brake test. Russ

Snowberger, driving a semi-stock car with a Studebaker engine, was moved from second qualifying position to the top spot.

Two drivers filed a protest and the technical committee disallowed the speed. In their attempt to rush the car onto the track, the pit crew failed to lock up the brake cables. Harry Hartz and Arnold contested the disqualification to the technical chairman Louis Schweitzer but eventually relented and accepted the committee's decision. This put Russ Snowberger back on the Pole.

Bill Cummings experienced equally bad fortune. Wild Bill posted the fastest time of the day at 115.001 mph on his initial lap. However, he was forced to abort the run because of a slipping clutch. Cummings returned later to qualify for the middle of the front row position. Rookie Paul Bost's run earned him the outside spot of row one, averaging over 112 mph. Deacon Litz, Ernie Triplett and Babe Stapp would start the race from row two. 17 cars would qualified.

Another contender for the Pole, former winner Louis Meyer saw his hope for the top spot dashed when his powerful 16-cylinder Sampson special crashed into the lower wall then rebounded into the outer wall. His foot had gotten caught on the accelerator. Louis would drive his car back to the pits but his frame sustained enough damage to prevent him from making a qualifying run over the weekend.

In an announcement that surprised many at the Speedway, Peter De Paolo stepped out of his Boyle Valve Special and gave his nod to Lou Moore to replace him. DePaolo indicated that since he has gotten used to front-wheel cars, he didn't like the feel of rear-drive cars. Moore made a qualification attempt but Pete waved off his slower-than-hoped-for run.

During the lull time, the crowd of 30,000 were absolutely flabbergasted by rookie Joe Russo's exhibition. He would drive his race car around the Speedway at 90 mph—-blindfolded!

Billy Arnold was able to salvage a bit of revenge by posting the fastest qualifying average of the field in his #1 Miller-Hartz Special. He obliterated Snowberger's Pole speed by nearly three and a half miles an hour with a qualifying run of 116.505 mph. However, as a day two qualifier, the defending champion would have to start the race in 18th spot behind the slowest first day qualifier, Dave Evans in the Cummins diesel. Tony Gulotta was the only other qualifier on day two with an average of 111.725 mph in a stock block Studebaker entry.

Paul Bost would headline a class of 12 rookies in the starting field of 40 qualifiers. The other notables of the 1931 rookie class included H.W. "Stubby" Stubblefield, Billy Winn, Joe Russo and Francis Quinn. In a surprise, Wilbur Shaw failed to qualify his Duesenberg but was tapped to drive relief for rookie Phil Pardee.

Joe Caccia, a 32-year old from Bryn Mawr, Pennsylvania, and his riding mechanic Clarence Grover, 23, from nearby Haverford were killed instantly as Caccia was preparing to qualify for the Race later in the afternoon. Skidding for 150-feet, his car had a horrendous impact with the retaining wall coming out of turn two, tearing down 28-feet of the eight-inch concrete wall. His car burst into flames as it hurtled 100-feet through the air, landing outside the track.

Caccia and Grover were hurled from their car and both struck a tree. Their race car would land on their bodies. Several drivers and mechanics hurried to extinguish the fire. The car wound up in the backyard of the house where Pop Myers resided.

Caccia was passionate about his racing career that spanned ten years, primarily on the East Coast. He forsook a successful taxi cab business that his mother owned to chase his dream. It was an added tragedy for his mother whose husband, two sons and daughter had recently died. Clarence Grover was an aspiring driver himself. Last year he was a mechanic on Zeke Meyer's car. His despondent mother stated, "I worried all the time about him, but I could not stop him. I was always afraid something like this would happen."

Legions of Ralph DePalma fans yearly had gotten their hopes up high that the 1915 Indianapolis winner would compete again in the 500 only to see it not materialize at the last moment. This year there was a buzz at the track that DePalma was driving his eight-cylinder Miller-Wehr Special from California to attempt to qualify for the race. The racing icon ventured on to the track on May 25 and was soon turning speeds near what was believed good enough to qualify for the race.

Down to the final minutes before sunset, the official ending of the final qualifying, DePalma pulls his rotary engine car onto the track to a thunderous roar from his fans that had waited all day to see the maestro drive again. Joe Huff, driving a Goldberg Brothers Special, was on his first lap of qualifying. Recognizing this, Ralph stopped at the starting line instead of making his run. AAA officials ruled he could not continue because the time for sunset had arrived. Fans jeered but to no avail. He would miss making the Race on an AAA technically of not starting before sundown. For a man use to disappointment at Indianapolis, Ralph just smiled and stated his typical response, "It was only Dago luck!"

Leon Duray, who had struggled all month with reliability issues in his new experimental 16-cylinder, two-cycle engine, became the last qualifier just at sunset with a disappointing speed of 103.131 mph for the two-time pole winner.

At 9:30 a.m. aerial bombs commenced firing at one-minute intervals Race Day morning. However, as a steady drizzle fell, it was quite apparent that the race would not start at its scheduled 10 a.m. time. Most observers felt the entire day would be a washout. Surprisingly, the sun peaked out and the brick surface began to dry. After nearly a two-hour delay past the traditional starting time, Eddie Rickenbacker and T.E. Pop Myers took a tour of the track and upon their return to the pits, pronounced the track ready for the start of the race.

As the green flag flew, rookie Paul Bost grabbed the lead of the race for the first two laps before being passed by Bill Cummings in his Cooper/Miller. Rapidly advancing through the field, Billy Arnold took command of the race on lap seven and proceeded to widen his lead with every lap, reminiscent to last year's dominance.

Francis Quinn was the first departure from the race, his Miller/Ford lasting just three laps. The talented Quinn had been denied the opportunity to drive as a relief driver for Frank Elliott because a medical exam showed him having a week heart. Herman Schurch, Leon Duray and Babe Stapp all were out of the running before lap ten.

The race's first accident occurred on lap six when Harry Butcher's car went over the NW wall. Joe Russo's car skidded to avoid striking Butcher's car. He suffered cuts and bruises to his right thigh. Surprisingly Butcher emerged with just lacerations and bruises. Dr. Horace Allen, in his medical report added, "I want to commend Russo for gallantry and for being a real good sport" for his efforts to avoid hitting Butcher's car and create a much more serious accident.

Showers fell again after 75 miles and it wasn't until the 150 mile mark that the track was dry enough for the starter to display the green flag.

Phil Pardee, complaining his car a Duesenberg Special that he felt was unmanageable to drive, was replaced by Wilbur Shaw in car #32 after 25 laps. Shaw went over the third turn wall on the 59th lap. Fred Winnai, who was closely following Shaw, attempted to slow down as Shaw went over the wall. He lost control of his car and also hurtled over the wall, pinning him and his mechanic, Clyde Dobyns, in the wreckage. Winnai suffered painful spine injuries and burns to his legs while Dobyns escaped serious injuries. Shaw received bruises to his leg. His riding mechanic, Walt Hannowsky, had lacerations to his head and leg bruises. Surprisingly sustaining only mild injuries, Wilbur would return to the pits and later take over as relief driver of the team car #33 Duesenberg Special being driven by Jimmy Gleason. Shaw drove the car 52 laps helping secure a sixth place finish.

Louis Meyer's quest for his second 500 crown ended on lap 28 when his Sampson Special developed an oil leak. During his schedule pit stop on lap 72, Meyer replaced rookie Myron Stevens, now running in the 15th spot. Myron, who was driving Meyer's Jadson Special, had started in 35th position. Louis would conclude the day with an impressive fourth place finish.

There were several other notable relief driver accomplishments. Peter Kreis drove Ralph Hepburn's #19 for 54 laps en route to a third place finish. Bill Cummings, whose Empire States Cooper would drop out after 70 laps with a broken oil line, returned to relieve Deacon Litz in #5 for 84 laps, advancing the car to third place before crashing on lap 177. Herman Schurch drove relief of rookie George Howie for 88 laps and finish just out of the money, in 11th place.

Also impressive relief stints were accomplished by two drivers who had never qualified for the 500. Bryan Saulpaugh drove 49 laps for Chet Miller in car #27 helping bring the car home to a tenth place finish. East Coast dirt track star James Patterson drove the ill-handling car #55 of Billy Winn's for 67 laps. At the end of the race the car was still running but was flagged off the track, completing only 138 circuits.

Arnold's blistering pace was slowed with the resumption of a slight drizzle and the cars maintained their position for the next 25 miles. Bill Cummings, a half lap behind in second position, dropped out of the race when his car suffered a broken oil pump on lap 70. The rain would cease and Arnold continued to run away from the field leading Tony Gulotta by more than a lap after 200 miles.

Arnold was making the contest another yawner in his quest to be the first person to win the 500 back-to-back. This would all change with a terrifying crash on lap 162 which had tragic consequences. Billy's car lost a left rear wheel, skidded sideways and collided with rookie Luther Johnson's car. Arnold's car crashed into the retaining wall, caught fire, then hurtled over the wall like a fireball. Their race car proceeded to crash through a low inside fence where Arnold and his riding mechanic were thrown from their car. Being ejected from their vehicle likely saved their lives as their car would burst into flames.

Initially Arnold and Matlock's injuries appeared not to be that serious. Arnold was unconscious for approximately 15 minutes. When he was revived, he dismissed his misfortune to the medics saying, "Just a tough break, that's all." However, upon further examination, Dr. Horace Allen listed Arnold's injuries as a double fracture of the right pelvis, severe burns to the right hip and a deep laceration on his left thigh which would result in the youthful Chicagoan spending a two-month stay in City Hospital. The fatalistic Matlock received a broken shoulder but he was released from the hospital the following day. Up unto the point of his accident he had led 155 of the 162 laps and earned $8,450 in lap prize money. Although he would require spending two months in the hospital while his double fracture of the pelvis mended, Billy lamented the loss of his car, virtually destroyed by the crash and fire. Luther Johnson escaped with cuts and bruises.

Spider Matlock, a self-professed fatalist, refused to carry any good luck charms. He firmly believed when your time comes, it comes. He pointed to the fact that he and Arnold were thrown clear of the wreckage as proof that their time "had not come." A Hollywood stuntman noted for being able to crash airplanes, he formed the group, "Thirteen Flying Black Cats of Hollywood." Only six members still survive.

Although three-plus laps in the arrears to Billy Arnold, Tony Gulotta, who was in a close battle with Louis Schneider for second place, crashed over the NW turn wall near the spot where Arnold's accident occurred. Tony's Hunt Special tore away a sizable section of the concrete wall. Fortunately the 27-year-old pilot from Kansas City suffered only cuts and bruises, but again for the popular Gulotta, it was another near miss at winning the 500-Mile Race. He was credited with an 18th place finish, out on lap 167. He blamed excessive oil on the track as the cause of his crash.

Bill Cummings, running in third place as relief driver for Deacon Litz, sustained cuts and bruises on the 177th lap when his car broke a wheel, skidded and crashed into the SW wall. He and his riding mechanic suffered only minor injuries.

Following Gulotta's crash, Louis Schneider had a comfortable lap lead over Fred Frame and he maintained a controlled pace until the finish, leading the remaining 39 laps. Ralph Hepburn, Louis Meyer and Russ Snowberger engaged in a close battle for third through fifth albeit five laps behind the winner. Jimmy Gleason, Ernie Triplett and Stubby Stubblefield would finish sixth, seventh, and eighth. And in a remarkable performance, Dave Evans drove the race non-stop in his Cummings Diesel. Owner Clessie Cummings stated the car consumed just $2.40 of fuel oil for the entire distance.

In Victory Lane, Schneider was joyous but exhausted. Virtually all the employees of Bowes Seal Fast, headquartered in Indianapolis, were there to great Schneider and his riding mechanic Jigger Johnson. On the forehead of the new 500 champion was a diamond-shaped smudge of grease. And Louis's face was very noticeably red from sunburn even though there had been threatening weather conditions all day. Schneider's first remarks were to ask about the condition of Billy Arnold. When informed both he and Matlock had survived the frightening crash, he responded, "wonderful". Schneider's victory was dubbed as a "surprise win" by the press.

Early on in his career, Louis Schneider got crosswise with Speedway General Manager Pop Myers when he took out onto the Speedway to run some practice laps in his passenger automobile. After becoming aware that this was happening, a furious Myers ordered Speedway motorcycle police to go arrest him. Schneider toyed with them—initially slowing down, then speeding up, before stopping. After discovering that Louis was an Indianapolis motorcycle policeman, they either could not or would not arrest him, angering Pop even more.

Despite finishing second in 1928 and third last year, Schneider had a stormy relationship with the AAA. Soon after he resigned from the police force in 1927, he would finish just out of the money in 11th. He was suspended by the iron-fisted sanctioning body for competing in un-sanctioned races and was forced to miss the 1929 race. Louis was reinstated for the following year and he placed third in 1930. For this years race, Schneider had purchased a new Miller racer but it really stressed his budget and he gave considerable thought to selling his investment just to be able to recoup some of his expenses. Schneider, like many other drivers, ate for several weeks on credit in Tom Beall's Speedway cafeteria. After winning Louis paid Beall off in full. He would earn $29,500 for his victory, considerable in the throes of the Great Depression but soon things began to crumble both in his racing career and his personal life.

It was an all-Indianapolis victory as Schneider, a former Indy motorcycle policeman who resided in the Wesley Hotel with his new 24-year old bride Barbara and their infant son Billy. Local company Bowes Seal Fast sponsored his car. They had been a local business since 1918.

In what was a tragic, freak accident, 11-year old Wilbur Brink was killed by a flying wheel from Billy Arnold's race car. Flung like a discus, the errant wheel traveled over two hundred feet sailing over two tall trees and the fence that enclosed the Speedway. It struck young Wilbur in the head as he and some friends were sitting on an ice box by a temporary refreshment stand his father, Harvey Brink, had set up in their front yard at 2318 Georgetown Road. The father had hoped to earn some extra money from race fans traveling to and from the track.

Brink was taken initially by ambulance to the Speedway's infield hospital where Dr. Horace Allen, Chief Surgeon, labored to save his life. Lewis Robbins, a Butler student who was a non-professional assistant in the track hospital and trained in the American Red Cross artificial respiration, volunteered to administer CPR. For more than two hours he continued his exact, regimented breathing while doctors tried in vain to save Wilbur. He accompanied young Brink to City Hospital continuing breathing for him. However, soon after arrival, he died of severe head injuries.

This was the second tragedy to befall the Brink family. The past December, Harvey Brink Jr., Wilbur's nine-year old brother, was critically injured by an automobile as he was sledding. Miraculously he would recover.

On Sunday, May 31, Louis and Barbara Schneider took their six month old son, William, to be baptized at Zion Evangelical Church. The ceremonies were performed by Reverend F.R Daries. Following the service Pastor Daries said a prayer for Schneider's protection on the race track.

June 23, 1931   WALT MAY DIES OF INJURIES AT SAN JOSE

A quartet of talented youngsters demonstrated excessive bravery as they battled each other up and down the California coast. Almost inseparable were Ernie Tripplett, Francis Quinn, Jimmy Sharp and Walt May. They cared almost as much for outdoing the others as they did winning. They traveled together. They partied together. They had a sizable bet on which one of the quartet would win the Indianapolis 500 first. Each of them knew they all would win the 500 but the big question was in what order. The revelry ended June 23, 1931, when Walt May died of injuries suffered on June 21 at the San Jose Speedway.

During time trials, the wheel of his car collapsed and his machine overturned. Walt suffered a brain concussion, fractured left shoulder and broken ribs. The surviving trio knew he was seriously injured but it shook them to their core when he died two days later. May had survived two serious accidents during the past year. At Ascot Speedway, he suffered a serious back injury when his car overturned. Later, again at Ascot, a flat tire caused him to crash into the wall and he was briefly listed in serious condition.

SEPTEMBER 12, 1931	JIMMY GLEASON KILLED AT SYRACUSE

The affable Jimmy Gleason's luck with brushes against death ended in a gory accident at Syracuse, New York in front of 10,000 spectators including his wife and eight-year-old son. Averaging 80 mph as he came out of the corner prior to the start of his qualifying run, he hit a soft patch of dirt on the track which caused his car to swerve to the right and crash into the outer wall. Gleason was thrown from his car onto the track. Tragically his errant car spun once then landed directly upon him. Earl Younger, his riding mechanic, was thrown across the wall and landed in the grandstands. Three spectators were injured by this human projectile.

Gleason was dead when the ambulance arrived. Younger was taken to the State Fair Hospital in critical condition but he would recover. Mrs. Gleason, unaware of her husband's condition, arrived at the track hospital before Jimmy was brought there and fainted when informed of his demise.

NOVEMBER 10, 1931   NEWLYWED HERMAN SCHURCH
                      DIES OF ASCOT INJURIES

Newlywed Herman Schurch, who had been absent from racing on the West Coast for over a year, proudly brought his new wife Florence with him. He had just married Miss Florence Turner on October 19. They would be in Los Angeles to see his brother Jack, a star guard on Occidental College's football team, play their arch-rival Whittier College. Four days after they arrived, the talented Swiss-American decided to race at Legion Ascot Speedway. Late on the morning of November 7, he went to the track to get some practice laps before Sunday's feature race.

While entering the south end turn, his brakes locked on his Cragar Special. Schurch's car catapulted over the wall, throwing Herman from his racer. He was taken to General Hospital in critical condition with a fractured skull, crushed pelvis and internal injuries. Herman would succumb on November 10. Schurch would be elected to the National Sprint Car Hall of Fame in 2010.

By virtue of their top three finishes in the Indianapolis 500, Louis Schneider, Fred Frame and Ralph Hepburn finished 1-2-3 in the 1931 AAA Championship car season. Schneider was also victorious in the Roby 100 at Roby (Hammond), Indiana, on June 21. Lou Moore captured two wins—the 4th of July 100-miler at Altoona, Pennsylvania, and the ill-fated Syracuse race. Also winning 100-miler events were Louis Meyer at Detroit and Shorty Cantlon in a September Altoona race.

December 13, 1931	FRANCIS QUINN DIES IN PASSENGER CAR ACCIDENT

Because the race at Oakland Speedway was rained out, Francis Quinn headed back to Los Angeles. Five miles north of Fresno, 28-year-old Russell Frasher suddenly swerved in front of Quinn's automobile and struck his car head on. Francis was thrown from his car and died on the roadside within minutes of a crushed skull. Claude French, who helped Quinn as a mechanic on his race car, was slightly injured. Deputy sheriff Harry Collins found a small amount of liquor in Frasher's automobile. Emergency attendants detected the odor of alcohol but Frasher denied being intoxicated.

A.C. Pillsbury, Quinn's manager, signed a complaint against Frasher, who would plead not guilty before Superior Court Judge T.R. Thomson. Two witnesses testified during the trial that Quinn passed them traveling in excess of 75 mph. Based on this testimony, Frasher was acquitted.

Quinn had been denied permission to race at Indianapolis by the Speedway medical staff due to an enlarged heart, which eventually proved inaccurate. In 2006, Francis was enshrined into the National Sprint Car Hall of Fame.

1931

Russ Snowberger

Pole Position. Finished 5th

1931

Louis Schneider
Winner
96.629 mph Average. Led 39 Laps

1932

JANUARY 1, 1932. RALPH HEPBURN, BRYAN SAULPAUGH HURT AT OAKLAND

Oakland Speedway opened the 1932 racing season with a New Years Day 100-mile race that would see both Ralph Hepburn and Bryan Saulpaugh suffer serious injuries in separate crashes. Saulpaugh had set a new qualifying record, traveling at a speed of 101.95 mph.

As Hepburn was entering the south turn his right front tire blew out. His car would plunge through a steel guard rail then travel an additional 25 feet before smashing through a board fence. He was taken to Hayward General hospital suffering a possible skull fracture, broken jaw, and broken knee cap, and he had several teeth knocked out.

After the ambulance had picked up Hepburn and the track was clear, the green flag was displayed even though rain had begun to fall. Immediately the 25-year old Saulpaugh, running second to Babe Stapp, lost control of his car on the wet surface and skidded into the officials' stand, which was perched on stilts 14 feet above the track. Its occupants were tossed onto the race track as the structure collapsed. Starter Fred Wagner, assistant starters George Theobold and Les Manning, AAA zone supervisor Hal Weller and former driver and race referee Bert Dingley were hurled 14 feet when the stand tumbled to the ground. All were fortunate to sustain only minor injuries.

Saulpaugh's car continued to careen 50 yards down the track, spinning twice before smashing into the guard rail by the pits. The impact tossed Bryan ten feet into the air, as many women shrieked in horror. Several fainted. Stapp, driving the late Francis Quinn's car, swerved to miss hitting the prone Saulpaugh. Bryan was unconscious when he arrived at Haywood General Hospital. Initially doctors were saying he has a "fighting chance" to recover having received a fractured skull, broken collarbone and suffering severe shock.

The race was stopped on lap 51 and Babe Stapp was declared the winner with Bill Cummings second and Ernie Triplett third. Hepburn's injuries were serious enough to cost him his chance of driving his own race car in the Indianapolis 500. His good friend Wilbur Shaw would pilot Hep's car in the race. Surprisingly Bryan Saulpaugh recovered and was at Indianapolis to attempt to qualify.

MARCH 1, 1932   CHARLES LINDBERGH'S BABY
                  KIDNAPPED

In the kidnapping that rocked the nation, American aviation hero Charles Lindbergh's 20-month old son, Charles Jr., was abducted from their home in Hopewell, New Jersey. The infant was asleep in his crib in an upstairs bedroom. On May 12, the child's body was discovered by a truck driver on the side of the road close to the Lindbergh home. A nation-wide manhunt ensued in search of the kidnapper. It would take two and a half years before Richard Hauptmann was arrested on charges of murder. He would be convicted of first-degree murder on February 13, 1935, and after all his appeals failed Hauptmann was put to death in the electric chair. Eddie Rickenbacker and Charles Lindbergh had a shared mutual respect for each others' accomplishments.

APRIL 27, 1932   BABE STAPP INJURED AT ASCOT

A Stanford University professor was working with Babe Stapp to streamline his race car with a fin-type design. They believed it would create more straightaway speed for their new Miller engine. However Stapp's desire to be the 1932 Indianapolis 500 winner were dashed after an April 27 crash at Ascot. A wet surface on the track caused him to lose control of his car and to hit the fence. His car ricocheted off the wall and turned over. Stapp was hurled from his car and would lie prone on the racing surface. Babe suffered a broken arm and shoulder and it was feared a skull fracture as well. He didn't regain consciousness until April 30. Initial reports indicated his injuries might prove fatal.

During his recovery, Stapp continued to say he planned to race the car in the 500, one-handed if need be. However, he did not receive a medical clearance and Stubby Stubblefield would eventually be assigned to his car.

With Babe hospitalized, Jimmy Sharp was selected as his replacement to drive the Gilmore Special in the May 8 100-miler at Oakland Speedway. This would be Sharp's first major race since his September 14, 1930, accident at the Fresno District Fair event. Jimmy was the current points leader in the AAA Pacific Coast Southwest championship. His car went through a fence tearing down a fifty-foot section. Sharp suffered a broken left arm and collarbone. Unfortunately, his arm failed to heal properly and he was absent from the cockpit for over a year. Francis Quinn would overtake Sharp for the points lead and ultimately capture the 1930 AAA Pacific Coast Championship.

Russell Frasher would plead not guilty to manslaughter charges in the death of Francis Quinn in Fresno Superior Court. The prosecution claimed he was driving at a high rate of speed down the wrong side of the highway. Frasher was free under $3000 bond and Superior Judge T.R. Thomson scheduled a court hearing for January 27. He would be found not guilty.

FEBRUARY 14, 1932   SHORTY CANTLON HURT AT EL CENTRO

Bob Carey, the Pacific Southwest champion, was leading the 60-mile event at El Centro for 31 laps when Shorty Cantlon and Ernie Triplett, running virtually side-by-side, both passed the pacesetter. Cantlon held the lead for the next ten laps with Ernie closely on his tail.

182

On lap 43, Triplett spotted a "sneaker" (the inner cord of the tire was starting to show through) in Cantlon's left rear tire and he made a bold move to attempt to pass him before the blow out. Cantlon's tire blew and he moved into Triplett's mount before Ernie could complete the inside pass. Upon impact, Cantlon's car rolled end-over-end three times toward the top of the race track. Shorty was tossed onto the track as cars sped toward him. Triplett's racer went through the infield. Bob Carey stopped his car to go to the aid of the injured Cantlon. In great pain with a fractured right thigh bone, Cantlon waved Carey back off the track. Triplett started to go to Shorty's assistance also, but he was told not to come. Once the yellow flag was displayed and the race cars slowed, the two drivers proceeded to assist him.

Shorty Cantlon suffered a broken leg in the El Centro accident while Ernie Triplett received and a minor facial cut to his head when he was struck by a piece of tire. Cantlon would try to get medical approval to drive his Lion Head Special in the Indianapolis 500 but would opt to have rookie Howdy Wilcox II drive. There were a lot of race fans that thought Wilcox II to be the son of 1919 500 winner Howdy Wilcox but they were not related.

(Howdy Wilcox son, Howdy Wilcox Jr. was instrumental in forming the Little 500 bicycle race at Indiana University. The 1979 Oscar nominated film, "Breaking Away", was a fictionalized story about four local boys—Dennis

Christopher, Dennis Quaid, Daniel Stern and Jackie Earl Haley—referred to as Cutters, compete in and win the Little 500. Steve Tesich won the Academy Award for Best Original Screenplay.

MAY 8, 1932   JIMMY SHARP KILLED IN HIS RETURN TO RACING

On May 8, 1932, Jimmy Sharp, hoping to dispel any concerns about his fitness to drive a race car, was killed at Oakland Speedway. He wanted to make a favorable impression with Indy car owners to help secure a ride for the 500, hopefully in Stapp's car. On lap 54, while running in a somewhat disappointing sixth place, he skidded in some loose sand and crashed through the guard rail at the south end of the treacherous Oakland track. Sharp was hurled 30 feet out of his car as it flipped end-over-end. His car soared approximately 30 feet in the air, then plunged down a steep embankment. Jimmy suffered a fractured skull, broken hip, broken collar bone and ribs as well as internal injuries. Two hour later he succumbed to these injuries at Fairmont Hospital without ever regaining consciousness. His close friend Ernie Triplett was victorious but bittersweet for Ernie, now that his racing compadres, Walt May, Francis Quinn and now Jimmy Sharp had been killed.

Despite his lackluster performance in last year's 500-Mile Race—qualifying 38th and finishing 14th—Lou Moore would return to drive for Chicago union boss, Umbrella Mike Boyle. On April 30, in a practice run at the Speedway, Moore turned a speed of 117 mph, casting him as one of the favorites to win the Pole. Lou told the media that he felt, after his car was fine tuned, he could run a lap over 120 mph.

In what came as a huge surprise, Cliff Durant agreed to drive for Harry Hartz, as a teammate to Billy Arnold. The 41-year old Durant last raced in the 1928 500-Mile Race. Hartz had built a new front-drive car, scavenging some parts from Tommy Milton's Detroit Special. After the car arrived late to the track, Durant reconsidered his plan, then stepped out of the car stating some other driver could do the car more justice. It had been Cliff's hope to be able to practice for a week to get re-accustomed to high speed driving.

Fred Frame, originally assigned to drive the Duesenberg that he had driven to a second place finish last Decoration Day, jumped at the opportunity to drive the new Harry Hartz creation built for Durant. Hartz would put Billy Winn, the dirt track driver extraordinaire, into Frame's machine. Winn's initial run in the 500 was mixed at best, qualifying 36th and finishing 21st last year. Frame was pleased to get the Durant ride even though the car wasn't ready.

Even with the gifted mechanic Jean Marcenac and crew working round the clock on fine tuning the car, Frame's chief mechanic had concerns about the car's reliability. Marcenac had worked several long weeks in Los Angeles to get it ready to be shipped to the

Speedway. As soon as they took to the track, they were immediately plagued with oil pressure issues. These problems were eventually remedied but they cost Frame the opportunity to qualify for the Pole. Finally on May 24, he was able to secure a spot in the field with a qualifying speed of 113.856 mph, good for 27th starting spot.

Still the prohibitive favorite to win his second 500 was Billy Arnold. The entire Hartz team felt Billy's late race crash gifted Louis Schneider with an undeserved victory. Schneider's win left an unpleasant taste in Hartz's mouth and Fred Frame was his insurance policy to make sure what transpired a year ago wouldn't happen again this year.

Studebaker entered a five-car team headed by Cliff Burger #22 and Tony Gulotta #25. The remaining trio included #18 Peter Kreis, #37 Zeke Meyer (no relation to Louis Meyer) and #46 Luther Johnson. Defending champion Louis Schneider would sport #1 on his Bowes Seal Fast Special entry. The Indianapolis manufacture would also sponsor #10 Bill Cummings and #24 Deacon Litz.

Shorty Cantlon arrived at the Speedway walking on crutches just days after his plaster cast had been removed. It turned out that he suffered a broken femur in his Valentine's crash with Ernie Triplett at El Centro, California. He was hoping that he could convince the medical staff to clear him to drive.

MAY 21, 1932   LOU MOORE WINS POLE

In a mild surprise, Lou Moore captured the Pole Position in an early evening run. Battling a stiff wind coming out of the North, his rear-drive Boyle Valve Special averaged 117.363 mph to become the fastest non-supercharged car to qualify. His final circuit was his quickest at 118.577 mph. Billy Arnold posted a disappointing average speed of 116.290 mph during a mid-day trial. He privately felt he'd average 118 mph. Rookie Bryan Saulpaugh, now nearly fully recovered from his January crash at Oakland, had an eventful day in securing the outside spot of the front row in his powerful 16-cylinder car.

While averaging 116 mph on his first qualification attempt, he spun. Fortunately he did not hit anything but his tires were flat spotted. After a change of tires and a consultation with Harry Miller, he went out and comfortably qualified at 114.369 mph. Although classified as a rookie, Saulpaugh drove 150 miles in relief for Chet Miller in 1931. Last year's Pole winner, Russ Snowberger, driving a near-stock car creation, was fourth fastest. Ira Hall would start fifth driving a Duesenberg and Howdy Wilcox II, in Shorty Cantlon's four-cylinder Lion Head Special, averaged 113.468 mph to fill out row two.

Former champion Louis Meyer, driving the 16-cylinder Sampson Special, was seventh fastest in a disappointing run of 112.471 mph. Billy Winn rewarded Harry Hartz for his confidence in him by posting the day's ninth fastest speed at 111.801 mph. Bob Carey, a rookie from nearby Anderson, Indiana, put Louis Meyer's Jadson Special in the field with a four-lap average of 111.070 mph.

Studebaker Corporation from South Bend, Indiana, fielded a five-car factory team and four drivers made successful runs led by Hollywood stuntman Cliff Bergere along with Peter Kreis, Luther Johnson, and surprisingly slowest, starting 20th, was Tony Gulotta. Zeke Meyer would qualify later in the month. All told 21 drivers qualified.

The second day of qualifications saw only two drivers post times. Wilbur Shaw qualified at 114.326 mph in a car entered by the injured Ralph Hepburn—the car Hep finished third with last year. Shaw's average was identical to Russ Snowberger's speed, but since he was a Day Two qualifier, he'd line up 22nd on Race Day. Al Aspen was the only other qualifier barely above 108 mph. Noteworthy, Leon Duray's powerful two-cycle, sixteen cylinder engine continued to have persistent problems. A gas connection broke on Duray's car on the backstretch and a brief fire erupted.

On Day Three of qualifications, Tommy Milton's protege Bob McDonogh became the first person to qualify a four-wheel drive race car with an average of 113.379 mph. His final lap was 114.635 mph, a speed faster than Bryan Saulpaugh's outside front row starting spot.

More impressive was the car didn't arrive to the track until Sunday.

Stubby Stubblefield, driving the four-cylinder Gilmore Special originally assigned to Babe Stapp, had a heartbreaking qualifying run. A bizarre final lap cost him having a shot of bettering Lou Moore's Pole speed of 117.363 mph average. Stubby's first three laps were outstanding——lap one 117.310 mph——lap two 117.570 mph——lap three 117.005 mph. On his final circuit, Stubblefield felt his tire was ready to blow so he slowed down on the backstretch. As he motored slowly down the main straightaway intending to stop before the start/finish line, he mistakenly drove passed it. His final lap fell to 101.088 mph which drastically dropped his qualifying average to 112.899 mph.

MAY 26, 1932   RIDING MECHANIC KILLED IN BENNY BENEFIEL CRASH

Harry Cox, a 28-year old riding mechanic from Indianapolis was killed, and driver Benny Benefiel was seriously injured when their race car hurtled over the south wall and smashed against a tree in a late afternoon practice crash. Going through the south turn, a left-front wheel broke causing the car to hit the inside retaining wall, then ricochet to the upper part of the track and over the top of the concrete wall. The car hit two trees, snapping off their branches, before dropping 18 feet to the ground. The wrecked race car eventually landed in the side yard of J.W. Stevens, a Speedway employee. His wife and son, sitting on their front porch, were the first to arrive at the accident scene. Benefiel and Cox were tossed from their car with Cox dying of a broken neck, broken left arm and internal injuries. They were driving the same car in which Joe Caccia and riding mechanic Clarence Grove were killed at the Speedway last year less than 200 yards from the Benefiel crash.

Benny Benefiel was taken to City Hospital in serious conditions with facial lacerations. So distraught over Cox's death, Benny refused to race again and would die in 1972 at age 66. Harry Cox was considered an expert parachute jumper and was a member of the Indiana National Guard 113th observation squadron holding the rank of sergeant.

Shorty Cantlon hoped to race his own car in the Indianapolis 500 or at least drive in relief for Howdy Wilcox II. He continued to lobby the Speedway medical staff saying "I can sit down to drive the 500-Miles so I see no reason why they don't let me tool my car." However, the doctors refused to clear Cantlon to drive.

MAY 27, 1932   MILTON JONES KILLED IN PRACTICE
                 CRASH

Early in the morning, Ira Hall, driving a Duesenberg, hit the NE wall when his throttle stuck. It was his second smash-up since the track opened. Then at 12:30 p.m. Milton Jones, a 38-year old rookie from Cleveland, lost control of his car #19 and headed up the track tail first, smashing hard into the concrete wall. The impact was so severe that a 15-foot section of the wall was torn away. Milton continued his backwards path over the wall before plunging down 15-feet. After striking the ground, the car somersaulted, throwing Jones and his riding mechanic Harold Gray from the car. Their racer would wind up a crumpled mess near the yard of Speedway General Manager Pop Myers.

The mortally wounded Jones, who was tossed into a weeded area, panically waved his arms to attract the attention of a Speedway guard. Jones pleaded, "Help me, for God's sake, please help me." When help arrived, he had lapsed into a coma and was rushed to City Hospital. He would die at 5:30 pm of a crushed chest and internal injuries. Harold Gray was seriously injured with a broken left arm, internal injuries and lacerations but he would survive.

Veteran mechanic Thane Houser was critical of Jones's driving skills. "Poor devil, he just drove over his head. He almost lost his car on the previous lap. Jones was driving the turn faster than he knew how."

Last year Milton Jones brought two new four-cylinder cars to the Speedway but opted to give the rides to Stubby Stubblefield and Frank Farmer. Stubby would finish eighth while Farmer would drop out after 80 miles with an oil leak.

Milton was known around the United States as "Dare Devil" Jones. He and his wife traveled the country for nearly two decades performing motorcycle trick-riding. His wife was billed as "Molly, The Mile-A-Minute Girl". Their most popular act was as silo-riders where Molly would stand atop the handlebars and Jones would steer his motorcycle with his knees. As he drove around the inverted bowl, Milton would grab an orange from his assistant who stretched out over the upper guardrail to hand it to him. Jones, an engaging storyteller, enjoyed holding court in describing some of his most frightening memories on the bike.

MILTON JONES——"I lost control of my machine once in Memphis, Tennessee. It threw my wife over the top rail while I crashed on the bottom of the pit. I wasn't hurt much but it was an extra thrill for the customers."

Ironically last week 19-year old Milton Jones Jr. was riding mechanic for Mauri Rose, when Rose crashed into the outside wall in the south turn, then slid down the sloping track. Although the car was extensively damaged, Rose and Jones Jr. escaped uninjured.

All told 12 rookies were among the 40 drivers to qualify for the race including front row occupant Bryan Saulpaugh. Howdy Wilcox II, subbing for the injured Shorty Cantlon, Bob Carey in Louis Meyer's backup racer, Al Gordon, Doc MacKenzie, Gus Schrader, one-legged Al Miller, Argentinian Juan Gaudino, and starting in last position, Kelly Petillo would headline the crop of rookie drivers.

During the lead up to the race, the newly-married Billy Arnold expressed his strong desire to join Tommy Milton as a two-time winner.

BILLY ARNOLD——"Today's race is worth more to me than any other driver entered. That broken axle a year ago and spill over the wall cost me $250,000 at one crack besides a $30,000 hospital bill. I am broke and just got married so I am out to snatch that first prize. Make no mistakes about that, I'll drive to win."

Unlike the traditions leading up to the start of today's Indianapolis 500——A bugler playing Taps, the singing of Back Home Again in Indiana, the release of thousands of multi-colored balloons and the command to....Start Your Engines, the start of the 1932 Indianapolis 500 followed a series aerial bombs exploding in the sky. At 10 a.m. the Lincoln Pace Car driven by Edsel Ford, the only child of Ford Motor Company founder Henry Ford, led the field of 40 cars down for a flying start. Gar Wood, motorboat water-speed record holder, waved the green flag to start the race.

Pole sitter Lou Moore led the initial lap before being overtaken by Billy Arnold who would quickly outpace the field. Rookie Gordon's car was sideswiped by Stubby Stubblefield on lap two causing Gordon's #26 Lion Tamer Special to go over the outer NW wall. Both Al and his riding mechanic were uninjured. Stubby's car was not damaged and he would continue on to finish 14th.

On the following lap rookie Gus Schrader crashed Harry Miller's four-wheel drive car and escaped unscathed. The four-wheel drive cars didn't last long enough to demonstrate their race worthiness as Bob McDonough would drop out four laps later with a broken oil line. Many felt Bob could be a serious threat to beat Billy Arnold.

Louis Meyer quest to be a two-time winner ended on lap 50 when his powerful 16-cylinder Sampson Special skidded in the south turn and was damaged. But unlike last year when Meyer quickly replaced Myron Stevens in his own Jadson Special after his car dropped out, Louis allowed rookie Bob Carey to continue his impressive run among the race leaders. And Bryan Saulpaugh, hoping to add his name to the list of rookie winners like Frank Lockhart, George Souders and Louis Meyer, would drop out on lap 55 with a broken oil line. Bryan's strong month only cemented Harry Miller's belief, he had a future winner driving his car.

In the early stages of the race, Billy Arnold and Bob Carey were already a lap ahead of third place Lou Moore and fourth place Ernie Triplett. Two laps behind were Howdy Wilcox II, Bill Cummings, Wilbur Shaw, Bryan Saulpaugh, Fred Frame and Louis Meyer. However, it would be a short-lived day for Arnold. As he entered the NW turn on lap 59, a car ahead of him fishtailed and Arnold purposely steered toward the outer wall to avoid a likely collision. Billy's racer struck the upper wall, tearing off its right front wheel. The car hurtled the wall and landed on its side outside the track. In a reverse of their previous years injuries, Arnold suffered a broken collarbone and his riding mechanic, Spider Matlock received a broken pelvis. Billy was taken to the Speedway track emergency hospital where his first request was for a cigarette. Spider was transported to City Hospital. Arnold had led from lap 2 thru 58 capturing $2800 in lap prize money before his accident.

Juan Gaudino, who had been trailing Arnold, came into the pits and through an interpreter told officials that Arnold had gone over the wall. His sportsmanship cost him several minutes but Juan would soon become a spectator as his car dropped out on lap 71 with a broken clutch.

Bob Carey, driving the Jadson Special owned by Louis Meyer, took the lead of the race after Arnold's crash on lap 59 and would appear to be cruising to an uncontested victory. At the 200 mile mark, Carey continued to be scored as race leader with a full lap lead over Lou Moore, who had just dropped out of the contest with timing gear issues. Unfortunately on lap 94, Bob Carey's car #61 blew a tire, spun around three times and hit the SE wall. Neither Carey nor his riding mechanic, Lawson Harris, were injured and Bob drove the crippled mount back to the pits to replace the tire—his car sporting a badly bent left front wheel. The frustrated pair waited impatiently for over ten minutes as technical committee members inspected his car for its suitability to continue.

Carey mounted one of the most spectacular charges through the field in Indy history. On two occasions he spun while attempting to pass rival cars in the turns. He was again called back into the pits several laps later to examine the car's shock absorber. The last 100 miles he was running speeds of 109 mph as he charged from tenth to fourth position. Most observers agreed if he had not lost 12 minutes in the pits, he would have been a rookie winner of the Indianapolis 500.

Ernie Triplett, who had started the race in 31st position, took the lead from Carey in his #7 Floating Power Special but the "Blonde Terror" from LA gave up the top spot when he pitted on lap 108. Triplett's promising day ended on lap 125 with a broken clutch. Defending champion Louis Schneider, who had moved from 30th to as high as third, as well as Chet Miller, would also see their day come to an end on the 125th lap.

Rookie Howdy Wilcox II would take the lead for one lap before he would be forced to pit. In a bit of a surprise, Ira Hall held the top spot from laps 110-115 after the frontrunners had pitted. Advancing from his 22nd starting spot, Wilbur Shaw took the lead in Ralph Hepburn's #3 Veedol Special and would lead the field until lap 125 when Wilbur would be forced to pit as well.

Fred Frame, in a team car to Billy Arnold, moved to the top of the charts on lap 126 and stayed there until he would return to the pits for more water. Shaw would again move to the top of the charts from laps 135-151. Looking like he was a sure winner, his hopes for victory were dashed when his car would not start as he tried to leave the pits. Wilbur would lose nine minutes before being restarted. This misfortune gave the lead back to Frame on lap 152 and Fred would lead the remainder of the race. Shaw eventually would get re-started but his day would end on lap 157 with a broken rear axle.

During the Race Frame's car broke an overflow pipe in his circulating system and his engine began to run hot. He stopped on lap 46 for 55 seconds for water. Again on the 74th lap he made a lengthy 2:30 minute pit stop to fix his car's radiator overflow pipe. A dozen laps later he was in the pits again for more water and a right front tire. On the 94th lap he needed another minute to add water. Frame was able to reach lap 133 before stopping again for water, this time costing him

1:10 minutes. Fred's final stop came on lap 167 for his radiator's last drink and a left front tire change.

Fred Frame slowed the pace to less than 100 mph his last two laps of the race allowing Howdy Wilcox II, now in second place, to narrow the gap between him and the leader. When the checkered flag fell, Howdy was 43 seconds behind the winner. Cliff Bergere was third, the highest finishing spot of the five-car Studebaker team. Earlier in the race Bergere's #22 spun twice, tapped the wall and stalled. Both Cliff and his mechanic hopped out, turned their car around and resumed the race.

With his aggressive charge, Bob Carey would move up to fourth place. He likely would have won the race had he not spent a total of 12:54 in the pits, first to repair the wheel damaged when he hit the wall. He also spent 5:04 minutes in the pits on lap 124 to repair a shock absorber. Russ Snowberger was fifth in his Hupp Comet Special. Ira Hall would slide down to seventh place in part because of Fred Duesenberg's decision to put Eddie Meyer in the car as a relief driver. Meyer lost ground to the front runners and was quickly yanked out of the car ten laps later. On the 182nd lap Hall's car slid in the SW turn wall but he kept going. Late in the race Tony Gulotta lost a wheel which bounded down the track and barely missed by Howdy Wilcox II's speeding race car.

Car #2 Duesenberg in which Billy Winn started the race, ended in ninth position piloted by rookie driver Jimmy

Patterson. Jimmy took over in relief and completed the final 103 laps. Sadly, the promising career of Patterson would end as a result of his fatal accident at Winchester, Indiana, on May 27, 1934. Also serving as a relief driver was Bill Cummings, who drove in relief for Bowes Seal Fast Special teammate Louis Schneider for nine circuits.

37-year old Fred Frame pulled his victorious #34 Miller-Hartz Special into the "Bull Pen" to a mob of photographers and press there to cover the driver who had just broken the track record of Pete DePaolo, set in 1925. Frame's first concern was about the condition of his teammate Billy Arnold and riding mechanic Spider Matlock. After receiving congratulations from his crew and fans, he departed toward the Speedway hospital tent to check on Arnold and Matlock but arrived there only to learn that they had been taken away by ambulance.

After his car was pushed to his garage he was greeted by his wife and his 16-year old son, Bob Frame. Bob towered over his dad, standing 6'3 and weighing 210 pounds. Bob has a passion to be a race driver but his mother wants him to become a doctor.

When asked how hard the race was on him physically, he told the press.

FRED FRAME——"It was not as hard as some of theaters
                I have driven in during the last fifteen

years, among them the races here in 1927, 1928, 1929 and 1931.

"The reason I think today's race was not so hard was because the track did not get so oily and slippery as it did in former years."

Harry Hartz, Fred Frame's car owner, would take permanent possession of the massive 7-1/2 foot silver Wheeler-Schebler trophy for being the first car owner to have his car lead at the 400 mile mark three consecutive years—Billy Arnold having led after 160 laps in both 1930 and 1931.

For the 1932 race, 108 laps were designated for the $100 prize as leader of the race. Whenever the race was run under the yellow flag, those laps were not counted and prize money was recalculated.

Billy Arnold did not learn until after he left the track hospital that his grandmother, Mrs. Eugenia Harrison, had died. Billy's mother forbade his younger brother or sister to mention her passing for concerns that would negatively affect his driving. After the race, Arnold and his new bride returned to their apartment on North Pennsylvania Street.

At the Victory Banquet Frame received checks totaling $32,050 from T.E. "Pop" Myers, General Manager of the Speedway, the Wheeler-Schebler trophy and the

L. Strauss & Company piece of art. Wilbur Shaw was presented with the Presto-O-Lite silver brick trophy as race leader at 300 miles. Billy Arnold, with his arm in a sling, attended the banquet and collected $2800 in lap prize money and $4545 of consolation money. His fellow drivers were surprised to see him. Billy told them, "I wasn't hardly hurt. Just broke a shoulder. It was set at the Speedway hospital and I drove home that night." Howdy Wilcox II's check for second place totaled $12,650. Cliff Bergere $6,600 for third place and Bob Carey's frantic charge up to fourth place netted him $5800.

Many felt Fred Frame lost the 1931 race because of getting bad instructions from his crew. Frame took the high road when asked that question.

FRED FRAME——"I drove my own race last year. This business of criticizing my pitman is not right. I always knew where I am and I am the boss of the situation."

AUGUST 28, 1932   FRANK FARMER KILLED AT WOODBRIDGE

Frank Farmer and Bill Neapolitan were killed in a qualifying heat at the renovated Woodbridge Speedway. The board track had been converted to asphalt. Farmer, a three-time participant in the Indianapolis 500, locked wheels with Neapolitan when he cut sharply to pass him on the inside. Farmer suffered a compound fracture of the skull. Neapolitan's car flipped four times and he was thrown from his car resulting in a crushed chest and extensive internal injuries. Both were unconscious when taken from their cars and were pronounced dead on arrival at Perth Amboy General Hospital.

This was the second accident in which Farmer was involved in just over a year. Last June at Langhorne Speedway, he suffered a brain concussion and fractured ribs when his car overturned after locking wheels with Herman Schurch. Farmer, who had set the 100-Mile record in 1930, did not have a ride for the 1932 Indy 500.

OCTOBER 1, 1932   BABE RUTH CALLS HOME RUN IN
                   WORLD SERIES

In the fifth inning of Game 3 of the World Series against the Chicago Cubs in Chicago, Babe Ruth made a pointing gesture toward center field, and hit the next pitch from Cub pitcher Charlie Root 440-feet to deep center to the spot he pointed. Billy Arnold was now being called the Babe Ruth of racing and he very easily could have won three consecutive Indianapolis 500s.

Bob Carey became the first driver to win the AAA National Championship in his rookie season. In addition to his impressive fourth place finish at Indy, he won 100-mile races at Detroit and Syracuse. His 815 points edged out Fred Frame's 710 points for the title. Other race winners were Stubby Stubblefield at Roby, Indiana, Mauri Rose at Detroit and Bill Cummings at Oakland.

A 150-Mile Championship season finale was held at the Oakland Speedway on November 13, 1932. Fred Frame went into this event with a scant 20-point lead over Bob Carey and 80 markers ahead of Howdy Wilcox II. This would mark the first appearance of the two-seat race cars since 1924.

Wild Bill Cummings captured the pole position with Howdy Wilcox II second, Carey third and Frame fourth. Les Spangler, the Harbor Typhoon, started fifth in Harry Hartz's car and popular Bryan Saulbaugh, returning to the scene of his near fatal accident in 1931, would start sixth. Ernie Triplett and Babe Stapp made up the fourth row. 15 drivers competed in the race.

Eddie Rickenbacker, Chairman of the Contest Board of the AAA, had flown in from Los Angeles to witness the crowning of a new champion. Earl Warren, district attorney of Alameda County was appointed race referee when Barney Oldfield had to cancel. (Warren would eventually become Chief Justice of the United States Supreme Court.)

Over 10,000 would watch Bob Carey finish in second place to Bill Cummings to become 1932 AAA National Driving Champion—a feat never before accomplished by a driver in his rookie season. A broken valve eliminated Fred Frame on the 18th lap ending his championship hopes. Carey had been dominating the later stages of the race, holding a three-mile lead over Cummings at the 100 lap mark. Motor problems started to develop for Carey forcing him to slow down. However, it would be a late race flat tire on the 145th lap which would cost Carey the victory. Wild Bill was able to make up the two and one-half mile deficit.

Early in the race the fans were aghast at Ernie Triplett's charge to the lead from his seventh starting position reeling in race leader Bill Cummings on ninth lap. He would continues leader until his right rear tire blew out on the 56th lap. Howdy Wilcox II would take command with Carey now in second. Triplett would recover and eventually finish third. Howdy would be a victim of a blown tire as well, but unlike Carey and Triplett, his motor would soon blow up ending his championship quest.

Lester Spangler and riding mechanic Spider Matlock had a nasty looking crash after their car broke a connecting rod on lap ten. His car overturned and slid down the straightaway causing Spangler to suffer a broken left arm. Matlock, thrown from the car, would receive cuts to his face and an injured arm. Both were taken to Fairmont Hospital.

NOVEMBER 8, 1932   FRANKLIN ROOSEVELT WINS PRESIDENCY

Promising a "New Deal" for every American Franklin D. Roosevelt beat incumbent President Herbert Hoover in a landslide. The former New York Governor was able to use the poor economic conditions of the Great Depression to score an impressive victory. Rickenbacker was not a fan of FDR and believed he'd push the country toward a socialistic pathway.

※ ※ ※

Just before Christmas three story lines occurred. 1) Barney Oldfield and Billy Arnold joined Plymouth to test their new Six model at the Indianapolis Motor Speedway. 2) In a calculated move, Fred Frame purchased the crashed race car of Billy Arnold from Harry Hartz, effectively blocking Arnold's chances of scoring his second Indy win in the car that had dominated the last three 500s. 3) Louis Meyer ended his association with Alden Sampson and struck a deal to drive Ralph Hepburn's car that Wilbur Shaw had led 27 laps battling Fred Frame for the Race lead.

Shaw, who had been driving Leon Duray's car on the West Coast over the winter, would agree to pilot it in next year's 500. And Chet Gardner, after his rookie year at the Speedway in 1930, did not compete in the 1931 and 1932 Indianapolis 500s, was selected by Alden Sampson to replace Louis Meyer to pilot his race car next May at Indy.

1932

Lou Moore

Pole Position. Led 1 Lap

1932

Fred Frame
Winner
104.144 mph Average. Led 58 Laps

1933

Fellow drivers were somewhat critical of Arnold's aggressive race pace believing he would have won three straight 500s had he slowed down after he got such a substantial lead.

One rumor going around was that his riding mechanic Spider Matlock ask him to slow down. When Billy refused, Spider reached down and tried to yank his foot off the throttle. Billy took one hand off the steering wall and smacked Matlock's jaw. Arnold denied this story and, if true, the tougher-than-nails stuntman/riding mechanic would have no doubt struck back.

Harry Hartz had no problem with the 1931 crash when Arnold's axle broke, but he was less than pleased with Billy's 1932 wreck. Arnold's explanation was that he took evasive action to miss one of the Studebaker cars that fishtailed. Others said the Studebaker spun in front of him and he made a quick maneuver to the right and up the outer banking of the track to avoid a collision.

Bob Carey told a different tale—that for a dozen of laps or so he successfully throttled Arnold's attempt to put him a lap down. A frustrated Arnold then attempted to pass him on the outer part of the track, lost control and crashed over the wall.

JANUARY 21, 1933   BILLY   ARNOLD   &   BARNEY
                    OLDFIELD HIRED BY PLYMOUTH

H.G. Moock, general sales manager of Plymouth Motor Corporation, announced the appointment of Barney Oldfield and Billy Arnold to be the safety advisors for the car company. Racing pioneer Oldfield was named as Highway Safety Advisor of Plymouth Motor Corporation and Billy Arnold was named his assistant. The two would serve as advisors in further development of Plymouth as the world's safest car. Oldfield was the first AAA champion and Arnold was the youngest AAA champ at age 24.

Billy Arnold along with Harry Hartz had worked with Chrysler Motors on several adventures. Recently they established 12 world records for Chrysler at Daytona Beach and Billy was part of their engineering staff. Both Arnold and Oldfield would be visiting Plymouth, Chrysler, Dodge and DeSoto through the country.

FEBRUARY 5, 1933   BOB CAREY WINS SEASON'S
                    OPENER AT OAKLAND

The Bob Carey/Ernie Triplett personal battle for supremacy resumed in the season opener at Oakland Speedway. Triplett, who had won back-to-back West Coast championships vs. Bob Carey, reigning AAA National Champion. Both had legions of vocal fans who were adamant that their driver was the best in the country.

Carey took off from where he left off with a dominating win. Starting from the pole, he beat Wilbur Shaw by one and one-half laps. Triplett and Bill Cummings finished third and fourth.

FEBRUARY 26, 1933   CAREY VICTORIOUS AT ASCOT

At Ascot, the Bob Carey/Kevin Triplett feud continued after Triplett had set a qualifying record, Carey was victorious in the two-lap helmet dash in record time. Carey won the 100-lap main event breaking Ernie's track record by more than a minute. Triplett ran second, Chet Gardner third. However, the "head games" would escalate. "Hollywood" Bill White, owner of Triplett's racer, in a somewhat professional wrestling bravo manner, emphatically stated that Triplett would not drive his car at Ascot's next race if it would remain a scheduled 150-lap feature.

BILL WHITE——"Automobile racing at Ascot should be a demonstration of speed and skill and not brute endurance. I have built Triplett's car with the view to enabling him to break speed records at Ascot and not to hang up a lot of tire endurance marks. In the last race at Ascot, Triplett broke the track record for qualifying and was breezing along ahead of Bob Carey when he popped a tire. The result was the luckiest driver, not the best one, won the race.

"If they want Triplett at Ascot in the future, they'll have to restart the distance to 100 laps. At that, I may enter him just for the Helmet Dash in order to afford him an opportunity to make a sucker out of Bob Carey."

A week later it was reporter that Carey and Triplett had made a truce in their verbal war of words.

MARCH 16, 1933   RICKENBACKER DEMANDS BOTH TO "CEASE AND DESIST"

However, Eddie Rickenbacker reached his boiling point about the squabbling over the 150-lap distance and he sent a truce telegrams to A.C. Pillsbury, West Coast Director of the AAA emphatically demanding that their remarks which he described as unsportsmanlike and unethical to cease-and-desist. Not wanting to ruffle the owner of the Indianapolis Motor Speedway feathers, White relented and entered Triplett in the 150-lap Ascot race.

MARCH 19, 1933   ERNIE TRIPLETT WINS ASCOT 150-LAPPER

Ernie Triplett scored a decisive record-breaking victory in the 150-lap Ascot race over Wild Bill Cummings with Wilbur Shaw third. The huge crowd left disappointed that the Triplett/Carey battle in the feature didn't go down to the wire like it did in the two-lap trophy dash with Triplett winning by inches. In the main event, Carey's car, running a close second, would drop out of the race after just 34 laps with a broken transmission. It was becoming a foregone conclusion that Ernie would capture his third straight Pacific Coast Championship. In a class B event, promising youngster Rex Mays won a neck-and-neck battle with Chris Vest, opening the eyes of many car owners over the youth's potential.

Billy Arnold would describe the extent of his injuries that never got fully reported immediately after the 1931 race. He escaped with a pelvis broken in three places, five broken vertebrae, a broken left leg where the bone pierced the skin above the knee, seven rib fractures, a cracked jaw, two teeth knocked out and a broken nose. He would be in and out of the hospital for nine months. Billy was also painfully burned when his gas tank exploded. It was too painful for him to lay in the hospital bed with his scorched body so physicians hung him with several straps in the air—trapeze fashion. After he described all his injuries he suffered he joke saying, "otherwise I was ok."

The day before the big 100-lap Easter Sweepstakes at Legion Ascot Speedway, Bob Carey received word that Babe Stapp challenged him to a match race.

BOB CAREY——"Sure, I'll race against Stapp any time, over any distance. If he is looking for competition, I think I'll be able to satisfy him tomorrow in the 100-lap race."

The Easter Sunday event would also mark the return of Les Spangler, the Harbor Typhoon, to the cockpit since receiving a broken arm last fall at Oakland. He would drive Danny DePaolo's #2 Red Lion Special. Many observers were of the belief that had Lester not been injured that he, and not Ernie Triplett, would have won the Pacific Coast Championship. Spangler was regarded as one of the most talented young prospects. Harry Hartz was so impressed with Les that he stated if his arm holds up at Ascot, he'd have a ride for Spangler at Indy as a teammate to Fred Frame. If that would happen, Billy Arnold would have to search for another car owner for the 500.

APRIL 16, 1933   DEFENDING AAA CHAMP BOB CAREY KILLED AT ASCOT

Like a meteor streaking suddenly across the sky, Bob Carey's meteoric ascension onto the big time championship racing season ended tragically on Easter Sunday while on his qualifying run at Legion Ascot Speedway. Driving a new $10,000 race car at nearly 100 mph, his foot throttle jammed and a steering knuckle froze as he headed into what had become known as "death curve". Carey's car crashed through the fence and sailed 30 feet through the air. After striking the ground, his car rolled end-over-end and landed upside down. Several drivers and mechanics rushed to pry him from the wreckage but the 28-year old champion succumbed en route to the hospital. Bob was driving for Joe Marks of Gary, Indiana. Bob's wife, Lennie Miller Carey, their eight-year old son Robert Jr. and his parents, Mr. and Mrs. Clifford Carey, were with him on that fateful Easter Day.

Steve Hannigan, IMS publicity director, remembered the champion.

STEVE HANNIGAN——"Bob Carey was practically an unknown driver when he entered the 500-Mile Race last year, but his sensational, spectacular and hard driving made him one of the most colorful pilots in the game."

Bob Carey was fearless and believed that racing wasn't that dangerous of a sport.

BOB CAREY——"Why it's like driving in the street. These fellows are careful and they don't want to get in any accident if they can help it. It's not so dangerous."

As a youth, Carey broke both of his legs when a motorcycle he was driving struck a telephone pole. A crash at Winchester, Indiana, in 1928 broke his neck but he was unaware of the extent of his injury and he raced the remainder of the summer. It was only during a physical examination later in the year that he learned of the injury to his vertebra. His doctor ordered him to wear a brace for several months.

Polesitter Babe Stapp was victorious in the annual 100-lap Easter Sweepstakes before a crowd of 7,500. Bill Cummings jumped Stapp at the start and led the first 36 laps but Babe swallowed him up and led the remainder of the race in record time. Cummings was second, a half-lap behind. The youthful Rex Mays, competing in one of his first AAA races, had car owners and fans alike shaking their heads in amazement about how talented the kid was driving a race car. Both Ernie Triplett and Wilbur Shaw were unable to have their cars ready in time to compete and missed the show.

APRIL 22, 1933   SAULPAUGH KILLED IN PRACTICE
                   CRASH AT OAKLAND

In less than a week, the racing world lost another potential superstar when Bryan Saulpaugh was killed in a Saturday practice crash at the Oakland Speedway for Sunday's 150-mile race. Babe Stapp, Howdy Wilcox II and Lester Spangler watched as Bryan's racer turned over three times after losing control in the south turn. Saulpaugh was tossed 15 feet and his car rolled over on top of him as it somersaulted down the track. His head and chest were crushed and he was unconscious when placed in the ambulance. He died en route to Fairmont Hospital. Ironically, he was driving the same car and on the same track that he was critically injured on New Year's Day 1932.

Bryan had recently gone into business in nearby Hayward, California. Immediately following Sunday's race he had planned to travel East to compete in the April 30 races at Reading, Pennsylvania, and to marry Miss June Casey of Henderson, Kentucky. She was notified by telegram of her fiancé's death.

Many race fans were upset when Ralph DePalma was suspended from competing in this year's 500 because he had made a test run without AAA sanction.

MAY 20, 1933.   BILL CUMMINGS WINS POLE

This year's run for the Pole had taken on a different qualifying format. Instead of the customary four qualification laps, it was now expanded to ten laps. More than 20,000 fans were in attendance to see Indianapolis native Wild Bill Cummings in #5 Boyle Products Special capture the Pole with a ten-lap average of 118.521 mph. This was the same car that Lou Moore had qualified in the front spot last year. Frank Brisko, driving the four-wheel car that Bob McDonough competed in a year ago, was second fastest qualifier at 118.388 mph. Many had predicted Frank would win the Pole. Defending champion Fred Frame was third fastest. Frame now owned the car that Arnold won with in 1930 and nominated Peter Kreis to drive it. He also entered a four-cylinder car for Paul Bost. Moore, who had switched to drive #37 Foreman Axle Special, qualified fourth quickest at 117.843 mph with Ernie Triplett and Louis Meyer filling out row two.

For a while, it appeared that misfortune had struck Cummings. Earlier in the day, after completing eight laps, six over 120 mph, his riding mechanic Earl Unversaw noticed that their right rear tire had severely blistered. He emphatically gestured to Wild Bill to abort the run. Heeding Unversaw's advice, Cummings pulled into the pits and replaced the badly worn tire. Over the eight laps he was averaging 119.5 mph with his fourth lap, a scorcher at 120.919 mph. Unfazed, Bill would return later to post the top speed of the day.

MAY 28, 1933   BILL DENVER & BOB HURST KILLED ON QUALIFYING RUN

Late in the afternoon on the final day of time trials, 32-year old Bill Denver (whose real name was William Orem) and his riding mechanic Bob Hurst ventured out to make a qualifying run in the #42 Ray Brady Special. This was the same car that Al Aspen had crashed on Monday, May 22, skidding a 1,000 feet before hitting the SW wall and tearing off a rear wheel. Al and his riding mechanic suffered only minor injuries but the Brady car suffered moderate damage. Perhaps disgusted that Aspen had crashed his car and it was going to cost a substantial amount of money and time to repair it, or because Bill Denver hailed from nearby Audubon, Ray Brady, the frugal businessman from Norristown, Pennsylvania, offered the ride to Denver. Bill's financial backers helped fund the rebuild costs.

As Denver took the green flag on his first of ten laps qualification run, his car vaulted over the NE wall near where Billy Arnold had crashed in last year's race. The car somersaulted three times throwing Denver and his riding mechanic Bob Hurst from the car on the first revolution. The car made significant impact with a tree outside the track and it burst into flames. Both Denver and Hurst laid unconscious near the burning car, their clothes on fire. Quick action by Speedway guards Ted Ross and Arlie Couple to yank their burning clothing off saved them from being incinerated. Sadly Denver had died of a broken neck before the ambulance had arrived. Hurst was rushed to City Hospital but succumbed in the emergency room of a skull fracture. Some felt that in his scramble to get the car on the track, Denver and his crew neglected to do a complete inspection of the repaired race car. Bill's first 500 was in 1930 when he finished 22nd in the #44 Nardi Special, dropping out after 41 laps. Last year Bill drove as a relief driver.

Hugh (Bob) Hurst, an Indianapolis resident, raced sporadically on local dirt tracks. When World War I started he enlisted the Marine Corps when he was only 14 years old—perhaps the youngest serving Marine. Later, he would join the Navy and sailed around the world on the future ill-fated USS Arizona. Bob's brother Francis told of Bob's premonition.

FRANCIS HURST——"Just yesterday at dinner here Bob said, 'If they wouldn't call me yellow, I'd quit and I wouldn't go back to the track.'"

His wife, Gladys "Happy" Hurst had a horror of the 500 and would refuse to go out to the track to watch her husband in the race. A week before he had mentioned to her, "Happy, I don't have any business on the Speedway."

Rain halted the time trials 48 minutes before sundown. Ralph Hepburn was making his qualifying run when the rains came. His last lap speed was barely above 98 mph pulling his average down to 106.700 mph for the 42nd and last starting position. Babe Stapp was the fastest qualifier of the final day of qualifications at 116.626 mph.

Track officials granted an extra 48 minutes of qualifying to make up what was lost on Sunday. Sam Palmer and Gene Haustein were bumped from the list of 42 starters. Phil "Red" Shafer and Ralph Hepburn would qualify their mounts. Yesterday Hepburn had driven his last five laps in the rain at a reduced speed. The Speedway management let him run the last five laps again on Monday and he jumped his qualifying speed up to 110.001 mph in his 16-cylinder Marmon Highway Parts Special.

Mauri Rose had a heartbreaking conclusion to his qualification run. For nine laps he was traveling a speed of 108.014 mph. On his final lap the right front spindle broke on his Iroquois Special DeSoto. Unfazed, he drove the car back to the pits. Leon Duray failed on two attempts to qualify his Morton Brett Special.

MAY 30, 1933   HOWDY WILCOX II NOT ALLOWED TO
                START RACE

42 cars, the largest field in Speedway history, failed to make the traditional 10 a.m. start due to an unprecedented incident that nearly ended the running of the Indianapolis 500 forever. Shortly before 10 o'clock, Dr. Horace Allen declared that Howdy Wilcox II had failed his physical and would not be permitted to participate in the race.

DR. HORACE ALLEN——"I found that Wilcox was suffering from diabetes and other ailments and simply had to be frank about it. Their souls have been in great danger from fatigue. I'm making the decision I was compelled to consider the other drivers as well as Wilcox. I am sorry about the whole matter."

For the first time in Speedway history, the start of the race was delayed. There was a controversy between the officials and drivers who would drive Wilcox's #3 Gilmore Special and where on the starting grid would it start. Howdy had qualified his mount on the outside of row two.

41 drivers submitted a petition to the officials demanding Wilcox be allowed to start the race or they would boycott the 500. Eddie Rickenbacker was more than irate at the suggested boycott. He said if he had to, he'd "get a car and be the only car in the race if need be." The crowd of 100,000 awaited nervously to see if the race would be run. Finally the impatient Eddie Rickenbacker gathered the drivers and their team owners and made this ultimatum.

EDDIE RICKENBACKER——"If this race does not start in five minutes, I will pay back every man, woman and child in this grounds their money and I will ask the guards to escort from these grounds every race car, every driver and I will padlock these gates and they will never reopened."

There was pushback on Mauri Rose to be the replacement driver. When hearing that Rose was to be Wilcox's replacement, riding mechanic Jimmy Chappell refused to ride with Mauri. Kermit Maynard then agreed to serve as his riding mechanic and Eddie Edenburn, head of the AAA Contest Board, ordered Rose to start at the back of the field because of him being a rookie and unfamiliar with the car. There were also rumblings that the drivers were also protesting over the reduced prize money that would be awarded and about the new rule limiting the amount of fuel that could be carried by each car.

The drivers relented and at 10:15 a.m. the race began. Byron Foy of Detroit drove the Chrysler Imperial Pace Car accompanied by Speedway General Manager Pop Myers. As fourteen rows of three completed the Pace Lap and received the green flag, the traditional aerial bombs exploded indicating the race was on.

1931 winner Louis Schneider was unable to complete one lap and to this day holds the distinction of who had the worst finish in the Indianapolis 500—42nd. Schneider would later relieve Deacon Litz in the #26 Bowes Seal Fast Special advancing from tenth to second place in just a few laps.

Pole sitter Wild Bill Cummings jumped to the front at the start and lead lap one by two car lengths. Frank Brisko, in the FWD Special, was second and defending champ Fred Frame third. Stubby Stubblefield pulled his #8 Abels & Fink Auto into the pits on lap one for a three minute stop. This lengthy pause could have cost him a chance to challenge for the win. Stubby would eventually finish in fifth place.

In an amazing charge through the field, at lap 20 Mauri Rose had advanced from 42nd to 6th behind Cummings,

Frame, Brisko, Shorty Cantlon and Louis Meyer. Ten laps later Rose's #3 was shown in fifth spot as Cummings held an 19 second lead over Frame with Brisko 3rd and Meyer 4th.

A three-minute pitstop near the 100-mile mark would drop Bill Cummings from the top spot. Fred Frame then assumed the lead and gave all indications that he might become the first driver to win back-to-back as Brisko ran 2nd, Meyer 3rd and Rose now 4th. Coming out of nowhere Louis Schneider, in relief of Deacon Litz, shot up to second spot after 125 miles behind Frame. Babe Stapp in #45 was now up to 3rd and Rose remained in 4th.

Frank Brisko's day would end on lap 47 running out of oil and a lap later Mauri Rose withdrew with timing gear issues. However, the cantankerous Rose made a positive impression with several car owners as someone who stood on the gas and who could possibly win the "500" one day.

Ernie Triplett, driving Bill White's Floating Power Special, dropped out with a burnt piston on lap 61 and Peter Kreis, driving Billy Arnold's 1930 winning car now owned by Fred Frame, lasted just two more laps and he was out with a broken universal joint. Kreis had been pegged as "dark horse" favorite to win and he was running in fifth position prior to his departure.

After Cummings's pit stop, the race lead changed hands back and forth between Fred Frame and Babe Stapp— Frame led laps 33-36, Stapp 37-38, Frame 30-50— At the 200 mile mark it remained Stapp, Frame and Meyer with Wilbur Shaw in 4th two laps down and Chet Gardner three in arrears.

The lead swapping continued with Babe Stapp out front from laps 51-63, then Fred Frame from laps 64-84. Frame would drop out of the race on lap 85 with a bad valve. During this battle for the lead between Frame and Stapp, rookie Mark Billman would lose his life in a gruesome accident on lap 79.

MARK BILLMAN KILLED

26-year old Mark Billman of Indianapolis was killed when his #64 Kemp-Menis Special hit the lower wall tail first then his car shot across the track and hit the outside wall in the SE turn. He had just moved into tenth position. Both Billman and his riding mechanic, Elmer Lombardi, were thrown from their car. Mark was pinned between his left front wheel and the concrete wall. His arm was badly mangled, both legs were broken and he also suffered internal injuries. Billman would lose a lot of blood during the 20 minutes it took to free him from the wreckage. He was rushed to the Speedway Emergency Hospital where in effort to save his life, his left arm was amputated and he was given several blood transfusions. Lombardi was taken to City Hospital and was fortunate to suffer only severe lacerations to his leg.

Since Mark Billman was a child, he dreamed about racing in the 500. Just 26 years old, he had been successful racing on dirt tracks throughout the midwest for eight years. Exhibiting some natural talent, last year he was victorious in ten races and he had captured over 50 wins in his career.

Billman attended Our Lady of Lourdes Catholic school in Indianapolis and following his eight grade graduation, he quit school to go to work at the local Ford Motor Company. He drove his first race when he turned 18 at the Hoosier Speedway, a half mile dirt track. Early in his career, he crashed with regular consistency. Billman turned a deaf ear to his parents, Nick and Ana's, request to stop racing. Despite multiple crashes in his career, he was only injured seriously once that occurring in a 1928 accident at Winchester, Indiana where he suffered a broken hip.

Mark Billman's car struck the outer wall with such a terrific impact, it tore out a "V" shaped piece of concrete wall. His car became airborne, and turned upside down, tossing Billman to the track and riding mechanic Elmer Lombard to the grass on the outside of the track.

With Fred Frame sidelined Babe Stapp took control and appeared to be pulling away while holding the top spot from laps 85-129. At the 300 mile mark, Babe continued to control the race over Louis Meyer and Wilbur Shaw. Stapp had the misfortune to run out of gasoline on the north turn. He would not only surrender the lead to Meyer but lose several laps to the new leader while returning his car to the pits to be serviced. When he did resume the Race he was in third place but his attempt to reel in the leaders would be short-lived and he was finished for the day on lap 156.

LESTER SPANGLER KILLED

On lap 132, a car spun in front of Malcom Fox in the SW turn. In his attempt to avoid a collision, Fox drove his car close to the outer wall. Lester Spangler, in Harry Hartz's #15, attempted to drive between Fox and the outer wall but he hit the rear of Fox's car. He and his riding mechanic G.L. Jordan were thrown from their car and landed on the brick surface. Fox told the press his account of the crash.

MALCOM FOX——"We were going along the straightaway just before the south turn when a car shot around me on my left and started to skid. I shot up toward the outer retaining wall. #15 Spangler was right behind me and he tried to go between me and the top of the wall. He couldn't make it and hit my rear left wheel. His car literally dove over my car and landed on top of the retaining wall. I went into another spin and the first thing I knew my car was dangling on the top of the outer wall."

At 400 miles Louis Meyer had nearly a full lap lead on Wilbur Shaw and then he put another lap on Shaw at the 450-mark. Meyer ultimately would have a three-lap margin of victory over Wilbur. Third place finisher Lou Moore lost nearly two-thirds of his exhaust pipe on lap 167. Cliff Bergere's car barely missed hitting it.

Louis Meyer and his riding mechanic Lawson Harris pulled his #36 Tyrol Special, sponsored by Tide Water Oil Sales Corp of Indianapolis, into the "Bull Pen" to receive the victory laurels. There to greet him was Ralph Hepburn, owner of the Tydol car. It was the car Ralph finished third with in 1931 and Wilbur Shaw led in last year. Meyer comment on his victory.

LOUIS MEYER——"I certainly am glad I won. Hep has had a lot of tough luck. He got in a terrible smash out in the coast last year and spent several months in the hospital. I am glad because I was able to drive his car through the race and win. Gladder for him than myself. You know how it is. A fellow has a tough break once, and if things keep on being tough, it is bad. But if things break right for him, why it makes a fellow feel good."

What would be debated was whether Ralph Hepburn would have won the Indianapolis 500 had he opted to drive his car instead of Meyer. Also with the huge lead Meyer held over Shaw in the late stages of the race, Hep could have been a co-winner had he ordered Meyer to the pits to relieve him for the final laps.

JUNE 28, 1933   BABE STAPP HURT AT ASCOT

Babe Stapp's flirtation with fate continued again at Legion Ascot Speedway. On the 26th lap of the feature event, his car crashed into the North turn fence in what would be regarded as one of the most spectacular spills at a track known for its terrifying crashes. Over 10,000 horrified spectators witnessed Stapp being thrown from his car. Babe tumbled head-over-heels nearly 100 feet down the middle of the track. Driver Mel Keneally described Stapp's terrifying accident.

MEL KENEALLY——"I could see Stapp's car but not him. There was so much dust that it was impossible to discern Babe in the car. I came barreling out of the North turn, and, seeing the car, figured I would go between the car and the wall. Just at that moment, a figure dashed out on the track. That was Pillsbury.

"In that instant I changed my course and went below the car. Had not

229

Pillsbury run out on the track, I would have headed for the inert form of Stapp, and well, I hate to think of what might have happened."

Prompt action by A. C. Pillsbury saved Babe. He was quick to run out on the track and pull the unconscious Stapp out of the way of oncoming race cars. The following week Pillsbury was presented with an expensive jeweled timepiece for his heroic efforts to drag Stapp to safety.

Ernie Triplett ended the youthful sensation Rex Mays five consecutive race winning streak at Ascot in a tense battle with Mays to win the 50-lap feature. That would set up a grudge match race for track superiority.

JULY 26, 1933   ERNIE TRIPLETT HURT AT ASCOT

For the third time in his racing career, Ernie Triplett luckily escaped the Grim Reaper as he and Al Gordon tangled at Ascot. The two-time Pacific Coast Champion was battling his nemesis Al Gordon for the lead when on the 33rd lap of the 50-lap feature event, the two cars locked wheels in the turn. Triplett's car flipped end-over-end for 75-feet before landing well outside the track. Amazingly, in what certainly appeared to be a fatal accident, the Blonde Terror escaped with just a broken shoulder and laceration to his forehead. Taken to White Memorial Hospital, physicians described his condition as fairly good. However, the painful injuries started him thinking about stopping racing other than Indianapolis. Gordon survived uninjured from his wrecked car. Rex Mays would chalk up another feature win.

AUGUST 26, 1933   RED SHAFER WINS ELGIN ROAD
                    RACE

After a 13-year hiatus, the AAA revived the historic running of the Elgin Road Race in Des Moines and nearly 30,000 witnessed a sensational conclusion. Phil "Red" Shafer, who first raced in the Indianapolis 500 in 1925 and finished third as a rookie, won the feature over Fred Frame in dramatic fashion. Leading by 51-seconds with just four laps until the finish, Red spun in the hairpin turn of the of the eight and a quarter-mile concrete and gravel layout. He lost the lead to Frame but that was short-lived for the 1932 Indy 500 winner was forced to his pit to change worn tires.

In his attempt to retake the lead, Frame drove with near reckless abandonment, first plowing through bales of straw. Then on the backstretch he lost control and hit the fence. These shunts sealed the victory for Shafer. Mauri Rose would place third. Earlier that morning, Frame won a preliminary stock car race. Now fifty years old and gray haired, Ralph DePalma finished tenth. He was the Elgin winner in 1912.

SEPTEMBER 11, 1933   BORZACCHINI KILLED AT MONZA

Three drivers were fatality injured at Monza, Italy. Italians Baconin "Mario" Borzacchini and Giuseppe Campari's cars skidded when they hit an oily section of the track and overturned during the Grand Prix de Monza. Campari died instantly in the crash. Borzacchini would succumb a half-hour later. Later Polish driver Count Stanislaus Czaichowski died of burns when his car caught fire.

SEPTEMBER 11, 1933   ARTHUR NEWBY DIES

One of the four original owners of the Indianapolis Motor Speedway, 68-year old Arthur C. Newby died at his residence at 4020 North Meridian Street, Indianapolis. He was passionate about bicycle racing and was one of the founders of the Indianapolis Zig-Zag Cycling Club, where prominent Indianapolis business people were members. Arthur and Charles Test started Indianapolis Chain and Stamping Company which manufactured bicycle chains. Prior to their entry into the market, most bicycles chains were made in Europe. They would eventually sell their company to the American Bicycle Company.

Arthur Newby would construct a quarter-mile high banked board race track which is now Central Avenue and Thirteenth Street. He had gotten to know Carl Fisher through the Zig-Zag Cycling Club. Later Arthur Newby would become a partner in the National Car Company. Carl Fisher would offer him an opportunity to be one of the owners of the Indianapolis Motor Speedway. In 1912 Joe Dawson would win the Indianapolis 500 driving a National. He gained notoriety as a quite donor gifting $50,000 to both Butler University and Earlham College. Newby also purchased 233 acres surrounding Turkey Run State Park to prevent it from being made into a commercial development. After thwarting the developers plans, Arthur then donated the wooded land for the expansion of Turkey Run. The only stipulation Arthur Newby would insist on was after making a charitable contribution, the recipients were not to reveal the source of the gift.

Bill Cummings would capture both the pole and the 100-mile races in the June 11 Detroit 100 and the September 9 Syracuse 100. Phil Shafer would win the non-championship Elgin National Trophy on the Elgin, Illinois road course. Fred Frame sat on the pole at Elgin. Even though he won twice, Cummings did not finish in the top five in the point standings. Louis Meyer would win his third AAA National Driving Championship with 610 points, Lou Moore was second with 530 and Wilbur Shaw third with 450.

ACE DRUMMOND

In 1933 Eddie Rickenbacker teamed up with illustrator Clayton Knight to create the comic strip "Ace Drummond".

It ran in the Sunday comic section from 1933 to 1939. At its peak, it appeared in 135 newspapers. Their final strip ran July 7, 1939.

In 1936 a 13-chapter serial would be filmed starring John "Dusty" Ford as Ace Drummond, Jean Rogers as Peggy Trainor, Noah Beery Jr. as Jerry and Lon Chaney Jr. as Ivan. Ace, a G-Man of the Sky, is sent to Magnolia to find the mysterious villain—The Dragon. A sub-plot has Ace volunteering to help Peggy Trainor search for her archaeologist father who has disappeared.

1933

Bob Carey

In Memoriam April 16, 1933
AAA 1932 National Champion

1933

Babe Stapp

Led 60 Laps. Runs out of Fuel

1934

JANUARY 10, 1934   JOE RUSSO MARRIES WEALTHY SOCIALITE

Joe Russo married Detroit socialite and sportswoman Helene Yockey in Martinsville, Indiana, on January 19, 1934. (Joe met his bride-to-be at a party in Grosse Point, Detroit a week earlier). She was a prominent horsewoman showing her horses throughout the country. At one time she was owner of "Just Gold" and later the famous five-gait horse "My Beloved." Joe had been working as a consulting engineer.

JOE RUSSO——"Mrs. Russo has no objection to my driving in this year's race but then, she has never seen a race and it may be a different story at the end of the 500.

If I could only win I am sure that it would help persuade her in favor of my sport. If she doesn't like me to drive, we'll take that up late in the afternoon of Decoration Day."

Two-time Pacific Coast AAA Champion Ernie Triplett surprised many of his fans when he announced he was going to retire from full-time racing and focus on racing in the Indianapolis 500 and selected road races like the upcoming Gold Cup race at Mines Field in Los Angeles on February 18. Following being seriously injured at Ascot last summer, the two-time AAA Pacific Coast champion admitted privately that he had lost his daring way of driving. He no longer drove with his breath-taking-abandon style. The AAA had just announced the car numbers assigned to the drivers for the upcoming season. Al Gordon would wear #1, Rex Mays #2, Ernie Triplett #3, Kelly Petillo #4 and Chet Gardner #5.

FEBRUARY 18, 1934   MINES FIELD 250-MILE GOLD CUP RACE

There was a buzz about a scheduled AAA 250-Mile Gold Cup Race to be held at Mine Field in Los Angeles (now where LAX Los Angeles International is now located). Over 75,000 packed the facility to watch Al Gordon win a bit of a snoozer event beating a field of 27 cars. Stubby Stubblefield finished second, Louis Meyer came in third. Peter DePaolo, who prior to the start of the race had asked AAA race officials that he be permitted to start last, drove a smooth race on the way to a fourth place finish.

Rex Mays would finish fifth despite two flat tires. He led the first 17 laps until he picked up a nail in his left rear tire. Ernie Triplett experienced mechanical issues early in the race. Two days later race results were reversed and Stubblefield was awarded the victory. Gordon elected to accept second place money and waive a protest. Stubby would be presented the Gilmore Gold Cup trophy by Earl Gilmore.

MARCH 5, 1934   ERNIE TRIPLETT DIES OF INJURIES AT EL CENTRO

On March 4, Ernie Triplett was critically injured and drivers George "Swede" Smith and Cambern "Hap" Happerly, a Hollywood garage owner, were killed in a spectacular four-car crackup at El Centro County Fairgrounds during their Midway Fair in Imperial, California. Triplett, "the Blond Terror" would succumb shortly after midnight of a skull fracture. The accident was triggered when Jimmy Wilkerson's car, after limping around the track for several laps, stalled in the north corner. Due to the tracks dusty conditions, Smith, when first spotting the crippled car, swerved sharply but he hooked a wheel of Wilkerson's racer. Swede's car rolled to the center of the race track.

Hap Happerly and several other crew members rushed from the pits to rescue Smith. Hap was struck by Triplett's car tossing him high into the air. Ernie, swerving sharply to avoid colliding with Swede's race car, lost control of his machine and would hit the guard rail. His car would overturn. Tossed like a stone out of a slingshot from his car, Triplett lay unconscious on the race track. Gordon's car would hit the fence near the judge's stand and also overturn. He suffered a severe cut to the head but otherwise escaped unharmed. Al Gordon and Triplett were in a tight battle for the lead.

Happerly would die soon after arriving at La Solana Hospital. The 35-year old Smith, regarded as Ascot's

Class B King, would die a few hours later of a fractured skull and internal injuries. The race was stopped and Gordon was listed as winner with Triplett in second place. The following day Herb Balmer was declared the winner, Al Reinke second and Rex Mays third.

There was a grand jury investigation of the accident. Their results concluded it was an unavoidable collision. They also pointed out the lack of AAA flagmen in the corners to display a yellow flag to alert drivers of an accident.

Rex Mays, a protégé of Ernie Triplett, was distraught enough about the loss of his tutor, he announced he was retiring from Coast racing and would compete on Eastern race tracks. Over a thousand mourners attended Triplett's funeral services on March 7 at the Little Church of the Flowers in Forest Lawn Memorial Park, Glendale, California. Mays, who was supposed to be a pall bearer, was too overcome with grief to participate. The beloved "Belvedere Bad Boy's" casket was covered with a checkered flag made of white and purple flowers. He was survived by his wife, Lillian, and their 4-year old daughter Doreen. Swede Smith and Hap Happerly funeral services were held the following day.

MARCH 8, 1934   HERB BALMER DIE TESTING STOCK
                  CAR ON LOS ANGELES STREET

On March 8, 28 year old Herb Balmer was critically injured in a bizarre highway accident at the intersection of York Boulevard and Verdugo Road when his V-8 stock car blew a tire, jumped the curb, hit a telephone pole and crashed into a concrete wall. Taken to Georgia Street Receiving Hospital, Herb would die at 6:05 p.m. of a basal skull fracture, crushed face, broken leg and internal injuries. His mechanic Ray Couch suffered a broken leg and arm. The previous week Balmer beat Al Gordon at Ascot, ending Al's record of seventeen straight wins.

The Los Angeles Examiner newspaper had gone on a crusade about all the carnage occurring in automobile racing and the growing number of driver fatalities. They were pushing to have the sport banned. The tragedy of three deaths on the El Centro race track really intensified the drum beat. From a race drivers perspective, this came to a head during the funeral cortege of Ernie Triplett.

The Examiner had sent James Lee, a reporter, and John Beenus, a cameraman, to cover the services. The boiling point occurred when Beenus attempted to take a photo at the burial site. Several drivers knocked him to the ground and repeatedly punched him in the face and kicked his body. His camera was damaged and the film removed from it. Driver Louis Tomei was the ring leader in the roughhousing of the bloodied Beenus. They forced him into his car and took his car keys. Lee was cornered by Babe Stapp and the talented young race driver Al Reinke and physically forced into a car against his own wishes. Both cars departed Forest Lawn and were driven to the Los Angeles Examiner offices. They were paraded to the executive office of Warden Woolard. They were adamant that the paper cease and desist on unfavorable articles on auto racing.

The following day James Lee filed charges with authorities that he and Beenus had been kidnapped. Stapp and Reinke would be arraigned on the charge of kidnapping Lee. A recently passed California statute providing for the death penalty for kidnapping when injury occurs suddenly became an alarming matter for both Stapp and Reinke. On March 13, both would be arraigned before Municipal Judge Joseph Chambers and ordered released on a $2500 bail each and set April 4 for trial. They would plead not guilty and ordered to stand trial before Judge Charles Burnell on April 26. In a separate matter, in a complaint issued by Deputy District Attorney Ferguson, Tomei was charged with a "felonious assault with means and force likely to produce great bodily harm" to John Beenus.

APRIL 11, 1934   TARGA FLORIO ROAD RACE AT ASCOT

The success of the stock car road race at Mines Field had helped fuel the buzz of the 150-mile Targa Florio road race at Legion Ascot Speedway. The uprising racing star, 22-year old Al Reinke, was eager to put the distraction of his pending kidnapping trial out of his mind. Reinke borrowed Louis Meyer's race car to take an "easy practice spin" to inspect the new circuit. The two-mile course had been recently coated with oil. Driving down a steep hill with a 25% grade, Reinke car slid into soft dirt and lost control. The car would overturn twice with Al and his riding mate Kenneth Dever thrown from the car. Dever, who suffered minor injuries, carried his next-door neighbor Reinke to the waiting ambulance. Reinke, landing on his head, would die fifteen minutes after arrival at the Georgia Street Receiving Hospital of multiple skull fractures, a crushed chest and internal injuries. The car Al Reinke drove to his death was the same car that Ernie Triplett piloted in the Mines Field race.

APRIL 22, 1934 LOUIS MEYER WINS 150-MILE TARGA FLORIO AT ASCOT

Louis Meyer, starting seventeenth out of a field of twenty, would win the 150-mile Targa Florio stock car race at Legion Ascot Speedway before a crowd estimated at 50,000. He was reeling in race leader Ted Horn before skidding into some hay stacks. Meyer, driving a Ford V-8 stock car minus a windshield and fenders, would recover and quickly catch Horn, who had led the majority of the race. Ted dropped back to second in the late stages of the race. Al Gordon ran third. Rex Mays would finish seventh, slowed twice with a flat tire. Meyer drove the car that Al Reinke had crashed to his death. This would be the only major race that Meyer would win in his career in Southern California.

APRIL 27, 1934   BABE STAPP PLEADS GUILTY TO
                  SIMPLE ASSULT

Babe Stapp escaped jail time by pleading to a lesser charge of simple assault before Superior Judge Charles Burnell and was fined $100. Louis Tomei was sentenced to six months in prison. Tomei, who pleaded guilty to beating and kicking John Beenus, asked for a suspended sentence but it was denied. The judge replied, "This may save your life."

※ ※ ※

Bill Cummings was again returning as lead driver for the Boyle Racing team in car #7 and he was teamed with rookie George Barringer #18. Wilbur Shaw and Kelly Petillo would be nominated to drive Joe Marks's and his mother-in-law, Mrs. Mary Falcone's, two race cars. The grocers from Gary, Indiana, bought the #3 Lion Head Special for Shaw and #17 Red Lion Special for Petillo. Louis Meyer would enter his own car #1 Ring Free Special and Ralph Hepburn would return to his own car #31 Art Rose Special that Meyer had won in last year. Frank Brisko was confident his #32 FWD Special would be competitive on an oily race track.

Ten days before the start of qualifications, the AAA technical committee shocked the race teams with the announcement that they would limit to three gallons of gasoline for their qualifying attempt. You would be required to make a flying start lap, ten lap qualifying run followed by a cool down lap. It appeared this requirement would benefit the four-cylinder race cars. One driver who did not have that worry was 1931 winner Louis Schneider. The AAA barred him from competing in the 500 because he had competed in a non-sanctioned race.

MAY 19, 1934   KELLY PETILLO & WILBUR SHAW
                 QUALIFY ONE-TWO

Two years ago rookie Kelly Petillo started last, 40th, in the 500. Last year, he started in 25th position. This year, his perception would not be that of a "field filler." Petillo and Wilbur Shaw would qualify one-two for the fledging race team owned by Joe Marks, a garage and grocery store owner, and his tight-fisted mother-in-law Mrs. Mary Falcone. Petillo's winning Pole speed was 119.329 mph. His fastest lap was over 122 mph and prompted his pit crew to frantically wave at him to drastically slow down. They had serious concerns he would fail to complete the ten lap run with the three-gallon gasoline allotment. Kelly's speed would break the 10-lap qualifying mark. This would be the fastest that a rear-drive car had qualified. Frank Brisko, the first driver to make a qualifying run, would complete the front row in four-wheel-drive FWD Special.

Mauri Rose, driving the car which Wilbur Shaw finished in second place last year, qualified Leon Duray's car fourth fastest. Chet Gardner, driving the 16-cylinder Sampson Radio Special, and Phil "Red" Shafer joined him in the second row. Tony Gulotta did not have a ride nor the promise of one this May. Late in the afternoon Chet Miller stepped out of the #8 Schroeder Special and within an hour Gulotta would qualify on the inside of the third row. Russ Snowberger was the slowest of the nine qualifiers at 111.428 mph.

During a practice session Joe Russo had to make a drastic swerve to avoid a rabbit that ventured on the track. Upon returning to the pits his crew discovered that he had jerked his steering rod loose and he would not be a Day One qualifier. Bill Cummings, last year's Pole winner, also did not qualify as he was struggling to find the balance of speed versus fuel consumption. Wild Bill was driving the car Babe Stapp drove in the 1933 Race. The same was true for Cliff Bergere, now driving the Bill White's Floating Power Special, that had originally been assigned to the late Ernie Triplett.

While traveling at a speed average of 117.632 mph after six laps of his qualifying run—good enough for a front row starting position—Deacon Litz's right front tire collapsed causing him to lose control in the south turn and make a hard contact with the wall. The car ricocheted across the track, striking the inner retaining wall. The car's frame was smashed eighteen inches out of line as it ripped out several yards of cement. In addition to the bent frame on Deacon's car, he discovered that part of his motor had been damaged which would even further delay his return back onto the track. Deacon and his riding mechanic were uninjured.

Bill Cummings became the fastest Day Two qualifier as he pushed his Boyle Products Special to a 116.116 mph average, good for the inside the third row starting spot. His final lap topped 117 mph. Ralph Hepburn posted the day's second best speed in the same car he let Louis Meyer drive to victory last year. Rookie George Barringer, a teammate with Wild Bill, qualified the second Boyle Special at 113.859 mph to round out Row Three.

Knowing that Hepburn intended to drive his 1933 winning race car, Louis Meyer built a new race car over the winter. He started his run with a speed of nearly 114 mph but his pace fell off and he would settle for a 112.332 mph average. The slowest qualifier was rookie Herb Ardinger driving a semi-stock creation powered by a Graham-Paige motor. Shorty Cantlon discovered his Sullivan & O'Brien Special had a cracked block so he struck a deal with Al Gordon to use his motor from the extra car that he had brought from California.

Eddie Rickenbacker, now vice-president of the aviation division of General Motors, arrived in Indianapolis two days earlier and would stay until after May 30. Almost the entire management of the Indianapolis Motor Speedway had been delegated to Pop Myers.

MAY 25, 1934   PETER KREIS KILLED

In what was described was the most unusual accident at the Indianapolis Motor Speedway, 34-year old Peter Kreis and his riding mechanic Bob Hahn were killed when their car hurtled the SW turn wall and struck headlong the trunk of a tree twenty feet from the track. The impact split the car in half at the cockpit and the two haves landed 25 feet apart. This was the same spot where Joe Caccia and Milton Jones had their fatal accidents. And it was the same tree that Benny Benefield had struck.

In a bit of irony, at 7:40 a.m. Cliff Bergere and Peter Kreis were driving over to the Speedway when they stopped at White River Boulevard and Michigan Street for a fatal accident in which Lewis Case was killed. After the ambulance arrived and they were told their assistance was not needed, they proceeded to the track. At the moment of Peter's accident, his watch stopped at 8:40 a.m. exactly one hour later.

Tossed from his racer, Peter died instantly of a fractured skull, crushed chest and both legs were torn from his torso. Hahn, pinned in the twisted wreckage, was barely alive when rescue workers arrived but would soon die of a crushed chest, fractured skull, fractured leg and broken arm. No one inside the track witnessed their accident. Kreis, a highly successful contractor from Knoxville, Tennessee, was doing warmup laps at about 90 mph at the time the accident occurred. Their badly mangled bodies were taken to the city morgue. The cause of the accident was not determined but it was believed to be a tire blowout or a tie rod had broken. The car had been rebuilt in Hartz Speedway garage over the past few days and Kreis had hoped to qualify later in the day.

Peter Kreis, often described by his racing colleagues as the "perfect Southern gentleman", was driving Harry Hartz's front-drive eight-cylinder racer that Fred Frame drove to victory in 1932. At the time of the accident Hartz was in his garage with a motion picture crew there to take pictures of his drivers and was awaiting Peter's return. Starter Seth Klein commented on his popularity. "He was one of the most popular men at the track—always a gentleman. He had a lot of hard luck, because he would rather break up a car in fast company than lag behind."

J. R. McCormick, an Indiana state policeman assigned to patrol the streets near the Speedway, witnessed the tragedy. "I saw the car riding along the top of the wall, practically straddling it. I couldn't believe what I saw. Then the car seemed to scoot over the edge and plunge into the tree."

Eddie Rickenbacker was addressing the Indiana Bankers Association when informed of the Kreis accident. He would comment,

EDDIE RICKENBACKER——"There is a price that must be paid for progress in the automobile industry. A serious accident occurred at the race track this forenoon and I deeply regret it. However, it is a thing that happens in every walk of life. Men are willing to take a chance in pioneering for progress and glory."

Peter Kreis worked as an engineer with his father and brother in the family's construction business. Their company specialized in building levees and railroads primarily in the South. Pete would take a month's vacation from his job to come and race in the Indianapolis 500. He did it for the thrill and love of the race and not the financial aspect of the sport. In addition to his love of racing, he was an aviation enthusiast and an accomplished pilot. Recently he made a forced landing in a southern river. Dr. Herbert Craig would come from Knoxville, Tennessee, to claim the body.

Bob Hahn rode with Harry Hartz from Los Angeles to Indianapolis. He had driven a few times at Ascot and aspired to drive in the 500 someday. Pinky Donaldson was Kreis usual riding mechanic but Hahn asked to take be taken on a ride to get a feel of the track for the future. No decision had been made as to whether he would have gotten to ride along in the 500-Mile Race.

Two and one-half hours later, the steering on Babe Stapp's Garcia Grande Special broke and his car would hit the inside retaining wall across from where the Kreis fatality occurred. Neither he or his riding mechanic were seriously hurt but Babe re-injured a previous leg wound, but he would remain mum about this to keep the track physician from barring him from competition.

Shorty Cantlon hustled his Sullivan & O'Brien Special around the Speedway on Friday with a ten-lap qualifying average of 117.875 mph, the second fastest overall speed. Rookie George Bailey also qualified. The tech committee disallowed Harry McQuinn's qualification run citing his car used a pint more gasoline than allowed. Both Cummins Diesel cars driven by Stubby Stubblefield and Dave Evans were both practicing over 100 mph but neither would make a qualification run. The Speedway had announced if either could qualify over a minimum speed of 95 mph they would be allowed to compete in the 500.

MAY 29, 1934   FRED FRAME FAILS TO QUALIFY

On Monday morning May 28 Fred Frame, while practicing the car in which Billy Arnold won the 1930 Race, broke a steering knuckle while he was coming out of a curve into the stretch, spun several times then crashed into the wall. Frame and his riding mechanic were uninjured but the car was moderately damaged. Fred, who had purchased the Arnold car from Harry Hartz two years ago, was fortunate not to go over the wall. Frame was able to repair the car but it arrived one minute after qualifications had officially ended at 4 p.m. Monday. Frame was philosophical when asked about the disappointment of missing the race.

FRED FRAME——"Well, I'm sorry. I thought you could qualify until sundown, as you had been. But it's O.K. with me. Maybe everything worked out for me the best.

Here was Pete, killed in the car in which I won in 1932. The cars have been closely linked. I drove the Hartz car in 1932 and 1933. Kreis drove my Arnold front-drive last year. I was to drive it this year. Maybe it was just as well. I'm not superstitious but, thinking it over, I'm not sorry they wouldn't let me qualify. I have two cars in the race anyhow, the one Rex Mays will drive and the one Johnny Seymour will handle. Maybe I can drive relief a few miles for one of them. Anyhow, I'm satisfied."

Babe Stapp switched to Leon Duray's two-cycle, 16-cylinder creation and with minimal time in the car was able to qualify it at a speed average of 109.648 mph. However, the AAA tech committee disallowed the speed for using too much gasoline.

MAY 30, 1934   LOCAL BOY BILL CUMMINGS WINS
                              INDIANAPOLIS 500

Bill Cummings was noted for his hard charging style of driving as soon as the green flag fell. With the greater fuel limitations placed on the cars this year—45 gallons of gasoline—very few of his competitors felt Wild Bill would lead a lot of laps but run dry on gas before the completion of the 500 miles. His car owner Mike Boyle took great pride in his going for the lead right at the get-go. Bill Cummings would win the 500-Mile Race in record time by driving a very "un-Bill Cummings like" race. As fans were exiting the Speedway grounds, many held the opinion there was never any more popular victory than what they just witnessed from the local boy who grew up just four miles from the track. Cummings would set a record speed averaging 104.865 mph.

It was a smooth race for Cummings except for one incident. "It came on the fourth lap. The car hit a bad spot of oil. We began to go sideways. I thought we were gone—that she was going to turn over. Then I managed to straightened her out and it was all over before I had time to get scared."

Starting tenth, Wild Bill was steady from the start and would move up gradually. Even though he had dropped out of the top ten after 50 miles, Cummings would advance to fourth place after 100 miles. Bill would take command of the race on lap 72 for eight laps. He would be shown in third after 200 miles, and second after 300 miles.

Cummings, driving the four-cylinder car that Babe Stapp looked so strong in during the early stages of last year's race, was accompanied by boyhood friend Earl Unversaw. Bill was such a pal he would name his first child Earleen, who he promised he would get a pony for if he won the 500.

Under a blazing sun, Cummings's face was caked with so much grease and grime they sent him to the infield track hospital following his Victory Lane accolades. It took two doctors and three nurses to totally clean his face with soap and rubbing alcohol.

Mauri Rose would finish second 27 seconds behind the race winner. Car owner Leon Duray would file an official protest that Rose should be awarded the Race win because Cummings gained track distance while the yellow flag was displayed. The protest would be denied. Lou Moore was third in the Foreman Axle Shaft Special. It was the same car he finished third in last year as well. Wilbur Shaw relieved Moore when he pitted on lap 76. When Shaw stopped for fuel on the 152nd lap, Moore returned to his car and drove it to the finish.

Deacon Litz rebounded from a early month crash to finish fourth. When Deacon pitted on lap 66, Babe Stapp jump in as relief driver. Late in the race, on lap 172, Litz climbed back into the Stokley Special and would complete the remainder of the 500 miles. Joe Russo's fifth place finish pleased his new bride enough that she didn't demand he retire immediately after the Race. Cliff Bergere's car would finish seventh. Bergere was relieved by Tony Gulotta on lap 118 and on the 130th lap, Tony returned to the pits where Billy Winn would climb in. One more stop was made on lap 161 and Bergere returned to the cockpit and drove the remainder of the Race. Cliff would have to make an unscheduled pit stop to replace riding mechanics when Aaron Vance fainted in the cockpit. It was a hot, sunny Race Day.

Deacon Litz apologized for need assistance from Stapp.

DEACON LITZ——"I guess I'm getting old. My car is better than I am. It could have gone much faster, but the old man couldn't drive it any faster. Fatigue got me. It's the first time."

Pole setter Kelly Petillo jump out in front at the start of the race and led the first six circuits. His teammate Wilbur Shaw had a short day in his #3 Lion Head Special. A crew member failed to tighten the car's oil drain plug and he lost all his oil and was sidelined on lap 15. Frank Brisko looked like a sure winner in the early stages of the race in his FWD Special passing Petillo on lap 7 and holding the top spot thru lap 71.

On lap 67 Al Gordon's car steering knuckle broke and he went into a wild skid before smashing into the inner retaining wall. Al would escape with minor bruises. His riding mechanic, Louis Sweet, would receive a severe burn on his hand as he tried to grip their slipping clutch. Kelly Petillo, trying to avoid Gordon's car, made an abrupt move toward the outer wall and his skillful driving avoided a crash. Louis Meyer made several stops because of oil troubles and would drop out after 92 laps. Later he would spell for Ralph Hepburn on lap 136 and Meyer moved Hep's car up into third place when a connecting rod broke on lap 164.

Mauri Rose would jump in front from laps 79-124. Frank Brisko would forge ahead from 110-113 but would steadily drop back from this point forward partially due to oil getting on the car's springs, making it hard to handle. During his pit stop on lap 129, he was replaced by Rex Mays. Rex could not get the car into high gear and drove an entire lap in 2nd gear and returned to the pits for assistance.

From this point on it became a two-car battle between Rose and Cummings with Mauri in first from laps 114-124. Cummings took over the top spot from laps 125-148. Rose would counter by leading the next 26 circuits, then on lap 175 Wild Bill would move to the front and remain there until he took the checkered flag. Cummings would make two pit stops totaling 3 minutes and 28 seconds. So reserved a Race did Bill run, he wound up using just 36 gallons and 2 quarts of gasoline. Rose would also make two pit stops totaling 2 minutes and 42 seconds.

Lap prize money was evenly spread with Frank Brisko leading two times for 69 laps, Mauri Rose led three times for 68 laps and the victorious Bill Cummings also lead on three different occasions for 57 laps. Brisko would soldier on to a ninth place finish and pole winner Kelly Petillo finished 11th. Petillo spent a total of 29 minutes and 30 seconds in the pits as the crew attempted to repair a leaking oil line and to fix his shocks. Herb Ardinger was the highest finishing rookie in tenth. Fellow rookie Rex Mays would drop out after 53 laps with a front axle failure and finish 23rd. Louis Meyer's hope to be the first to win consecutive 500s never materialized and he was out before the halfway point with an oil leak.

Three early race accidents slowed the pace of the Race. On lap eleven Chet Miller's #46 Bohnalite Ford Special skidded going into the SW turn. Zigzagging through the turn, his car somersaulted, then climbed, front first, over the wall. The car rested briefly atop the wall, before harmlessly dropping on its wheels on the outside of the track. Neither Miller or his riding mechanic was hurt. Chet would be credited with a 33rd place finish.

On lap 13, rookie George Bailey would lose control of his Scott Special and crash over the outer wall. He would receive a fracture of the left wrist and numerous body bruises. His riding mechanic, James Johnson, had four teeth knocked out as well as suffering lacerations on his face and head. Two laps later Doc MacKenzie, while attempting to avoid contact with Gene Haustein's skidding car in turn three, threw a tire and his car would smack the wall before coming to rest in the center of the track. Neither Doc or his riding mechanic were injured. Leon Duray would file an immediate protest that during the eight minutes it took the safety crew to remove MacKenzie's stalled race car from the track, three drivers, one being Bill Cummings, ignored the yellow flag and picked up three-quarters of a lap on his driver, Mauri Rose.

Following the race, Wild Bill's mother, Mrs. Minta Brown, tells a story of how her seven-year old son could hear the sounds of the race car motors from their home at 1806 North Alabama Street. "Mother, that's Barney Oldfield. I know the sound of his motor. I'm going to do that. I'm going to win that race."

MINTA BROWN——"Bill always wanted to be a race driver. When he was just a little fellow, his father—you know he was a race driver too, and was called 'Wild Bill' Cummings—made him a tin Marmon like the one Ray Harroun drove. Bill would whittle out a little wooden cigar, turn his cap with the brim to the back of his head, cock that cigar at an angle and say, 'Mother, I'm Barney.' It's a wonderful thing for a boy to grow up to be just what he thought he wanted to be when he was small."

Rumor was rampant that notorious bank robber John Dillinger could possibly attend the race blending in with the 140,000 race attendees. Numerous plain clothed policemen were on the lookout for him. A hitchhiker notified law enforcement that he saw Dillinger driving north towards Indianapolis on Highway 31. When quizzed how he was so positive it was Dillinger, he stated that he had a machine gun on his lap.

W.D. Edenburn, chief steward, W.G. Wall, steward and A.C. Pillsbury conducted a six-hour review of the timing recording tape in response of Leon Duray's protest. Besides the prestige of winning the Indianapolis 500, there was a large difference between first place, $29,075 against $14,250 for the runner-up. They issued a written report:

"We, the stewards of the 500-Mile Race, have reached the following decision in regard to the protest of Entrant Leon Duran, owner of car No. 9, against the Boyle Products Company entry, car No. 7; That the protest is hereby denied.

260

"First, that the yellow flag was displayed from the starter's bridge on the seventeenth lap of the leader and remained displayed until the twenty-fourth lap of the leader.

"Second, during this interval car No. 7 did not change its position with regard to other cars or pass any competitor and gained on car No. 9 approximately four seconds.

"Third, that the record shows that the yellow flag was displayed from the thirteenth lap at the over-head bridge on the North stretch to the leader's seventeenth lap and, further, that car #7 in the interval gained three positions and approximately twenty seconds in time on car #9 and that further this is not a violation of Article 11, Page 116 of the A.A.A. contest board rule book, as practiced under the ground rules of the Indianapolis Motor Speedway and in accordance with the instructions given the umpires by the starters."

An incensed Duray immediately appealed to the National Board:

"To the stewards of the twenty-second annual Indianapolis 500-Mile Race, May 30, 1934, A.A.A. Contest Board sanction No. 3,000:

"Please be advised that I, the undersigned, do hereby protest the decision of your body this date with reference to the protest entered by me on May 30, disputing the relative position of my car and other cars in the above race.

"I request that the payment of first and second place money be withheld in escrow until such appeal to the contest board under the rights granted me in Secs. 323, 324 of Chap. 20 of the A.A.A. Contest Board Rules Book.

Yours respectfully,

LEON DURAY,

Entrant Car No. 9."

The National Board would rule against Duray.

For the first time in the history of the Indianapolis Motor Speedway the winner's check and trophy were not presented because first and second place prize money was being disputed. The banquet was held in the ball room of the Indianapolis Athletic Club.

Eddie Rickenbacker announced at the banquet that there would be no radical rules changes for the 1935 500-Mile Race. He did indicate that the national technical committee should lower the 45 gallon fuel limit. Their next meeting was scheduled for July in Detroit. He also mentioned the improvements in tires and that only nine tires were changed during the race.

JUNE 10, 1934.   JOE RUSSO DIES OF INJURIES FROM LANGHORNE CRASH

Not given the ultimatum to quit driving race cars by his wife, the 32-year old Joe Russo headed to Langhorne, Pennsylvania. On that 38th lap of the 50-lap feature, Russo hit the fence and began a series of pinwheels down the track. The Foreman Axle Special, owned by Lou Moore, broke into two pieces and Joe was tossed 75 feet. He was unconscious when picked up by the medical attendants. Helene Yockey Russo witnessed her husband's accident and would follow the ambulance to Harriman Hospital in Bristol, Pennsylvania. Al Gordon won the 50-lap feature and George "Doc" MacKenzie ran second.

Joe Russo sustained fractured skull, a broken jaw, severe internal injuries and fractures of both ankles. He would undergo an emergency operation. Doctors listed his condition as serious but Joe took a turn for the worse Saturday evening. At 4 p.m. on June 10, Russo would die without regaining consciousness. Mrs. Russo remained at his bedside.

Having resided in the Spink-Arms Hotel in Indianapolis, Joe recently moved to Detroit where he joined the Payroll Company as a consulting engineer. His new bride, Helene, was a prominent Detroit socialite and sportswoman. She had inherited a successful furniture business when her first husband was killed in a passenger automobile accident. Joe had told friends he was set for life and was considering retiring from driving. In addition to his wife, Joe left an eight-year old son Eddie and brother Paul, also a race driver.

JULY 1, 1934   BERT KARNATZ KILLED ON LOCAL TRACK

Promoters of the Veterans of Foreign Wars Speedway, Eight Mile Road and Schoenherr Roads, Detroit planned to honor local hero and race driver Bert Karnatz on Sunday July 1, 1934. He would be presented with a gold watch in recognition of his seven straight victories at their track. Motor problems ended his streak last Sunday. The event would be publicized as Bert Karnatz Day. However, it was a painful day for the popular Indy 500 driver. He injured his shoulder when his car's steering gear cracked and he went hurtling over a ten-foot bank as the crowd looked on in horror.

Despite his shoulder injury, he told the promoters that he planned to get back in his winning form the following Sunday. On the first lap of a 30-lap feature the 29-year old Karnatz was fatally injured when car locked wheels with Windy Jennings's racer. Bert's car flipped end-over-end and it landed on top of the embankment that surrounded the track. He suffered a broken neck and a fractured skull. Karnatz also sustained severe cuts about his eyes and face from the glass of his broken goggles. Bert would be pronounced dead at 7:35 p.m. in Saratoga General Hospital. Earlier on he had won the first heat race, a five-lap dash against the four fastest qualifiers. Jennings's car would roll over several times but he escaped from the car with minor injuries.

Bert Karnatz was single and live with his mother in Dearborn, Michigan. He worked in the engineering department at Chrysler Corporation. Two years ago he was seriously injured at Salem, New Hampshire suffering a fractured skull and broken right arm.

JULY 22, 1934   JOHN DILLINGER KILLED LEAVING
                 BIOGRAPH THEATER

31-year-old public enemy number one John Dillinger was killed by BOI agents as he left the Biography theater in Chicago. He was accompanied by Ana Sage and Polly Hamilton to watch "Manhattan Melodrama" starring Clark Gable and Myrna Loy. He had been accused of robbing 24 banks. Melvin Purvis and agents moved in to arrest Dillinger as he was leaving the theater. He attempted to flee and ran down an alley but he was shot four times. Souvenir hunters dipped handkerchieves in his blood. Dillinger loved attending the Indianapolis 500 where he could blend in amongst 125,000 spectators.

※ ※ ※

Billy Winn would be the beneficiary of Johnny Sawyer's misfortune in the Springfield 100 on August 25. Sawyer started on the Pole and would lead the entire way before dropping out on the 93rd lap. Billy Winn inherited the lead and went on to edge Russ Snowberger. Mauri Rose and Frank Brisko came in third and fourth.

Shorty Cantlon would win the Syracuse 100 on September 9. George Brayon was killed when he was thrown from the car and was struck by Frank Brisko. Then his car, which had been turned around in its skid, also ran over Brayon's body. Frank, unaware that he had struck George, went on to finish second. Billy Winn finished third.

Kelly Petillo would get an early Christmas gift when he won the December 23 Mines Field road race before 50,000 spectators. (This is the location where Los Angeles International airport would be constructed.) Doc MacKenzie started on the pole and had worked up a considerable lead. For five laps his pit crew held up a five gallon gas can but Doc ignored the signal to pit. His engine would sputter and the car would come to a stop on the backstretch. While a tow car was bringing a crew member with a can of gasoline, Wilbur Shaw, Kelly Petillo, Ralph Hepburn and Chet Gardner all would pass MacKenzie's car. Doc would lose five laps to the leaders before he could resume the race.

Bill Cummings won the 1934 AAA National Driving title with 681.7 points. Mauri Rose was second with 530. Kelly Petillo, Russ Snowberger and Joe Russo would all tie for third with 300 points.

1934

Ernie Triplett

In Memoriam March 5, 1934

1934

Bill Cummings
Winner
104.863 mph Average. Led 57 Laps

1935

With the prize money that Kelly Petillo made from winning the Mines Field last December 23, Petillo was of the mind set, why share race winnings with a car owner—build yourself your own car for the Indianapolis 500 and you would make twice the income. So Kelly would spend the winter building a race car that others ridiculed as built of parts from a junk yard.

Mike Boyle would enter three Boyle Products Specials, #1 for Bill Cummings, #4 for Al Miller and #3 for Russ Snowberger. Russ was optimistic that his switch to such a powerful team was his path to Victory Lane. Youthful St. Louis businessman, Gil Pirrung, entered two cars and nominated Wilbur Shaw for car #14 and George "Doc" MacKenzie for car #8 to be his drivers.

Louis Meyer would be in the #36 Ring Free Special in his quest to be a three-time winner. Mauri Rose had replaced Frank Brisko in the now-numbered #2 FWD Special while Brisko move to the #41 Art Rose Special. Leon Duray landed Bowes Seal Fast as a sponsor and picked Tony Gulotta to drive his #44 and defending AAA Eastern Champion rookie Johnny Hannon for car #45. In addition to Hannon, there was a promising collection of rookies hoping to qualify for their first race including #22 Floyd Roberts, #62 Harris Insinger, #43 Ted Horn, #37 George Connor, #39 Jimmy Snyder, #26 Louis Tomei, now free from prison, and Clay Weatherly in the #56 Cresco Special owned by Jack Schmidlapp of Cincinnati.

MAY 18, 1935   YOUTHFUL PHENOM REX MAYS WINS POLE

23-year old daredevil Rex Mays, the 1934 AAA Western Champion, captured the Pole Position with a 25-mile qualifying average of 120.736 mph. He had posted an unofficial record yesterday over 122 mph. But it wasn't a way Mays would have liked to capture to top starting spot. Kelly Petillo, last year's Pole winner, took to the track near sundown and electrified the crowd of 25,000 with a new one-lap 122.416 mph and ten-lap 121.687 mph track records. His speeds would be disallowed by the AAA technical committee who determined he used five-eighths of a pint too much gasoline. (Rules allowed three gallons, with a tolerance of one pint). It was too late for Kelly to readjust his carburetor to make another qualification attempt before sundown.

Shorty Cantlon and Lou Moore also experienced hard luck. Shorty was averaging 117 mph after nine laps but he was forced to quit on his final lap. His speed would have placed him in the middle of row two had he completed his run. Moore was averaging 116 mph but broke a ring gear on his seventh lap.

It was an ideal day for qualifying but only nine drivers would post speeds. Al Gordon, driving car Bill White's #6 Cocktail Hour Cigarettes Special, would start second and rookie Floyd Roberts, despite having driven minimal practice laps, surprised many people by landing the outside position in row one with a speed of 118.671 mph in his Abel-Fink Special. Louis Meyer, Bill Cummings and Tony Gulotta filled row two. Gulotta was driving the car that Mauri Rose finished a close second in last year. Former winner, Fred Frame, made up for the sting of missing last years race by qualifying in the middle of the third row. Fred was flanked by Ralph Hepburn and Chet Gardner, the slowest first day qualifier at 114.556 mph.

Eddie Rickenbacker arrived in Indianapolis for the First Day of Qualifications. He inspected the track and was quite pleased with the green and yellow safety lights placed in six different locations around the track.

MAY 19, 1935   JOHNNY   HANNON   ESCAPES FRIGHTENING CRASH

On Sunday May 19, Johnny Hannon, the 1934 AAA Eastern Champion, had a spectacular accident at Milwaukee. His car crashed through the infield fence, overturned twice and landed upside down in a five-foot ditch. His head hit a concrete retaining wall, splitting his helmet.

Surprisingly, he escaped with only a loss of a tooth and bruises. Doc MacKenzie would win the race. Johnny had also gotten upside down and suffered a bruised back in an April 28 smashup at Reading, Pennsylvania.

Mauri Rose and Russ Snowberger made the race on Day Two. On Rose's first qualification attempt, he was flagged into his pit after his first lap because his oil pan was dragging. Rose would go out later in his FWD Special and qualify with an average speed of 116.470 mph with his quick lap of 117.447 mph. Snowberger, the former Pole winner, posted a somewhat disappointing speed of 114.209 mph. The track closed early at 5 p.m. Intermittent showers had shut down the track in the afternoon.

MAY 20, 1935   JOHNNY HANNON KILLED ON HIS INITIAL LAP

May 20, 1935 was a black day at the Indianapolis 500. Two race drivers and a riding mechanic would lose their lives in separate accidents. The morning started off with rookie Harris Insinger losing control of his car and hitting the retaining wall in turn three. Harris was not hurt and his car sustained slight damage.

Johnny Hannon had arrived from Milwaukee to the needling by his crew for tearing up a race car up there. First car owner Leon Duray took Hannon on a familiarization ride of the track trying to convey that driving on bricks was quite a bit different than driving on dirt tracks. Next teammate Tony Gulotta took the wheel and proceeded to drive Johnny at laps above 117 mph for him to get a feel for that kind of speed. Now it was time for the former professional boxer to test the car and possibly qualify later in the day similar to what Floyd Roberts had done a week ago. No riding mechanic had been officially assigned to the #45 car, so Duray asked Harold (Shorty) Reeves, who was to ride with Chet Miller, to take a ride with the rookie.

The AAA Eastern Champion didn't complete a lap. Johnny Hannon entered the NE turn traveling at an excessive speed. His car went into a long skid and the violent impact tore out four feet of concrete wall. It would land upright with Reeves unconscious in the car. Hannon was thrown 50 feet from his racer, his head and chest crushed. Johnny would die minutes later as Leon Duray arrived at the crash scene.

Now semiconscious, Reeves would be taken to City Hospital in serious condition suffering spinal injuries and severe lacerations. Virginia Whetstone, Shorty's girlfriend, read about his accident in the newspaper and rushed to the hospital to be by his bedside. His parents had been try to dissuade him from riding in this year's 500. When not serving as a riding mechanic, Reeves was an accomplished trap drummer and had performed with several orchestras in Indianapolis.

Drivers blamed Johnny Hannon's inexperience for his fatal accident. A troubled Tony Gulotta would say he told him to take it easy until he got the "feel" of the car and the track. An examination of the car showed there were no mechanical failures and track officials put the cause of losing control due to his unfamiliarity with the race track.

Hannon, who won 13 of 14 professional boxing matches before taking up race car driving as a career, entered the National Sprint Car Hall of Fame in 2006. He left his wife Mary and two daughters.

More misfortune be struck Kelly Petillo. On his second qualification attempt, he had turned in nine solid laps averaging 116.8 mph. On his final go-around his motor broke a connecting rod, cracked three cylinders and cut the crankcase in two. He would coast back to his pit. Petillo had sunk all his money and then some in his home-built car. He had borrowed money from his father's fruit business, and ran up a huge debt throughout Indianapolis living on credit.

He made an emergency call to C. W. Yount, head of the Eagle Machine Company at 635 East Market Street in Indianapolis. Pleading that he needed the motor rebuilt in time to qualify, Yount put his best men on the project. They would weld the case, install three cylinder sleeves, and align and bore the case so the crankshaft had a precision fit. Kelly also placed a rush order for a new rod that was fitted into the motor as well. The workmen completed the project on Saturday May 25.

Babe Stapp, driving the #17 Marks Red Lion Special, was the day's fastest qualifier with a speed average of 117.847 mph but would start twelfth on Race Day. His teammate, rookie George Connor, would qualify the #37 Lion Head Special at 114.321 mph on his second attempt.

MAY 20, 1935   STUBBLEFIELD AND MECHANIC
KILLED ON QUALIFYING RUN

During a late afternoon qualifying run, W. H. "Stubby" Stubblefield and his riding mechanic Leo Whitaker were killed when their car leaped over the outer wall in the SW turn. Their crash occurred in almost the identical spot where Peter Kreis' fatal accident occurred last year. The 27-year old Stubblefield had just completed his seventh lap and was averaging 114.709 mph. Something in the steering apparatus apparently broke on Phil Shafer's Victor Gasket Special as there were no skid marks left on the race track. Despite both wearing crash helmets, each died from fractured skulls. Whittaker expired as he was being placed on a stretcher at the accident scene. Stubblefield would die before he reached City Hospital. He would leave a wife. Stubby was enshrined into the National Sprint Car Hall of Fame in 1997.

50,000 race fans, what was called the largest Pre-Race crowd in the Speedways history, witnessed Shorty Cantlon qualify at 118.205 mph, the fourth overall fastest speed. After his initial lap logged at 119.506 mph, his pit crew signaled for him to slow it down. Knowing he was okay on his gas consumption, he put the pedal down on his final lap speed, posting a 119.760 mph lap—faster than Al Gordon's average qualifying speed. Harry McQuinn would achieved a speed that will never be matched at Indy—111.111 mph. Wilbur Shaw finally got his #14 Pirrung Special in the field with a 116.854 mph and would start in 20th position.

Just before sundown Kelly Petillo, a born mechanic and machinist, took to the track for what was his third and final attempt. He would make a measured run and qualify with a 115.095 mph speed average. There were some anxious moments as the officials measured his fuel consumption. When the AAA tech team gave their O.K. a huge cheer went out to Kelly.

Frank Brisko, whose speed was disallowed last Saturday for exceeding the three-gallon and one-pint fuel requirement by a quart, easily made the show with a 113.3 mph average.

24-year old Clay Weatherly kept begging Leon Duray for him to be able to drive the now-repaired car of Johnny Hannon. Mechanics had worked feverishly to repair the car. Eventually Duray relented and let the promising dirt track driver take a ride in car #45. Clay immediately left the #56 Cresco Special owned by Jack Schmidlapp of Cincinnati. Weatherly would qualify at an impressive speed of 115.095 mph—the fastest qualifier of the day. He would start the race in 25th position.

Harry Mack, manager of the Ford Motor Company's plant in Dearborn, Michigan, drove the Ford V-8 Pace Car to lead the field to the green flag and as expected Rex Mays grabbed the lead at the start and would lead the first 63 laps. Tony Gulotta followed at the 50 mile

277

mark, with Louis Meyer third and Babe Stapp fourth. Stapp would trail Mays for the next one hundred miles and Kelly Petillo had advanced through the field to now run third.

The initial round of pit stops shuffled the field with Stapp forging out in front from laps 64-67 when Mays went in for servicing. Petillo would take the lead on lap 68 for six laps when Babe pitted. Rex Mays would again resume the lead on 74 and continue out in front through lap 99, but on the next lap Petillo would go back on top and have the honor of leading at the half way point. Louis Meyer was again running in third place with Wilbur Shaw now up to fourth.

Soon after the 250-mile mark, Tony Gulotta, who had been consistently in the top three in his #44 Bowes Seal Fast Special, dropped out of the race with a bad magneto on lap 102. One lap later Mauri Rose's day would end in the FWD Special with studs being listed for his departure. Rex Mays believed Kelly Petillo's patched up motor wouldn't match the swift pace he tried to set but on the contrary it was Mays whose day would end on lap 123. With Kelly's main worry now on the sidelines, he led comfortably through lap 139 when it was time to make his second pit stop. Wilbur Shaw would take the lead for the first time in the race for five laps then surrender it back to Petillo on lap 145.

Intermittent showers brought out the caution flag for a number of laps at 450 miles. This kept the hard charging

Shaw at bay and the diminutive Italian-American would lead the remainder of the way to win the 23rd Indianapolis 500. Wilbur Shaw, frustrated in his inability to close in on Petillo's lead the last 50 laps due to the rain, finished second. Bill Cummings, trying to replicate the conservative, steady pace to took him that Victory Lane last year, mis-guessed the pace of the Race and would finish third. Rookie Floyd Roberts month ended well with a fourth place finish and Ralph Hepburn, with 68 laps of relief help from Gene Haustein, would round out the top five. All told Petillo, who had worked all night until 4 a.m. in the morning on his car, led three times for 102 laps. Rex Mays was out front twice for a total of 89 laps. Kelly would set a new speed record for the race of 106.240 mph in his four-cylinder, rear-drive Gilmore Speedway Special.

The first words Petillo would say in Victory Lane was, "How did Shaw do? That guy had me worried. He was after me all the time." When told he finished second, Kelly would say in almost disbelief, "This was the first time a car ever stayed together for me!" Not one to enjoy large numbers of people crowding around him, his crew quickly pushed his car back to his garage. Petite, 4'10" Mrs. Valentine Petillo and her eight-year old son Kelly Jr. tried to push and shove themselves back to her husband's garage through the throng of people. When asked was she worried, the relieved wife would just smile and say, "When I saw Kelly out in front I knew he would win if he didn't run out of gasoline. I just held my breath and waited for him to get the last lap finished."

Kelly, who years ago earned the moniker "King of the Ridge" for being the person who could drive the treacherous Ridge Route between Los Angeles and Bakersfield faster than all others in a truck, was asked if he would continue to race. He responded in the affirmative,

KELLY PETILLO——"Three years ago I begged for a chance to drive when I came here. I've only started to win races. I'm going to win more of 'em—that is, if Pete DePaolo remains as my pit manager to do the thinking for me while I do the driving."

Jimmy Dunham, Petillo's riding mechanic, discovered his shirt was completely torn off one shoulder because of the wind. When he went over to the Speedway Hospital, a nurse ask him how he felt, he responded, "Baby, what are you doing at 8 o'clock tonight?"

MAY 30, 1935   CLAY WEATHERLY KILLED

Clay Weatherly quickly advanced to a top ten position in the early stages of the race. Leon Duray was so terrified he personally grabbed a large chalkboard and wrote "Slow Down!" Bordering on the edge of being out of control, on lap eight Clay lost control of his

#45 Bowes Seal Fast Special coming out of the NW corner. His car shot diagonally across the track, ripped through a wooden fence and flipped end-over-end before landing on the grass in full view of thousands of horrified spectators in grandstand H. Several women spectators fainted as they watched Weatherly and his 23-year old riding mechanic Francis Bradburn being tossed from their racer. Clay was dead of a fractured skull and crushed chest before medical attendees arrived. His mother, Mrs. Elizabeth Baxter, learned of her son's death when she purchased a newspaper on her way home from work. She collapsed and was taken to her home by friends. Neighbors quickly collected money for her to pay for the cost of a train ticket from Los Angeles to Dixon, Illinois, where burial would occur.

Francis Bradburn, an employee at Leon Duray's garage, was unconscious and his helmet was battered and blood stained. Taken to the infield emergency hospital, doctors determined he suffered a fracture of two vertebrae in the middle of his spine. His first concern was about his family saying, "Don't worry, mom, I'm O. K." Francis was placed in a plaster cast then transferred to Robert W. Long Hospital. When the announcement of the accident was made, his parents called the Speedway and immediately hurried over to the track's emergency hospital. Bradburn's mother would comment,

MRS. IVAN BRADBURN——"He was wild over airplanes and race cars. He was so thrilled about getting the opportunity to ride in the Race, although he had never met Clay until he came out for the Race. An odd part of the whole thing was that he was slated to ride with Johnny Hannon and then he was changed. We were so thankful that he wasn't with Hannon after that accident. It seemed strange that he escaped one accident and was in another."

Ross Ormsby, editor of Speedway Magazine, witnessed the crash and put the blame squarely on Weatherly.

ROSS ORMSBY——"He was driving over his head. He was going too fast. You could see his pit crew signaling to him to slow down. He started out in 18th position and I think he was fifth when he crashed, and that was after only 33 miles."

The 24-year old Weatherly found great pleasure assisting his friend Philip Muehlfelder, who promoted midget car races at Coney Island in Cincinnati. Clay had recently been appointed as track manager and vowed after the 500-Mile Race he would devote full time to this position.

Shorty Reeves, recovering from his broken back at City Hospital from the Johnny Hannon crash, said he believed the car was jinxed.

SHORTY REEVES——"I don't know whether there's anything wrong mechanically with that car, but I'm inclined to believe it wasn't. Certainly a man who knows his race cars as well as Leon Duran and has the interest of his drivers at heart as much as he has, wouldn't let the car go into the race in bad mechanical condition. But you just look at the record of that car. It's fast and has been under excellent management and it's never been dogged by trouble, mechanical or otherwise. That makes me think it's being followed by a jinx that won't be defeated at any cost."

On his 16th lap, 33-year old Al Gordon was involved in a nasty-looking crash that he was fortunate to survive. Gordon lost control of his #6 Cocktail Hour Special going into the NW turn, hit the outside wall, straddled it, then hung suspended upside down atop the wall. Rescue workers pulled Al from the wreckage. His riding mechanic, Frank Howard, was thrown from the car. Unlike last year when Gordon would spend several days in the hospital, this time he escaped with minor injuries. Howard's injuries were superficial also. Both were taken to the infield medical center in the fire battalion chief's automobile and would walk from the car to the hospital. Mrs. Gordon would weep with joy after seeing that her husband was uninjured. Al accepted entire blame for the accident. "It just got away from me, that's all." His helmet was crushed on its side. He was anxious to get to the pits to see if he could serve as a relief driver.

Bob Sall, who started 33rd in the race, would drop out of the race on the 47th lap with steering problems and finish 29th. This would mark the 1933 AAA East Coast Champion's only appearance in the 500-Mile Race. He would be enshrined into the National Sprint Car Hall of Fame in 1992.

Rex Mays impressive charge effectively ended on lap 123, when during his pit stop a technical committee member spotted a broken front spring shackle.

Pete DePaolo, the 1925 Indy winner, would serve as pit manager for Kelly Petillo. He kept trying to keep Kelly believing he could win despite all the misfortune he experienced during the month.

PETE DE PAOLO——"This year is going to be another Italian year. In 1915, Ralph DePalma, an uncle of mine, won

284

it. In 1925, I won it and now the ten-year cycle comes around again and some Italian out there at the Speedway should win. I don't know who it will be—maybe Tony Gulotta, maybe Kelly Petillo, maybe Al Gordon, whose real name, I think is Al Gordino.

"Remember my prediction after the race.

"Kelly, you've the ability and you got the car. You do the driving and let me do the thinking here at the pits, and I don't want you to miss a single signal."

Petillo and his wife were virtually penniless for two weeks leading up to the race. They were living in a small white garage in Speedway City.

Wilbur Shaw's race calculations were based on his belief that Kelly Petillo's patch-quilt rebuild of his blown motor could not last 500 miles. He further felt, correctly so, that Petillo would not be able to resist the temptation to push his car to the limits, to lead the race and capture as much lap prize money as possible. The laps that were ran under caution late in the race due to the sudden rain shower, were not part of his calculation. In hindsight, he wish he had pushed Kelly much harder.

Another stroke of luck for Petillo, even though it didn't seem so at the time, was when on the last lap of his ten lap qualification run, his engine blew. Had the motor lasted one more lap for a successful qualifying run, Petillo's car might have been an early retiree. Fears of fuel shortages proved unfounded as Kelly confirmed he had two gallons, three pints remaining. Wilbur Shaw finished with three gallons extra but most impressive was Floyd Roberts with just over five gallons. Shorty Cantlon, driving the #9 Sullivan & O'Brien Special, got every last droplet out of the 42 1/2 gallons of allotted gasoline. Shorty ran out of gas and coasted across the finish line in sixth place.

Kelly Petillo's gamble to be his own car owner, which pushed him to the brink of financial ruin, paid off as was awarded $30,600 at the awards banquet at the Indianapolis Athletic Club. In addition, he was presented with a DeLuxe Ford V-8 roadster by the C.D. Warnock Company, a year's free meal ticket at Wheeler's cafeteria, the L. Strauss trophy——two European pieces of art work——(from Milan, Italy, a pair of heroic urns, symbol of victory, and from the "Left Bank" in Paris, a superb clock) presented by A.L. Block, president of L. Strauss & Company. Mrs. Petillo was especially thrilled over the prize from the Norge Company, an electric refrigerator.

As leader at 300 miles, Kelly also won the Presto-O-Lite silver brick. Wilbur Shaw was awarded $13,150 as the race runner-up, Bill Cummings $6,700 for third place. Kelly had promised pit manager Pete De Paolo that he would follow his instructions and he would say, "I kept my promise to Pete and I'm the happiest man in the world for doing so."

Kelly would take $2000 from his prize earnings from the Mines Field race and put it toward building his own car for the 500. His competitors needled him about his "mongrel" car, calling it "Kelly's Folly", implying it was a piece of junk. And there was some truth to that. Petillo was a scavenger in search of used parts from old airplanes, junk tractors, and crashed race cars. Portions of the car were literally held together with baling wire.

Joining Eddie Rickenbacker at the awards banquet was popular Hollywood actor Richard Arlen. Arlen starred in the Oscar winning film "Wings", the first movie to win the Academy Award for Best Picture. It was during the banquet that Rickenbacker remarked he would be in favor of making all cars stock entries, causing a murmur from the audience. He also expressed a hope that New York City, Los Angeles, Chicago and Miami Beach would also construct Speedways.

Petillo along with Floyd Roberts, Doc MacKenzie and Chet Miller, by virtue of completing all 500 miles, qualified for membership in the Champion Spark Plug's 100-Mile an Hour Club.

Because of the numerous fatalities over the past three years, Eddie Rickenbacker decided that the inclined surface in the four corners needed to be redesigned to reduce the likelihood of cars going over the wall. During the summer, the Speedway would spend a considerable sum of money on the reconstruction of the upper ten feet of the track to greatly reduce the angles in the turns. During the four month project, patches of asphalt were placed over various sections of the track in their efforts to smooth out the track's rough sections.They also added a dirt apron on the inside edge of the track on the turns.

SEPTEMBER 9, 1935   HARRIS INSINGER KILLED AT
                      OAKLAND

Currently in second position for the Pacific Coast Championship, the talented 26-year old Harris Insinger had hoped to score a victory in the 50-lap main event at the wickedly fast Oakland Speedway to narrow Al Gordon's point lead. As a rookie in this year's Indy 500, the Germantown, Pennsylvania, pilot had made an impressive advance from 31st starting position to finish 14th. Sadly his career ended on lap three when Insinger, riding in third position, attempted to pass second place Gordon. Harris and Al locked wheels coming out of the turn onto the backstretch. Insinger's car rolled over three times throwing him onto the track surface and crushing him when his car struck his body. Harris was barely alive when track attendants reached him but would be pronounced dead upon arrival at Fairmont Hospital. Gordon's car skidded when the two cars locked wheels but he managed to avoid crashing and resumed the race.

Very intelligent, Insinger had been an engineering student at the prestigious University of Pennsylvania before starting his racing career in earnest. He had several major crackups including at Ascot where he broke his back.

Kelly Petillo would capture the 1935 AAA National Championship with 890 points over Bill Cummings with 630, Wilbur Shaw 530 and Floyd Roberts 510. In addition to his winning the Indianapolis 500, he also scored victories in the July 4 St. Paul 100 and the October 13 race at Langhorne. Billy Winn, despite being victorious in the August 24 Springfield 100 and the September 2 Syracuse 100, would finish only fifth in the standings with 408.2 points. Louis Meyer won the September 7 Altoona 100 and Rex Mays came home first in a non-championship race on December 15 in the Ascot 125 to end the season.

1935

Al Gordon

Qualified 2nd. Crashed on Lap 17
In Memoriam January 26, 1936

1935

Kelly Petillo
Winner
106.240 mph Average. Led 102 Laps

1936

Even though Ted Horn ran a nondescript Race in 1935, Harry Hartz selected the 27-year old Horn to drive his car in the 500. The father of a 2-1/2-year-old daughter, Ted would drive the car that Fred Frame drove to victory in 1932.

In 1928 the Glendale American Legion Post took over the promotion of Sunday races at the Ascot track. Later they would expand to hold races on Wednesday nights under the lights. Midget racing was becoming quite the trendy thing and because its popularity, attendance at Ascot had seen a steady decline. The American Legion would bow out of promoting races at Ascot in early 1935. In an effort to spur interest, a 200-lap race using the two-seater cars that raced in the Indianapolis 500 was scheduled for January 25, 1936. The track had been re-named the Ascot Motor Speedway.

Over 10,000 fans packed the grandstands to see the two-seater cars in action. Fresh off his 1935 AAA West Coast Championship, Al Gordon was now focused on reversing his bad luck at the Indianapolis Motor Speedway and winning the 500 and the AAA National title. Being able to drive his Indy car at Ascot would be the opportunity to get his race car ready before May. Spider Matlock would be joining him as his riding mechanic.

Gordon ran close to race leaders Rex Mays and Louis Meyer until lap 117 when he blew his right rear tire. He lost valuable track position as he drove back to the pits on the rim. Al would roar back to the track after a quick wheel change and commenced a frantic charge to make up lost ground.

His banzai drive both thrilled and terrified the Ascot attendees but it would end tragically nine laps later. Coming high off the south turn, he apparently hit a slick spot causing his car to spin. Gordon's racer would crash backwards through the fence and disappear from spectators view as he careened down a 12-foot graded embankment. Helen Gordon, Al's wife, and the elder of their two young sons, witnessed the origins of the crash.

Gordon, who on numerous times, had escaped the Grim Reaper, finally had fate catch up with him. Track attendants placed Al's broken body on a stretcher and rushed him to nearby Good Samaritan Hospital. However, he would succumb shortly after arrival due to a fractured skull and crushed chest. Spider Matlock, known as "The Man of a Thousand Crackups "was listed in critical condition at the hospital. The movie stuntman would die the following day.

Gordon's death surprised nobody. It was common to hear, "His days are numbered" and "He'll kill himself some day." Al had told a Los Angeles Times reporter just a week before his fatal accident,

AL GORDON——"I'm not afraid to die. When it comes, well, it'll just come. It may come

Sunday, or next week, or next year. We all have to die some time. So what difference does it make."

Al Gordon was inducted into the National Sprint Car Hall of Fame in 1999.

Spider Matlock, also a fatalist, had a most interesting career. He appeared as himself in an uncredited role in the popular racing movie "The Crowd Roars" starring James Cagney. Matlock was successful real estate salesman, a champion motorcycle racer and a wing-walker on barnstorming bi-planes.

Rex Mays would win the race with a quarter of a lap victory over Louis Meyer. Rex had been in a neck-and-neck battle with Floyd Roberts until Roberts car blew a tire on the backstretch. Floyd would recover and go on to finish third ahead of Bill Cummings and Chet Gardner.

FEBRUARY 1936   NEW THE BORG-WARNER TROPHY

The Spaulding-Gotham Company of Chicago crafted the sterling silver Borg-Warner trophy. It featured bas-relief sculptures of every Indianapolis 500 winner. Unveiled at a February 1936 banquet in New York, it was presented to Eddie Rickenbacker. The trophy stood 52 inches with an original value of $10,000. Rickenbacker indicated it would be permanently housed in the Detroit Athletic Club.

APRIL 26, 1936   ASCOT SPEEDWAY GRANDSTANDS
DESTROYED BY FIRE

On April 26, 1936 the grandstands at Ascot Speedway were destroyed by fire. The track had been closed since the deaths of Al Gordon and Spider Matlock. A.C. Pillsbury, Pacific Coast director of the AAA, said the track would not be sanctioned until improvements were made to the facilities. They estimated the loss to be $75,000. Initially the fire was believed to have started from a short circuit in the lighting system. Further investigations indicated an arsonist burned down the abandoned Ascot grandstands. Seven years later Linden Emerson, the racetrack janitor, confessed to setting the fire.

※ ※ ※

In an attempt to better prepare rookie drivers to be able to successfully compete at the Indianapolis Motor Speedway, Eddie Rickenbacker would require every first-time contestant, regardless of their racing experience, to demonstrate their competency with ten-lap phases at 80-90-100-105 and finally 110 mph. This would become known as the "rookie test."

MAY 6, 1936   KELLY PETILLO RETIRES FROM RACING

In a startling development, defending Indy 500 winner Kelly Petillo suddenly announced his retirement from racing. He boasted he had sufficient amount of money to allow another driver do the work. He selected George "Doc" MacKenzie, Eastern Driving Champion, to pilot his car. Petillo had entered the car the previous week listing himself as driver. MacKenzie was slated to drive Ira Vail's car. Kelly, known as "King of the Ridge" from his days when he would drive his father's fruit truck faster than anyone over the treacherous California route.

As MacKenzie was preparing to climb into the Petillo race car, Kelly pointed to the Van Dyke-bearded driver and exclaimed, "There's the winner of the race May 30." Then he did a quick reversal demanding, "Just a minute. Give me a crash helmet and goggles, I'll take it." He ordered Doc to move to the riding mechanic seat. The defending champion then proceeded to click off several progressively faster laps, his final circuit topping 114 mph. Then Petillo told MacKenzie, "Let's see what you can do."

Wasting no time Doc was traveling at speeds approaching Rex Mays's pole speeds of a year ago. Kelly found it to be a lot more terrifying riding along at 120 mph than driving the car. Whether it was begging or an order, Petillo yelled to Doc, "Hey, slow it down!" MacKenzie was loving it, telling his boss, "Nothing doing, it's my turn now!" The East Coast Champ would be one of the favorites to capture the Pole Position.

MAY 10, 1936   BILLY DEVORE SERIOUSLY INJURED
                 AT ATLANTA

Billy Devore's quest to become the first father-son combination to race in the Indianapolis 500 was nearly snuffed out when the 25-year old Devore was seriously injured at Atlanta's Lakewood Speedway. His vision hindered by the dusty conditions, Billy hit the turn one wall and was thrown twenty feet, landing on the track surface. His condition was initially listed as serious with a broken vertebra but no paralysis. He would remain hospitalized several days for observation. Mauri Rose won the feature with Chet Gardner second and Bob Sall third.

MAY 15, 1936   TONY GULOTTA IN FRIGHTENING
                 CRASH AT SPEEDWAY

On his initial appearance onto the track in preparation for tomorrow's battle for the Pole Position, Tony Gulotta, driving the Pirrung Special, hit the SW wall after a steering arm bolt broke. He then skidded, turning over twice, before coming to stop on the safety apron. Tony ducked down in the cockpit and had a death grip hold on the steering wheel. Gulotta and his riding mechanic Carl Riscigno were rushed to Methodist Hospital painfully injured but X-rays proved negative. Tony suffered a deep cut to his nose, mouth and chin. His back and shoulders were burned as they slid over the bricks.

Riscigno was tossed from the car on its impact with the retaining wall but escaped with minor injuries to his arm. AAA officials attributed Gulotta's survival due to his wearing a new crash helmet. As he slid upside down, his metal crash helmet scraped along the brick surface. The top of his helmet was worn down to the thickness of a dime. Fellow drivers felt the recent reconfiguration of the turns helped prevent Gulotta from going over the wall. Car owner Gil Pirrung initially believed the car would not be able to be repaired in time to qualify but Tony's crew were determined to rebuild the car.

Later in the day, Mauri Rose spun into the turn two wall in his F.W.D. Special when his car's steering arm broke. Rose and his mechanic Earl Frost were fortunate to escape with minor injuries. The car's front axle was bent and a wheel was torn off but the car would be repaired for qualifications later in the month.

Eddie Rickenbacker instituted even tighter fuel requirements for this year's ten-lap qualification run—reducing the allotment of gasoline to two and one-half gallons down from the previous year's mark of three gallons with a pint tolerance. No tolerance would be permitted this year. Most teams were frustrated by the decision to lower the amount gasoline except for Wilbur Shaw, who's new streamlined racer was not having fuel mileage issues at all. Former Pole winner Russ Snowberger was believed to have found the secret to run fast and stay within the fuel limit boundaries.

Even with the tightened restrictions, Rex Mays and Bill Cummings were favorites to with the Pole Position.

Millionaire rookie driver Joel Thorne had commissioned ten gold belts made that were inlayed with sterling silver and rubies. Thorne gave one to Preston Tucker of the Packard Indianapolis Company. He intended to present the Pole winner with one of his stylish belts also.

MAY 16, 1936   REX MAYS WINS BACK-TO-BACK POLE POSITIONS

Rex Mays, the 1934 and 1935 Pacific Coast Champion, became the first driver to win back-to-back pole positions as he sped to a 10-lap qualifying average of 119.644 mph in his four-cylinder Gilmore Special as a crowd of over 20,000 cheered his run. Mays fifth lap was his quickest at 121.065 mph. It was the same car he drove last year but with a new engine. Chickie Hirashima was his riding mechanic. The day's biggest disappointment happened just before sundown. 1934 Indy 500 winner Wild Bill Cummings excited the crowd with his 10-lap run of 119.845 mph to unseat Mays for the top spot. However, his speed was disallowed when it was determined his car had consumed a pint too much gasoline. Cummings fastest lap speed was 120.643 mph in his Boyle Products Special.

Babe Stapp, driving the #21 Pirrung Special which Wilbur Shaw drove to second place in last year's race, qualified in second position averaging 118.945 mph. Stapp's car was owned by the wealthy young St. Louis sportsman Gilbert Pirrung. And despite driving an eight-cylinder car, Chet Miller was third fastest in his Boyle Products Special. It was the car which Billy Arnold won with in 1930 and which he crashed while leading the 1931 and 1932 500s.

Doc MacKenzie rewarded Kelly Petillo for the confidence the defending champion placed in him by qualifying on the inside of row two with an average speed of 116.961 mph in the Gilmore Speedway Special. The quiet, well spoken MacKenzie sported a Van Dyke beard for good luck. He vowed he would never shave it off until he won the Indianapolis 500. George Connor in the Marks-Miller Special and Herb Ardinger, driving the Bowes Seal Fast Special, filled out the remainder of row two. MacKenzie, the reigning Eastern AAA Champion, quickly departed the Speedway to drive to Langhorne, Pennsylvania to compete in Sunday's 50-mile race.

Floyd Roberts, runner-up in the Pacific Coast Championship in 1934, and Deacon Litz qualification runs were also disallowed for using too much fuel. Roberts had an impressive run, averaging 118.633 mph while Deacon would post a 115.328 mph average. (Speedway rules required a warm-up lap, the ten lap qualification run and a coasting lap not to exceed the 2 1/2 gallon limit). Louis Meyer was averaging over 118 mph before a cracked block ended his run on his fifth qualifying lap. He had a new motor rushed from Los Angeles. Louis Tomei was the slowest of the eight qualifiers in the Wheeler's Special, the car which had originally been assigned to Billy Devore. Tomei was selected as replacement driver after Devore was seriously injured the previous week in a crash at Atlanta.

MAY 17, 1936   HEPBURN UNINJURED IN A HARD CRASH

During the morning practice session before the start of the Second Day of Qualifications, Ralph Hepburn, riding alone, lost control of his car coming out of turn four. His racer made hard impact four times with the upper retaining wall, tearing out a chunk of concrete. Hep's car then slid down the track where it ripped through the inner rail, knocking down 50-yards of wooden boards before coming to a stop. All though badly shaken up, Hepburn sustained no injuries. Later he indicated that his crew should be able to repair the smashed rear end of his racer in order to qualify the following week.

Many fans of Wilbur Shaw were disappointed that he did not make a qualifying attempt for the Pole in his personally designed streamlined racer. Shaw opted to make his qualifying run in his "catfish" shaped car on Sunday. He had a blistering run underway—one lap at 120.064 mph—when he made an uncharacteristically huge error. Wilbur mistakenly thought he had completed his ten-lap qualification run, when in reality he had logged only nine laps.

Later he would return to make a second attempt. Surprisingly his first lap was a very disappointing, 111.815 mph, but he would immediately step up the pace. His fourth lap was 119.617 mph and he finished as the Second Day of Qualifications fastest qualifier averaging 117.503 mph. He appeared to effortlessly qualify his streamlined machine. Savvy race people felt Wilbur could have posted a 121 mph lap had he chosen to drive the car all out. What really startled his competitors was that he use less than two gallons of gasoline during his 25-mile qualifying run—a quart under the imposed gasoline limit. Wilbur had put all his money into this car and he believed it would average 15 miles a gallon for the entire race. His competitors were very worried that they would only be able to average 13.46 mpg.

Shorty Cantlon, driving Bill White's Hamilton-Harris Special, was the day's second fastest qualifier at 116.912 mph. This was the originally slated for the late Al Gordon to drive in the 500. Ted Horn, driving for Harry Hartz, was third quick at 116.564 mph but he had a fast lap at 119.332 mph. And Bill Cummings and Floyd Roberts re-qualified at 115.221 mph and 112.403 mph respectively. Both remained annoyed that their initial fast speeds were rejected by the AAA.

MAY 17, 1936   DOC MAC KENZIE WINS LANGHORNE
                        50-MILER

Before a crowd of 40,000 Doc MacKenzie would capture the 50-mile feature after race leader Vern Orenduff dropped out in the waning stages of the race. In victory lane, the classy MacKenzie acknowledged the fine race Orenduff drove over the public address system.

DOC MAC KENZIE——"This afternoon I got the greatest break that ever came to a driver on this track. Orenduff was out there with more stuff than I had and was driving a marvelous race that had me licked when his engine failed him."

Hearing the praises being said about him, Orenduff went to victory lane to congratulate MacKenzie and in a fine display of sportsmanship responded.

VERN ORENDUFF——"A couple of weeks ago, it was me who got the breaks and I won as MacKenzie went through the fence. Considering the fact that "Doc" drove all night to get here in time for this race, leaving Indianapolis late on Saturday, he sure piloted his race car in fine style."

MAY 20, 1936   RALPH DE PALMA NAMED REFEREE
                 FOR 500-MILE RACE

Ralph DePalma was appointed Referee of the 500-Mile Race by Eddie Rickenbacker. The 1915 winner intended to serve as pit manager for Henry Banks. DePalma had built the car for his youthful portage. Banks's father William, a former racer from England, agreed to manage his son's pit. Ralph, who had returned to competition in 1934, gave positive remarks about the further reduction in gasoline for the qualifications and the race.

RALPH DE PALMA——"Undoubtedly this will be the safest race in the history of the 500-Mile event since 1911. The few accidents, none serious, which occurred before qualifying and the increased speeds despite fuel economy requirements seem to me to present the most spectacular set up in years."

In a surprise decision by the AAA Contest Board, famed stunt driver E.M. (Lucky) Teter was denied permission to attempt to compete in this year's race. They declared Teeter ineligible saying that he had not competed in any AAA events during the past year nor did he hold an AAA drivers' certificate.

Tony Gulotta was released from Methodist Hospital on May 22. He had a bad cut on his face that was stitched up. He also had very painful shoulder injuries that were badly skinned by contact with the brick surface of the track. Gil Pirrung had his car repaired but Tony could not find enough speed to qualify and was signaled back to the pits. The crew would take the engine and put it into another car but Gulotta could only reach a speed of 108 mph.

A strong wind kept the number of qualifiers to four on Monday, May 25, bringing the field total up to 28 starters. Rookie Ray Pixley of Fullerton, California was the fastest qualifier averaging 116.703 mph with a fast lap over 117.7 mph. Deacon Litz, Harry McQuinn and Ray Painter also qualified. A late afternoon rain shower prevented Lou Moore and Mauri Rose from making their time trial run. Louis Meyer lost another motor.

MAY 25, 1936.   BORG-WARNER TROPHY UNVEILED

The Borg-Warner trophy, what would become the symbol for winning the Indianapolis 500 for future generations, was presented to Captain Eddie Rickenbacker by the Borg-Warner Corporation at an informal dinner held in the ballroom of the Indianapolis Athletic Club. Borg-Warner had commissioned a 5-1/2-foot silver trophy to be designed which included the sculptured bust of the 23 previous Indianapolis 500 winners that would surround the trophy. Charles S. Davis, President of Borg-Warner, presented Rickenbacker with the trophy valued at $35,000 (originally said to be $10,000) and indicated each future winner's bust would be added to the trophy. A smaller trophy of similar design would awarded to every new Indy 500 champion. The winner would also receive $100 a month for a year. Former winners in attendance included Ray Harroun, Ralph DePalma, George Souders and Peter DePaolo.

Tommy Milton, two-time Indy 500 champion, was selected to drive the new Packard One Twenty Pace Car to start the race. Milton, currently employed as an engineer with the Packard Automobile Company, announced the winner will receive the Pace Car as one of his prizes. When asked if he would consider a return to the cockpit, Milton declared, "I've quit in body but my mind still lives on the track." He said despite all the glory of winning the 500-Mile Race, he doesn't miss the burning feet baking near the engine.

The Speedway management drew the ire of its drivers and teams by slashing the amount of gasoline they could use from 42 gallons to 37.5 gallons. This would require the race cars average 13 miles per gallon to finish the race.

Many drivers had their distinct good luck charms. Doc MacKenzie had his Van Dyke beard. Mauri Rose had his dog Prince.

MAURI ROSE——"Why that dog knows when my car goes by. And every time he's been at the race track, I've come into the money. So this year, Prince, is going to watch his first 500-Mile Race."

Rose had been becoming a much smoother race driver at the Speedway than when he first arrived. The cerebral Rose quickly figured out, "Many dirt track racers have a tendency to 'drive over their heads' on the Speedway, a problem which I had to overcome in my first couple of years." He felt confident his four-wheel drive car would carry him to Victory Lane based on Frank Brisko's success in it in 1934 when he lead 69 laps, more than any other driver in the 1934 500-Mile Race.

Hollywood stuntman Cliff Bergere has "doubled" as a driver in the movies. Very popular with star-struck movie fans, Cliff would be constantly asked what was harder, driving a race car or doing Hollywood stunts for films. His response would surprise many people.

CLIFF BERGERE——"The Indianapolis Race is a mild adventure compared to the stunts required in Hollywood. I don't mind changing planes in midair or crashing onto a fence, but a stunt that's certain to fail isn't worth trying."

One of the favorites to win the 1936 Indianapolis was George "Doc" MacKenzie. He enjoyed tell the story of how his cousin, named George W. MacKenzie, both got into the racing game together. They both got hooked on racing after attending a small fair race near Bristol, Pennsylvania. Both young men decided they wanted to be race drivers so they pooled their resources and built a race car in a farmer's stable near their homes to hide it from their parents. Doc, whose uncle was a distinguished surgeon, tells of their early racing days.

DOC MAC KENZIE——"We raced in several fair meets, saving enough money to buy a better car. Later at Langhorne, we saw the car we wanted. It had just won the feature race, so we dug up $1600 and bought it. We tossed a coin to see who would drive and George won. The car went through a fence in a race next day and he was badly injured."

Doc would drive the repaired race car and hone his skills to become a serious contender to win the 500-Mile Race.

MAY 30, 1936   LOUIS MEYER BECOMES FIRST 3-TIME WINNER

It was biting cold in the early hours on Race Day morning, but the sun would come out and many spectators would leave the track sunburned. Before a crowd of 170,000, 32-year old Louis Meyer became the first three-time winner of the Indianapolis 500 averaging a record-breaking speed of 109.069 mph to beat Ted Horn by 2 minutes 17 seconds. The top five finishers bettered last year's record race average.

After Louis Meyer pulled his winning #8 Ring Free Special into the "Bull Pen", he was handed a bottle of cold buttermilk, his personal preference. To quench his thirst, he quickly chugged the entire bottle commenting, "Gee, that's swell. I'll be back next year for more." By happen chance, a photo of Louis drinking his beverage of choice appeared on the front page of a local paper and a representative of the Dairy Association spotted this photo and decided to make "milk" an annual tradition for the 500 winners to drink in Victory Lane.

Most of his fellow drivers expected Meyer to have a short day in the race as he had been beset with motor problems throughout the month. Two days before Pole Day, Meyer cracked a motor block and it had to be welded together. On May 16, the First Day of Qualifications, his car went five laps on his qualifying run before he cracked the block again.

Meyer had a spare block with him that his crew installed but on May 24, while on a morning practice run before the start of time trials, he cracked this block too. On Monday May 25, Louis would be forced to wire Los Angeles to have a new block shipped out via air. It arrived Tuesday and was installed and Louis was successful in qualifying in the afternoon of Wednesday

May 27—the final day of qualifying. His "safe" qualifying speed would earn him 28th starting spot.

The saga continued when his crew discovered on Friday morning May 29, that the engine had little compression because both valves and piston head had been damaged during his qualification run. Meyer telephoned the Century Tire Company in Indianapolis and told them that he needed a rush job to smooth the heads off. It was 4 p.m. when they were delivered to Meyer's garage to start yet another engine re-build.

There was a Speedway rule that a driver could no longer work on his race car after 8 p.m. the night before the race. The completion of the task was left to his mechanics Lawson Harris, Dale Drake and Carl Effman. Former driver Frank Elliott, who Louis Meyer had ridden with as riding mechanic in the 1927 500, also lent a hand. Meyer arrived back at the track Race Day morning at 7:30 a.m. to help in the final assembly. It was 9:15 a.m. when his car was "buttoned up." Louis car would be the last one pushed to their starting spot, less than twenty minutes before the starting bombs. The crew were not able to run the engine prior to the start.

Starting the race back in 28th position due to a myriad of engine problems throughout the month, Louis steadily worked his way up through the field. He would first appear in the top ten at the 125-mile mark. Kelly Petillo, not pleased with MacKenzie running in seventh position, relieved Doc on lap 141. Petillo would steadily advanced the car up to a third place finish. Originally Mauri Rose was scored in third, but following a review from timing and scoring of the Race, Mauri would be drop one position to fourth in his #36 F.W.D. Special. Rose was fortunate as his day almost came to an early end. On lap 74, his FWD Special went into a skid and his wheel grazed the wall but Mauri didn't lose control. Chet Miller would finish fifth but he ran out of gasoline before he could complete his "cool down" lap.

Harry McQuinn, driving the #28 Sampson Radio Special, ran out of gasoline on the backstretch, costing him a sixth place finish. Rookie Ray Pixley, the pride of Fullerton, California, drove a consistent race to finish sixth. Shorty Cantlon was snakebit in the late stages of the race. While running in third place on his 193rd lap, Shorty's #7 Hamilton-Harris Special would run out of gasoline causing him to finish out of the money in 14th position. Likewise, Floyd Roberts saw his day come to a halt on lap 182 when his car ran out of gas. Roberts was never lower than seventh in the race. It was a particularly impressive drive for Roberts considering was driving with a broken arm that he hid from Speedway medical officials. Rex Mays would come back from his long early race stop to advance up to sixth position but he, too, would run out of gas on lap 192.

As expected 23-year old Rex Mays jumped into the lead on the opening lap in his #33 Gilmore Special with Babe Stapp in second and Wilbur Shaw in third. Setting a record pace, Mays held that position until he was forced into the pits on his 13th lap when a clevis pin dropped from his foot throttle. Rex would spend twenty minutes in the pits as his crew made repairs. When he resumed the race he had lost several laps. He then had to make a second stop to get another pin replacement. Now driving like a demon, Rex would work his way up to 6th place before running out of gasoline.

Babe Stapp in the #21 Pirrung Special would inherit the lead as a result of Mays' misfortune and would establish a new track record at 50 miles, averaging 116.125 mph. Wilbur Shaw was two seconds behind in second, Chet Gardner third, Chet Miller fourth and Billy Winn fifth. Wilbur was gaining on Stapp and would nose ahead on lap 32. Both Shaw and Stapp thrilled the crowd with their back-n-forth lead swapping which they carried on for several laps. Gardner's car dropped out on lap 38 with a bad clutch. Billy Winn would advance to third before a broken crankshaft forced him out on lap 67.

Wilbur Shaw, the pre-race favorite in his streamlined Gilmore Special, took the lead from laps 32 thru 82. On lap 83 he would stop for a right rear tire and fuel allowing Babe Stapp to again re-take the lead. Wilbur was confident he would not have any sort of a fuel issue to complete the 500 miles. He even good-naturedly laughed when a crew member accidentally spilled some gasoline and he reassured him, "Don't worry. I'm getting along ok and will have plenty."

However, misfortune was about to strike Shaw. Pressure underneath his hood was building up and it would tear loose the front hood fastenings. Wilbur was forced to stop on lap 88 to wire up the hood rivets that had loosened. Then on lap 89, Stapp's car would stop on the backstretch with a broken rear axle. With Babe's departure, Louis Meyer took the lead.

Shaw was in the pits for 11:47 minutes to wire down the hood. That proved only temporary and he'd be forced to return to the pits on lap 103 for an additional 4:43 minutes to repair the hood again. That corrected the problem. Late in the race, Shaw would make his final pitstop lasting 1:20 minutes for enough gasoline to make it to the finish. All told Wilbur would spend 19:30 minutes in the pits leaving him frustrated of what could have been.

On lap 119 Al Miller, running in seventh place, skidded sideways on the straightaway for 100 yards before hitting the inside railing on the main straightaway due to a broken steering knuckle. Miller was thrown from his cockpit into the inside guard rail. Al suffered a fractured hip and head injuries. It was the first time since 1911 that there had been an accident on the main straightaway.

Al Miller was in a great deal of pain as he lay in Methodist Hospital suffering from a compound fracture of the hip. Dr. E.B. Mumford was concerned about possible injuries to his spine as well. Miller showed some wit when his sister greeted him in the emergency hospital at the Speedway. "Don't worry. It's the same old bad leg." His knee had been amputated below the knee following a motorcycle accident years before.

When Louis Meyer pitted, Ted Horn in the #22 Hartz Special took the lead for 16 laps from 131-146 but Meyer re-took the lead when Horn was forced to the pits. Louis would slow his speed down to 98 mph the last eight miles of the race to save gas. Horn also slowed to make it to the finish as well.

Bill Cummings had bad luck from the very beginning when he could not get his #2 Boyle Products Special going. His clutch was slipping and Wild Bill rolled only a few feet before stopping. His crew worked feverishly to repair the clutch. A half hour later they finally stopped their efforts. This was the first time in Speedway history that a driver was out of the race before the flying start. Cummings's friend actor James Dunn, who would win Best Supporting Actor for his role in "A Tree Grows In Brooklyn", would needle him saying, "I came 3,000 miles to see this guy race and look what he did to me." Fred Frame's #46 Burd Piston Ring Special lasted only four laps before being sidelined with a burnt piston.

Jimmy Snyder, after his #43 Belanger Miller Special had dropped out of the race, took over as a relief driver for Emil Andres #19 Carew Special on lap 53. Tony Gulotta, who failed to qualify for the race after his frightening crash, took over Cliff Bergere's #42 Bowes Seal Fast Special on lap 59. Ralph Hepburn's #9 Art Rose Special developed a small leak in the line to the oil gauge. While in his pit, Hep borrowed a pocket knife from a fan and he carved a quarter-inch wooden peg to plug the hole and he was back on the track.

Three times Louis Meyer had to replace motor block after motor block. The last one was sent by plane from Los Angeles and it arrived just in time to mount it and qualify before the final deadline. As late as Friday night, May 29, Meyer and his crew worked late into the night to install a new piston. In Victory Lane, he credited his crew for the victory.

LOUIS MEYER——"The car ran wonderfully. It was a nice day and nice race. When did I think I had it in the bag? Not until that checkered flag. You never know about this one. But when I went into my reserve gas with only four laps to go I knew I had enough. Be sure to give the crew plenty of credit. If it wasn't for them, I would have never won. My car was in perfect shape."

JUNE 1, 1936.   MEYER NETS $31,255 AT VCTORY BANQUET

The following evening, Louis Meyer received $31,255 at the awards banquet held at the Indianapolis Athletic Club for his 500-Mile win. Ted Horn pocketed $13,775 for his second place finish. Meyer would also receive a smaller version of the new Borg-Warner trophy along with a $100 check each month for a year, a Norge refrigerator, a Gruen-Curvex wrist watch, the L. Strauss trophy "Grace"—a piece of art bought in Europe by Charles Mayer for the Strauss Company, the Payroll trophy and Wheeler's Cafeteria free meal ticket good for one year. Starter Seth Klein would present Louis the checkered flag waved to him—the first time in Speedway history for such a presentation. And also for the first time, Meyer would receive the keys to the Packard Pace Car, presented by Tommy Milton. Louis drew laughter when he said he won two races at the Speedway and "one economy contest." He added he hopes to come back and "win his third race." Rex Mays was also the recipient of a Gruen-Curvex wrist watch for winning the Pole Position.

JULY 12, 1936.   DOC MAC KENZIE, FLOYD ROBERTS HURT AT READING

Doc MacKenzie, Floyd Roberts and Frank "Wild Man" McGurk were injured while warming up their race cars before the start of time trials at Reading, Pennsylvania. As McGurk slowed to enter the pits, MacKenzie and

Roberts were speeding behind Frank and both crashed into the rear of his car. Doc and Floyd were rushed to Homeopathic Hospital with serious injuries. MacKenzie suffered a concussion, broken thumb and burns. Roberts leg was broken.

JULY 18, 1936   REX MAYS SERIOUSLY HURT AT READVILLE SPEEDWAY

Two-time Pole winner Rex Mays was initially reported to be dying at Forest Hills Hospital as a result of a four-car crash at Readville Speedway, outside of Boston. Driver Wesley Johnson was killed, Vern Orenduff and Henry Angeloni were also injured. The accident occurred during the midway point of the 25-mile feature race. Battling thick dust, Johnson, who was a lap behind, lost control of his car and struck a post, then slid back onto the track, crosswise. Mays and Orendorf were battling for the lead as they rounded the turn at full speed. Their cars skidded and crashed into Johnson's race car and overturned. Angeloni, directly behind Rex and Vern, swerved sharply to the right to avoid the pileup. His car crashed through the guard rail.

Preliminary medical reports described Mays condition as serious with a crushed chest, two broken ribs and lacerations. Orendorf received lacerations of the face, a fractured rib, abrasions and contusions of the body.

JULY 20, 1936   DOC   MAC   KENZIE   MARRIES
SWEETHEART IN HOSPITAL

George "Doc" MacKenzie married Miss Verna Mather of Langhorne, Pennsylvania while confined to Homeopathic Hospital bed suffering from a brain concussion and broken hand from his racing injuries at Reading the previous week. Doc is the nephew of Dr. George W.M. MacKenzie, a prominent Philadelphia ear, nose and throat specialist. Uncle George had received the gold medal of the University of Vienna for his surgical work in 1932. A prenuptial agreement was that Doc shave off his trademark Van Dyke beard. The couple had first met at Langhorne Speedway in 1931. MacKenzie was 30, Verna 22.

DOC MAC KENZIE——"The beard has been my lucky charm, but off it comes if the girl friend says so."

Floyd Roberts, MacKenzie's hospital roommate, served as Best Man. Floyd, a former Sunday school teacher, would sing "Oh Promise Me" to begin the simple evening ceremony. Rev. Albert T. Broek, Pastor of the Calvary Reformed Church, performed the 7 p.m. ceremony. After he pronounced, "Whom God hath joined together, let no man put asunder," the new bride burst into tears.

Dr. George Kirk, the attending physician of MacKenzie and Roberts, said Doc should be confined an additional week to ten days. He informed MacKenzie that he would not be able to return to the race track this season. Doc disagreed.

DOC MAC KENZIE——"I'll be around soon and back behind the wheel of a new job, a new high-powered car now being built. But maybe the boss will want me to retire, but I don't think so, because she is a real race fan. I'm going to be back in the racing game in three weeks or a month, at the most.

As soon as this hand heals and my head injury clears up, I'll be back at the wheel again."

Doc MacKenzie would be dismissed from the hospital on July 28.

On August 22, 1936, at Springfield, Illinois, MacKenzie set a new track record of 38.67 in time trials in his return to the cockpit. During the race Doc would lead the first 56 laps before being forced by exhaustion to withdraw and turn his car over to Tony Willman. Two laps later, Tony lost a wheel and Wilbur Shaw would take the lead and go on to win. Willman was able to salvage second place.

AUGUST 23, 1936   DOC MAC KENZIE KILLED AT
                    MILWAUKEE

34-days after shaving off his trademark Van Dyke beard, which he considered his lucky charm, and his marriage to Verna Mather, Doc MacKenzie was fatally injured in a 25-mile state fair race at the Milwaukee State Fairgrounds Park. Doc's car crashed into a rail and then turned over four times. Race leader Billy Winn had just passed George Connor on an inside move. MacKenzie followed Winn's car but his right rear wheel caught Connor's left front wheel sending the car into the rail where it ripped out 20 feet of fence. Doc was thrown from the car. He died shortly after 7 pm, three hours after his crash, of a punctured lung, scalp and neck lacerations and other injuries. Doc MacKenzie had told friends before the Springfield race yesterday,

DOC MAC KENZIE——"I have had my share of driving troubles this year, culminating in the smash at Reading. According to the law of averages, I should finish the season without further trouble, and I believe I will."

MacKenzie, who gave up medical school to drive race cars, was very popular with race promoters who knew if Doc was advertised to race, it would be a success at the gate. A Philadelphia Inquirer "In Memoriam" article recalled their native son. "MacKenzie was far above the average run of automobile drivers in the matter of intelligence. Well educated, the scion of a distinguished professional family, 'Doc' succumbed to a mania for speed in his early youth. He realized that an automobile pilot must add to his driving skill an element of showmanship in order to achieve success. MacKenzie became the sport's leading showman." George "Doc" MacKenzie was enshrined into the National Sprint Car Hall of Fame in 1991.

AUGUST 30, 1936   RAY PIXLEY KILLED AT ROBY SPEEDWAY

Before a crowd of 20,000, the promising career of 29-year old Ray Pixley ended when he was fatally injured while competing in a 10-mile qualifying race at Roby Speedway, in Hammond, Indiana. During the qualifying heat race, Ray Pixley's car collided with George Connor's racer. Pixley was thrown from his car as it rolled over three times, crushing him. Ray died en route to St. Mary's Hospital in Hammond, Indiana, of internal injuries and broken ribs. Connor was uninjured and his car was not badly damaged. A good friend of Pixley's, George refused to race any more events that day. The race was won by Billy Winn, Chet Gardner was second and Tony Willman third.

SEPTEMBER 20, 1936   GEORGE CONNOR SERIOUSLY INJURED

Ironically, less than a month after his buddy Ray Pixley was killed at Roby Speedway, where the two of them had tangled, George Connor was seriously injured on the same track. Driving the car that Pixley was killed in, George spun, crashed into the inner guard rail and rolled over twice. Thrown from the car, Connor was unconscious when picked up by the ambulance crew. He suffered internal injuries but would recover to resume racing the following season.

No two drivers did as extensive preparations to their race cars over the winter than Wilbur Shaw and Bill Cummings. Shaw believed he was denied victory when rivets holding the hood on his race car snapped after leading 51 laps. Cummings could not wait until May to return to the Speedway to amend the embarrassment of not being able to pull away at the start. Both drivers spent months improving their race cars to make sure that unlikely gremlins would not deny their chances to win the 1937 Indianapolis 500. And their precise preparation showed.

1936

Ted Horn
2nd Place. Led 16 Laps

1936

Doc Mac Kenzie

3rd Place. Relieved by Kelly Petillo
In Memoriam August 23, 1936

1937

Perhaps the biggest switch of rides occurred when defending champion and three-time Indy 500 winner Louis Meyer joined the Boyle stable. He'd drive #2 Boyle Special and team with #16 Bill Cummings and #7 Chet Miller. Wilbur Shaw spent the entire winter improving his streamlined #2 Shaw-Gilmore Special. Rex Mays would switch to the #14 Alfa Romeo with Bowes Seal Fast sponsorship. Rex would seek to win his third consecutive Pole Position. Shorty Cantlon, in car #34, also would run the Bowes Seal Fast colors.

Jimmy Snyder would be in the #5 Sparks six-cylinder powerhouse funded by millionaire Joel Thorne. Thorne would also enter cars for Floyd Roberts #62, rookie Floyd Davis #32 and Al Miller #42 as well as a car for himself. Ralph Hepburn figured he would be very competitive in the #8 Hamilton-Harris Special. Babe Stapp would be teamed up with promising rookie Ronney Householder in the #15 and #23 Topping Specials.

Billy Devore, now fully recovered from his Atlanta injuries of a year ago, would drive the #28 Miller hoping to become the first father/son combo to have raced in the 500. Two incredible midget drivers were ready to tackle Indy for the first time. Tony Willman would drive #26 the FWD Special, replacing Mauri Rose and the most feared midget racer, Bob Swanson, would attempt to qualify #32 Fink Auto Special. Mauri Rose would sport #1 on his Burd Piston Ring Special. Chet

Gardner #31 and Tony Gulotta #38 would also drive under the Burd Piston Ring banner.

MAY 15, 1937   WILD BILL CUMMINGS WINS POLE
                FOR SECOND TIME

Wild Bill Cummings and Wilbur Shaw would qualify one-two for the race. Cummings, winning his second Pole Position, set both one-lap and 25-mile qualifying marks. Wild Bill, the 1934 Race winner, hustled his #16 Boyle Valve Special setting new track records, 1-lap 125.139 mph and 10-lap 123.455 mph in front of 28,000 cheering spectators. Shaw's qualifying average was 122.751 mph. Herb Ardinger's fast qualifying run was a surprise as he captured the outside spot of the front row at 121.983 mph.

Billy Winn, who's racing bio now lists him as a furniture executive from Detroit (via his marrying into Helen Yockley's furniture fortune), was fourth fastest at 119.922 mph. The colorful Winn's moniker was the "Red Devil" for he would drive wearing a bright red helmet and red silk shirt. Regarded as, perhaps, the finest driver on dirt tracks, he yearned for respect at the Indianapolis Motor Speedway.

Louis Meyer, hoping to become the first back-to-back race winner and first four-time winner, qualified in the middle of the second row with 119.611 mph while Ralph Hepburn qualified for the outside of row two. Mauri

Rose, the 1936 AAA National Driving Champion, would start eighth, flanked by Tony Gulotta and Chet Gardner.

Former University of Chicago student Jimmy Snyder, who drove a milk wagon while he was working his way through college, was hampered by a strong wind from qualifying on Day Two. Earlier in the day, Jimmy turned an eye-popping speed of 123.247 mph in Art Sparks's new six-cylinder supercharged racer in a practice run. The highlight of the day was when the legendary winner of the 1915 Indy 500, Ralph DePalma, drove two laps before he was flagged back into the pits for not wearing a crash helmet. This year there was a slight revision to the qualifying schedule where trials would be scheduled from 1pm to 7pm—gone was the sundown deadline.

MAY 22, 1937   JIMMY SNYDER SET 1-LAP NEW
                 TRACK RECORD

An early afternoon downpour shut down the track and it appeared that would end all chances of seeing activity on the track but by 4:30 p.m. the track had dried sufficiently to allow 18 cars to go out and practice. However, no one wanted to tempt fate and become the 13th qualifier. Fortunately, the rains stopped shortly before 7 p.m. Jimmy Snyder took his Art Sparks 6-cylinder car onto the track. In a superlative show of speed, Snyder obliterated the 1-lap track record posting a speed of 130.495 mph. His next two laps saw a drop off in speed due to reduced visibility—lap two at 129.4 mph followed by a 127.3 mph third lap.

Jimmy aborted his sensational run when he deemed it too dark to complete the 25-mile run.

On Sunday six more drivers qualified with Chet Miller the fastest speed of the day at 119.213 mph and would start on the inside of row five. 60,000 race fans waited until dusk to see if Jimmy Snyder would take to the track but he elected not to do so.

Floyd Roberts broke the big bone in his arm while clowning around in a bicycle race for drivers eight days before the grind. Keeping the painful mishap to himself, he would drive in the race with his arm taped and braced with a leather strap. As a kid, Floyd used to race his neighborhood buddies on a bicycle. At age 16, he started to race motorcycles a North Dakota county fairs.

MAY 26, 1937   JIMMY SNYDER SET 10-LAP NEW
                 TRACK RECORD

Both Jimmy Snyder and former winner Kelly Petillo both broke Bill Cummings Pole speed as ten more cars qualified. Early rains prevented many cars from taking to the track to practice and qualify. Snyder would average 125.287 mph (his fastest lap during this run was 127.1) to establish a new 10-lap record. Even though it was a NTR, Snyder was disappointed that he didn't top his previous blistering speeds of a week ago. Petillo, driving the car he sped to victory in 1935, would muscle into the field with an average speed of 124.129 mph.

Local driver Harry McQuinn ran three laps at better than 125 mph but he would come into the pits because of a rear tire problem. This set the stage for his third and final attempt to make the race. McQuinn made a cautious run averaging of 121.822 mph. Southern California rookie driver Bob Swanson had been running impressive speeds only to see his speed drop off to a 121.920 mph average the #33 Funk Auto Special.

Before the start of the month of May, many felt Rex Mays would be the first driver to win the Pole Position three consecutive times but he turned a disappointing speed of 119.968 mph driving the #14 Bowes Seal Fast Special Alfa Romeo. 6'6 foot millionaire rookie Joel Thorne qualified with the slowest speed of the day, averaging 115.602 mph. He had inherited a vast amount of money when his parents died while he was an infant.

May 28, 1937   INFERNO IN THE PITS

At 1:40 pm Overton "Bunny" Phillips, while practicing before he would make a qualification attempt in his J.L. Mannix Duesenberg, triggered a freak, fatal accident. Traveling down the main straightaway, his car broke a crankshaft strewing motor parts down the track. His car exploded in flames when gasoline from a severed gas line sprayed on the hot magneto.

The blazing car then slid toward the pits striking the #68 Ray Brady Special that Vern Orenduff was to take out later to qualify. Overton and his passenger, Walter King, a Cornell University medical student, were tossed from their flaming car upon impact the Brady machine. King was not an AAA registered mechanic in violation of track rules. He was a friend of riding mechanic Jimmy Louden, who offered King that experience, as he stood listening to Phillips's motor as he circled around the course.

Standing beside the Brady car were George Warford, Anthony Caccia and Otto C. Rohde. All three were struck by the blazing car. Flames rose the height of the grandstand. The 42-year old Warford, who had taken his physical at the Speedway Medical Center yesterday, had been selected to drive one of Joel Thorne's entries. George was a rookie but he had served as a riding mechanic in 1931. He would die in City Hospital admitting room. Caccia, brother of the late Joe Caccia killed driving at the Speedway in 1931, was working as a mechanic on the Brady car. He was listed in serious condition with burns and a broken leg.

Otto C. Rohde, VP and chief engineering of the Champion Spark Plug Company, was tossed over the wall where he laid burned and unconscious. He was taken to City Hospital in critical condition with severe head injuries and burns. Otto would succumb on June 2. Rohde was one of the founders of the prestigious Champion

100-Mile-An-Hour Club and was regarded as one of the greatest authorities on motor spark equipment. Overton Phillips suffered a fractured pelvis and severe leg burns while Walter King was painfully burned. Both would survive along with Caccia. Both cars were welded together from the intense heat.

Jimmy Louden, riding mechanic with Overton, had just gotten out of the car two laps prior so his friend Walter King could experience the thrill of riding in a race car at Indianapolis. He was timing Phillips with a stopwatch and listening to the motor. Louden told reporters,

JIMMY LOUDEN——"We had to jump to get out of the way when the car crashed. The crankshaft went out, the car spun sideways and the insides of the car were thrown out on the track. When the gas lines were torn out, the gasoline hit the magneto and an explosion and fire resulted. The car was in flames when it hit #68 and that took both of them in a flash. The men around #68 didn't have a chance. We were close by but were watching Phillips and jumped just in time."

Wilbur Shaw's car was parked next to the Brady car. He commented,

WILBUR SHAW——"My back was turned and I was lifting the hood of my car when I heard a terrific impact against the wall. I wheeled about and the blazing machine appeared to be heading directly at me. I had no time to jump. Then it careened just ahead of where we were standing and smashed into the Brady machine #68 less than ten feet away piling up Rohde, Warford and Caccia with the wreckage. I had just ask Rohde to look over my spark plugs but he still was busy on the other car."

MAY 28, 1937 RIDING MECHANIC KILLED WHEN FRANK McGURK'S CAR CRASHES

At 6:30 p.m., Frank "Wildman" McGurk, driving the Belanger-Miller Special, was attempting to be the first qualifier of the day. He had completed four laps at better than 119 mph. Entering turn one, a connecting rod cracked and his wheels locked. His racer swerved sharply to its left and struck a wooden bridge. A huge dust cloud was stirred up and observers saw the race car flipping end-over-end upwards, to 30 feet in the air. Various sizes of timber went flying. 26-year old Albert Opalko, McGurk's riding mechanic, was tossed from the car and was killed. Frank's condition was listed as serious with head lacerations and a broken arm, but he would eventually recover.

Drivers and car owners were exhilarated when they learned the IMS was ending the limit of fuel they could use in the race. They would now be allowed to use as much gasoline as needed. The Speedway did mandate that only commercial gasoline that the public could purchase at a gas station would be permitted.

Wealthy 22-year old driver Joel Thorne, who was bumped from the field, tried to buy his way into the starting field. When qualifications ended, Thorne was the second alternative with the slowest speed of 115.602 mph. Emil Andres, the first alternate, had his Kennedy Tank Special withdrawn by owner Phil (Red) Shafer. Red announced that a broken torque tube connecting with the differential was damaged and not repairable before Race Day. Thorne notified the AAA Board that he had purchased from George Lyons the Midwest Red Lion Special qualified by Cliff Bergere. Joel planned to withdraw the Lyons car and start his own car. Thorne offered Bergere $400 to stop complaining but Cliff protested to the AAA. Thorne responded,

JOEL THORNE——"It's strictly an overboard business proposition. We're all professional drivers and owners here to make money. I have a right to protect my investment as I see fit."

An angry Charles Merz, Chief Stewart of the AAA Contest Board, emphatically said Bergere was going to drive the car. Period! Joel Thorne would be permitted to serve as a relief driver any of his five cars in the race.

Mechanics for Bob Swanson's car worked all night to install a new crankshaft in his car. Herb Ardinger was considered the "dark horse" to win the race.

This was the first time that the Speedway posted qualifying prizes. Jimmy Snyder won $2000, Kelly Petillo $1000, Bill Cummings $800, Herb Ardinger $600, Bob Swanson and Harry McQuinn $500 and George Connor, Rex Mays and Bill Winn $250. Ten of the drivers made runs faster than the 1936 Pole winner.

The last qualifying period, from 1 to 4 p.m. Saturday afternoon, saw Ted Horn finally qualify for the race in the same Hartz-Miller Special he drove to second place last year. Horn struggled all month to get the car up to speed.

MAY 31, 1937 WILBUR SHAW WINS INDIANAPOLIS 500

After seven attempts to win the Indianapolis 500, twice bridesmaid, 34-year old Wilbur Shaw won the twenty-fifth anniversary race. It was the closest race in Speedway history as Shaw edged Ralph Hepburn by a mere 2 and 16/100 seconds. Hep's car was the same one Louis Meyer drove to victory last year. Shaw set a new race record averaging 113.580 mph despite extreme heat that had many drivers stopping for relief.

Hepburn was relieved mid-race by Bob Swanson during his first regular pit stop. Swanson's car had dropped out after 125 miles with carburetor issues. Ralph would return to the cockpit when Swanson brought the #8 Hamilton and Harris Special in for its second pit stop on lap 163, leading the Race. Despite the intense 90-degree heat, Shaw refuse to take relief. Ted Horn marched his Miller-Hartz Special from 32nd to 3rd. Louis Meyer in the #2 Boyle Products Special finished 4th. George Barringer took over from Cliff Bergere, who was overcome by the 90-degree heat, and finished 5th.

Herb Ardinger, starting on the outside of the front row, would lead the first two laps in the #54 Chicago Raw Hide Oil Special. Quickly carving his way to the front from his seventh row starting spot, Jimmy Snyder took the lead and held the top spot for the next 24 circuits until his transmission broke on lap 27. Wilbur Shaw then took control from laps 27 thru 74 while Snyder's interesting day was just beginning. Jimmy took over for Herb Ardinger, who was running in fifth place. Not long after Snyder took over Herb's vehicle, a steering arm broke causing the car to spin going into the SW turn. Jimmy Snyder described the incident, "The wheels locked and at the end of the skid, the rear end grazed the wall. It was only slight damage." Snyder would drive three cars in the race. At 300 miles, Jimmy took over

Tony Gulotta's #38 Bird Piston Ring Special and would soldier it home to an eighth place finish.

Rex Mays had a short day. He brought his #14 Bowes Seal Fast Special into the pits on lap 14 for oil and water. Ten laps later his day was over as his car was leaking oil. Soon Mays would relieve Shorty Cantlon in the #34 Bowes Seal Fast Special. At 150 miles (60 laps) Shaw had built up a 52 second lead over Bill Cummings. Kelly Petillo was a lap behind in third.

Ralph Hepburn, who took the lead from laps 74 thru 83 after Shaw pitted, would also be overcome by the heat as well. Relieved by Bob Swanson on his 112th lap, Hep was taken to the emergency hospital for treatment. The attending physician also treated him for bruises to his hips. After being treated, Hepburn went atop the Speedway medical hospital's roof to watch Bob Swanson's progress. Shaw had regained the lead from lap 84 thru 120. Then suddenly rookie Bob Swanson was leading the race. He continued out in front from laps 130 thru 163 before darting into the pits. Hepburn told Swanson, "I'm all right. I'm a little sore but I want to get in there and win that race. You did a swell job, Bob." Their pitstop lasted 2 1/2 minutes. But instead, Hep's car started to lose ground to Wilbur. Many believe had they left the "Midget Driver Extraordinaire" in the car to finish the race, then Bob Swanson would have gotten the checkered flag.

In the later stages of the race, Shaw began to experience a loss of oil pressure. Wilbur did a mental calculation of how much he could slow down and maintain his lead to the finish. Hepburn could smell blood. He mounted a banzai-type charge to catch the leader as a crowd of 170,000 stood cheering him on. With each lap, Ralph whittled seconds away from Wilbur's lead. With two laps remaining Shaw had a 14-second lead. Most likely Hep would have won if the Race was one or two laps longer. However, this day was Wilbur's day. Despite the intense, 90-plus heat, he refused relief assistance and he shattered Louis Meyer's track record by over 4 1/2 miles, averaging 114.580 mph.

Ted Horn, who would make four pit stops, pitted with one lap to go to be certain he would have enough gas to finish the race. It was extremely difficult to get his car re-started but finally it roared to life and he would finish third. Louis Meyer, despite his pit crew discovering he had a broken magneto switch, finished fourth. Experiencing both spark plug issues and shock trouble, Bill Cummings would make six stops en route to a sixth place finish. On Lap 134, Wild Bill was replaced by Chet Miller then Fred Frame took over on the 157th lap.

In Victory Lane, Wilbur Shaw and his riding mechanic Jigger Johnson were near exhaustion. He would tell his adoring fans and the press,

WILBUR SHAW——"I've never was so dog tired in all my life. I'm so weak I can hardly stand up. But it was worth it. All I want is water, water, water. I guess I've gone a long way since I raced a goat at the Shelby County Fair about 25 years ago. And boy, what a close shave. I knew I was going to win but Ralph Hepburn was only a hundred yards behind. That checkered flag was the sweetest thing I ever saw in my life. I'm going home and get a couple hours of sleep then I'm going out and drink a bottle of champagne at Earl Gilmore's expense!"

Shaw and his wife Boots (the former Miss Cathleen Stearns from Vernon, Indiana) lived with his mother and step-father, Mr. and Mrs. Charles Morgan, at 516 East 31st Street in Indianapolis.

The race was accident free until after the checkered flag was displayed to Shaw. Floyd Davis's #32 Thorne Special, on his 189th lap, skidded in the NE turn, spun four times and hit the wall. Mechanic Dee Toran was thrown onto the track and lay semi-conscious on the hot brick surface while Floyd slumped unconscious, pinned in the cockpit. Guards carried Toran over the track wall and he was taken to City Hospital. It took nearly a half hour for an ambulance to reach Davis.

He was taken to the Speedway hospital. Both suffered head injuries.

Wilbur Shaw would make two pit stops—on lap 74 for 3:09 minutes for a right tire and gas then on lap 130 for 2:40 minutes. Each time he was doused with ice cold water. His car developed an oil leak and both Wilbur and his riding mechanic Jigger Johnson were sprayed with hot oil. Shaw's and Johnson's shoes splashed with oil and their trousers were soaked with it from their knees down. Wilbur's right leg was burned. The oil got so low that his gauge showed no pressure during the final stages of the race. Shaw said had Hepburn tried to pass him for the lead, he would have pushed his car to the limit. Surprisingly Wilbur had nearly a quart of oil left.

Later various members of the media and friends gathered at the home of Wilbur's mother. He would tell how painful his foot was burned.

WILBUE SHAW——"The heat was bad, and then this foot of mine kept getting worse toward the last. It was blistered by the heat from the transmission although there was more than one inch of asbestos packing in-between.

I'll tell you, this winning just proves what I've said all along—that if it's your time to win, it's your time, that's all there is to it. Last year everything seemed right and I lost. This year everything went wrong and I won."

A crowd of over 500 gathered at the Claypool Hotel in downtown Indianapolis watched Wilbur Shaw receive a check for his win of $35,075 and Ralph Hepburn's prize totaled $15,930. Wilbur's badly burned and blistered foot would cause him to skip the 100-Mile event at Roby Speedway on June 6.

JULY 2, 1937   AMELIA EARHART PLANE DISAPPEARS OVER PACIFIC

Amelia Earhart, during her attempted a circumnavigational flight of the globe, disappeared over the Pacific Ocean on June 2,1937. She was accompanied by her flight navigator, Fred Noonan. Earhart was flying a Lockheed 10-E Electra. Rescue efforts proved futile as they searched for signs of life near the Howland Islands. Eddie Rickenbacker respected Amelia for her flying accomplishments and was honored at her accepting his invitation to attend the Indianapolis 500 as Honorary Referee.

SEPTEMBER 27, 1937   TED HORN INJURED AT NASHVILLE

Ted Horn was injured, originally reported in critical condition, and Howdy Cox killed in a four-car smashup on lap 20 of a 25-lap feature event at the Tennessee

State Fairgrounds track in Nashville. Accounts of the accident varied significantly. One version had race leader Duke Nalon's rear axle cracked causing him to spin as he exited the turn and entered into the backstretch. Howdy Cox then crashed into Nalon's car. Howdy was tossed high into the air, then landed on his head. Vern Orenduff side-swiped the pile-up then skidded under the outer guard rail. Horn would also crash into Cox's car. Taken to General hospital, Dr. O.W. Harris treated Ted for head cuts and a knee injury and Orenduff for a lacerated nose and chin. There conditions were reported as non-serious.

Duke Nalon's vision differed. While at General Hospital, Duke said he was about to lap Cox, when Howdy skidded through the corner, and onto the backstretch into the path of Nalon. Horn and Orenduff piled into the wreckage. Ted was thrown from his car and he had one leg pinned underneath it. None of the three were notified that Cox had been killed. Numerous spectators watching from outside the track scaled the barbed wire fencing and rushed to try and extricate the injured drivers as race cars were still racing. They ignored the pleas of the public address announcer to remain off the track.

A third version said that the race leader Nalon skidded and was struck by the car driven by Orenduff. Horn and Cox then rammed into their race cars. Cox had a reputation as being a reckless speedster on the turns.

OCTOBER 7, 1937   BOB SWANSON SERIOUSLY
INJURED AT GILMORE STADIUM

25-year-old Bob Swanson, the 1935 Pacific Coast midget racing champion, was seriously injured in a spectacular crash on the 49th of a 50-lap midget feature at Gilmore Stadium in Los Angeles. A crowd of 16,000 watched in horror as Ronney Householder skidded and Swanson crashed into his car and somersaulted. He was pinned underneath his car for several minutes. Bob suffered a broken right leg, fractured shoulder and there were some initial concerns of a possible spinal injury but no paralysis. It would take several months to totally recover. Sam Hanks won the feature.

OCTOBER 30, 1937   CLIFF DURANT FATAL HEART
ATTACK

Wealthy racer/playboy Russell "Cliff" Durant suffered a fatal heart attack at 5:30 p.m. in his apartment at 1289 North Crescent Heights Blvd. in Beverly Hills, California. His wife, Charlotte Phillips, called for medical assistance but Durant was dead before a physician could arrive. He was the son of William Durant, founder of General Motors. Cliff had been accused of extra-marital affairs and physical abuse by his first three wives——Lena Pearl McFarland, Adelaide Pearl Frost, and Lea Gapsky. He drove in six Indianapolis 500s beginning in 1919 through 1928. In 1923 he fielded six cars in the Indianapolis 500. Cliff had announced he would drive in 1932 race but reconsidered and Fred Frame would drive the car to victory.

Cliff Durant was one of the principal investors that also included noted Hollywood film director Cecil B. DeMille in the Beverly Hills Speedway high-banked board track. (where the Beverly Hills Hotel is located today). Cliff was an accomplished musician with the violin, trumpet and piano.

1937

Wilbur Shaw
Winner
113.580 mph Average. Led 131 Laps

1937

Ralph Hepburn
2nd Place by 2.16 Seconds
Led 9 Laps
Relieved by Bob Swanson Laps 108-163

1938

Virtually every race fan was excited for the Speedway's mandate to return to the single-seat race cars. One owner, Lou Moore, built a new car and he chose Floyd Roberts as his driver. Most of the cars were modified two-seaters. Russ Snowberger believed a stock-block motor would not give him a good chance to win in 1938. He opted to drive the D-X Special. Defending champion Wilbur Shaw would again drive the car he was victorious in a year ago, but modified for him alone.

Rookie Frank Beeder, Eastern AAA Champion, was a taken for a familiarization run by Shorty Cantlon. Beeder picked Friday the 13th to break his "jinx" of four recent crashes. He would go out and drive 77 incident free laps. Frankie would comment, "I think the jinx is broken."

MAY 21, 1938   FLOYD ROBERTS WINS POLE POSITION

In what the press labeled as a "Dark Horse" Pole winner, 38-year-old Floyd Roberts would set a new 10-lap qualifying record of 125.506 mph to erase Jimmy Snyder's mark of a year ago. 25,000 spectators tolerated an early afternoon heavy rainstorm. However, the track would dry in three hours. They were rewarded for their patience with exciting late-day activity.

Ten minutes after Roberts broke the qualifying record, Kelly Petillo, in a modified version of his 1935 winning car, took to the track with hopes to top Floyd's speed.

An excited crowd watched the '35 winner post nine laps that averaged 126.361 mph. However, as he came down the main straightaway to start his final lap, his right rear tire blew. Kelly would stop on the backstretch, cursing his luck, then drive his car back to the pits on the flat tire. His crew put on a new tire but he was not permitted to go back out for another attempt because the 7 p.m. qualifying deadline had been reached.

Russ Snowberger would average 124.027 mph to earn a spot in the middle of row one. And Rex Mays, in his Alfa Romeo, accepted a speed of 122.845 mph and would start third. Mays could have easily have captured his third Pole Position. In his first qualifying attempt, Rex was averaging 126 mph for his first six laps when his rear tire blew causing his car to go into a skid in the SE turn. His car would spin around three times without making contact with the wall.

Sentimental favorite Tony Gulotta had high hopes that 1938 would finally be the year he would win the Indianapolis 500. He was nominated to drive #17 Hamilton-Harris car that Louis Meyer won with in '36 and which Ralph Hepburn finished second last year. He would start fourth with a 122.499 mph speed. Before the rains came, Chet Miller was averaging 125.201 mph but blew a front tire on the backstretch on his final lap. He'd return to qualify fifth at 121.898 mph. Ted Horn would start sixth. Wilbur Shaw, Babe Stapp and Mauri

Rose comprised row three. Rose was driving an Italian Maserati with only 91 cubic inch piston displacement.

In what was a disappointment to his numerous legion of fans, Wild Bill Cummings would not make a qualifying attempt in the Mike Boyle 8-cylinder front-drive car. He had practiced over 128 mph earlier in the week. A defect in the steering arm was detected that morning. Jimmy Snyder, driving the Sparks-Thorne six-cylinder beast, had hard luck as well. Snyder was averaging over 125 mph when his engine started to heat up on lap nine and he pulled into the pits.

※ ※ ※

There was a huge buzz around the Speedway when word got around that Italian ace Tazio Nuvolari was coming to Indianapolis with hopes to drive in the Race. Known as the "Man who has a contract with the Devil," Tazio was bantamweight in size, weighing only 112 pounds. He sent a cablegram to Pete DePaolo.

TAZIO NUVOLARI——"Preparations with my car delayed in Italy. I come with my racing helmet, gloves and goggles which have been victorious in places all over the world. Is it possible for me to have a car to participate in coming Indianapolis race? Arriving New York May 25, stopping at Hotel

Ambassador, and trust you will make reservation of said request."

PETER DE PAOLO——"I know one of his great desires is to win to 500-Mile Race. He told me that in New York when I was there in 1936 and won the Vanderbilt Cup race on the Roosevelt raceway."

Ronney Householder, a neighbor of Floyd Roberts, broke his track record with a ten-lap average of 125.796 mph before a Sunday crowd over 40,000. His fastest lap was his third at 126.706 mph. However, since he was a Day Two qualifier, he would start tenth. Kelly Petillo was spectacular again but misfortune continued to stalk his car. On his second qualifying attempt, he posted a 130.246 mph on lap three but his engine lost power and he aborted the run.

Having been plagued all month with chronic overheating, Jimmy Snyder failed to qualify on his second attempt while boss Joel Thorne, on his third and final attempt, made the race. Louis Meyer would qualify with a disappointing 120.525 mph average.

Making a brief appearance at the Speedway was the long awaited arrival of Harry Miller's rear-engine car. However, it only made it as far as the infield. It was without question the most innovative race car to ever to appear at the Indianapolis Motor Speedway. It had 4-wheel drive and the driver sat in front of the motor! Ralph Hepburn agreed to drive the car. Hep was eager to take it out on the track, but they opted to make a short test run down the Speedway's infield road. A faulty fuel pump quickly ended their day.

Eastern AAA dirt track champion Frank Beeder was selected to drive Leon Duray's Barbasol Special replacing Billy Devore. The second-generation driver jumped to the Midwest Red Lion Special.

Jimmy Snyder, having the pressure of attempting to qualify on his third and final strike, led five qualifiers with an average of 123.506 mph in his 6-cylinder supercharged racer. Bill Cummings (122.392) and Chet Gardner (120.435) also made the field. Rookie Frank Beeder, on lap three of his qualifying attempt, hit the wall in the SW turn. He escaped injury but the rear end of the car was damaged. Car owner Leon Duray felt it would be repaired by Saturday to make a qualifying attempt.

In 1935, rookie driver Floyd Roberts qualified on the outside of the front row. He was one of the drivers pictured on the Indianapolis News Race supplement. An aunt living in Youngstown, Ohio, saw this and sent the paper to her family in Casey, Illinois. They contacted the Speedway and the communication department gave Roberts notification that lost relatives were searching for him. Floyd's father, Floyd, Sr., moved from Casey to

North Dakota nearly 40 years ago and began to farm the land. He died 15 years later and Floyd's mother moved the family to California. A few years later his mom died and he was orphaned at age 16. Roberts then began a career driving race cars in the West Coast and he progressed to become the runner-up in the AAA Pacific Coast championship.

He would return to Casey to be reunited with his 88-year old grandmother, Mrs. Emezetta Roberts, Uncles Amos, Henry, James and Otis plus numerous cousins. Grandma Roberts told him that she knew he would win this year's race since her birthday is June 1.

Tazio Nuvolari's late arrival greatly narrowed his choice of cars to drive in the race. Bill White, owner of Rex Mays Alfa Romeo, allowed Nuvolari to drive Rex's car a few laps. Tazio had driven that car in Europe a few years before. Mays was confident that the Italian champion would be successful in the 500.

REX MAYS——"There are only four turns and they are all alike. You don't have to use your brakes on this track, you simply shut off at a certain spot and put your foot down at the other one. Tazio will catch on in a hurry."

Joel Thorne offered Tazio a ride in one of his cars but he declined because he had never driven a front-drive race car before. Nuvolari climbed into Herb

Ardinder's car which had been qualified the previous Sunday. Attempting to leave the pits, he would strip the transmission gears as he was driving down pit row and the car stopped before it exited the pits. When it appeared that no other top line equipment was available, he gladly accepted Eddie Rickenbacker's invitation of being the official starter for the race.

85 loud-speakers had been installed all around the track. Rickenbacker's goal was that wherever you might be at the Speedway, you'd be able to hear what's going on, just as you could if you were seated at the start/finish line.

Kelly Petillo, on his third and final attempt to qualify, drove cautiously for the first nine laps then finished his final lap over 125 mph. Shorty Cantlon, Al Miller and rookie Al Putnam also made the Race. The Speedway received a telegram from Fred Frame that he was en route from California towing his Hulbert-Duesenberg Special. However, Fred did not arrive in time to attempt to qualify.

Hollywood film director Henry King arrived at the IMS and he brought a camera crew to film background shots of the track in advance of a new racing movie he will be making later that year. King had just completed "Alexander's Ragtime Band" with Tyrone Power, Don Ameche and Alice Faye. Eddie Rickenbacker offered King an invitation to serve as one of the judges for the race.

Leon Duray was a man short of patience. After Frank Beeder's two qualifying attempts were waved off, George Bailey was assigned to Duray's Barbosa Special and George responded with a successful qualifying run of 116.393 mph. Billy Devore, Cliff Bergere and rookies Henry Banks and Duke Nalon would fill the field before the closing gun.

Ralph Hepburn's attempt to qualify Harry Miller's revolutionary six-cylinder, rear engine car ended in disappointment. Having trouble starting his car, he was finally pushed away a few seconds after the 4 p.m. deadline. He would be given the red flag, signaling him back to the pits as disqualified. Billy Winn also failed to find enough speed to qualify two other 4-cylinder Harry Miller cars.

Borg-Warner hosted its Pre-Race corn beef and cabbage dinner at the Indianapolis Athletic Club. C.S Davis, President of Borg-Warner, served as toastmaster. Tazio Nuvolari addressed the crowd in his native Italian language while Peter De Paolo translated. Tazio would say that he loved coming to Indianapolis to look the track over and promised that he would return next year to compete. (The war in Europe prevented his return to the Speedway.)

Wilbur Shaw and Rex Mays were listed as 4-1 favorites to win the 500. Bill Cummings, Floyd Roberts and Tony Gulotta 5-1. Louis Meyer and Ronney Householder 6-1, Jimmy Snyder and Kelly Petillo 8-1. The drivers' meeting was held at 2 p.m. May 29 at the Press Pagoda. Passes and credentials were issued.

Eddie Rickenbacker had introduced a new distribution of prizes for this year where every driver shared in the purse with last place netting $500. The gates opened up at 6 a.m. and the first person to enter was John Ventura of Cleveland, Ohio. He had been waiting at the gate for 28 days.

A proud Eddie Rickenbacker brought his dapperly dressed adopted sons to the race—David, age 12, and Billy, age 10. Attendance was down with some of the grandstands not filled to capacity when the starting bombs were fired. The weather had been threatening early in the morning but the sun peeped out at the start. Stuart Baits, first VP and general manager of the Hudson Motor Company, was the driver the Hudson 112 Pace Car. He was joined by Theodore E. "Pop" Myers, General Manager of the Speedway.

MAY 30, 1938   FLOYD   ROBERTS   WINS INDIANAPOLIS 500

Picked as the "dark horse" for the race, 38-year old Floyd Roberts from Van Nuys, California, drove his #23 Budd Piston Ring Special to a record-setting victory. The partial bald, 210- pound Roberts had worked as an assembly lineman at the Lockheed air plant in Burbank, California before quitting to race at Indianapolis. Roberts drove Lou Moore's car to a dominant two-lap victory over Wilbur Shaw. Chet Miller, who was running second behind Roberts during the last 125 miles of the race, was forced to stop on the 199th circuit for a 30-second splash of gas. Shaw would move into second while Chet pitted. Miller would finish third, 7 1/2 miles back. Ted Horn, driving the #2 supercharged Miller-Hartz Special, was fourth. Chet Gardner in this #38 Burd Piston Ring Special came in fifth.

Rain had threatened all day but held off. It began drizzling on Roberts 192nd lap but race officials elected not to display the yellow flag. After Gardner finished in fifth place, a downpour began and the race was declared ended.

Roberts, scoring his first major victory in his 22-year career, benefited by making only one pit stop. On lap 107, the crew changed a right front tire and filled up the gas tank in the bright red #23 Budd Piston Ring Special in 30 seconds. Contrast that with Wilbur Shaw's pit stop for three tires and gas costing him 2:45 minutes.

As expected, Rex Mays took command at the start of the race, leading the first 14 laps. Louis Meyer in the #5 Bowes Seal Fast Special had to pull in the pits on lap one. His foot throttle was sticking. Jimmy Snyder was rapidly advancing through the field in his #6 Thorne-Sparks Special. Starting 15th, Jimmy was running second by lap three and he would pass Mays at the 37-mile mark. Rex would re-take the lead for two laps on the 32nd circuit only to be passed again by Snyder, who would lead at the 100-mile mark. Mays trailed by three seconds. However, Mays began signaling to his pit that he was having motor problems and his day would end after 112 miles.

With Mays's departure, Snyder's teammate, Ronney Householder, moved into second place just two and a half seconds behind. It was while Householder made his first pit stop, Floyd Roberts would move into second place and he'd take the lead for the first time when Snyder pitted on lap 75. Kelly Petillo and Wilbur Shaw now ran second and third. Jimmy would recapture the lead on the 111th lap followed closely by Roberts, Householder, Meyer and Chet Miller. A euphoric Art Sparks would say, "Looks too good to last!"

Jimmy Snyder, appearing headed to victory, would see his day end when a hose connection came loose on his supercharger. 15-laps later Billy Winn, driving for Householder, dropped out with exactly the same thing as Snyder. From then on it was easy sailing for Roberts and at the 400-mile mark he led Chet Miller and Wilbur Shaw by three laps. Despite his disappointment, Jimmy Snyder displayed class in his post-race comments saying, "That's the breaks one has to look out for. We had it in the bag." The two Art Sparks/Joel Thorne race cars would be used in a movie that was being filmed at the Speedway by Twentieth Century Fox.

Emil Andres, a partner with Snyder in a Chicago tavern, skidded on the 42nd lap in the SE turn, spun around three times and crashed through the inside guard rail. Andres was thrown from his car and was unconscious when the track ambulance arrived. Emil was taken to Methodist Hospital suffering from chest injuries and a broken nose.

Everett Spence of North Terre Haute was killed outright when a wheel from Andres car sailed 200 feet and struck him as he sat on a truck parked in the fourth row from the track. A platform had been installed on the truck on which Spence and his wife sat in the second row of chairs. The Spences had come to the track to celebrate their 14th anniversary. Everett was knocked from the top of a truck. He was the first spectator to be killed at the Speedway since 1909 when Charlie Merz, current Chief Steward of the 500-Mile Race, ran into a crowd and fatally injured two bystanders.

Bill Cummings had radiator problems early in the race. He stopped on lap 23 yelling at his crew to stop the leak. Cotton Henning, his chief mechanic, worked frantically to repair it. Having lost three laps while repairs were made, Cummings had trouble getting his car restarted. On the 72nd lap, Wild Bill would call it a day due to an unrepairable leaking radiator. Another former winner, Kelly Petillo, had worked his way up from 21st starting position to second place. However, just past the half-way mark, his car stopped in the NW turn with a broken camshaft. Soon afterwards, Petillo would relieve Tony Gulotta in car #17. Kelly would complete only one lap in the car before the car stopped on the backstretch on lap 131 with a broken connecting rod. Gulotta was unaware that his father Marco had died Sunday night. The family did not want to notify him until after the race.

Russ Snowberger, riding in fourth place, would drop out at 140 miles with a broken connecting rod. Later he would replace Herb Ardinger and drive it home for a sixth place finish. Rookie Henry Banks persevered— pitting eight times before dropping out on the 110th lap with a broken connecting rod. After 372 miles, Louis Meyer stalled his engine in the pits and lost 18 minutes. His troublesome day would finally end on lap 149 with a broken oil line. Time limitations prevented Louis from working out all the bugs in his newly built creation. Afterwards Meyer would say, "It will be a good car next year."

A throng of press and well wishers crammed the bull pen. An euphoric Roberts would comment on his win.

FLOYD ROBERTS——"The last twenty laps of the race were the toughest. The car rode like a Dream when I was driving around 120 mph but when I slowed down to 116 mph for the last part of the race, it was a handful. I wasn't tired at the finish. I will be back here next year and Lou Moore will build a new car just like this for the 1939 500-Mile event. I'm going to buy a farm too. It will be around 600 acres in either northern California or Oregon."

When race credentials were distributed to the drivers and crew members, Floyd Roberts's mechanic Lew Webb received badge #123. Floyd felt it was an omen. "That '23' corresponded to my car and that '1' in front of that meant it couldn't be anything else but first for us." Car owner Lou Moore debunked that superstition and credit himself for the victory.

LOU MOORE——"That '123' stuff sounded all right to me, but I think Floyd's victory is partially due to that upholstering job. I put that in personally and feel that making Floyd comfortable had a lot to do with it."

Roberts, a former Sunday school teacher, was speechless when he first pulled into the "birdcage" to face the mass gathering of media and well wishers.

FLOYD ROBERTS——"I am naturally the happiest man in the world. I am happy for myself but more so for that good little wife and those two kids back home in California."

Roberts would celebrate until the wee hours of the morning with his racing buddies at Stein's Tavern at 1121 North Meridian Street. He expressed no interest in retiring.

FLOYD ROBERTS——"I love racing. I've always wanted to win at Indianapolis and I've finally made it. I don't see why I shouldn't be racing, with good clean living, until I'm 50 years old."

Floyd's children, Betty Louise, 10, and Billy, 8, relatives and friends gathered at the Roberts's home at 14135 Kittridge, Van Nuys, California, listening for updates of the race. Mrs. Roberts was working at her job with the Van Nuys Telephone Company. She would leave work early saying it was too hard to concentrate on her work. Her husband had this superstition that a black cat was good luck. Once one crossed his path on the day of a race and he would go on to win. On his way to Indy from California, another black cat crossed his path. This convinced Floyd that he would win. There was a rumor that once he defeated Rex Mays at Ascot after he had walked the streets all night in search for a black cat.

Jimmy Snyder went to Methodist Hospital to visit Emil Andres, his partner in a Chicago nightclub. Emil suffered a broken upper jaw, right collar bone, cracked ribs and he lost several upper teeth. Andres remained unconscious. Afterwards Snyder expressed his frustration on his car's failure to finish. "That's the breaks one has to look out for. We had it in the bag."

Tazio Nuvolari was ecstatic on what he had witnessed.

TAZIO NUVOLARI——"This was the greatest sporting event in the world without question. Will I be here to race next year? I'll guarantee you that and I'll be here a month earlier."

Floyd Roberts would receive $31,950 at the Victory Dinner along with the Borg-Warner trophy, the L. Strauss trophy, a watch and a Norge electric refrigerator. Floyd expressed regret that his wife and two children could not attend the banquet. Wilbur Shaw earned $14,450 for second place. Roberts told the crowd how he almost didn't take Lou Moore's offer to driver his car.

FLOYD ROBERTS——"When Lou Moore first talked to me about driving his car I told him I didn't think a car without a supercharger could get any place in the Indianapolis race. I finally decided to try it, though, and now I want to thank Lou for talking me into it. And I'll be back next year!"

An opportunity to be interviewed over the National Broadcasting Company network in Chicago caused

Floyd to cancel plans to race in Milwaukee Sunday June 5.

AUGUST 20, 1938   BILLY WINN DIES OF INJURIES SUFFERED AT SPRINGFIELD

James M. (Billy) Winn, regarded as one of the top dirt race drivers ever, died of injuries suffered at the Illinois State Fair 5th annual 100-mile automobile race at Springfield. Tony Willman was victorious, Ted Horn finished second. The race had been delayed until late afternoon to allow Winn's car to be repaired after he had experienced oil trouble issues. A fan favorite, he was victorious in the 1934 and 1935 Springfield 100-mile races.

On lap 4, his car threw a tire and turned end-over-end. Winn was hurtled high in the air and landed head first on the track surface. He was unconscious when taken to the hospital listed in serious condition with a fractured skull, broken ribs and internal injuries. He was immediately placed in an oxygen tent. Billy would die shortly before midnight without regaining consciousness. Winn's mother and stepfather, Mr. and Mrs. U.E. Withrow, would take the body back to Detroit.

In 1935, Billy married the wealthy socialite Helen Yockey of Detroit. She had inherited her first husband's successful furniture business in Detroit after he was killed in a passenger car crash in 1933. In January

1934, she married race driver Joe Russo, who was killed at Langhorne, Pennsylvania, in June, 1934.

Billy Winn, known as the Red Devil, was rumored to be conducting an affair with Yockey prior to Russo's death. After their marriage, he became an executive in her furniture company. Both Winn and Yockey were exceptional horsemen. In contrast to most race drivers who would rent a bedroom from a family in the Speedway area in May, the financially well-heeled Mr. and Mrs. Winn lived at the Spink Arms hotel leading up to the race. James M. "Billy" Winn would be enshrined into the National Sprint Car Hall of Fame in 2003.

T.E. (Pop) Myers released a statement in behalf of the Indianapolis Motor Speedway.

POP MYERS——"I regret Billy's passing very much. We'll miss him here a lot. He was courageous, had real ability and was an able mechanic. He had a nice personality. It's too bad."

SEPTEMBER 3, 1938   CHET GARDNER HERO, DIES AVOIDING CHILD

Before a crowd of 7,000 spectators, 40-year old Chet Gardner from Long Beach, California, was killed when his car overturned and he was thrown out, crushing his head. Chet was dead when officials arrived at the scene. Major E.B. Allen, president of the fair association stated, "Gardner swerved his car to avoid hitting a child who ran across the track." He was praised for his unselfish heroism. Seated in the officials' stand in the infield, Gardner's wife witnessed her husband's fatal accident. She immediately ran to the accident scene.

Promoter Ralph Hankinson indicated the steering apparatus in Chet's car locked as it swerved. The two had walked the half-mile track together earlier in the day. When they got to the start/finish line, Gardner reached down to pick up a penny. Pleased, he would tell Hankinson, "I guess it is my lucky day."

As he headed out to begin his qualifying attempt, the public address system announced that Gardner was "one of the oldest drivers in the game." The 12-year veteran of auto racing, Chet had the reputation as being one of the safest drivers on the track. He had won the Milwaukee 100 race the week before. Chet and his wife would live in Indianapolis during the racing season staying with friends, Mr. and Mrs. Paul Whiteside of 323 East 30th Street. Chet Gardner was enshrined into the National Sprint Car Hall of Fame in 2000.

SEPTEMBER 24, 1938   CRASHES FINALLY CATCH UP
                       WITH FRANKIE BEEDER

Frankie Beeder, former AAA Eastern champion, tangled with Mike Little during the 15-lap main feature on the half-mile dirt track at Allentown, Pennsylvania. Beeder, who held the track record at Allentown set in

1937, was thrown clear of his car. He was rushed to a hospital in critical condition with two fractured legs and lacerations. Frankie would die from injuries sustained in the crash on September 27. Earlier in the day Roy Lake was killed when he crashed into the first turn fence. He was thrown against the steering wheel and died within an hour.

Floyd Roberts would win the AAA National Driving Championship which consisted of two races—the Indianapolis 500 and the Syracuse 100. Tony Willman and Chet Gardner were victorious in non-championship races—Willman on August 20 in the Springfield 100 and Gardner in the Milwaukee 100 on August 28. Jimmy Snyder would capture both the pole and the 100-mile race in the abbreviated season finale in the Syracuse 100 on September 10. By virtue of their finishing positions at Indianapolis, Floyd Roberts, Wilbur Shaw and Chet Miller finished 1-2-3 atop the AAA National Championship point standings.

1938

Floyd Roberts
Pole Position & Winner
117.200 mph Average. Led 92 Laps

1938

Chet Miller
3rd Place Finish

After watching Floyd Roberts dominate the 1938 Indianapolis 500, it was very clear to Wilbur Shaw his "pay car" would not stand a chance of winning again. It was during his participation in the Vanderbilt Cup races that Wilbur became convinced a Maserati would be the combination he needed to become a two-time winner. He was successful in convincing Mike Boyle to purchase a Maserati for the 1939 race.

In late January Wild Bill Cummings stopped by the office of Blaine Patton, sports writer for the Indianapolis Star, all excited about his prospects of winning the 1939 Indianapolis 500. He would again be driving Mike Boyle's eight-cylinder, front-drive Miller that he captured the Pole Position last year and that was running well in the race with before a broken radiator sidelined him.

Equally optimistic was Wilbur Shaw. He was able to persuade Boyle to purchase the bigger 183-sized Maserati motor for this year's race. Cotton Henning was dispatched to Maserati's headquarters in Italy to supervise the purchase and shipment of the car back to the United States. Shaw selected Mauri Rose to drive his "pay car" in the 500. Chet Miller, still stinging from the last lap pit stop that dropped him from second to third, would run the third Boyle car. Each Boyle driver were convinced this would be "their" year to get to Victory Lane. Deacon Litz would drive the small 83 Maserati.

No doubt the biggest coup was when multimillionaire Joel Thorne persuaded Rex Mays to leave Bill White and the Alfa Romeo team and be a teammate with Jimmy Snyder in the super fast #15 Thorne Engineering/Sparks six-cylinder thoroughbred. Thorne would drive his own #8 and midget standout Mel Hansen rounded out the four-car team.

Bill White would replace Rex Mays in his Alfa Romeo with Babe Stapp believing all the kinks had been worked out to now compete for the win. Defending champion Floyd Roberts car would carry #1 symbolic of his winning the 1938 AAA National Driving Championship. Roberts would again be driving Lou Moore's Burd Piston Ring Special—last year's winning mount but with a new engine which Floyd believed would be the perfect combination to become the first driver to win the 500-Mile Race back-to-back. Roberts wanted one more big payday so he could purchase a large farm and retire from racing. Tony Willman would also drive under the Burd Piston Ring banner.

Equally as confident was Louis Meyer in his quest to be a four-time winner. Louis and Myron Stevens had spent the winter perfecting his #45 Bowes Seal Fast Special that held so much promise a year ago. After a year to refine his rear-engine creations, Harry Miller selected George Bailey to drive his car #17 and 42-year old Johnny Seymour to drive the sister car. No driver had been picked for the third rear-engine mount.

One of the pre-race favorites was the powerful 16-cylinder Stevens/Sampson car that Bob Swanson was tapped to drive. Swanson was so unwavering in his belief that he would have beaten Wilbur Shaw to the finish line in 1937 had Ralph Hepburn not opted to climb back into the cockpit of the Hamilton-Harris Special for the final stint of the race. Now that there were no fuel limitations, the 16-cylinder beast could outpace the competition. And Hepburn, after missing last year's race, had returned back to the Hamilton-Harris camp still obsessing over what could have been in 1937 had there been just one more lap in the race. All told, this had the makings of being the most competitive Indy 500 to date.

FEBRUARY 6, 1939   BILL CUMMINGS DIES FROM
AUTOMOBILE ACCIDENT

Returning home on the evening of February 6 from his Lucky Seven tavern, Wild Bill Cummings's automobile skidded on a slippery pavement into the soft shoulder. When he tried to swerve back onto the road, his car overturned several times and plunged down a steep embankment into Lick Creek—just east of Emerson Avenue on highway 29. His car tore out 30 feet of steel plated guard rail. Wild Bill was thrown from his car and he landed face down in knee-deep, icy-cold water. His automobile landed upright and came to rest in the soft mud—its headlights still burning and its roof crushed. Nearby residents Reuben Behlmen, Calvin Burton and

William Frank spotted the bright headlight beams and they ran to the crash site. They pulled the unconscious champion from the water, carried him roadside and called an ambulance.

Deputy sheriffs Herbert Stevens and Richard Stewart stated had not been for the valor of these three pedestrians, Cummings would have no doubt drowned. Their report indicated that Wild Bill's car shot 50 feet into the air and cleared several small trees before landing in the creek.

Bill's wife, Mrs. Leoda Cummings, arrived from their nearby home by Five Points just as the ambulance attendees were placing the critically injured Cummings on a stretcher and she rode with her husband to Methodist Hospital. The happy-go-lucky Cummings suffered a severe brain concussion and was not expected to live. Doctors operated on him Tuesday morning to relieve pressure on his brain. His condition began to deteriorate late Tuesday afternoon. In an attempt to stabilize his condition, physicians injected insulin into his into his blood and Cummings heart briefly responded favorably to the treatment. However, the popular Indianapolis 500 champion would succumb at 6 o'clock in the morning on Wednesday, February 8. His wife and several close relatives were at his bedside. In addition to his wife Leoda, the 32-year old Cummings was survived by his daughter, Miss Earlene

Ann Cummings, his father William Cummings and his mother Mrs. Arminta Brown.

Saturday February 11, 1939

Funeral services were held at Royster and Askin Mortuary at 1902 N. Meridian Street where Reverend Raymond Hoestra, pastor of Calvary Tabernacle church, officiated. An overflowing crowd of over 700 mourners came to pay their respects. Pallbearers were Deacon Litz, Chet Miller, Lou Moore, Wilbur Shaw and Russ Snowberger. A close friend, Bill Breitensteur, composed a brief poem and sent it air mail from Miami, Florida. Pastor Hoestra would read:

Red Sails in the Sunset,
Purple Haze on the Hill
Checker flag on the highway,
Bon Voyage, Bill

In the summer of 1938, they were pouring a concrete road leading from the garage to the track. Inspired by Grauman's Chinese Theater where famous actors and actresses put their hand and footprints in wet cement, Cummings told Lawson Harris, "Hollywood stars do this and we're the only stars here." They both put their footprints in the wet concrete and initialed and dated them.

In recent years Cummings developed a love for flying. He had been given flying instructions from Lawrence

Genaro, who was an inspector for the Civil Aeronautical Authority. Just before being lowered into the gravesite, Genaro flew a circular pattern, then dipped his plane low to drop a cascade of flowers from the sky.

Several days later, Mike Boyle would select Ted Horn to replace Bill Cummings. Harry Hartz countered by naming Herb Ardinger as his new driver.

The first serious accident of the month of May occurred Friday afternoon May 12 when Ronney Householder, traveling at 118 mph, lost control of Leon Duray's #26 Barbasol Special in turn one. His car spun and crashed through the inner guard rail. The racer would then flip and land upside down in the turn one infield creek. Householder held onto the steering wheel as his head was submerged in water. Miraculously, he was able to crawl from his wrecked race car before the track rescue team arrived. Uninjured but extremely shaken, Householder was taken to Methodist Hospital where he was soon released suffering only minor injuries. The medical team credited his use of a crash helmet for preventing much greater injuries. The crash really unnerved Ronney for racing at the Speedway and Leon Duran would replace him with Billy Devore. He would never race in the 500 again but instead focus on his love, midget racing. Later in the year he captured the first track championship at Soldier Field in Chicago.

Ronney Householder joined Chrysler Corporation in 1955 and would eventually become the high performance director for their stock car racing program. He would succumb to lung cancer November 11, 1972. He was posthumously inducted into the National Midget Auto Racing Hall of Fame in 1984.

Just minutes after the 10 a.m. opening of the track, a crowd estimated at 50,000, the largest to witness the First Day of Qualifications, would watch Louis Meyer, driving the #45 Bowes Seal Fast Special, break the track qualifying record with a speed average of 130.067 mph. However, Jimmy Snyder made it a short-lived track record as he piloted his Thorne Engineering/Sparks six-cylinder machine to establish a new four-lap qualifying average of 130.138 mph to win the Pole Position. The former milk wagon driver also broke his one-lap record with a speed of 130.737 mph. Meyer would start the race in second position while Wilbur Shaw, in his new Mike Boyle Maserati, would round out the front row with a speed of 128.977 mph.

Rex Mays, driving a similar six-cylinder car to teammate Snyder, posted two laps over 130 mph during his qualifying run, then aborted his run on his third lap. Rex would later express his dissatisfaction with the performance of his motor. He would qualify the following Thursday with a disappointing average of 126.413 mph. His first two laps topped 128 mph but his final lap dipped way down to 124.035 mph and really hurt his qualifying average.

Soon after Jimmy Snyder's record run, there was a spectacular, fiery crash involving Johnny Seymour, the 42-year old Grosse Pointe, Michigan, veteran. Seymour was making a practice run in one of the Harry Miller rear-engine cars. His car went into a 200-foot slide before hitting the NW outer wall and flipping over. Upon impact with the wall, the "pontoon-type" gasoline tanks, mounted next to the cockpit, exploded. Fuel that had splashed on Johnny's clothing ignited. Johnny either jumped or was thrown from his car. Seymour first tried to beat out the flames on his clothing to no avail. Then he ran and jumped the outer wall and rolled on the ground before being picked up by an ambulance and taken to Methodist Hospital. Both his hands and legs received second degree burns. The car was destroyed by the fire. From his hospital bed, Seymour told reporters about his accident.

JOHNNY SEYMOUR——"I went into a long spin and lost it. The car hit the wall and caught fire and I got out. Then I jumped over the wall and rolled in the dirt and grass."

Earlier in the day, George Bailey qualified a sister rear-engine car to Seymour's at an impressive speed of 125.821 mph, good for sixth starting spot. Boyle teammates Ted Horn and Chet Miller would qualify fourth and fifth—Horn posting a 127.723 mph speed. Mauri Rose qualified Wilbur Shaw's "pay car", the

Wheeler Special, at 124.896 mph good for the middle of row three and Horn's replacement in the Miller-Hartz Special, Herb Ardinger, would earn the ninth fastest spot with 124.125 mph average.

On Sunday, May 21, intermittent showers curtailed Day Two of qualifications with only one driver, Babe Stapp, driving Bill White's Alfa Romeo Special, made the field with an average of 125.000 mph. He would start 16th on Race Day. Kelly Petillo had made a wager with Louis Meyer that he would break Jimmy Snyder's track record, confident he could run a 132 mph lap. On a warm-up lap, Petillo shut off his engine as he headed down the main straightaway but still topped 129 mph. During a later qualifying run, he took the green flag but would pull into the pits after just one lap complaining the course was too slippery.

Finally Bob Swanson was able to get his 16-cylinder Alden Sampson into the field with the third-best speed of the month at 129.431 mph. On his final lap he topped the 130 mark. Defending champion Floyd Roberts broke a crankshaft and a replacement had to be shipped from California. Lou Moore's crew was able to get it installed and Roberts would post a 126.998 mph average but would have to start 23rd. Always having a flair for the dramatic, Kelly Petillo on his "third strike" qualified over 123 mph to make the field. Russ Snowberger, Tony Willman and Tony Gulotta also joined the '35 winner in making the field.

On the final day of qualifications, rookie driver George Robson, driving the Deacon Litz Special, qualified his car at 116.305 mph but his speed put him on the bubble. Somewhat amazing was in just a few hours prior to his qualifying run, Robson had just finished completing his rookies' test. Leon Duray replaced Ronney Householder with Billy Devore in the Barbasol Special and the second generation driver narrowly bumped his way into the field with a speed of 116.527 mph. Duray and crew had worked more than a week, day and night, to repair the car from Householder's wreck.

Since 1938, more new asphalt had been added to the track.

May 29, 1939

At the drivers meeting the day before the Race, Eddie Rickenbacker announced that Chief Steward Charles Merz was named assistant to T.E. (Pop) Myers. Merz would continue as Chief Steward as well. He was president of Merz Engineering Company. Ted Doescher was appointed Assistant Chief Steward. Former heavyweight boxing champion Gene Tunney would serve as honorary starter for the race.

In the 500 Race Day edition of the Indianapolis News, a broadly smiling Floyd Roberts poses holding a black cat, what he believed was a good luck charm for him. Before the start of the race, a confident Roberts stated he'd be the first back-to-back winner.

FLOYD ROBERTS——"Before last year's race, I said I'd win and I'm going to tell you the same thing this year."

Floyd had stated to friends this would be his last 500-Mile Race which pleased Mrs. Roberts to no end. He had used a majority of his winnings to purchase a farm in the Van Nuys, California, area. She would say, "Floyd has always wanted to return to a farm and I have always agreed with him. He's always wanted to do it as soon as he had enough money. I am sort of hoping he will do it now since he's reached his goal, but of course, that's up to him."

Rex Mays's car #15 caught fire in his garage early on Race Day morning while the crew was doing a tune-up. Rex's engine backfired igniting fumes in the exhaust. Flames spread to the carburetor but his mechanics quickly smothered the flames.

Because of the zapping heat that he endured during the 1937 race, Wilbur Shaw had devised a plan to keep himself cool for this race. In his pit was a refrigerator with a spare helmet, gloves and water bottle where they were kept chilled. On top of his helmet, he kept a moist sponge to further cool his head. He also installed a large thermos bottle in his car with a small rubber hose that he could sip as the race progressed.

Rumors were circulating throughout Gasoline Alley that the ever-calculating Wilbur Shaw may set an early blistering pace in the race hoping that his chief competitors would follow challenge his car, and if his Maserati would break down, he'd drive in relief of Mauri Rose in his "pay car". Shaw would dispel these rumors.

WILBUR SHAW——"Of course, if the Maserati had been forced out of the race, and Mauri seemed to be tiring, the natural thing for me to do would be to give Mauri help. But I would not take the car from Mauri if he felt all right."

Just before the start of the race, Floyd Roberts, who had promised his two children he would win again, eluded confidence.

FLOYD ROBERTS——"I have the car that can do it. Tonight I'll have twenty grand in my kick, and you won't hear any more about a driver not being able to win two-in-a-row."

With the nervous excitement of the start of the 500, Mrs. Louis Meyer, who was standing on the top row of the grandstands, nearly toppled from her vantage point when she saw her husband take the lead. Friends grabbed her before she tumbled to the ground.

As expected, Jimmy Snyder shot to the lead at the start of the race. After 50 miles he was on top of Louis Meyer by three seconds. Wilbur Shaw was 3rd, Ted Horn 4th,

Bob Swanson 5th, Rex Mays 6th, Chet Miller 7th, Floyd Roberts 8th, Cliff Bergere 9th and George Bailey, in the rear-engine Harry Miller creation, 10th. Jimmy Snyder would lead the first 36 laps.

Bob Swanson's powerful 16-cylinder car had been sidelined early, dropping out after 19-laps with a burned clutch and finished in 31st position. Hoping to recapture the magic of two years ago, Swanson again replaced the exhausted Ralph Hepburn in the #25 Hamilton-Harris Special on lap 107. Hep would say, "Good luck, Bob." But there was only very bad luck, almost instantly. Bob would only make it past turn two when his car began to swerve left, then right. Rapidly approaching the Swanson car was Floyd Roberts's #1 Bird Piston Ring Special. While Bob was fighting to save control of his car, Roberts's left-front wheel hit Swanson's right-rear wheel.

Floyd Roberts's car immediately darted to the right and plowed through the outside fence, splintering the board guard rail, and somersaulted into the Speedway golf course. Roberts was thrown from his car and he would lay unconscious near his wrecked machine. His bludgeoned face made it quite apparent that he would not survive the accident. When the ambulance crew arrived, they placed a sheet over the defending champ's body from the neck downward and carefully struggled to lift the 200+ pound driver onto a stretcher. Floyd was transported immediately to Methodist Hospital where he would soon be pronounced dead of a brain concussion and multiple injuries. He was the first Indianapolis 500 winner to be killed at the Indianapolis Motor Speedway.

The Los Angeles Times penned a gruesome description of Roberts crash. "Roberts's car careened off Swanson's machine and plowed through the outside board fence, coming to stop in the adjoining golf course. The impact with the boards ripped and tore the flesh off Roberts body. He was picked up unconscious and rushed to the hospital, dying within an hour."

Floyd's wife, Mrs. Edna Roberts, was attending her first Indianapolis 500. She did not see her husband's accident. Speedway officials promptly reached her and she was taken to Methodist Hospital. Her husband died before her arrival. Edna's two children Betty Louise, age 11, and Billy, 9, were at the Van Nuys, California, home of their uncle, Harvey Roberts, intently listening to the radio fully confident their father would repeat as race winner. Later they would hear the announcement that their father had died.

Swanson's car rolled over when it was hit by Roberts's vehicle. Being tossed from the Hamilton-Harris Special, Swanson slid down the center of the track ripping his skin from his back. He would come to a stop next to his flaming race car. Both his shirt and pants caught fire causing painful burns on his back and legs. Quick responding state police pulled Swanson away from the edge of the car, no doubt saving his life as the car would catch fire and burn ferociously. Many spectators, unaware of the driver change, believed in was Ralph Hepburn burning inside the raging inferno.

Chet Miller, driving the #3 Boyle Special, swerved to miss the prostrate Swanson on the race track but he would strike Bob's car. Miller's vehicle would then smash through the inside wooden guard rail destroying several hundred feet of it. Chet was tossed out of his racer, which would overturn in the infield. The yellow flag was displayed for 31 and 1/2 minutes for cleanup of the three-car crackup.

Miller would be taken to the Speedway hospital then transferred to Methodist Hospital suffering a fractured collarbone and broken ankle. Erroneously, he was initially reported in critical condition, but soon after was described to be in fair condition. He would spend nearly a month in Methodist Hospital recuperating.

Two women, Mrs. Fern Milliken and Martha Ponelite, were struck by the flying debris from Miller's crash. Mrs. Milliken was watching the Race on a truck platform 150 feet away. As the pieces of splintered boards sailed toward her, she clutched her six-year-old daughter, Jacqueline, and turned to shield her from harm. She received compound fracture of her left leg. Miss Ponelite sustained head and shoulder injuries.

Aware of the blown engine that sidelined his teammate Rex Mays on lap 146, Jimmy Snyder began nursing his six-cylinder Sparks engine to hopefully make it to the end of the race. Running in third position, he basically conceded the top two spots to Meyer and Shaw. Up until that point, Snyder looked poised to be the winner. He led the initial 35 laps then would regain the lead from laps 75-103. Mays was running in second 15 seconds behind and gave every indication they would finish one-two in the race.

Louis Meyer, driving the #45 Bowes Seal Fast Special, appeared on his way to becoming the first four-time winner. However, on lap 130, his car went into a skid in the NE turn. Meyer did a masterful job of keeping his car from making contact with the wall and continued as race leader. At the 455 mile mark, Meyer was leading Wilbur Shaw by a lap and was two laps ahead of third place Jimmy Snyder. But the race would change dramatically for Meyer as his car blew a RF tire going into the first turn. It couldn't have come at a worse part of the track as he had to drive his racer more than two miles on three wheels back to his pit. Fast work by his crew had him back out on the track in 35 seconds but he had now dropped to second position behind Wilbur. Valiantly charging after race leader Shaw, Meyer would go into another spin in the SE turn on lap 197. In what appeared a frightening crash, his car would smash through the inner guard rail destroying 200-feet of two-by-eight wooden planks before coming to a stop.

Meyer surprisingly received only slight injuries from the nasty-appearing crash. After being taken to the Speedway infield hospital in an ambulance, he realized he was missing his shoes. The track clean-up crew located them close to his damaged race car. Luckily escaping the Grim Reaper, Louis decided it was time for him to retire as a race car driver.

Johnny Moore of Firestone said the bad slide Louis Meyer took on the NE turn on lap 130 was the contributing factor of what caused his RF blow out on lap 182 and caused Meyer's car to go in a spin. Up until that point he had been leading Shaw by over a lap. According to Moore, the three-time Indianapolis 500 winner locked his wheels while attempting to correct his slide which damaged all his tires. Eventually the RF wore through, causing the spin. Johnny indicated that Meyer's final spin on lap 197 was due to oil on the track.

There was high drama during Wilbur Shaw's final pit stop on lap 191 when he came in for a splash of gas. His crew attempted to start his motor three times before it roared to life. In his hurry to rejoin the race, Wilbur ran over two crew members. Fortunately neither were injured.

Wilbur Shaw would lead the remaining eight laps to capture his second win in three years, duplicating Tommy Milton victories in 1921 and 1923. His Maserati was the first victory for a foreign car since 1919. Trailing Shaw to the checkered flag by 1:48 minutes was Jimmy Snyder, who was not in position to challenge for the lead due to fears his motor would blow like his teammate Rex Mays's did. Cliff Bergere was third, Ted Horn fourth and Babe Stapp, in Bill White's Alfa Romeo, fifth. Multimillionaire Joel Thorne would finally qualify for the Champion 100 Mile-an-Hour Club with his seventh place finish. Mauri Rose nursed Shaw's "pay car" home to eighth. Mel Hansen, the only rookie in this year's race, crashed on lap 113 and finished 19th. All told, Louis Meyer lead on three occasions for 79 laps, Jimmy Snyder twice for 65 laps, Wilbur Shaw twice for 51 laps, Ted Horn once for 4 laps and Rex Mays 1 lap.

Upon his arrival in Victory Lane, Wilbur's first request was for water, water! Upon quenching his thirst, he inquired who was involved in the three-car crackup in turn two and the drivers conditions. When told of Roberts demise, he lowered his head momentarily, in silent tribute to a good friend. Shaw told the media that he was fortunate to win.

WILBUR SHAW——"I never would have won that race if Louis Meyer hadn't spun. If Lou hadn't thrown a tire and lost a lap or two, I wouldn't have stood a chance of winning. Lou, up to that time, simply was setting a pace I couldn't keep."

A reporter ask Shaw, what victory was more special. Wilbur would say, "I think I got more of a thrill out of this victory than I did in 1937. In 1937, I figured I had it in the bag, but I wasn't sure this afternoon until Lou had tough luck."

Joining his son in the "Bull Pen" to celebrate his second victory, Wilbur's father, James Shaw, told the press of his sons first race—a goat race—at the 1922 Shelby County fair. 15 goats were entered. When asked where he finished, James Shaw would say, "First, of course. Where else could he have finished?"

As they were ready to move Shaw's winning car from the "Bull Pen" back to the garage, he was asked about his future racing plans. Shaw was adamant, "This is a screwy business, isn't it? But I wouldn't ever do anything else. I'll be back next year trying to become a three-time winner."

To cool Wilbur off in Victory Lane, a crew member accidentally poured a tin pitcher of lemonade over Shaw's head. Some of it got into his eyes, and it really stung for several seconds until he was doused by a pitcher of ice water, thoroughly soaking him.

The race was ran under bright sunshine—ideal for the fans—but it played havoc on the tires. The entire top ten finishers changed at least one tire. Shaw would change both RF and RR.

At the Indianapolis Athletic Club the following evening, Wilbur Shaw accepted the winner's prize of $27,375. He again humbly referenced Meyer's misfortune.

WILBUR SHAW——"I can assure you it gave me no pleasure when I came down the straightaway and saw Meyer's mishap. Louis drove the winning race and there's no question about it."

Jimmy Snyder pocket $15,587 for second place. Eddie Rickenbacker was not in attendance and Pop Myers announced there would be no more Victory Dinners.

JUNE 10, 1939   FLOYD ROBERTS FUNERAL

Funeral services were conducted Tuesday June 10 in the Central Christian Church in Van Nuys before an overflowing crowd of 1000 people gathered to pay respects. Reverend J.C. Carmichael would say in his eulogy:

REV. CARMICHAEL——"Floyd Roberts went to the races, knowing he must contend not only with his fellow drivers but death. He was a brave man. He chose the hazardous way of life. But his life was formed in two circles. In one circle were his wife, his children and home. In the other was the race track, the race track that fascinated him, the track that brought him death. When death with the black flag shall wave us off the track, let us hope we shall go with the same feeling held toward us as those gathered here today to mourn Floyd Roberts hold for him."

Rev. Carmichael was visibly shaken, having married the Roberts 14 years ago. The widow and her children wept unconsolably as their Pastor delivered his eulogy. Floyd was a deeply religious and emotional man who had once been a Sunday school teacher.

After setting new qualification records at the Indianapolis Motor Speedway and nursing home an ailing motor for a second place finish in the 500-Mile Race, Jimmy Snyder had now achieved super-star status at the highest level of his sport. Although 30 years of age, he had a youthful appearance of someone in his early 20s and an exuberance that made fans instantly like him.

Snyder was very smart and super athletic earning 11 letters at Englewood High School in Chicago. Upon graduation he enrolled in the University of Illinois to study medicine and to play halfback for the Fighting Illini. He believed he'd be the noted Dr. James L. Snyder M.D. or the person who replaced Rogers Hornsby as the Chicago Cubs second baseman or being selected

All-American on the gridiron. His God-given talent made each dream a realistic possibility.

However at the U of I, Snyder clashed with coach Bob Zuppke, primarily on how to carry the pigskin. So Jimmy made the decision to transfer to Oglethorpe University in Atlanta telling Coach Zuppke,

JIMMY SNYDER——"If I can't use my own style then I'm quitting Illinois. You'll feel sorry about it someday. I'm going to Oglethorpe to complete my education in medicine and when you read of 'Dr. Snyder' curing a lot of patients, you'll remember that he's the boy you didn't think could play football."

When Snyder finally internalized the amount of years it would take to establish himself as a doctor, he decided he didn't want to invest that amount of time. So he returned to Chicago and landed a job as a milk wagon driver.

Jimmy Snyder shared his unlikely plunge into auto racing to sportswriter Sid Keener of the St. Louis Star and Times after attending the Indianapolis 500.

JIMMY SNYDER——"Something grabbed me inside when I heard the hum of those cars whizzing around the track.

It gave me the thrill of my life. I leaned over to Mrs. Snyder and said, 'Honey, your Jimmy is going to be in that race car one of these hot May days.' She laughed at me. I didn't say anything about a career as a racer for two years. I saved my money, with one thought, I'd buy a car and see how fast it would travel. I purchased a second-hand thing in 1934, tuned it, tested it, and entered a stock car event at Evanston Speedway on the outskirts of Chicago. Mrs. Snyder didn't know about my debut in the racing game, but when I returned home that night and handed her $250, my prize as winner, she agreed that her Jimmy should become a speed racer."

JUNE 29, 1939   JIMMY SNYDER KILLED IN MIDGET
                 RACE AT CAHOKIA, ILLINOIS

Doing a favor for a race promoter, Jimmy Snyder was killed competing in a midget race at the Cahokia, Illinois, Speedway, three miles south of East St. Louis on highway 3. Twice postponed due to rain, this was the opening program of the season. Running second on lap 13 to Ronney Householder, the "Flying Milkman" got up into the loose dirt going into the south turn of the

394

quarter-mile banked track. He hit the wall then began a series of barrel rolls before coming to a stop upside down in the middle of the track. Three cars managed to miss Snyder's crippled vehicle. Paul Armbruster, who recently had started racing under the pseudonym Don Army, lost control of his car and crashed into Snyder's racer. The impact stirred up a large cloud of dust, which obscured the seriousness of the accident to many of the 4,000 spectators.

The race was stopped and track officials rushed to aid Snyder and Armbruster. Jimmy was rushed to St. Mary's Hospital in East St. Louis but he was pronounced dead on arrival due to a broken neck and internal injuries. Armbruster was burned. Snyder was very popular in the St. Louis area having won championships at Walsh Stadium and the Arena.

The previous Tuesday Snyder captured the 50-lap feature at Walsh Stadium sponsored by Father Timothy Dempsey Charities. Father Jimmy Johnston, head of the Dempsey Charities, had spoken to Snyder that evening and Jimmy mentioned his intention to retire from racing. Fr. Jimmy Johnston, "He told me Tuesday night that his chief ambition was to win the Indianapolis race so he could retire from the game."

JIMMY SNYDER——"I'm set for life if I win the big race just once. This is an awfully dangerous game and I want to get out of it. I've got a wife and three kids to think of."

His children ranged in ages: Grace Louise, age 11, Jimmy Jr., age 4, and Lois Ann, 16 months. A grief-stricken Pete DePaolo commented about his good friend's generosity.

PETE DE PAOLO——"No race was too small, no purse to meager, no luncheon club too inconspicuous, when the call came, Jimmy responded. Jimmy's greatest failing was that of not being able to say no. He always was willing to accommodate anyone who might desire his service. And it's my guess that he drove in his last race trying to help some promoter who urgently asked for Jimmy's appearance, in order that he could capitalize on the fact that Jimmy was a second place winner at Indy, and for which Jimmy would have received the equivalent to a large sack of peanuts.

"During one of my last conversations with Jimmy, prior to the last Indianapolis Race, the subject of his competing in the future midget races came up and I urged him to stay out of this type of racing, pointing out that he was too valuable a driver for the 500, where at least he would be better remunerated for his services, but in his usual jovial manner he replied, 'Well Petey, I've got three little bambinos and have to buy them baby shoes!'"

In addition to his racing success, he and Emil Andres owned a popular racing-themed tavern in Chicago. He played professional football with the St. Louis Gunners several years ago. (The Gunners were founded in 1931 and folded in 1940.) Jimmy was also employed as an ice skating instructor at a rink operated by Earl Reflow, promoter of midget races in St. Louis.

JULY 15, 1939   CARL FISHER DIES

Indianapolis's own version of P. T. Barnum, 65-year old Carl Fisher, died at 3:55 p.m. in St. Francis Hospital, Miami, Florida, of a gastric hemorrhage on July 15, 1939. He had been in poor health the past several years. It was Fisher who first conceived the idea of building a super-sized Speedway for manufacturers to be able to test their automobiles. By using his business contacts, he was able to persuade James Allison, Frank Wheeler and Arthur Newby to join him as investors in the two and one-half mile Indianapolis Motor Speedway. After two years of hosting a series of races of varying lengths, the Founding Fathers decided to host just one event a year for 500 Miles.

Fisher was instrumental in both the Lincoln Highway, (from New York to San Francisco) and the Dixie Highway (from upper peninsula of Michigan to Miami) being built. He would transform 3,500 acres of mangrove swamp into Miami Beach. Nearby Fisher Island bears his name. The stock market crash of 1929 and the Great Depression left him virtually penniless as he had sunk most of his $100 million fortune into developing the eastern tip of Long Island—Montauk—into the "Miami Beach of the North". The final development project he built was the Caribbean Club at Key Largo, Florida, in 1938.

SEPTEMBER 20, 1939   LAWSON HARRIS KILLED IN
                        TEST AT THE SPEEDWAY

In a bizarre incident at the Indianapolis Motor Speedway, Lawson Harris was killed while riding with Babe Stapp during a tire test for Firestone Tire and Rubber Company. The car they were riding in was Mike Boyle's and had been driven in the past 500 by Ted Horn. Running speeds in excess of 116 mph, a rod broke in the car as he was entering turn one and it shot straight for the retaining wall. It bounced 20 feet along the concrete wall, then swerved another 25 feet before coming to a stop. Some witnesses thought that Harris was attempting to exit the car when it hit the wall. His helmet hit the concrete wall multiple times and his shoulder was crushed by the impact before being thrown from the car.

It was reported that one of his shoes was ground into the bricks. Harris' clothing was shredded and his blood-stained helmet, torn from his head, rolled down the track. An ambulance transported him to Methodist Hospital but he would die soon after arrival. Babe Stapp, who received a severe cut to his lip, stopped the car and rushed to Lawson's aid. Unable to speak due to the severity of the laceration, Stapp gestured for a pencil and paper as the attending physician started to examine his badly bruised leg. Babe wrote, "Get away from that leg. It's already been broken two or three times!" Dr. E. Rogers Smith indicated that Stapp had no broken bones.

OCTOBER 5, 1939.   "INDIANAPOLIS   SPEEDWAY"
                    MOVIE OPENS IN INDY

The new Hollywood feature film, "Indianapolis Speedway," starring Pat O'Brien, Ann Sheridan and John Payne opened at the Lyric Theater, 121 North Illinois, Indianapolis. Ozzie Nelson and his band along with singer Harriet Hillard would perform live on stage following the film. The Lyric, with its ivory and gold lobby, was regarded as one of the finest theaters in the state. The plot had Joe (Pat O'Brien) racing to put his younger brother Eddie (John Payne) through college. Joe is involved in an accident where Spud Connors (Frank McHugh) is killed. McHugh revived the role he played in the 1932 classic starring James Cagney in "The Crowd Roars" where he suffered the same fate. (McHugh is best known for his performance as Father Timothy O'Dowell in the Oscar winning film "Going My Way"). In 1940, Pat O'Brien would star in his signature role playing Notre Dame's legendary football coach, Knute Rockne. In 1947 Payne would star as attorney Fred Gailey who successfully defends Kris Kringle (Edmund Gwenn) as the one and only Santa Claus in the Christmas classic, "Miracle on 34th Street".

On the strength of his Indianapolis 500 victory, Wilbur Shaw would capture the 1939 AAA Driving Championship over Jimmy Snyder and Ted Horn. Babe Stapp was victorious in the August 27 Milwaukee 100. Mauri Rose won at Syracuse on September 2 and in a non-championship event at Springfield, Illinois. Emil Andres was also victorious.

Bob Swanson's survival from the spectacular crash in the 500 and painful recovery went on deaf ears as a judge ordered him to begin a 30-day jail sentence for speeding at 60 mph through a boulevard stop. He was also fined $25. To lend some support, his wife Lillian, the widow of Ernie Triplett, said let's focus on the good things to come—a New Year and a New Decade. They both looked to rid themselves of all their ill-fortunes that occurred in the 1930s.

DECEMBER 15, 1939   PREMIER OF GONE WITH THE WIND

Eddie Rickenbacker chartered one of his Eastern Airline airplanes to fly fifty business associates, stockholders and close friends for the Pre-Premier Gala on December 14 in Atlanta and to see the most sought-after premier showing of "Gone With The Wind" at the majestic Lowes Theater. Over 300,000 cheering fans lined the parade route to see Clark Gable, who starred in the role as Rhett Butler, accompanied by his wife Carole Lombard and Vivian Leigh, who portrayed Scarlett O'Hara. Rickenbacker would state, "This is the most colorful thing I've ever seen." A private cocktail party was also held for Rickenbacker and his entourage.

1939

Jimmy Snyder

Pole Position & 2nd Place
Led 65 Laps
In Memoriam June 29, 1939

1939

Tony Gulotta
13th & Final Indianapolis 500

1940

Frustrated after several unsuccessful shots at the brass ring, Babe Stapp decided to build a "featherweight" race car over the winter that he believed would finally help give him that illusive 500 victory.

BABE STAPP——"The race cars I have driven all weighed around 2000 pounds and I was so tired afterwards I could hardly stand. But my car weighs only 1400 pounds and is the lightest in the race. I'll be able to handle it more easily and it won't wear me down like a heavier car would."

After 12 frustrating attempts to win the Indianapolis 500, Babe was sure the new light-weight car wouldn't be jinxed by his 13th appearance. Stapp had led the race on four different occasions for 106 laps but had only a fifth place as his best finish.

The car considered the one to beat at Indianapolis was the #33 Bowes Seal Fast Special. It was the car that Louis Meyer had come so close to winning in last May. After Meyers nasty-looking crash on the 197th lap, he retired as a driver and took a position with Ford. When Robert Bowes was sure Meyer's retirement was an absolute, he formed a partnership with Alvin Jones, who had an Indianapolis De Soto dealership, and collectively they convinced Rex Mays that he was the only one who could maximize the horsepower produced by the eight-cylinder supercharged motor. Bud Winfield, regarded as the top authority on carburetors, would take the crashed Meyer racer and totally rebuild it over the winter. Ralph Hepburn would be Mays' Bowes Seal Fast teammate, assigned to drive the updated four-cylinder racer, that Cliff Bergere had finished third in last year.

Equally confident he would become the first to win the Indianapolis 500 back-to-back, Wilbur Shaw would return to drive the maroon Boyle Maserati, now sporting a #1 on the cowling. Ted Horn would be his teammate in the #3 Boyle Special. And in a bit of a head-scratcher, Frank Wearne would be added to the three-car stable after Chet Miller quit the Boyle team.

Elgin Piston Ring would sponsor three cars: #7 Mauri Rose, #16 Frank Brisko and #38 for rookie Paul Russo, younger brother to the late Joe Russo. Other promising rookies hoping to make the Race were Sam Hanks in #28 Duray Special, Tommy Hinnershitz, the dirt track extraordinaire, in # 9 Marks Special and Joie Chitwood in #42 Kennedy Tank Special. After George Bailey's 6th place starting spot in last year's race, many tabbed him as a "dark horse" to win this year's race. Harry Miller had spent the winter making improvements to his rear-engine creation. Early in May, Rex Mays was impressive setting an unofficial track record of 132 mph.

MAY 7, 1940   GEORGE BAILEY DIES OF BURNS

In a fiery accident eerily similar to Johnny's Seymour's crash of Harry Miller's revolutionary rear-engine car last year, 38-year old George Bailey crashed the sister car with tragic consequences. Bailey, taking to the track for a practice spin, entered the SE turn too high, lost control of his race car and slid into the inner guard rail. His car ripped out over 150 feet of wooden guard rail which pierced his "pontoon-shaped" gasoline tank mounted on the side of the cockpit. There was an immediate fiery explosion and moments later there was a second explosion as his other gasoline tank ignited. With his car totally engulfed in flames, Bailey managed to leap from his burning race car, his clothes ablaze. Trying to run away from the inferno, he would fall four times.

Fellow driver Floyd Davis and track photographer Eddie Hoff were two of the first responders to come to Bailey's rescue, stripping the flaming shirt and trousers from his body. Hoff tried to beat out the flames with his camera bag. As George was placed on a stretcher, he screamed to Mike Davis, the ambulance driver, "My back is still burning." Davis quickly removed smoldering fragments of what remained of his shirt, singed himself in the process.

Bailey was taken to Methodist Hospital where he would die 45 minutes later. Speedway medical chief Dr. E. Rogers Smith indicated that although his cause of death was due to third degree burns, Bailey also sustained a fractured hip, and a wooden plank from the guard rail had pierced his leg.

Just prior to the accident, the five-time 500 veteran had posted a speed of 128.5 mph. Ironically, two years previous his car caught fire during a practice run, but fortunately Bailey was able to bring it to a stop and leap uninjured from his racer.

George Bailey was a bachelor and lived in Detroit with his mother. When he was not racing, he was employed by the Hudson Motor Car Company as an experimental driver. Like the Seymour machine, Bailey's car was destroyed by the flames too.

Pete De Paolo had predicted the front row to consist of Bob Swanson, Rex Mays and Wilbur Shaw and that Swanson would set a new track record of 132 mph. Pete was only part correct. A crowd of over 35,000 there to watch the battle for the Pole Position were brought to their feet in excitement as Rex Mays set an unofficial of 132+ mph lap—an unofficial track record. However, a strong East wind and high humidity hampered any chance of breaking the track record.

Soon after Wilbur Shaw had posted the day's quickest speed of 127.065 mph, Mays set out on his qualifying run but a light shower on the backstretch halted his quest for his third Pole after posting an opening lap of 128.590 mph. Within a half hour the track dried and Mays would complete the remaining three laps to average 127.850 mph. Mauri Rose, now Lou Moore's driver replacing the late Floyd Roberts, qualified Moore's 4-cylinder machine 125.624 mph, barely edging out

Ted Horn in the Boyle Special for a front row berth. Beside Horn in row two were Mel Hansen in the Harry Hartz Special and Cliff Bergere, the day's first qualifier, driving a car he had purchased from Lou Moore.

The expected pole showdown between Rex Mays and Bob Swanson in his "Big Bertha" powerful 16-cylinder racer failed to materialized as Swanson could not reach a speed high enough to qualify, then saw a 5 p.m. heavy downpour quenched any hope of topping Mays's speed. Later in the week when time trials resumed, Kelly Petillo, who threw a rod prior to Pole Day, would battle the still-persistent strong wind to earn the unlucky 13th qualifying spot with a four-lap average of 125.331 mph.

George Barringer, driving a rear-engine team car to the late George Bailey's, completed a solid 222.5 mph run in the Hollywood Pay-Day Special. Again weather interfered with the day's qualifying efforts, as an early afternoon rain shower shut down the track until 5 p.m. Rookie Sam Hanks, driving for Leon Duray, impressed his hard-to-please boss with an average speed of 123.064 mph.

Finally, after days of adjusting the carburetor on the 16-cylinder Sampson Special (actually two 91-cubic-inch Miller motors), Bob Swanson posted a speed of 124.619 mph, the day's fast speed. However, they were extremely disappointed that they could not reach last year's speed of 129.4 mph. Ralph Hepburn, Mays's

Bowes Seal Fast teammate, was the second fastest qualifier at 123.860 mph.

Two Frenchmen, Rene Dreyfus and Rene LeBerge, serving on the front line for the French army, were granted a leave of absence to drive Italian Maseratis in the 500-Mile Race. Both drivers struggled to reach qualifying speeds of 118 mph. Dreyfus, the first to qualify, stated he was unaware that he could be bumped if he was one of the first 33 qualifiers. Wilbur Shaw circulated a petition that would have allowed him to be able to start the race but it was denied. Dreyfus would be allowed to serve as a relief driver for LeBeque in the other Lucy O'Reilly Schell Maserati. (After World War II, Rene Dreyfus and his brother Maurice started the famed French restaurant La Chanteclair in New York City). Argentine road racer Raul Riganti, returning to the Speedway after a seven-year absence, qualified his Italian Maserati at 121.827 mph.

All told six rookies would qualify for the race—Sam Hanks, George Robson, Rene LeBeque, Joie Chitwood, Tommy Hinnershitz and Paul Russo, the late Joe Russo's younger brother. Russo had broken a differential in the morning and a frantic call was made to Chicago to rush a new part. It arrived 42 minutes later and was installed in time to qualify at 120.809 mph.

Billy Devore, a Top-Ten finisher in his previous attempts in the 500, qualified Wilbur Shaw's "Pay Car." Tony Willman and Henry Banks failed to qualify for the Race.

Louis Meyer would accept the position of team manager for Rex Mays. Many felt that with Meyer's skill of keeping a race car running the complete 500 miles, he'd be the missing ingredient to finally get Mays into Victory Lane. When asked if he'd sooner be driving his car this year, the philosophical Meyer responded.

LOUIS MEYER——"Remember the smashup I had last year? I do, because it provided one of those heart-stopping moments when it was touch and go between a driver and Gabriel with his horn. I've been in accidents before but that was the first one I definitely knew was caused by me, and not by any fault in the machine. Right then, I knew it was time for me to quit. When I got an offer of a good job I didn't need any persuading to take it."

Before the drivers meeting, Eddie Rickenbacker announced that Chief Steward Charlie Merz would be promoted to Assistant General Manager to T.E. (Pop) Myers. The congenial Ted Doescher would replace Merz as Chief Steward. Rickenbacker also stated that contrary to the rumor circulating that this would be the last running of the Indianapolis 500, the race would continue May 30, 1941.

Quite a few people were surprised by Louis Meyer's retirement from racing. Henry McLemore of UP asked

411

the three-time winner why he was passing up a great chance to win his fourth Indy this May.

LOUIS MEYER——"I'm thirty four, and this is a youngster's game...a game for a thin, hard, tough kid who can take the awful beating holding a wheel for 500 miles at high speed. I just got tired—running down the backstretch I remembered I should check my tires before hitting the dangerous turn. I looked at my right front. I looked at my left front. Then—and this was the lapse—I looked at each of the back ones without taking a look at the track and where I was going. When I did look up, the crowd was right on top of me and the car was in a spin. When a racing car gets out of hand, there isn't a thing you can do but hold on, pray and get ready to jump. The next thing I knew I was on the track, all alone, and just about to be run over by all sorts of cars.

"That lapse cost me the race, if not my life. So I'm through, let the kids tool 'em around."

Race fans arrived at the Speedway wearing top coats. It was one of the coldest 500 mornings in the history of the 500. The temperature was in the mid-fifties. In a display of sportsmanship, August Duesenberg and several dedicated crew members worked around the clock for 48 hours to repair the crankcase of #49 Schell Special, owned by Mrs. Lucy O'Reilly Schell and driven by Frenchman Rene LeBeque. Just after completing his qualifying run, a rod went through LeBeque Maserati crankcase casting concern if the motor could be repaired by the start of the Race. (On February 24, 1946 the 32-year old LeBeque was accidentally asphyxiated by gas leaking from a defective water heater in his bathroom.)

Shorty Cantlon was noticeably intoxicated on Race Day morning and Speedway officials refused to let him drive in the race. Car owner Fredrick Surber helped Cantlon save face by stating he had influenza. Surber selected Babe Stapp, who failed to qualify his ultralight race car, to be Shorty's replacement. Stapp's wife wasn't thrilled and only agreed to permit Babe to drive if he would turn the car over to a relief driver, Tony Willman.

As he had on three previous occasions, Rex Mays jumped to lead at the outset and would lead the first 33 laps closely followed by Wilbur Shaw and Mauri Rose. Mays was adhering to Louis Meyer's team orders not to try and lap the field but rather wait until after 400 miles to turn it loose.

True to his promise he made to his wife, Babe Stapp would drive just 12 laps then turned the car over to Tony Willman. However, it was a short-lived day for

Willman. On lap 64, his car lost its oil cap and it ran out of oil.

On lap 24, Argentina's Raul Riganti's #29 Maserati spun in the SE turn and he had a spectacular crash over the inside fence that had fans sensing the popular 47-year old Riganti wouldn't survive. He was tossed from his car and over the inner guard rail. His somersaulting racer landed four feet from his head. Surprisingly he only suffered a wrenched back, scratches and bruises. Raul, who finished in 33rd, would describe the accident to the press while resting in Methodist hospital.

RAUL RIGANTI——"I went in at 400 rpm and hit a spot of oil. The car spun and it hit the inside rail. I was thrown out on the grass and the car came tumbling after.

"It almost hit me. There was a big hole in the fuel tank, but fortunately the car did not burn. I think my escape was miraculous."

On the 32nd lap, while driving down the main straightaway, rookie Tommy Hinnershitz's crankshaft broke and his engine locked up. His car abruptly turned and crashed several time into the low retaining wall. After bringing his car to a stop, the crowd gave him a thunderous ovation. Believing he had escaped uninjured, he was surprised to learn from Dr. E. Rogers Smith that he had broken a small bone in his right arm.

Wilbur Shaw would take the command of the race, leading laps 34 thru 73 before Mays would re-take the lead from laps 74-99. Pit manager Louis Meyer had originally planned to have Rex pit for fuel and tires after the halfway mark but he began to fret that Mays might run out of gas on the backstretch, so he ordered him in on the 99th lap. All four tires were changed and the car refueled. Mauri Rose would take a momentary lead at the half-way point, leading laps 100-104.

While Mays was in the pits, Shaw greatly upped his pace to where he could afford to make an extra pit stop and still be the race leader.

Then on the 151st lap, a cold drizzle began to fall and the yellow flag was displayed. The Bowes Seal Fast team's strategy to charge hard in the final stages of the race had backfired. The remainder of the race was run under caution. Shaw would receive the checkered flag running only 96 mph. He was 2:15 minutes ahead of Mays at the finish and immediately the red flag was displayed. Mauri Rose finished third, Ted Horn was flagged off the course in fourth place, completing only 199 laps. He had completed the entire 500 miles the previous four races. Joel Thorne raised eyebrows with his fifth place in a one-car effort. Bob Swanson was four laps off the pace in sixth position.

Wilbur Shaw would pit twice—on lap 73 for a RF tire and gas for 2:30 minutes and on lap 143 for gas in just over a minute. He became the first to win back-to-back 500s and joined Louis Meyer as a three-time winner. Wilbur had been so dominant the past eight 500-Mile Races—first three times 37-39-40, second three times 33-35-38, and seventh in 1936 when he was en route to victory until his hood rivets loosened. Only in 1934 did he have a DNF, and he started second in that race.

In Victory Lane Wilbur Shaw would say, "I'm feeling fine. It was the easiest race I ever drove."

Asked if he was going to retire, Shaw was adamant that he wasn't considering that as an option. "Certainly not. I'll be back next year trying to make it four victories— three of them in a row."

Many of the fans left the Speedway grounds after the conclusion of the race disgruntled about Rickenbacker ordering the yellow light to remain on for the last fourth of the race. Louis Meyer refuse to lambast the Speedway owners decision.

LOUIS MEYER——"Eddie, you did just right. There was no earthly sense in taking a chance.

"Lives of kids mean a lot. Rex and I are satisfied with second dough. Hell, $10,000 ain't oil."

At the Indianapolis Athletic Club, Rickenbacker responded to his decision to keep displaying the yellow flag. "Before I ever try to make a dime at the risk of one man's life, they can burn the joint down." Wilbur Shaw would receive $31,875, the Studebaker Sedan Pace Car, the L. Strauss trophy, a Wheeler's meal ticket good for one year and a Norge refrigerator. Rex Mays was awarded $15,950, Mauri Rose $7,187 and Ted Horn $4,575.

JUNE 12, 1940   BOB SWANSON KILLED IN MIDGET RACE AT TOLEDO

Most tragically, Lillian Swanson became a racing widow for the second time when her husband Bob was killed at the Fort Miami Speedway in Toledo, Ohio. The midget race car he was driving hit a rut then overturned several times during a qualifying race. The 27-year-old Swanson's body was crushed as he was thrown from his racer. Bob was unconscious when rescue workers arrived. Rushed to Community Hospital in nearby Perrysburg, Ohio, he would die at 5:37 a.m. the following morning of internal injuries. The Swansons were married in 1935. Bob Swanson would be enshrined into the National Midget Hall of Fame.

The Los Angeles Times described Swanson as, "The greatest drawing card Southland automobile racing has ever known." He had few peers while driving midgets. In 1934, he won the Inaugural Turkey Night Grand Prix. He helped pack Gilmore Stadium where the crowd would jeer him as the villain because he won so many times." Perhaps sensing a premonition, Swanson recently told friends,

BOB SWANSON——"I don't want to die any more than the next man does, less in fact. But if I have to go within the next few years, I'd rather go out in the seat of a racing car than any other way."

Duke Nalon won the Langhorne 100 on June 16 in record time. Nalon took the lead when pole sitter Tony Willman was forced into the pits to replace a blown front tire on lap 48. Returning to the track in second place behind Duke, Willman would re-take the lead on the 58th lap. However Tony's day was short-lived as his car broke two laps later. When the checkered flag fell, Nalon had a commanding four-lap lead over Ted Horn.

AUGUST 12, 1940 BABE STAPP SERIOUSLY BURNED

Babe Stapp was seriously burned with first, second and third degree burns on his face, hands and legs when a gas line in Mike Reaser's midget racer burst showering Babe with flaming gasoline. Stapp was trapped in the burning car while he was testing the race car on South Garfield Avenue in Monterey Park, California. Reaser had intended to race the car the following day at Atlantic Speedway in Los Angeles. Stapp would spend weeks recovering at Glendale Research Hospital. During his recuperation, his first child, Steve, was born on August

19, 1940, and he decided to retire as a driver. In 1994, Babe was enshrined into the National Sprint Car Hall of Fame and his son Steve was inducted their Hall of Fame in 1999.

Rex Mays would win the rain-delayed Springfield 100 at the Illinois State Fairgrounds over Al Miller on August 24. Rex followed up that performance on September 2, 1940, as he would drive to a dominating victory in the Syracuse 100. In doing so Mays captured the AAA National Championship in the season finale at the New York State Fairgrounds. George Robson finished second. On lap 17, Lou Webb of Los Angeles was killed when his car collided with Kelly Petillo and turned over three times. He was declared dead upon arriving at the hospital. The day before, Al Putnam was critically injured during practice but he would recover.

With Wilbur Shaw busy as the Firestone Tire and Rubber safety speaker traveling the country and speaking to the nation's youth. Rex Mays would capitalize on his second place in the Indy 500, earning enough points to win the 1940 AAA National Driving Championship. Mays's total for the season was 1225 points compared to Shaw's 1000 that he earned by winning the Indianapolis 500.

1940

Rex Mays
Pole Position & 2nd Place
Led 59 Laps

1940

Bob Swanson

In Memoriam June 12, 1940

1941

FEBRUARY 27, 1941   RICKENBACKER SERIOUSLY INJURED IN ATLANTA PLANE CRASH

For all the combat missions Eddie Rickenbacker had flown during World War I, he was never involved in any sort of serious crash. Even when the airplane he was a passenger in crashed upside down upon landing in Cheyenne, Wyoming, he escaped basically unscathed. This would all change during the early morning hours of February 27, as an Eastern Airlines sky sleeper twin-engine plane bound from New York to Atlanta crashed five miles SE of the airport.

Seven people were killed including the pilot James E. Perry, co-pilot L.E. Thomas and United States Congressman Rep. William D. Byron (D-MD). The Eastern Airlines plane, flying on the beam, but unexplainably at only 50-feet altitude, sheared off the top of a pine tree near a farm field. (It should have been at 800 feet altitude as it swung toward the airfield.) 13 passengers were asleep in their deluxe berths. The plane then continued plowing through a grove of trees before it came to a stop upside down. The wings had been sheared off and one motor was discovered 100 feet away.

Survivors, who were tossed clear or crawled from the aircraft, shivered outside beside the crumpled plane. They could hear the moans of fellow passengers unable to free themselves. Most were wearing sleeping garments. It was pitch dark and a bitterly cold, damp February night.

Eddie Rickenbacker was unable to free himself as he lay pinned atop the dead body of cabin steward Clarence Moore. Although seriously injured and in great pain, Eddie was very much in control. Aware of the amount of high-test gasoline that had seeped from the plane's fuel tanks, Rickenbacker barked orders, "Don't strike a match. It will explode the gasoline." He also kept repeating, "I'm sorry this had to happen to you boys."

It was rough terrain where the plane finally landed. A pajama-clad passenger, Jesse Rosenfeld, painfully made his way to a nearby farm house and was able to call for emergency help. He detailed to the media his ordeal to get help for the crash victims.

JESSE ROSENFELD——"I was feeling fairly strong. We could see lights of automobiles in the distance, and figured we were near a road. I had no shoes, so I asked Mr. Sewell for his. I said I'd try and get some help. Sewell's shoes were too big for me, but they covered my feet. I stepped along pretty gingerly, going in the direction of the road. I stumbled into a ditch. I tried to climb out of it, but it was too slick. There was nothing to do but wait until daylight. I remained in the ditch until the first streaks of dawn made it possible to see.

"There were some branches jutting from the side of the ditch—it was like a ravine—and I grabbed those and climbed out. I began to walk across the fields. I came to a man's house and told him there had been a plane crash and I wanted to phone for help. He had a car and we got in it and drove to Morrow, Georgia. I phoned from a store there. Ambulances came and I directed them to the wreckage."

Rescue workers had a difficult time traveling the rough terrain to reach the victims. Rickenbacker would be the last person removed from the airship. The side of the plane had to be cut away before rescue workers could extricate Eddie. Laverne Raymond was one of the rescue workers trying to free Rickenbacker.

LAVERNE RAYMOND——"Not many men could have stood what that man took. Boys, there's a man. He was lying under a mass of twisted wreckage. All we could see was his face and that was covered with blood. Right in front of him were the bodies of the pilot and co-pilot. He groaned and talked in a low voice."

Rickenbacker was taken to Piedmont Hospital where a pint of blood plasma was rushed to his attending physician. Doctors thought it was amazing that he did not lose consciousness as he suffered a broken left hip, several cracked ribs and a huge gash on his forehead. His condition was listed as serious.

When learning of the accident, Mrs. Adelaide Rickenbacker immediately drove from where she was visiting in Charlotte, North Carolina, to Atlanta over slick roads. Family elected not to inform Mrs. Elizabeth Rickenbacker, Eddie's mother, of the crash, due to her being in ill health. Eddie's fractured hip was attributed to a re-break from an old racing accident.

※ ※ ※

As the month of May approached, race fans had an eye toward the war going on in Europe and whether President Franklin Roosevelt would have us join forces with the Allies against Nazi Germany. However, the 500 would proceed and at the center of attention was Wilbur Shaw and whether he could he win three consecutive 500-Mile Races. Wilbur would again be at the wheel of his maroon #2 Boyle Special Maserati that Cotton Henning had massaged over the winter. For sure, Wilbur exuded confidence that he could accomplish the feat. Chet Miller would return as a Boyle teammate after his one year sojourn with the Alfa Romeo in 1940. Somewhat surprisingly George Connor landed a spot in the third Boyle Special, which was his best ride opportunity in his six previous 500s. Miller would drive car #14, Connor car #41.

Rex Mays was exhilarated to finally carry #1 on his car representative of his winning the 1940 AAA National Driving championship. He would also arrive at Indy convinced this would be "his" year to win the Indianapolis 500 in the Bowes Seal Fast Special. Ralph Hepburn would again be his teammate in the #54 Bowes machine.

Lou Moore had purchased the Maserati that French rookie Rene LeBeque had finished in tenth position last May from Lucy O'Reilly Schell. Moore knew what Wilbur Shaw was acutely aware of, that the Maserati was the fastest car at the Speedway. Moore virtually rebuilt the car using American parts. Pleased with Mauri Rose's third place finish from a year ago, the bantamweight speed demon would drive the #3 Elgin Piston Ring Maserati. Floyd Davis, a three-time starter with mediocre success, was tabbed to drive Rose's car from the year before, now the red-and-blue-painted #16 Noc-Out Hose Clamp Special. Cliff Bergere would be piloting the #34 Noc-Out Hose Clamp Special. The Hollywood stuntman envisioned winning the 500 by driving the entire race without a pit stop.

After a two year stint with Boyle Racing, Ted Horn was lured over to drive the #4 T.E.C Adams/Sparks entry owned by millionaire Joel Thorne. After Joel Thorne's fifth place drive of a year ago, fellow drivers were reluctantly acknowledging that Thorne might be a race car driver after all, and not just a wealthy playboy. He would drive the sister car, the #5 Thorne Engineering Special.

Kelly Petillo selected the diminutive 1940 Pacific Coast Racing champion Roy Russing to drive his car. Petillo, who hoped to secure a fast Maserati ride, was full of praise for Russing.

KELLY PETILLO——"This boy is gonna be tough here. He's been cleaning up on the Coast and when he hits here, he's gonna make people sit up and take notice.

"He might not be a fast qualifier but that's not what I'm interested in. He'll show his stuff when the chips are down and that's what counts with me."

Russing had showed a lot of grit when returning to dominance in the midgets following a serious crash on September 24, 1936, at Gilmore Stadium in Los Angeles. Roy suffered a crushed chest, fracture of the left shoulder and head injuries. Originally, he was listed in critical condition.

The racing community were speculating whether Eddie Rickenbacker would recover sufficiently to be able to attend the 500-Mile Race. In mid-April, Steve Hannigan arranged a dinner at the opulent Dinty Moore's restaurant on West 46th street in New York City for a large gathering of Eddie Rickenbacker's closest friends. Hannigan had a "talking movie" made of Rickenbacker giving a 20-minute talk while propped up in his hospital bed. Capt. Eddie graphically told how he was pinned under a section of the aircraft's wing and how he could hear his ribs crack as he struggled to free himself from the wreckage. Particularly gruesome was him telling how he lay atop the dead body of the plane's cabin steward. The horror of the crash was forever etched into his memory, "I never lost consciousness but there were many times I prayed for just a few minutes of total oblivion."

Speedway General Manager Pop Myers traveled to Atlanta on May 7 to visit his boss and to learn if he would be able to attend the 500-Mile Race on May 30. Myers discovered that the day before Rickenbacker began using a walker for the first time since the accident. Eddie had suffered a fractured hip, which had been a re-break of what was an old racing injury.

Doctors told Rickenbacker that it would be at least three weeks before he could leave the hospital. The G.S & S. Railroad has ensured the Captain that they would have a private car available if he would need it to travel back to Indianapolis for the race.

Kelly Petillo's confidence in his rookie driver Roy Russing's ability to master the Speedway abruptly changed on May 13. Russing, while on lap eight of the final phase of his 115 mph rookie test crashed in the SE turn. Ripping out 50 feet of lower guard rail, his car would overturn, then bounce upright. Thrown from the car, the 36-year old Russing miraculously escaped with only bruises. And Petillo's car, despite the serious looking nature of the crash, was not damaged enough to prevent it from being repaired to qualify the following week. Petillo, habitually strapped for cash and not able to land a ride in a Maserati, fired Russing and opted to drive his own car. Later Roy would drive the Marks Special but would fail to qualify for the race.

Roy Russing would return to California where he would repeat as the 1941 Pacific Coast Champion. He also won the 1940 & 1941 Turkey Night Grand Prix. After World War II, he purchased the first of the Kurtis Kraft Offy race cars and he felt he'd dominate in America's return to auto racing. Tragically, on April 21, 1946, Russing was killed instantly in a practice crash as his car plowed through two barbed wire fences at the San Joaquin County Fairgrounds in Stockton, California. He was nearly decapitated from the impact of the crash. His wife and 12-year-old son were in the grandstands and witnessed the fatal accident.

Rex Mays was favored to win his second consecutive Pole and fourth over all but a stiff North wind contributed to much slower speeds and only 12 drivers would complete qualification runs. In a mild surprise, Mauri Rose would put his Maserati on the Pole with an speed average of 128.691 mph, bolstered with a remarkable second lap of 130.152 mph, despite the less-than-favorable conditions. Mays settled for an average of 128.301 mph with Wilbur Shaw snaring the outside front row spot at over 127.8 mph.

The entire second row was an unexpected surprise. Harry McQuinn, driving Bill White's Alfa Romeo, was fourth fastest at 125.499 mph. Doc Williams, the day's first qualifier, would line up fifth with a 124.014 mph average, strengthened by a quick lap of 125.9 mph. Williams helped finance a new motor by selling racing photos of himself. Frank Wearne and Cliff Bergere would qualify with the exact same speed of 123.890 mph. However, since Wearne made his qualifying run first, he would start from the outside of row two, Bergere from inside of row three. Cliff was driving Floyd Roberts's 1938 winning car. Rookie Everett Saylor, a former school teacher from Ohio, was the slowest of the twelve qualifiers and the only driver who failed to top the 120 mph speed barrier. Saylor had graduated from Ansonia Normal and began teaching rural grade schoolers in Ohio.

Six more drivers would qualify on Day Two before a Sunday crowd exceeding 40,000. Shorty Cantlon, driving the 16-cylinder Sampson Special, broke a rod just before reaching the starting line on his qualifying run and the yellow flag was displayed. Cantlon's foot was burned and blistered as hot oil splashed on him. Shorty would never reach the hoped-for speed out of the car and was eventually replaced by Deacon Litz.

George Connor was the day's fastest driver in the third Boyle Special at 123.984 mph but would have to start in the "unlucky" 13th spot. George Barringer excited the crowd with his qualifying run in the #35 Miller Special rear-engine machine, but George was disappointed that he didn't go faster. And Floyd Davis could only get 121.106 mph out of Lou Moore's Noc-Out Hose Clamp Special that Mauri Rose had been so successful with a year ago.

Former Indy 500 driver Carl Marchese of Milwaukee entered a car with the smallest motor of all contestants—a piston displacement of just 135 cubic inches. He selected Paul Russo as his chauffeur and portly Paul became the fastest qualifier of the day as he averaged 125.217 mph with a fast speed of 126.3 mph. Kelly Petillo was back in his 1935 winning mount and made a solid run of 124.417 mph.

Surprisingly Ted Horn struggled to get his T.E.C. Special to any sort of quick speed during the month in the late Jimmy Snyder's Sparks racer. However, they were able to find some speed and became the 31st qualifier at 124.297 mph. His third lap speed of 125.104 mph gave indication that he would be formidable on Race Day.

Still suffering from the effects of his Atlanta plane crash, Eddie Rickenbacker chose not to attend the Indianapolis 500. This would be Rickenbacker's first race he would miss since the inaugural 500-Mile Race in 1911. After the annual drivers meeting the day before the race, the track was open for anyone wishing to make a last-minute test run. It became a painful decision for Sam Hanks to take to the track. Driving the #28 Tom Joyce 7-Up Special, a connecting rod broke, causing his back wheels to lock. Sam's car went into a spin in the SE turn before making hard contact with the wall. The 26-year old Hanks was unconscious when medical help arrived. Dr. E. Rogers Smith said Sam had a concussion, and injuries to his back and left leg. He would regain consciousness at the hospital. The car was damaged enough to be declared out of the race.

On the Night Before the 500-Mile Race, Peter DePaolo returned to his downtown hotel to discover a $2500 diamond ring, presented to him for winning the 1925 Indianapolis 500, $100 cash and a sports coat had been stolen. The ring was inscribed with his name.

The gates to the Speedway had been opened for an hour when at 6:59 a.m. Race Day morning, a massive fire broke out in the south section of Gasoline Alley. It rapidly spread through 24 of the 30 garages. It was believed the fire started by a static spark as mechanics were draining gasoline from their car. Fire fighters battled for two hours before the fire was extinguished. Three race cars were destroyed in the fire including the #35 rear-engine car of George Barringer, now owned by Eddie Offutt, valued at $50,000. The cars of Joe Marks and Milt Marion, which failed to qualify, were also completely burned.

Despite the intense flames, crew members braved the fire and rushed to pull over a dozen race cars from their garages. Seven men were burned but not seriously. Because of the heavy Race Day traffic driving to the track, fire engines had difficulty getting to the Speedway.

The power lines to the electrical timing device were burned causing a one-hour delay from 10 to 11 a.m. for the start of the race as repairs were hurriedly made. The fire caused an estimated $150,000 in damages. Several teams lost race equipment and their tools. Other teams demonstrated great sportsmanship sharing their tools with the unfortunate teams.

The fire began in the garage of the #35 Miller Special to be driven by George Barringer. As crewmen Reid Henderson and Lloyd Barnes were draining gasoline from the tank of their car, an explosion occurred. Barnes received burns on his face, hands and legs.

Four successive explosions would follow as flames and black smoke shot high into the air. A patriotic soldier ran to save the American flag from being destroyed by the fire. Russ Snowberger lost $157 that he had in a pair of trousers hanging in the garage. Former driver Marion Trexler repeatedly braved the flames driving his tow truck back and forth into the flaming garages to haul out several race cars.

Car #9 Fageol Special driven by Mel Hansen had a magneto failure and his car was forced back to the pits before the start of the race. Quick repairs proved just temporary as Mel's day would end on the 12th lap.

As was expected as he had on four previous occasions, Rex Mays jumped to the lead on the opening lap and he would lead through lap 38. On lap four Louis Tomei's car #53 tangled with Emil Andres driving the #19 Kennedy Tank Special. Andres was attempting to get out of the way of Joel Thorne. Thorne's car climbed the rear axle of Andres, then hit the NE wall. Joel was sprayed with hot fuel from Emil's car. Climbing out of his wrecked machine, Thorne was desperate to remove his clothing. A reporter would take a pail of water and douse the hot fuel mixture on Thorne's clothes. Tomei's car would remain in the race and would finish in 11th place.

At 150 miles, Wilbur Shaw led Rex Mays by 10 seconds. Harry McQuinn had moved into third, Doc Williams ran fourth and Frank Wearne fifth. 50 miles later, despite Wilbur having to stop for tires and fuel, he continued to lead by a quarter of a lap. The top five were on the lead lap with Harry McQuinn now in 2nd place, Cliff Bergere 3rd, Ted Horn 4th and Ralph Hepburn 5th.

After Mays led the initial 38 laps, Mauri Rose would take a short-lived lead on lap 39 thru 44 before engine issues cropped up. He pitted on lap 54 to change plugs, then he returned the pits on the following lap for a carburetor adjustment. Finally, Mauri would drop out of the race on lap 60 due to an injection failure in his Maserati. Shaw would take command on lap 45 and began dominating the race, leading through lap 151.

With Rose's Maserati out of the race, Lou Moore grew increasingly impatient with Floyd Davis. Now in 12th place and averaging 111 mph, Davis was falling even further behind the race leader Shaw, who was running speeds of 114 mph. Finally Lou Moore had enough and ordered Davis into the pits, even though their pre-race strategy was to run the entire race without making a pitstop. Rose was told to get into Davis's machine. In his hurry to leave his pit, Mauri struck two crew members but they were uninjured. Immediately he began to reel in the race leaders as he averaged over 115 mph. From laps 120 to 150 he ran in fourth position then moved to second at the 160-lap mark.

By 300 miles, Shaw had a lap lead over Cliff Bergere who, in turn, was up a lap over Rex Mays. At the 350 marker, Shaw still led Bergere by a lap followed by Mays, Rose and Hepburn. Ted Horn was in 6th place three-laps behind. Wilbur Shaw felt confident he was on his way to his third consecutive victory. He held a lap lead over Bergere, his tires were O.K. and he had enough fuel to finish the race. Then came misfortune on the 151st lap. Going into turn one, a spoke gave way and the car's wheel collapsed. Wilbur's car slid hard into the SW concrete retaining wall.

Upon impact, his gasoline tank burst. Nearby spectators were drenched by the spray from high octane fuel that shot 50 feet into the air. Wilbur was temporarily paralyzed and could not climb from the cockpit.

Shaw's racer hit with a tremendous impact and his collision could be heard above the race car motors. Sobbing unceasingly, Wilbur was carefully removed from his car and placed face down atop the retaining wall then carefully rolled onto a stretcher. He assured the attendees that was alright.

On lap 155, 36-year old Everett Saylor, who for a brief stint had moved up to seventh place in the Race, lost control of his car, the #47 Bowles Special, owned by Dr. Mark Bowles of Cincinnati, in the NW turn. His car skidded across the track and tore through the inside wooden rail. Saylor was tossed from his car as it turned over. Everett's vehicle would continue to slide upside down and crash into two parked passenger automobiles. State guardsmen pulled Saylor away as his car erupted in fire. It was quickly extinguished. Two men who were sitting atop the guard rail had just left the spot where Everett's car struck. The semi-conscious Saylor was taken to Methodist Hospital in serious condition suffering from a skull fracture, crushed chest and lacerations.

Everett Saylor's wife, Ruth Ann, and their six-year old daughter Connie were sitting in the grandstands but did not witness the crash. Saylor's pit crew rushed them to the hospital. Three days later Everett's condition worsened. He developed pneumonia and was placed in any oxygen tent and would also receive a blood transfusion from Floyd Davis. Wearing a shoulder brace and chin strap to keep his broken jaw in place, Everett was released from Methodist Hospital on June 22. Almost immediately he began plotting his return to racing. Doctors had ordered him not to race again this season but Everett wouldn't heed their advice. On August 23, while driving Lucky Teeter's mount at Altamont, New York, he was injured again in a crash and would break several ribs.

Mauri Rose would take the lead on lap 162, averaging laps from 121 to 123 mph, and continue to lead the remainder of the race with Rex Mays finishing in second place. Making three pitstops was Rex Mays undoing and cost him the race. On lap 65 he stopped for 64 seconds to change his LF and RR tires and get gas. He returned to the pits on lap 117 for 79 seconds for gas and tires then, finally, on lap 152 for 57 seconds for more gasoline. All told Rex spent three minutes and thirty seconds in the pits whereas Rose's winning car stopped just one minute on pit row. Mays would finish second to Rose by 1:30 minutes.

As the race neared its finish, Rose's fast pace started to worry car owner Lou Moore. He tried to slow Mauri down but Rose kept pushing the car at 120 to 122 miles-per-hour laps.

In the final 50 miles of the race, Mays, who had fallen to fourth place, was able to pass teammate Ralph Hepburn, then got around Ted Horn to finish in the runner-up spot for the second year in a row. Driving Floyd Roberts's 1938 winning car, Cliff Bergere had planned to drive the entire race without a pit stop. His strategy nearly succeeded and he was very much in the position to win after Wilbur Shaw's crash on lap 151.

After Shaw's accident, Bergere now assumed the lead and remained out front from laps 152-161. However, the 44-year old was tiring and fumes from the motor were making Cliff nauseous. Being overcome by the fumes, his pace slowed and his driving became more erratic as he struggled to keep his car off the wall. He would fade to fifth place and upon returning to the pits, he was so exhausted that his pit crew had to assist removing him from his race car. Concerned about his health, Bergere was placed in a wheelchair and taken to the Speedway infield hospital. Cliff became the first person to ever drive the entire 500 miles without a pit stop in a gasoline-powered car.

Starting nineteenth, Kelly Petillo quickly advanced through the field but his day was short-lived. His #22 Air Liner Sandwich Shop Special dropped out of the race after 48 laps because of a broken connecting rod. However, he was able to relieve Harry McQuinn on lap 97 and help pedal it home to a seventh-place finish. Petillo and Chet Miller had a spirited battle for sixth position with Miller edging out the '35 winner by 18 seconds. Louis Tomei continued on from his fourth lap shunt to finish 11th and Al Putnam, the last car running, placed 12th.

Mauri Rose made a classy gesture when he stopped near the end of the pits to pick up Floyd Davis, so together they could take the turn into the "Bird Cage". It was a bit of an confusing scene in Victory Lane with Rose in the spotlight and Floyd Davis, joyfully but awkwardly joining him. Reaching for his customary long-stemmed pipe, Rose acknowledged after a couple speechless minutes, how fortuitous it was. "All I can say is that if it wasn't for Wilbur's bad luck, we couldn't have won, but that's racing. Just luck, that's all."

Rose would quickly down a pint of milk, with much of it running down his chin. His wife Ruth, stunningly dressed in a navy blue outfit, had given him both a rabbit's foot and a four-leaf clover yesterday for good luck. Mauri's victory kiss left a sizable grease smear around her mouth.

The 5'6" Rose, who wore a size 12 shoe, gave high praise for the car he drove to victory. "It would run all day. Those Maseratis, they let you down. Not this one." It was the same car that he drove to a third place finish last May. Riding on Firestone tires, Rose's car became the first to complete the entire 500 miles without a tire change. When Lou Moore made the driver shift after 71 laps, the pit crew added five gallons of gasoline just to play it safe.

Col. Roscoe Turner picked up the Borg-Warner trophy and placed it in the seat of the red-and-blue winning car between the two drivers. When asked what he thought of being replaced by Rose just 70 laps into the Race, Floyd Davis, a general contractor in Springfield, Illinois, was diplomatic and intelligent enough to know not to criticize Lou Moore's decision, at least in public.

FLOYD DAVIS——"I think most of the credit is due to Mauri Rose. He'd driven the car 500 miles before and I felt he could do better in it than I could."

Lou Moore would heap praises on Mauri. "He's the only driver I know that could have done what he done today." Rose indicated he would return next year as defending champion and that he'd be back to work tomorrow morning at Allison's. Mauri had an exceptional work ethic and would schedule his practice runs at the Speedway during his lunch break, then return back to the track after he got off work. He would qualify on his day off.

Mauri and Ruth were married in March 1940 and a seven pound son, Mauri Jr., was born on April 3, 1941, at Methodist Hospital. They reside at 1315 North Ewing Street along with his spouse's parents, Mr. and Mrs. R.E. Rickets. He has been employed at Allison's Engineering Division of General Motors for three years. Much of the year he traveled throughout the country where he met with airplane manufacturer executives who used the Allison engine.

Chief Steward Ted Doescher indicated that the official listing of the final results of the 500-Mile Race would be delayed until the 24-hour protest period had elapsed. It was unclear whether Davis or Rose would be declared winner or would they be listed as co-winners like in 1924 when Joe Boyer relieved L.L. Corum and sped to victory.

Mr. and Mrs. Robert Kirby, big fans of the winner, named their newly-born daughter Mauri Rose Kirby. When asked about the honor, Rose chuckled.

MAURI ROSE——"There's another youngster named for me. Several years ago a boy in Huntington, Indiana, was named Mauri

Cummings Stewart after myself and Bill Cummings. That was the only time I ever got ahead of Bill."

A cocktail party at the Indianapolis Athletic Club was the venue for the distribution of the prize money. Rose worked until noon at Allison's then left to collect his paycheck of $29,735. Needing to be in Philadelphia at 10 a.m. the following morning for a business trip, he left the party soon after picking up his winner's prize. Rex Mays received $15,625 for second and Ted Horn's third place finished earned him $6,863. Wilbur Shaw, by virtue of leading 107 laps, pocketed $5875 for 18th place. Chet Miller was presented with the prestigious Carl Wallerich Sportsmanship award—a gold split-second watch. In 1939, the selection committee had overlooked the fact that Chet intentional crashed his car to avoid striking Bob Swanson, who had been thrown onto the race track and they wanted to recognize the feat of heroism. There was no recipient in 1940.

Lou Moore would tell the attendees, "I pulled a sneaker on the rest of the boys by planning to go through the 500-Mile Race non-stop. A special large gas tank and heavy tires did it. Rose drove a beautiful race." Pop Myers estimated the crowd exceeded 160,000, making it the largest to watch the race.

Interviewed in his room at Methodist Hospital, a dejected Wilbur Shaw shared his thoughts on what exactly happened to cause his crash.

"WILBUR SHAW——"I was running right on schedule. I had the race all mapped out, and I was one lap and seventy-eight seconds ahead of Cliff Bergere. Then something happened. I guess the wheel had been taking too much punishment. But the tire did not give out."

Extremely uncomfortable with the pain of two pinched vertebrae, Wilbur theorized that when he was balancing tires the day before the race, one would not balance and he marked the rim with chalk saying "use last." He felt that may have been washed away when firemen were fighting the huge blaze that destroyed much of the south garages in Gasoline Alley. Shaw promised to be back next year.

Dr. E. Rogers Smith, Speedway Medical Director, anticipated Wilbur would remain hospitalized for five days.

DR. E. ROGERS SMITH——"You know the x-rays show definitely that one of the vertebrae was hurt yesterday. But the other vertebra might have been injured years ago. He probably didn't know about it until he was hurt this second time. But he's getting along fine."

Wilbur, a Murat Temple member, was to have driven in a special 6-car, 50-mile exhibition race at the Speedway on June 9 as part of the entertainment schedule for the Shriners National convention.

JUNE 4, 1941   HARRY McQUINN & CHET MILLER WIN
                 SHRINERS RACES AT IMS

To speed the recovery of his fractured vertebrae, doctors applied a body cast around Wilbur Shaw's spine. They also diagnosed that Wilbur had sustained cracked ribs in a smashup. Shaw was bound and determined that even though he couldn't participate in the 6-car exhibition race at the Speedway for the Shriners Convention, he'd be there to serve as Master of Ceremonies. Doctors would discharge him the day before the race.

3,500 Shriners and their wives attended the exhibition races at the Speedway which were delayed one and a half hours for the track to dry from late morning showers. Many attendees had never seen the Indy 500. The first race was won by Harry McQuinn and Chet Miller was victorious in the second event, a 50-miler in which the crews were to make a tire change. The largest cheer went out to Wilbur Shaw as he was driven by the start/finish line.

On June 27, with the money earned over the past seven years of racing, Wilbur Shaw purchased for himself and his wife Kathleen a 300-acre farm on the banks of Sugar Creek, situated seven miles SE of Crawfordsville. They planned to divide time between living in Akron, Ohio and there.

OCTOBER 12, 1941   TONY WILLMAN KILLED IN
                      MIDGET SEASON FINALE

A week after capturing the 100-lap National Midget Championship race on the half-mile dirt track at Williams Grove Speedway, Tony Willman of Milwaukee was killed in the season finale 100-lap midget race at the Thompson Speedway in Thompson, Connecticut. Before 12,000 spectators, the popular "Flying Dutchman" race car's rear end appeared to lock and Willman crashed into the top guard rail. Not one to wear a safety belt, Tony was thrown from his car directly into the path of Howard "Bumpy" Bumpus. He was killed instantly when Bumpus's front axle struck Tony's head, fracturing his skull. He had started last, in 20th position, and in two laps had passed 16 cars.

A half-hour earlier Tony had set a new record for midget cars on a half-mile track. Tony was very much a family man who never smoked, drank or gambled. His hometown fans affectionately called him "The Mayor of South Milwaukee." Willman would compete in the Indianapolis 500 on four occasions—1937, 38, 39 and 41 but he was sidelined with mechanical failures each year with his best finish being 14th in 1939, dropping out after 188 laps because of a fuel pump failure. Driving relief for Harry McQuinn, he finished seventh in 1938. Tony Willman was inducted into the National Sprint Car Hall of Fame in 1992. He is also a member of the National Midget Hall of Fame.

Tony's wife, Lorraine, and their 12-year old daughter witnessed the accident from the grandstands. She would later say, "Tony was in a financial position where he didn't have to race, but he loved the track too much to quit."

(On June 16, 1946 32-year old Howard "Bumpy" Bumpus was fatally injured on the Flemington, NJ, Fairgrounds when his race car crashed through a fence on the backstretch during the final qualifying heat. His car climbed the rear of race leader Frank Bailey's car, and was catapulted into the air. Bumpy was thrown from his car and suffered a broken neck. He was pronounced dead on arrival at Somerset Hospital in Somerville, NJ.)

OCTOBER 22, 1941   GUS SCHRADER KILLED AT
                     SHREVEPORT, LOUISIANA

The Hankinson Fair Circuit season finale was held at Shreveport at the Louisiana State Fair on October 22 where Gus Schrader and Jimmy Wilburn were battling for the title. A very disappointing small crowd was in attendance for the Wednesday, October 22, showdown. The 46-year-old Schrader had confided with close friends that he would retire at the end of the season, champion or not. He seemed more focused to get away from Louisiana and back to his home in Cedar Rapids, Iowa, as fast as he could. Gus and his wife were to leave to go on a hunting trip in Winnipeg, Canada.

Schrader ran all the Fair Circuit races in a $15,000 chromium-plated racer nicknamed the "Riverside Offenhauser" that he built over the winter in Hollywood, California. Schrader and Wilburn would both start the feature from the front row. The navy veteran, often referred to as "King of the Dirt Tracks", snookered Jimmy and initially jumped out in front. Wilburn caught up and the two raced hub-to-hub. Although very dusty, race officials believed Schrader's right rear wheel locked with Wilburn's left front. The two cars briefly locked wheels and Schrader was thrown 15 feet in the air and over the race track fence. As he was hurled from his car, he lost both his helmet and shoes. Gus would land on his head suffering a fractured skull. He was transported to the Tri-State Sanatarium where he would die two hours later of a cerebral hemorrhage. Eunice Schrader, Gus's wife, was in attendance. Officials felt that he would have survived the crash had he not lost his helmet. His race car wound up on the other side of the outer fence but it sustained minimal damage.

For nine of the past ten years, Schrader reigned as National Champion of the Fair Circuit and was highly popular in Shreveport. He drove only one time in the

Indianapolis 500, escaping unharmed after crashing after just seven laps in turn four. Gus was credited with a 39th place finish. Last year he broke his neck and back but he was back racing soon afterwards. He was inducted in the inaugural class of the National Sprint Car Hall of Fame in 1990.

DECEMBER 7, 1941   JAPANESE SNEAK ATTACK OF PEARL HARBOR

Life in America changed dramatically on December 7, 1941 after the Japanese sneak attack on Pearl Harbor. Five battleships were destroyed and there were 2,403 casualties. President Franklin Roosevelt would go before Congress to declare war on Japan and Nazi Germany.

DECEMBER 29, 1941   RICKENBACKER SUSPENDS INDY 500 UNTIL AFTER THE WAR

On December 29, 1941, Eddie Rickenbacker would announce in New York that the Indianapolis 500 would be suspended for the duration of the war.

EDDIE RICKENBACKER——"Tradition and priorities demand we again voluntarily abandon the annual 500-Mile Race at the Indianapolis Motor Speedway in the interest of a full-out victory effort. Back in 1917 the men of automobile racing immediately answered the call to colors and served magnificently. Now again, the call has come. Today tools and motors are as important as men and priorities demand that we make the decision to call off the race despite a definite feeling that the majority of sporting events in the country should be maintained in the interest of morale."

"The Indianapolis Motor Speedway has always been the outdoor laboratory of the automotive industry. It's contributions to the modern motor are a matter of record but conduct of the 500-Mile Race calls for the expenditure of rubber, fuel, oil and many intricate motor parts as well as mechanical brains and we, who are responsible for the operation of the IMS, believe that

such an expenditure of man
and motors can be applied
toward our ultimate victory."

On December 30, Lou Moore, president of the
Indianapolis Automobile Racing Association, stated
that the proposed 100-mile AAA championship event
planned to be held on June 21 at the Indiana State
Fairgrounds could be moved to the May 30th date with
a purse of $15,000.

LOU MOORE——"Our action will depend entirely upon
the decision of the contest board
of the AAA. If other circuits of the
organization continue to operate, we
will go ahead with plans to give the
motor fans a 100-mile championship
event using the same type big cars
which are used at the Speedway.

"Many of the drivers and owners
have been working on their cars ever
since the completion of the race last
May and have practically their entire
earnings invested in their mounts.
This includes rubber tires not good for
commercial use."

1941

Mauri Rose

Co-Winner with Floyd Davis
115.117 mph Average. Led 39 Laps
Rose Replaced Davis on Lap 72; Car in 11th Place

1941

Cliff Bergere

Sickened by Fumes & Exhaustion
Drops From 1st to 5th
Led 10 Laps

JANUARY 5, 1942   SPEEDWAY OFFICES CLOSED

On January 5, 1942, in a startling announcement, Eddie Rickenbacker ordered the closure of the Indianapolis Motor Speedway offices at 444 North Capitol Avenue for the duration of the war. All Speedway personnel's employment would be terminated including General Manager T.E. "Pop" Myers. A fixture at the Speedway for the past 31 years, many couldn't imagine Myers not being behind his desk on the SW corner of the IMS office. There had been rumors circulating that Rickenbacker might consider selling the facility to a land developer. He was focused on running Eastern Airlines and now World War II was occupying his mind. Immediate speculation was that Charlie Merz, his top assistant, would assume control of the facility at the conclusion of the World War II.

Pop Myers was very popular with the drivers and he considered them all his boys. He would have sandwiches and coffee in his office at the Speedway for any driver, mechanic or crew member hungry because they were in a financial pinch. He loved being able to pass out all the checks at the Victory Banquet as much as he did being the passenger in the Pace Car to lead the field down for the start of the 500. Pop rode shotgun from 1928 thru 1941 and always had his trademark sailor straw hat in hand.

Myers most recently was involved in the supervision of the rebuilding project of the garages in Gasoline Alley that were destroyed this past Race Day morning. They were on schedule to be completed before the 1942 Indianapolis 500. Pop would make a statement about the closure and his future. "My health has been bad and I'm going to rest up and get myself in shape. After that, I don't know what I will do."

APRIL 12, 1942   PETILLO'S CAR HIT BY TRAIN

Kelly Petillo was in serious condition with a brain concussion and head and face injuries after his passenger car struck a Pacific Electric train in the early morning hours at Main and Lanzit Streets in Los Angeles. Petillo was treated at Georgia Street Receiving Hospital before being transferred to Mission Bell Hospital.

MAY 31, 1942   EVERETT SAYLOR KILLED AT CAPE GIRARDEAU, MISSOURI

One year and a day after being seriously injured in the 1941 500-Mile Race, the former Ohio school teacher was killed in a race in Cape Girardeau, Missouri. Driving Floyd "Pop" Dryer's race car, the 32-year old Saylor lost control of his car, hurtled a bank and crashed into a pole. Suffering from a compound skull fracture, he was taken to a local hospital. His will to live surprised doctors as he battled to survive before succumbing at 8:15 p.m. without ever regaining consciousness. The track's dusty conditions may have obstructed his vision and was believed to be the contributing cause of his accident.

On Saturday Saylor's wife, Ruth Ann, accompanied her husband to Milwaukee for a Memorial Day race. Engine problems made it a short day for Everett and they would head back to Pop Dreyer's shop in Indianapolis. Mrs. Saylor would return to their home in Dayton, Ohio to be with their 10-year old daughter Consuela. Saylor would ride over to Cape Girardeau with Dryer. He had told his wife, "when I die, it might as well be in a race car." In 2002, Everett Taylor was inducted into the National Sprint Car Hall of Fame.

Everett never smoked or drank alcohol and for a period of time did serious exercises and roadwork to become a professional boxer. But the lure of racing won out. He had been hospitalized six weeks from his Indianapolis crash, and nearly died of complications from pneumonia at one point. Saylor ignored doctors orders not to race again for the remainder of the season. Soon after his return to the cockpit he was injured again at Altamont, New York.

On numerous occasions, Saylor would state that he had no fear while driving a race car.

EVERETT SAYLOR——"I never think of that accident at the Speedway. I drive to win every time. When you're a race driver, it's in your blood and you don't worry about what has happened. Race drivers are never afraid. Once fear gets them, they're done."

JULY 5, 1942   LUCKY TETER KILLED AT INDIANA STATE FAIRGROUNDS

The War had put a moratorium on all State Fairs. This was a huge disappointment for stunt driver Earl M. "Lucky" Teter, whose favorite place in America to perform his Helldriver's Show was at the Indiana State Fairgrounds in Indianapolis. When the Army Relief Fund ask if he would headline a four-show, two day performance, the nearby Noblesville native jumped at the opportunity to be part of the benefit. "LUCKY TETER AND HIS HELLDRIVERS" would pack the grandstands.

Both Saturday performances and the Sunday matinee went off without a hitch before 12,000 race-starved fans. The grand finale of the evening featured the daredevil driving a 1938 sedan up a ramp, soaring 150 feet over a large yellow truck, then landing on the opposite downward ramp. Teter called the act, his "Rocket Car Leap." After the previous shows, he made the distance five-feet longer. Lucky wanted to give his fans a "send off gift" of a new record distance jump so that they could remember him accomplishing spectacular until the war ended.

Recently, he had purchased a pair of brown boots. For the past nine years he had worn an old pair of black boots. Before his last performance, Lucky removed his new left boot and put back on his old black boot. He joked that he was changing back to one of his old boots because it brought him luck. He would tell the fans over the public address system,

LUCKY TETER——"I want to thank the officers and soldiers in Indianapolis and I'm dedicating this last stunt not only to the soldiers here but to all the boys in Uncle Sam's armed forces throughout the world."

The car traveled at a high speed up the ramp and cleared the truck. However, his car would plummet prematurely and would jam up against the heavy wooden ramp. Frantically rescue workers rushed to save Teter's life. They would need an acetylene torch to cut him from the car. His father, mother and sister watched his fatal accident. His wife Edna was in Philadelphia. Initially it was announced that Teter was being taken to Methodist Hospital. When it was apparent that he was deceased, they would go to City Hospital instead. County coroner Dr. Herbert Collins said he died of a broken neck and internal injuries.

Cliff Bergere, Hollywood stuntman and 500 Race car driver, was a special addition to the program. He would perform a crash through a double wooden barricade.

CLIFF BERGERE——"This was to have been his last stunt for a long while. Lucky was going into the army right away. Like the rest of us, he was abandoning the amusement game for the duration. He put on the show here because it was at the Indiana Fairgrounds and because it was for Army Relief."

SEPTEMBER 22, 1942   LOUIS SCHNEIDER DIES

40-year old Louis Schneider, the 1931 Indianapolis 500 winner, died of complications from an injury suffered in 1938 racing accident in San Diego. His left arm was mangled and crushed in the accident and it was reported that he developed tuberculosis of the bone. He also developed a drinking problem. Schneider had been ill for two years and hospitalized in the Flower Mission Hospital for three months. Louis was in and out of trouble with the AAA for competing in unsanctioned races. In 1924-25, he was an Indianapolis Motorcycle policeman. He was survived by his two children, Miss Mary Ellen Schneider and William G. Schneider.

OCTOBER 21, 1942   RICKENBACKER'S   PLANE MISSING IN SOUTH PACIFIC

On October 21, 1942, while flying on a secret mission for Secretary of War Henry Stimson, 52-year old Eddie Rickenbacker and a crew of seven were forced to make an emergency crash landing in the South Pacific. Their plane was en route from Hawaii to the South Pacific war zone when they strayed off course due to a faulty compass and would run out of gasoline. Mrs. Rickenbacker voiced hope, "Eddie will turn up. He's too old a hand to get lost in any airplane now." They were to spend 23 days adrift inside three rubber rafts.

Although never particularly religious, Rickenbacker would always carry with him a small crucifix and a St. Christopher medal. When all looked bleak, an hour after a communal prayer, a seagull landed on Rickenbacker's head and he was able to capture it. That was the first food they had eaten other than four oranges. It's innards were used as bait which they caught several fish. Sgt. Alexander Kaczmarezyk, crazed by intense thirst, disobeyed orders not to drink the seawater and would succumb on the eleventh night. Rickenbacker led his burial at sea.

Pilot Captain William T. Cherry's raft was first to be spotted on Friday November 13. His rescued then intensified the search for the remaining missing crew members. The next day a Navy PBY Catalina flying boat spotted Eddie Rickenbacker, Col. Hans Anderson and Pvt. John Bartek's raft in the waters north of Samoa and the rescue at sea was successfully accomplished. The third raft with crew members Lt. John De Angelis, Lt. James Whitaker and Staff Sgt. James Reynold were found on a small deserted island.

Mrs. Eddie Rickenbacker would say she never lost hope even though it was a foregone conclusion they could not have survived the crash and/or that many days adrift.

ADELAIDE RICKENBACKER——"I never lost faith and knew that he would be rescued. I was worried a little the last few days because he might be exposed to the winds and the sun, and I was worried about his physical condition."

After a brief period to recuperate, Rickenbacker would join another crew and complete his mission for Secretary Stimson. (NOTE: For detailed information of their ordeal at sea read "Seven Came Through, Rickenbacker's Full Story" by Eddie Rickenbacker and "We Thought We Heard The Angels Sing" by James C. Whittaker.)

※ ※ ※

On October 10, 1944, Wilbur Shaw addressed the Shriners Club of Cuyahoga Falls, Ohio, dinner and he told the audience that Eddie Rickenbacker favors selling the Indianapolis Motor Speedway because new taxation guidelines would create a lot of hard work and nothing to show from it because Uncle Sam would take most of the profits. He told of the American Legion's interest in purchasing the track from Rickenbacker. Wilbur indicated that since the Legion is a non-profit organization, they could operate with minimum taxation and a minimum of profits. Shaw felt the sale would go through.

OCTOBER 25, 1944　　RICKENBACKER　　MEETS WITH AMERICAN LEGION TO SELL IMS

On October 25, Eddie Rickenbacker began conversations with the American Legion to purchase the Indianapolis Motor Speedway from him and to restore the annual Memorial Day event. The proposal would have their subdivision, the Indianapolis Voiture No. 145 of the 40 and 8 Society, a.k.a. the Forty and Eight, head the management of the track and the race. A committee was formed with Norman Coulon appointed as chairman. After a meeting with Wilbur Shaw, Robert Bowes, Cotton Henning, Harry Hartz and V.A "Army" Armstrong, the Indiana American Legion executive committee met to discuss the feasibility of staging the return of the Indianapolis 500 on May 30, 1945. It was their collective opinion that proper tires and gasoline would not be available by May 1945. Shaw would state,

WILBUR SHAW——"No tire manufacture will stick his neck out far enough to supply synthetic tires for an automobile race, and few drivers would risk driving on them at high speeds. The engineering of synthetics has not progressed to the high degree

> necessary for 100-mile-an-hour
> speeds."

Regrettably their recommendation was that the resumption of the Indianapolis 500 should be delayed to May 30, 1946.

The Forty and Eight had strong reservations about having the race staged on Memorial Day, May 30, due to their patriotic reverence for that date. They strengthen their argument of moving off that date by showing race attendance historically was greater when it had been held on Saturdays. They were of a strong opinion to schedule the next 500-Mile race on the Saturday closest to Memorial Day.

NOVEMBER 20, 1944   AMERICAN LEGION TO BUY
                      SPEEDWAY

Norman Coulon announced that the option to purchase the Indianapolis Motor Speedway by the Forty and Eight had been extended until December 15. He indicated that "certain legal difficulties will be ironed out soon" so the sale could be completed by December 15. He also announced that applications had been filed with the Securities Exchange Commission and the Indiana Securities Commission to receive approval of a bond issue to finance the purchase. They also have intentions to use the Speedway for other entertainment and sporting events. Coulon stated that profits earned from the race will be directed to veterans rehabilitation programs and child warfare.

DECEMBER 15, 1944   AMERICAN LEGION'S OPTION
TO PURCHASE EXPIRED

Even though the option to purchase the Indianapolis Motor Speedway by the Indianapolis Voiture No. 145, American Legion Society of the 40 and 8 had expired, they stated they have a "Gentleman's Agreement" with Rickenbacker and are still going forward with plans to finalize the purchase. Chairman Norman Coulon stated there have been legal snags with the Federal Securities and Exchange Commission which has caused a delay in the approval of a $1,000,000 bond issue. The bond was specified for financing the purchase and renovation of the Speedway. Coulon concluded, "I'm sure Rickenbacker will understand the delays and will permit us to go ahead with the plans."

Because the Securities Exchange Commission determined that the Indianapolis Motor Speedway was a commercial proposition, the bond issue was denied. Coulon stated new briefs have been prepared and have been sent to the SEC headquarters in Philadelphia. Coulon's Speedway Purchase Committee is incorporated under Indiana laws as a non-profit corporation for the sole purpose of raising funds for charitable purposes. The plan is to issue 15-year maturity bonds up to $1,000,000 total with a 10-year call feature.

MARCH 12, 1945   WILBUR SHAW TESTS SYNTHETIC RUBBER TIRE AT SPEEDWAY

Throughout World War II there was a pressing demand to create a wartime synthetic rubber tire as a replacement for the traditional rubber tire. The Firestone Tire and Rubber Company, with the approval of the government, had Wilbur Shaw conduct a 500-mile test of their new synthetic tire to see if it could withstand the rigors of high speed driving over a rough brick surface. On this cold March day Shaw managed to drive his test car the entire 500 miles at an average of 102 mph without a blowout. Wilbur gave high praise to the new tire but emphases that "low speed driving is vitally important to conserve civilian tires."

WILBUR SHAW——"Many persons doubted the ability of synthetic rubber tires to give a sustained performance at high speeds. The test run showed that they could adequately withstand real punishment. Super-speed tire construction developed for the Speedway has been made mandatory for all military aircraft tires."

Wilbur Shaw was quite depressed after leaving the track. His "beloved" Speedway had fallen in a state of disarray with deteriorating grandstands and waist-high weeds grew throughout the entire complex. He had heard rumors of Rickenbacker wanting to sell it to a building developer and now he quickly understood why that rumor was realistic.

Wilbur would promptly schedule a meeting with Rickenbacker at his Eastern Airlines headquarters in New York. Eddie was direct with Wilbur that he would rather sell the Speedway than commit the kind of monetary investment it would take to completely restore the facility. Shaw asked, "How much money will it take to buy the Speedway?"

EDDIE RICKENBACKER——"I will sell it for exactly what I've put into it and I will let you examine the books, so you'll be able to present an accurate picture of the financial possibilities to any prospective investor."

After leaving Eddie Rickenbacker's office, Wilbur Shaw felt there now was hope of saving the Indianapolis Motor Speedway. With his friendships at Indiana National bank, they were in agreement that $750,000 would be a realistic dollar figure to secure loans to complete a sale. Wilbur knew Rickenbacker wanted to sell it but also he would entertain an offer from any interested party that intended to return the 500 to its past glory and beyond. Both Wilbur and Eddie were cool to the idea of the American Legion and their subsidiary, the 40 and 8, hosting several races at the track and moving

Race Day from the traditional May 30 date. They held the option to purchase the Speedway.

Armed with realistic bank figures Wilbur sent out proposals to over 30 companies. Shaw also sought to attract a group of investors so he could purchase the Speedway, similar to how Rickenbacker gathered Detroit financiers to acquire the Speedway in 1927. Whether it be himself as owner, another sportsman, or company, he wanted to save the Speedway and the 500-Mile Race from going by the wayside to a commercial developer.

Quickly letters of interest started to arrive but Wilbur would soon become disillusioned with their self-interest responses. It each case, they wanted to be the sole source of their product and eliminate rival companies from being able to use the race to showcase their products as well.

JUNE 19, 1945   "CAPTAIN EDDIE" PREMIER

20th Century Fox released "Captain Eddie" starring Fred MacMurray as Rickenbacker, Lynn Bari as Adelaide, and an all-star cast including Charles Bickford, Thomas Mitchell, Lloyd Nolan, James Gleason and Spring Byington about his plane crash in the South Pacific and 23 days lost at sea. It would receive one Oscar nomination for Best Special Effects.

Eventually an exasperated Shaw would meet with an investment banker friend, Homer Cochrane, and express his growing frustration in not finding a proper suitor. Cochrane recommended he contact Anton Hulman Jr., a successful businessman and sportsman from Terre Haute, Indiana.

HOMER COCHRANE——"Tony is the head of Human & Co., at Terre Haute. He's a sportsman as well as one of Indiana's most able businessmen. He's becoming increasingly active in civic affairs and he has the financial background to swing the deal if you can interest him."

After fulfilling Firestone tire test obligations at the Bonneville salt flats and the Nevada's Tonopah Highway, Shaw was able to schedule a meeting with Tony Hulman and his key lieutenants including Joe Cloutier. Shaw was thoroughly prepared with charts and graphs demonstrating how Hulman could turn a reasonable and sustainable profit. To Wilbur's surprise, Tony would respond,

TONY HULMAN——"I don't care whether or not I make any money out of it. The Speedway always has been as much a part of Indiana as the Derby is part of Kentucky, and the 500-Mile Race should be resumed. But I don't want to get into something requiring additional capital each year to keep it going.

"I'd like to be sure of sufficient income to make improvements each year and build the Speedway into something everyone could really be proud of. We'll drive over to Indianapolis soon to take a good look at it, and then let you know what we think of the idea."

NOVEMBER 14, 1945   RICKENBACKER   SELLS SPEEDWAY TO TONY HULMAN

Late Wednesday afternoon, November 14, 1945 at the Indianapolis Athletic Club, Eddie Rickenbacker completed the sale of the Indianapolis Motor Speedway to Anton "Tony" Hulman, Jr. of Terre Haute, Indiana for a reported $750,000. (Rickenbacker and his Detroit investors had purchased the Speedway from Carl Fisher and James Allison for a reported $700,000 in 1927). The 44-year old Hulman, a sportsman and financier, owned Clabber Girl Baking Powder Company and other successful businesses. Wilbur Shaw was named president and general manager of the Speedway. Shaw, who had been serving as sales manager for the Firestone Aircraft subsidiary of Firestone Tire and Rubber Company in Akron, Ohio, indicated he intended to resign immediately. He would state later that evening on WIBC radio that he would not drive in the Indianapolis 500 anymore.

T.E. "Pop" Myers, would return as vice president. Two Terre Haute associates of Hulman's were given executive positions—Leonard Marshall, attorney and president of the First National Bank of Terre Haute, was selected as secretary and Joseph Cloutier, vice-president of Clabber Girl Baking Corp, would become the Speedway's treasurer. Tony, a Yale University graduate, indicated work would commence immediately and they planned to resume running the 500-Mile Race on May 30, 1946. Their stumbling block was the potential shortage of labor and materials.

TONY HULMAN——"Our first aim will be to look to spectator comfort and convenience and to provide a track and competition that should be an invitation and a challenge to the best race drivers in the world. We think the fans in Indiana will be glad to know that the Speedway is home-owned now."

The sale was somewhat melancholy for Rickenbacker. He would state the reasons for making the decision to sell the Speedway to the media.

EDDIE RICKENBACKER——"When the Speedway was available for sale in 1927, I became interested because of my early association with automobile racing and, fortunately, was able to obtain financing in Detroit which enabled me to take over the operation. Since that time I was able to not only plow back earnings into it but also give the city a $100,000 golf course and accomplish some $250,000 work of improvements to the track itself.

"However, I have always felt that the people of Indiana should have had more than an observation interest in this great state institution. The demands of running Eastern Airlines makes it impossible for me to give the Speedway the attention which it demands and it is fortunate that I am able to dispose of my interest to Mr. Hulman.

471

"Mr. Hulman and Shaw will bring to the track 'hometown' ownership which it deserves along with Shaw's knowledge of racing which he learned the hard way on the track itself. I have no doubt that the new ownership will continue its successful operation. It is fitting that Hoosier management and Hoosier capital should continue the most famous venture in mechanical competition.

"Wilbur Shaw is of the track, as I was, and brings to it not only sound ability to carry on the top traditions of racing in America but the sincere affection that is so necessary for the proper conduct of this international event."

Rex Mays, who was in Indianapolis, expressed his hope Tony Hulman would resurface the track because the brick track is too rough now.

1945

Tony Hulman buys Indianapolis Motor Speedway from Eddie Rickenbacker for $750,000.
Wilbur Shaw named President and General Manager.

MAY 30, 1946   GEORGE ROBSON WINS
                 INDIANAPOLIS 500

Tony Hulman's concern that fans might not show up for the resumption of the Indianapolis 500 proved unfounded. Ticket sales were strong and on Race Day traffic was so congested that many motorists were unable to get inside the track before the now 11 a.m. start. George Robson, driving Joel Thorne's six-cylinder car, was viewed as a surprise winner, even though he would lead 138 of the 200 laps. Ralph Hepburn, who obliterated the former one-and-four lap track records, was the crowd favorite driving the supercharged Novi.

Cliff Bergere would sit on the Pole, Paul Russo, driving a car with two-engines (one engine in the front of the car, the other in the back), would start in the middle of row one and Sam Hanks completed the front row.

All told an estimated 165,000 fans would watch Tony Hulman's first Indianapolis 500 as new owner. An in the early stages of the race, the usual list of characters would lead the race. Mauri Rose, starting in ninth place, would lead the first eight laps. He would crash on lap 40. The first driver eliminated was Paul Russo who crashed his twin-engine machine on lap 16. Rex Mays passed Rose to move into the top spot for three circuits on lap nine. Mays's day was short lived as Rex would drop out of the race on lap 26. Ralph Hepburn, who had started 19th and was mounting a sizzling charge to the top, blew past Mays on lap 12. Hep would promptly stretch out a large lead as front runner through lap 55 when he was forced to the pits. It was at this point George Robson first took the race lead. He would lead a total of 138 laps en route to Victory Lane. This was his first major win in his racing career. George had the added joy of being able to compete against his rookie brother Hal, who would finish 25th, out with a broken connecting rod.

The Indianapolis 500 had returned and the positive way that race-starved fans responded left no doubt in Hulman's mind he made a smart decision to purchase the Speedway. George Robson had an outstanding pay day with total earnings reaching $42,550. He would get the keys to the Lincoln Continental Pace Car that Henry Ford II would lead the field down to begin "The Tony Hulman Era." The 36-year old Robson would also be given a round-the-world air ticket on Trans-World Airlines by L. Strauss. Not wanting his wife Margaret to miss the experience, he would exchange that prize for a trip to Cairo, Egypt for he and his wife to see the Pyramids in October.

※ ※ ※

During the next decade, ten drivers from the "Eddie Rickenbacker Era" would die tragically——George Robson, George Barringer, Al Putnam, Howdy Wilcox II, Shorty Cantlon, Ralph Hepburn, Ted Horn, Rex Mays, Wilbur Shaw and Joel Thorne.

SEPTEMBER 2, 1946.   GEORGE ROBSON & GEORGE BARRINGER

Since Joel Thorne almost never ran any of his race cars on dirt race tracks, Indianapolis 500 winner George Robson wouldn't be competing in his winning 500 mount in quest of the 1946 AAA National Driving Championship. Not wanting to pass up appearance money that goes for being the new King of Indy, George would drive the Noc-Out Hose Clamp Special to compete in the Labor Day AAA National Championship 100-mile race at Lakewood Park Speedway in Atlanta. This was the car that Cliff Bergere had qualified for the Pole Position at Indianapolis in May. George "Tex" Barringer would drive the car Wolfe Motors Company of Tulsa Special owned by Irwin Wolfe. Only eleven cars started the race.

As the race was nearing it conclusion, Billy Devore, driving a car with a damaged drive shaft slowed down to 20 mph. For several laps Devore motored around hugging the inside of the race track. With each passing lap dust was being churned up from the dry red clay surface, obscuring both the drivers and spectators vision. Accounts vary on what happened next.

On lap 98, as George Robson was speeding down the track in the Noc-Out Hose Clamp Special, he apparently didn't see Devore's slow moving vehicle due to the swirling dust. George swerved abruptly to miss Billy's car, but tragically, direct into the path of the hard charging Barringer. There was a terrific impact.

Robson's car flipped end-over-end, tossing him onto the track. Another version claimed Robson, who was bleeding profusely, jumped from his car. A larger cloud of red dust was stirred up by their collision, obscuring the vision of the drivers even more so.

There were three different accounts to what caused George Robson's fatal injuries. First, as the stunned Indy winner was sprawled on the race track, he was struck by two race cars in rapid succession. The Indianapolis Star reported that Robson was hit by Bud Bardowski and Emil Andres. Secondly, The Indianapolis News account differed indicating George Connor was believed to have hit Robson as he was attempting to find his way to the rail. Third, some fingered blame on Ted Horn who would admit afterwards that he hit "something" on the race track. Horn's damaged race car was quickly loaded on the trailer and promptly departed.

The now-driverless Robson car smashed into Billy Devore's racer and the second generation driver would land upside down into a nearby lake. Trapped briefly beneath the water, Billy would escape with a broken collar bone and broken shoulder. Devore was fortunate not to have drowned.

Mrs. Margaret Robson and her sister-in-law were sitting near the judges stand when the accident occurred. George Robson would be taken to Grady Hospital but would die soon after his arrival of massive injuries. The

Robson's were parents of a 12-year-old son George Jr. and 6-year-old daughter. They resided at 3924 E. 53rd Street in Maywood, California.

42-year old "Tex" Barringer would also succumb soon after his arrival at Grady Hospital. Tex's wife Velma and their young son Billy were also watching the race. The Barringers resided at 1322 North Gale Street in Indianapolis and Tex worked for Allison Division of General Motors.

Ted Horn said he "couldn't see a thing" as he sped into the turn and that he saw an upturned car "just a second or so before I smacked into it." Horn would extricate himself from his damaged race car and frantically wave his arms to warn his colleagues of the accident. Six races cars would crash or be damaged in the melee. Afterwards Horn was quite critical of Billy Devore for continuing to stay out on the race track.

TED HORN——"I just missed Devore's car two or three times on previous turns and I think he should have been taken out of the race because of poor visibility. I couldn't see a thing when I roared into the turn and saw an overturned car just a second or so before I hit it."

Initially, Ted Horn was declared winner but that decision was reversed giving George Connor the victory. The AAA would also exonerate Billy Devore of any wrong doing stating that he was driving according to the association's rules that allow a car to continue in a race providing that they hug the inside rail and maintain a steady, reduced speed. Billy would say he had driven about 25 miles at that pace and all of the fellow racers had passed him several times before Robson swerved to pass his car.

SEPTEMBER 15, 1946   AL PUTNAM

The superstition that "things happen in threes" prove to be the case two weeks later when Al Putnam was killed at the Indiana State Fairgrounds for a 100-mile AAA race promoted by Lou Moore. As he was preparing to make a qualifying attempt, Al had just taken the green flag and was rounding the NW corner, when his car skidded twenty feet in loose dirt. The 37-year old Putnam crashed through the wooden inner guard rail tearing out a twenty foot section. His race car would then collide head-on into an abutment of an underpass. Two Indiana State Policemen were the first to arrive at the scene and they removed Putman from his race car. Al died instantaneously when his steering column pierced his chest. He also received a fractured skull.

Al Putnam was a four-time starter in the Indianapolis 500, his first race being in 1938. His best finish was twelfth in 1941 when he completed all 200 laps. This past 500-Mile Race Al finished fifteenth, dropping out after 120 laps with a faulty magneto. On September 2, 1940, Putnam was injured during a race at Syracuse,

New York, when his race car hit a rail and overturned several times. Originally listed in critical condition with a severe head injury and broken right arm, he would recover in time to race in the 500 the following May.

Mrs. Pearl Putman, Al's wife, witnessed the crash from her grandstand seat. She hurried to the first aid station at the Coliseum and was there when an ambulance carrying the body of her husband arrived. The popular Indianapolis resident was active in several civic organizations including the Speedway Masonic lodge, the Scottish Rite of Indianapolis and the Murat Temple Shrine. Al was also a member of the Indianapolis Athletic Club and would frequently work out several hours daily in their fitness center. Al was the father of two sons, Norman and Jackie, from a previous marriage. Al and Pearl resided at 5144 Winthrop Avenue in Indianapolis.

NOVEMBER 13, 1946   HOWDY WILCOX II

In a bizarre accident, Howdy Wilcox II, the second place finisher in the 1932 Indy 500, was killed while serving as a flagman at the Converse, Indiana, fairgrounds. As Jimmy Wilburn was coming down to receive the white flag being waved by Wilcox, indicating one more lap in the 20-lap race, Howdy was struck by the car driven by Kenneth Wines from Kokomo, Indiana. In the last nano-second before being struck, Wilcox tried to dodge Wines swerving race car. He couldn't react fast enough and he was killed instantly as his body was tossed 25 feet. The accident occurred at dusk.

Wines would comment, "I saw him standing on the track just before I hit him but I didn't have a chance to miss him. I know he never saw me." He indicated it was impossible to spin his race car fast enough to miss Howdy. The half-mile dirt track was primarily used for harness racing.

Wilcox was survived by his widow, Mrs. Hazel Pritchard Wilcox and their three daughters. They resided at 940 Tulip Avenue in Indianapolis.

MAY 30, 1947   SHORTY CANTLON

Starting fifth in the #24 Automobile Shippers Special, Shorty Cantlon believed this was the year that he would finally win the Indianapolis 500. The 5'4 1/2, ten-time Indy 500 veteran was driving the powerful 16-cylinder owned by Louis Rassey. The start of the race was a disaster for Shorty. Following the command to start their engines, Cantlon's orange racer would not start nor did the cars of Mel Hansen and Joie Chitwood. Finally before the field had come all the way around to complete their first lap, all three cars were able to get started and took off to join the starting field of cars. A huge roar from the crowd roared as Shorty was finally able to pull away from his pit a half-lap behind the field.

On lap 41, rookie Bill Holland, the Race leader in the #16 Blue Crown Special, spun going into turn one. The 43-year old Shorty Cantlon, swerving toward the top of the track to avoid hitting Holland's car, spun around four times and made hard contacts with the SW turn wall. His car caromed off the retaining wall and stopped on the upper part of the race track. Immediately Shorty slumped in his cockpit, motionless. The car began leaking gasoline which trickled down the track but it did not catch fire. Rescue workers had difficulty reaching Cantlon as they had to dodge race cars whizzing by Shorty's vehicle. Finally reaching the car, they made the grotesque discovery that the force of the crash pushed the engine back into Shorty's lap.

Shorty Cantlon would die of a crushed chest, a fractured leg and internal injuries caused when the steering wheel pierced his chest. The popular Cantlon was a successful used-car dealer in Indianapolis.

MAY 16, 1948   RALPH HEPBURN

In 1947, Cliff Bergere qualified his Novi in the middle of the front row. He would lead the first 23 laps but his car would drop out early in the race. Car owner Lou Welch, impatient with Herb Ardinger's performance, would replace him with Bergere as his relief driver. Cliff would advance the car to a fourth place finish.

Pleased by his performance, Bergere was selected to drive the Novi again in 1948. On the Friday before the First Day of Qualifications, Bergere had slowed to 80 mph as he was preparing to come into the pits. His Novi did a three-quarter spin when Cliff applied the brake. The tail of the Novi smashed into a utility pole. Tempers flared between Bergere and Welch——Bergere would say he quit the ride, Welch said he fired Cliff.

To replace Bergere, Ralph Hepburn was offered the ride in the Novi which he had set the track record two years ago. Hepburn, the president of the American Society of Professional Auto Racers (ASPAR), led the boycott of drivers to holdout for larger prize money in 1947. It was finally resolved when Bill Fox, sports editor of the Indianapolis News, brokered an agreement between the Speedway and ASPAR. However, Hep opted not to compete in the 1947 500-Mile Race.

Now 51 years old, Ralph had not driven a race car in two years but he knew the powerful Novi gave him what might be his last, best chance to win that elusive Indianapolis 500. Chet Miller would be his teammate, driving the newer Novi built last year.

While out practicing before the start of the Day Two Qualifications, as Hep was going into the NE turn, his Novi began to fish-tail. It swerved into the dirt by the inside of the track, lost control and shot across the track hitting the concrete outer wall head-on. He would die instantly of a fractured skull and crushed chest. A grieving Chet Miller would step out of the second Novi and was replaced by Duke Nalon. Last year, Hepburn took a position as Western sales manager for the Tucker Motor Corporation. Ralph, his wife Ada, and daughter Jo Ann resided at 4718 Worster Street, Van

Nuys, California. Ralph Hepburn was inducted into the Indianapolis Motor Speedway Hall of Fame in 1970.

OCTOBER 10, 1948   TED HORN

On August 21, 38-year old Ted Horn won the Springfield 100 and captured his third consecutive AAA National Driving Championship—1946, 1947, 1948. The season was to conclude with a return to Du Quoin, Illinois, and even though the race would not affect the national standings, he was very popular at the southern Illinois track.

On the second lap, a spindle broke on Horn's race car causing him to lose control and he swerved into the car driven by Johnny Mantz. Ted was thrown onto the race tracks just before his car hit Mantz's racer. Horn would suffer a brain concussion, crushed chest and fractured left leg. Rushed to Marshall-Browning Hospital, he would die twenty minutes later. When hospital attendants removed Horn's left shoe, his "lucky" dime fell on the emergency room floor. His right shoe, in which he would always carry three pennies for good luck, came off during the accident. Mantz was slightly injured.

H.C. "Cotton" Henning, who Horn drove his Maserati the past three years in the Indianapolis 500, had recently signed Horn to drive for him in 1949. He would state, "Ted Horn undoubtedly was the greatest day-after-day driver I ever saw." Henning blamed a pre-race sabotage cost him from winning this past May.

Cotton claimed someone put a foreign substance into the engine. Ted's record at Indianapolis was a model of consistency—1936 second, 1937 third, 1938-39-40 fourth, 1941 third, (1942-45 no race), 1946-47 third and 1948 fourth. This season Horn posted ten straight victories on the dirt.

Ted Horn, who neither drank or smoked, refused to quit driving until he won the Indianapolis 500. Early this year, he divorced his wife Theresa. One reason she cited was Ted wouldn't stop racing. 17 days ago Horn was married to former Geraldine "Gerry" Horn. She witnessed her husband's accident. Early in 1949 their daughter Gaylee was born. Ted had a daughter, Loretta, from his previous marriage. Race driver Lee Wallard would accompany Ted's body back to Clifton, New Jersey.

More than one thousand mourners visited Quinlan Funeral Home to pay their respects. Harold Mohn wrote a tribute to Ted Horn and sent it to his widow. Rev. Charles Child of Trinity Episcopal Church in Patterson, N.J. officiated. He read Mohn's poem.

The Speed world morns the passing
Of the blonde and blue eyes Ted.
The brightest star the sport has known.
In many a year is dead.

Ted was inducted into the Indianapolis Motor Speedway Hall of Fame in 1964.

MARCH 7, 1949   L.L. CORUM SUICIDE

1924 Indianapolis 500 co-winner L.L. "Slim" Corum was found hanged in his garage by his mother at 33 North Kealing Avenue in Indianapolis. His body was suspended from a rafter by a clothesline. Dr. Joseph Jewett, deputy Marion County coroner, said he took his life two days before being discovered. The 50-year old Corum had been in ill-health since the death of his son Robert of rheumatic fever in March 1945.

NOVEMBER 6, 1949   REX MAYS

There had been an absence of Champ Car racing in southern California since 1934. There was great enthusiasm when the announcement was made that the AAA would conclude their 1949 racing season with a 100-mile race at the famed Del Mar, California, race track. One of its principal investors was Bing Crosby. It opened in 1937 and on opening day Bing was there to greet each spectator. It would grow into the place for Hollywood stars to go for summer horse racing. The race was scheduled for Sunday November 6.

On race day morning Rex Mays and Duke Nalon accompanied by AAA officials took a tour of the track in the pace car. One things that was glaring concern were the posts on the infield side of the track. Mays, who pronounced the track race ready commented,

REX MAYS——"The posts won't bother us any. The top railing has been taken off and if anybody should happen to slide to the infield, they'll just snap off the post like matchsticks. The first turn always takes a beating and usually digs up a little.

"But I'm more worried about the west turn where it narrows down a little bit.

"We should have an official there with a flag to remind the boys to keep down."

On the 13th lap of the 100-lap feature, Rex Mays was killed after he was thrown from his Wolfe Special and was run over by trailing cars. Running in second place behind Jimmy Davies, his car brushed the racer driven by Johnnie Parsons as they went into the backstretch. (Others believed Rex's car caught a rut causing the car to lose control.) Rex's car darted out of control and into the inside wooden fence where it knocked down 200 feet of barrier and several rail posts before snapping off a furlong post. The car then flipped end-over-end twice ejecting Mays from his cockpit onto the middle of the race track. Mays was one of a very few drivers who didn't wear a seat belt.

At least two cars would run over his prostrate body. The Indianapolis News reported that Mays was struck by cars driven by Hal Cole and George Connor before rescue works could safely reach him. Death was instantaneous. A track physician stated he had a broken neck from landing head first onto the track. Rex was taken to Scripps Memorial Hospital in La Jolla, California where he was pronounced dead on arrival.

The Los Angeles Times published a series of photos that were taken by Phil Bath, a Times photographer. The captions stated:

PHOTO——FIRST BLOW—The prostrate Mays has been struck by car #22 George Connor as Mays's car has landed on its wheels a second time.

PHOTO——HIT AGAIN—Mays's body again is hit, this time by car #24 Paul Russo, as driver is unable to swerve out of the way of sprawling body.

PHOTO——LAST CRASH—Mays's helmet flies through air after he has been hit for the third time, by car #14 Hal Cole going by.

Dorothy Mays, Rex's wife, was in attendance. They had two children, 10-year old Rex III and 4 1/2-year old Sue. During World War II, Rex was a Captain in the Army Air Force Transport command at Long Beach, California. His assignment was to fly war planes from the factory to the fighting front. Rex was a Captain in the 731st bomb squadron, 452nd bomb wing. In 1946, Rex would compete in the famous Bendix Classic air race.

A sad irony occurred last year in Milwaukee. Driver Duke Dinsmore crashed his car and he was tossed onto the race track. To avoid hitting Duke, Mays swerved his car and crashed into the retaining wall. Dinsmore survived. Just recently at Dayton, Ohio Speedway, Rex's race car crashed through the outer wall and was thrown from his car. The race car continued to plummet down a 30-foot bank. Emerging with just a sprained ankle, it reinforced in his mind that it was safer if you were tossed from the vehicle.

Three time Indianapolis 500 winner Mauri Rose would say, "Rex was the number one man I raced against." Mel Hansen, who had been paralyzed in a midget crash in Detroit in early September, told about his good friend Mays's fatalistic viewpoint, "Rex figured that when your number comes up, that's it." Rex Mays drove in 12 Indianapolis 500s and sat on the Pole four times. Mays would finish in second place twice, in 1940 & 1941. Rex was inducted into the Indianapolis Motor Speedway Hall of Fame in 1963. In 1990, he was a member of the first class enshrined into the National Sprint Car Hall of Fame.

MAY 15, 1953   CHET MILLER

In 1952, Chet Miller would set an unofficial track record of 140.187 mph and there was great excitement when he would go out to make a qualification run—hoped he would again capture a new track record for the Novi. On his first lap he would set a NTR with a speed average of

139.600 mph followed by a low 139 lap. Suddenly Chet slowed and he would return the powerful Novi back to the pits, his motor had burnt a piston. Two days later he would make his second qualification attempt and instead of playing it safe, he would set a new four-lap speed record of 139.034 mph but he would start way back in 28th starting spot. All month Miller was dogged with carburetion problems. Race Day would be short lived for the diminutive 5'5 inch fan favorite as his Novi would have a supercharger failure after 41 laps.

In May 1953, the now 50-year-old Chet Miller would again return to drive the Novi in what he hoped would be "his" year—win the Pole and the Race. Chet was determined to be a first day qualifier. In 1951, his speed rank in the starting field was third fastest and last year he was the fastest qualifier overall but he would start 27th and 28th the previous two years. He had never won the Pole and had only started from the front row once at Indy—3rd in 1936.

On Friday May 15, the day before Pole Day, Chet ventured out on the track. His sleek, white Novi had just turned a lap at 139.5 mph when he went into to turn one too low. The Novi would briefly fishtail, then for an instant it appeared that Chet had his racer under control, only to see it abruptly shoot toward the outer retaining wall. The Novi made a hard, head-on impact. The car would smack the wall four additional times as it traveled another 300 feet before coming to a halt in the short stretch. Miller was dead of a basal skull fracture when the ambulance arrived. His fuel line ruptured and fireman were quick to douse the Novi with CO_2 before a fire erupted.

Chet Miller wrestled with the idea of retiring. After last year's race, he had told friends that was his last 500. However, the lure of sipping milk in the Winners Circle brought him back one more time. The persistent question, "When are you going to retire?" would typically come up during every interview.

CHET MILLER——"It might be this year. If I go out there and it doesn't feel right, that's it.

"Nobody will know but you. I promised my wife Gertrude this year would be my last."

A stunned Lou Welch would say, "I never thought it would happen to Chet." Another buddy and fellow competitor Lou Moore was so saddened about Miller's demise, he stated this was definitely going to be his last year as a car owner in the Indianapolis 500.

LOU MOORE——"When you see your old buddies get knocked off, it takes all the fun out of it.

"I bet I didn't get an hours sleep last night. I think it is up to the AAA to put an age limit on this thing. Louis Meyer had enough sense to quit. If he hadn't, the same thing would have happened to him."

It's almost unfathomable that during his 16 years of competition at Indianapolis, Chet never led a lap with over 5,000 miles driven. Chet was inducted into the Indianapolis Motor Speedway in 1995.

OCTOBER 30, 1954   WILBUR SHAW

If anyone has a love or even an appreciation of the Indianapolis Motor Speedway, then they owe Wilbur Shaw a huge thank you. Wilbur's passion for his "beloved Speedway" is what saved it from a virtual certainty of being turned into a housing development for returning servicemen from World War II. While at the Indianapolis Motor Speedway to conduct a 500-mile test for Firestone's new synthetic tires, he was shocked and highly troubled at the sight of the Speedway having fallen into a state of disarray. Soon he was able to arrange a meeting with Eddie Rickenbacker to determine what price he would sell the Speedway to him or other investors. Wilbur did everything to save the track and eventually found a willing buyer, Anton Hulman, Jr., with a Hoosier background to purchase the facility and to restore the running of the 500-Mile Race. Tony Hulman installed Wilbur as President and General Manager in November 1945 and the Indianapolis 500 continued to grow in popularity and attendance from 1946 thru 1954.

In 1947 Wilbur Shaw decided to add some "Hollywood" glamour to the race and the Speedway partnered with Borg-Warner to bring a movie starlet to kiss the new Indy 500 winner in Victory Lane and to present their famous trophy to the new champion. Carole Landis first appeared as the Borg-Warner Queen in 1947 and would give the grease-stained Mauri Rose not just one kiss, but multiple smooches. It was a big success and it developed into an annual tradition with Barbara Britton in 1948, Linda Darnell in 1949, Barbara Stanwyck in 1950, Loretta Young in 1951, Arlene Dahl in 1952, Jane Greer in 1953 and Marie Wilson in 1954. (The tradition would continue five additional years—1955 Dinah Shore, 1956 Virginia Mayo, 1957 Cid Charisse, 1958 Shirley MacLaine and 1959 Erin O'Brien.) From his days of racing at Ascot in Los Angeles, he befriended many Hollywood celebrities and he would invite them to watch the 500-Mile Race, including Clark Gable and Jack Benny.

All this would change tragically on October 30, 1954. Wilbur Shaw, noted 500 racing artist Ernest R. Roose, and pilot Ray Grimes would die when their gray and green, single engine Cessna 195 aircraft crashed in a corn field three and one-half miles west of Decatur, Indiana. They were returning from Detroit to Indianapolis.

The trio had left Sky Harbor Airport, NE of Indianapolis at 9:05 a.m. for Ann Arbor, Michigan airport, arriving at 11:30 a.m. They were taken directly to the Chrysler Proving Ground where Wilbur would conduct a high-speed test drive of the new 1955 Chrysler Imperial over their 4.7 mile course. After completing the test Shaw stated, "This is safer than flying an airplane."

After their test was completed they listened to the Michigan-Indiana football game in Ann Arbor. The Hoosiers, winless in the Big Ten, shocked the Wolverines 13-9 to hand the Maize and Blue their first conference loss.

Wilbur Shaw had flown the Cessna up to Ann Arbor and it would be Grimes, a veteran of 13 years of flying, turn to fly back to Indy. Ray had piloted charter planes for Wilbur the past several years. The weather reports were favorable and Shaw was excited to return home for tomorrow was not only Halloween but would be his 52nd birthday. However, the weather started to deteriorate. The skies became dark with visibility between two and three miles. Rain and snow flurries formed. Uncommon for late October, it was snowing in nearby Decatur.

Homer Ginter was driving a tractor in his field when he heard a roar. He would look and see a plane break apart 20 feet above the ground. Immediately he went to the crash site to try and rescue the victims. It was apparent they did not survive. When the fuselage smacked the ground, it skidded 150 feet, through a fence and into another farmer's field. Debris from the wreckage was scattered over a wide area. There was no fire.

Aviation experts discounted the notion that the plane broke apart before striking the ground. It was their opinion that Ginter most likely witnessed the Cessna rebounding after impact. A woman would inform County Coroner Harmon Gillig that she saw the airplane explode. Adams County Sheriff Robert Shraluka received notification of the plane crash at 4:15 p.m. and he and State Trooper Walter Schindler were the first authorities to arrive at the scene of the accident. Shaw and Grimes were identified by their pilot licenses and Roose by his drivers license. Mrs. Loretta Roose was initially told her husband wasn't aboard the plane.

Tributes world poured in from around the world. Harvey S. Firestone, Jr., Chairman of Firestone Company, would memorialize his former employee.

HARVEY FIRESTONE, JR.——"The death of Wilbur Shaw came as a great shock to me and my associates. His friendship and dynamic personality will be greatly missed by all who knew him. His intense interest in the automobile and tire industries contributed in a large measure to their progress."

Wilbur Shaw was close friend with the entire Firestone family. After Shaw suffered a near-fatal heart attack while acting as the honorary referee at the National Soap Box Derby in Akron, Ohio, in 1951, Wilbur would recuperate at the home of Raymond Firestone in Akron. He loved the Soap Box Derby and he loved youngsters. Still today, located at 2200 W. 30th Street, is the Wilbur Shaw Soap Box Derby Hill.

Wilbur Shaw was inducted into the Indianapolis Motor Speedway Hall of Fame in 1963 and the National Sprint Car Hall of Fame in the inaugural class in 1990.

OCTOBER 17, 1955   JOEL THORNE

The words "wealthy" and "playboy" were typically attached in an opening paragraph of articles about Joel Thorne. People described him as daring, reckless and careless. Very tragically, it caught up with him on an overcast October evening as his single-engined Beechcraft Bonanza aircraft, which he was piloting, crashed into a two-story apartment house at 11948 Magnolia Boulevard in North Hollywood, California. Thorne and two residents were killed instantly and nine others were injured. The death toll would grow to eight residents over the next two weeks.

Witnesses said they heard the plane "buzzing" the area on three occasions two minutes before the fatal fiery crash. Thorne had just departed ten minutes earlier from Lockheed Air Terminal in route to Las Vegas. Will Chappel heard what sounded like repeated buzzing by a plane and he went to his back yard to observe.

WILL CHAPPEL——"It became apparent that the pilot was swooping down to attract the attention of someone, then climbing. On that last dive he lost a wing and went into a spin seconds before the crash and explosion."

Mrs. Daniel Dewberry also hear what she thought was a plane buzzing the neighborhood.

MRS. DANIEL DEWBERRY——"Although I had the radio turned on, the buzzing sound of the plane was so loud, I just turned the radio off and looked out the window. The plane seemed to be flying at dangerously low altitude, revving its motor as if buzzing deliberately the homes around my North Hollywood home. It circled the immediate area several times, then went off in the direction of Studio City.

"I didn't hear it anymore and was relieved that it had stopped buzzing."

Even though some stated that he buzzed the area, others claim the saw a wing fall off the plane before its fatal plunge. An off-duty fireman, Ralph Frazier, had been attending a night class at North Hollywood High School. He had just come outside to head home and witnessed the plane circling no more than 200 feet above the apartment buildings. Frazier would describe the accident, "One of the wings dropped off. Then part of the other wing fell into the street a few minutes later. The aircraft plummeted down at a steep angle and through the roof of a six-unit apartment. There was a tremendous explosion." The detached wing was discovered 150 feet away in a neighboring apartment house. Federal regulators had cited Thorne about his buzzing activities in the past.

Killed was a bride of two months, Mrs. Betty Jean Wolf. Just 18 years of age, she was an accomplished violinist with the Burbank Symphony Orchestra. Seven-week old Sheryll Preston, who had just recently been baptized, also died instantly. 7-year-old John Marchica succumbed to burns 22 hours later. Tragically seven members attending the baptism party for baby Sheryll would die of complications from their burns.

Joel had celebrated his 40th birthday the day before. Although married, the 6′ 6″ Thorne recently became engaged to 21-year old Jo An Burdick. The blue-eyed fitness instructor, who stood 6-foot tall barefoot, wore a diamond horseshoe ring that matched the style Joel wore to his death. They had discussed a Valentine's Day wedding if his divorce would go through. The CAA announced that Thorne did not have instrument rating certification and stated that he should not have been allowed to take off under the weather conditions that existed on the evening of his plane crash. Thorne was survived by his estranged wife, Johnsie Eager Thorne, and their 13-year old son Jonathan.

THE TRAGIC UNRAVELING OF KELLY PETILLO

Initially wildly popular with race fans, Kelly Petillo began a slow fall from grace with a series of run-ins with the law that ruined his career and life.

AUGUST 10, 1941   SMACKS COP

Annoyed that a nightclub located at 1710 N. Las Palmas Avenue refused to let him in to their establishment, Kelly Petillo would show up at police headquarters in Hollywood demanding they send cops to raid a club that was violating the liquor curfew. He also insisted they give him a receipt of the conversation. Police Sergeant E. D. (Roughhouse) Brown told him, "We don't give receipts for such things" and suggested Petillo notify the State Board of Equalization. Without warning, Kelly punched Sergeant Brown in the eye, shattering his glasses and giving him a black eye. Brown punched back, blackening both of Petillo's eyes.

Kelly was then charged with assault. Both Petillo and Brown were treated at Georgia Street Receiving Hospital. The attending physician stated that Officer Brown was fortunate not to have lost his eye in the attack. Petillo was held at Central Jail before being released after posting a $500 bond.

On August 20, John S. Cooper, Petillo's Defense Attorney, accused Brown of not only being rough but also ferocious. Municipal Judge Wilbur Curtis dismissed the case stating there was no felony assault. Afterwards Brown stated he would not file misdemeanor assault charges against Petillo. The two would shake hands but "Ferocious" became Brown's new nickname.

MAY 19, 1943   ASSAULT AND BATTERY SUIT FILED

Attorney Emmett Tompkins, in behalf of Harry Palmer and his wife Margaret, filed suit in Superior Court charging assault and battery against Kelly Petillo and demanding $35,445 in damages. Mr. and Mrs. Palmer complained that Petillo struck them with a wooden club and his fists in a cafe he owned on the 9000 block of South Vermont Avenue. Kelly's attorney would get this settled out of court.

JULY 15, 1943   MRS. PETILLO FILES FOR DIVORCE

After 19 years of marriage, Valentine Petillo sued her husband Kelly for divorce in Superior Court. She charged him with cruelty. On August 20, she asked the court not to recognize a property settlement agreement that she originally signed for $9500. She claimed Petillo deceived her on the value of community property, stating its true value being over $25,000. Petillo responded that his wife was fully aware of the extent of his holdings.

On July 12, 1944 Mrs. Valentine Petillo would tell Superior Judge William S. Baird,

VALENTINE PETILLO——"He was out all the time and when he did come home it was three or four in the morning. He associated with other women, was continually drunk, and he didn't like married life. Sometimes he wouldn't come home at all, and when he did he wouldn't say where he'd been, and would start an argument."

The community property valued at $50,000 was divided equally in the property settlement agreement. Judge Baird gave her custody of their two children, 17-year old Kelly Jr. and Darlene, age 3, and issued a speedy divorce decree.

AUGUST 21, 1943   PETILLO BOOKED FOR SPEEDING

Kelly Petillo was charged for excessive speeding—driving 50 miles an hour in a 25-mile zone—as he drove toward his night club located at 10901 S. Vermont Avenue by California Highway Patrolman N. C. Barkalow. Petillo refused to sign a citation and was charged with resisting arrest. While writing out the speeding citation, jumped out of his car and knocked the officer to the ground breaking one of the policeman's teeth. Two sheriff deputies, patrolling the neighborhood, would respond and take Petillo into custody. Kelly was released on $500 bail.

On September 15, Petillo appeared before Judge Frank Carrell of the Gardena Justice Court and he was convicted of three charges—speeding, battery and resisting arrest. Kelly claimed he was traveling 37 miles an hour and Officer Barkalow hit him first. On October 11, Judge Carrell sentenced Petillo to 90 days in jail, suspended for two years, provided he pay Officer Barkalow $300 to cover his dental expenses and pay a fine of $300.

SEPTEMBER 29, 1943   ACQUITTED OF STRIKING A
                      WOMAN

Kelly Petillo was acquitted of striking Mrs. Musette Capaci in his night club in Judge Frank Carrell's Gardena Justice court.

APRIL 18, 1944   PETILLO FACES CHARGE OF ASSULT

A warrant was issued by Judge Frank R. Carrell of Gardena Justice Court charging Kelly Petillo with assault by hitting 35-year old Thomas Tyree over the head with a bar stool inside Petillo's night club on Vermont Avenue. Kelly admitted to police officers that he did strike him but did so in self-defense after Tyree pulled a knife on him. Bail was set at $500.

JANUARY 25, 1945   ASSAULTS ANNA GRIMET

On the evening of January 25, 1945, Kelly Petillo invited 25-year old Anna Grimlet over to his apartment at 1031 W. 37th Place, Los Angeles to "look at some racing pictures". Grimlet said Petillo got "that look in his eye" and when the attractive waitress rebuffed his advances Kelly gave her two black eyes. Judge James Pope refused to dismiss battery charges even though Grimlet indicated that the whole thing was a mistake. Petillo wrapped his arm around her and told the judge, "This is going to be my next wife." He would get off with probation.

JULY 1, 1945   ASSAULT WITH INTENT TO COMMIT MURDER OF A MARINE

Marco's Cafe at 912 W. Pico Blvd., Los Angeles, was Kelly Petillo's new business venture. As it was nearing midnight, Petillo told two Marines, John Yount and James Lunsford, to leave his bar. They refused to and

Kelly hit Yount over the head with a wooden chair then proceeded to go to the kitchen and get a Winchester rifle. He fired "a warning shot" at them. The next day he was charged with assault to commit murder. Petillo would tell the officers, "I was only trying to scare the Marine and his buddy so I could close the bar by the midnight state curfew hour."

On September 21, 1945 Kelly was cleared of two counts of assault with a deadly weapon by Superior Judge Myron Westover. Petillo had claimed he acted in self-defense when the two Marines assaulted him when he had ordered them to leave his tavern. Neither witness was able to attend the hearing because they had been both been recently shipped overseas.

JULY 5, 1945   "BRIBES" POLICE DETECTIVE

Veteran detective, Sgt. Heber Skaggs was charged with accepting a $500 bribe from Kelly Petillo to "fix" an assault-to-commit murder charge. As he walked out of Petillo's cafe, he was arrested by Deputy Chief W. J. Bradley for carrying $500 in marked money given to him by Petillo. Police said Skaggs admitted to taking the money but insisted the "fix" was first brought up by Kelly. It was unfortunate for Skaggs who had served on the force for 20 years and was ready to retire from the force.

On April 12, 1946 Heber Skaggs argued that he was double-crossed and that he was working up a case against Petillo for offering him the money. He claimed Kelly thrust the marked bills into his hands. The jury of 10 women and two men did not believe the story and found him guilty of taking a $500 bribe. On April 18, 1946, Petillo testified that Skaggs offered to have the charges against him dropped in exchange for a $500 payoff. Superior Judge Thomas Ambrose sentenced Skaggs from one to 14 years in San Quentin. The case was appealed and on August 12, 1947, Superior Judge William McKay freed Skaggs of bribery charges stating that the officer was merely gathering evidence when he allowed Petillo to give him $500 to "fix" the pending felonious assault case against Kelly.

JUDGE WILLIAM McKAY——"There is nothing more than a mere suspicion in the case against Sgt. Skaggs. It would be a flagrant miscarriage of justice to send a man with 21 years as a law enforcement officer to the penitentiary on mere suspicion."

NOVEMBER 25, 1945. MARIE COOPER BEATEN BY PETILLO

Kelly Petillo and his friend James Theriac were booked for an attack on an Ohio resident who had moved to Los Angeles three weeks earlier. They were behind bars in an El Segundo jail for their attack on Miss Marie Cooper, a 44-year old from Ohio. Police had spotted a vehicle stopped in the middle of a deserted, unpaved road. When they stopped they notice all three occupants partially unclothed. Miss Cooper was screaming and trying to fight off their advances. Her clothes were torn, her lips cut and her eyes blackened. Marie told the police she had lost her purse in downtown LA and had asked directions back to her sister's apartment. Miss Cooper accepted a ride in Petillo's sedan on Pico Boulevard. Kelly would call it a "bum rap" and said he did not want any negative publicity since he was attempting to build a new super-sized speedway in Los Angeles to challenge the Indianapolis Motor Speedway in prestige.

DECEMBER 5, 1945   PETILLO   CHARGED   WITH BURGLARY

In a complaint issued by Deputy District Attorney Don Avery, Kelly Petillo was charged with the burglary of an electric portable phonograph. Kelly was alleged to have stolen the phonograph on November 24 from the room Kenneth Lee of Los Angeles for payment of a past due bill. Lee informed Detective Lt. Harvey Burch that it was his roommate that owed Petillo $20 for his bar bill and that the defendant had mistakenly been led to believe the phonograph belong to the roommate. Municipal Judge Joseph Chambers dismissed the charges on December 17.

MAY 23, 1946   PETILLO SUES SPEEDWAY

Attempting to enter a car for the 1946 Indianapolis 500, Kelly Petillo's entry was rejected by the Speedway. He would file a laughable damage suit demanding $50,000 in Marion County Circuit Court. Petillo accused Wilbur Shaw of "attempting to control the outcome of the 1946 race by keeping him from participating this year." He claimed he was denied entry "by reason of his ability, daring and competency is feared as a contestant by many race drivers." He further added in his charge that the Speedway, "circulated among other drivers and the public at large that this plaintiff is incapable of driving a race car, although they well know that he is the best equipped and most competent race driver in the world." His attorney, William Miller, filed the lawsuit.

MAY 7, 1947   SUED BY CREDITORS

The race track that Kelly Petillo had hoped to build fell through and left him with 22 creditors going to court for payment of work completed. Nathan Moore, a Los Angeles contractor, brought suit against Kelly in San Diego Superior Court claiming the former driver owed him $11,741 for labor and materials on his speedway construction. The judge sided with Nathan Moore. This was on top of Superior Court Judge Charles Haines April 3 decision that 21 creditors were owed $52,482 from a previous suit.

Kelly Petillo's darkest moment occurred in the early morning hours in the Roosevelt Hotel, at the corners of Capitol Avenue and Ohio Street, in Indianapolis. Petillo had checked in the hotel at 2:30 A.M. using an alias of Joe Melo. He then informed David Milligan, a bellhop, to go to the room of Mrs. Naomi Shofner, his former secretary and girlfriend, to let her know "an old friend just checked in and wants to talk to you." The bellhop did as requested and brought the attractive 25-year old blonde down to Petillo's room on the second floor. Shofner would tell police of the terrifying incident.

NAOMI SHOFNER——"I attempted to awaken my husband Roy, but he was sleeping soundly, so I went down stairs with the bell-boy. Kelly opened the door and pulled me into the room and put his arms around me. He tipped the bell-hop and locked the door. Kelly became enraged when I said I just got married. He said, 'Why did you do me like you did?' He slugged me then slashed me with a knife."

Petillo had inflicted a deep cut from her temple to her chin. She screamed as blood gushed from the slashing. The bellhop heard the scream and returned. After he broke open the door, he called the police. Petillo had vanished. He notified her husband and they were rushed to Methodist Hospital. Mrs. Shofner identified Petillo as the assailant. Hotel records showed that Joe Melo arrived at 2:10 a.m. and checked out at 3 a.m.

The daughter of W. E. McGinnis, pastor of the Lebanon Pilgrim Holiness Church, Naomi had traveled to California with Petillo and worked for him as a secretary for 25 months . During this timeframe, Naomi, who was married to Charles Roberts, and she and Kelly romantically involved. (Last December, she divorced Charles Roberts, her first husband. They had two children—Larry age 8 and Mickey age 4).

The former Indy winner was charged with assault and battery with intent to kill. Shofner claimed Petillo had beaten her often after they had first met in January 1946. Soon after, they moved from Indianapolis to California and would not return back to Indiana until May 1947 for the Race. After the 500, "he blackened both of my eyes when I refused to return to California with him. Then he sent a lawyer to see me saying he would marry me if I would go back with him. Like a fool, I did." (No marriage occurred.)

Naomi also told detectives that she had received several written threats against her life and heard Petillo threaten "to scar her for life." The Saturday before the 1948 Indianapolis 500, a car without headlights drove up in front of the Roosevelt Hotel as she stood outside. "Two men jumped out—one was Petillo. They each struck me in the face, leaped back in the car and sped away. He was jealous and infuriated because I left him."

Two arteries were cut in Naomi's neck and physicians would require 40 stitches to close the gaping slash on the left side of her face. She would required a pint of blood.

Two days later, the FBI joined local authorities in search for Petillo. All local hotels stated they had no sighting of him. They expanded the manhunt into neighboring states. The 1935 500-Mile Race winner was barred in competing in the Indianapolis 500 and at all other AAA sanctioned race tracks. He had to resort to running the "outlaw circuit."

JULY 4, 1948   WINS 100-MILE RACE IN MICHIGAN

Although he drove to a dominant win of a 100-mile July 4th stock car race at Owosso, Michigan, he would receive a paltry first place prize of $113. And a pair of handcuffs as well. Deputy sheriffs were there to arrest Petillo in victory lane. Shiawassee County Sheriff Duane Near had his deputies arrive early at the track and were stationed in the pits and in the grandstands. "I gave the deputies permission to let him race." Petillo's appearance as star performer in the race had been widely publicized in newspapers and on radio. He bragged, "Why I even had been on a radio program here advertising this race. I plan on racing quite a bit up around here. I'm broke and need the money."

Kelly first threatened to fight extradition from Corruna, Michigan, to Indiana but on the advice of his attorney, T. Ernest Maholm, (uncle of the late Howdy Wilcox), agreed to surrender to Indianapolis detectives Edwin Bowers and Casper Kleifgen. Petillo said he could prove he was at the Harbour Hotel at 617 1/2 North Illinois Street during the time of the alleged cutting.

KELLY PETILLO——"I didn't beat her up. The last time I saw the girl was 10 days ago. She's got a lot of enemies. Any one of four or five guys could have done it.

"Why a couple of 'muscle men' started to beat me up twice during the last month and I think she had something to do with it."

JULY 6, 1948   BOUND OVER TO GRAND JURY

Naomi Shofner signed the warrant against Kelly Petillo. He would appear before Municipal Court Judge Joseph Howard who ordered bond set at $1500 on the charge of assault and battery with the intent to kill. His attorney, T. Ernest Maholm, waived a preliminary hearing. Kelly was bound over to the Marion County Grand Jury. Mrs. Mary Maio, a long-time friend of Petillo's, signed the $1500 bond.

NOVEMBER 22, 1948   JAILED BY JUDGE

Judge William Bain in Criminal Court, Division 1 raised Petillo's bond to $5000. After Mrs. Mary Majo said she no longer wanted to be the surety for Kelly because he was to hard to locate, he ordered the 1935 Indianapolis 500 winner jailed. Petillo said he had to be away to fulfill racing contracts in California and Florida. He told the court he was broke and could no longer afford an attorney. (T. Ernest Maholm had withdrawn from the case.) Public defenders William Wilson and John Lewis were assigned to his case. Kelly would be taken to the Marion County Jail.

JANUARY 17, 1949   GIVEN 1-10 TERM IN
                    FACE-SLASHING

Mrs. Shofner, possessing a deep scar on the left side of her face, appeared in court and watched the prosecution pick away at Petillo's defense. She had to listen as her past life was brought forth including the damning acknowledgement that she had been arrested 11 times on a variety of charges including child neglect. The defense made a motion for a directed verdict of not guilty on the grounds that the weapon used in the slashing was never located. That was denied and Kelly would be sentenced to a 1-to-10-year prison term. When Petillo begged Judge William Bain to reconsider the evidence, an angry Judge Bain scolded him saying, "There can be no question about who inflicted the wound. The only question is whether you did it with intent to kill her. By registering at the hotel under an assumed name indicates you planned the attack." Petillo immediately requested that they appeal the decision. He began serving his sentence at the Indiana State Prison in Michigan City on January 18, 1949. Kelly would have eight parole hearings and each one would be denied. Several appeals were made over the years but were rejected.

JANUARY 26, 1949   FILES MOTION FOR A NEW TRIAL

Aiding Kelly Petillo voluntarily, attorney Lawrence Ammons filed a motion for a new trial. Ammons said if the appeal was granted, Petillo would need a public defender because Kelly was without funds.

In November 1954, Petillo was transferred to Robert Long Hospital in Indianapolis to undergo treatment for a lung ailment. He was promptly returned back to Michigan City.

JULY 23, 1955   PAROLE APPROVED

Hugh O'Brien, State Correction Board Chairman, announced that the parole board of the State Prison in Michigan City approved Kelly Petillo's parole request subject to finding a sponsor and a place to live. They would approve the parole when his son Dr. Kelly Petillo, Jr., a Los Angeles dentist, agreed to let his father live with him. The 51-year old Petillo was officially released from the Indiana State Correctional Facility in Michigan City on August 29, 1955.

MAY 3, 1957   HUNTED AS PAROLE VIOLATOR

Hugh O'Brien announced that Kelly Petillo faced return to the State Prison for parole violation. He left California without permission. His son, Dr. Kelly Petillo, Jr., told State Parole Chief Joseph Sullivan that he believed his father was headed to the Indianapolis Motor Speedway. O'Brien indicated that when apprehended, Petillo would have to serve his remainder of his 1-to-10-year sentence. Speedway officials inquired throughout Gasoline Alley and no one had seen him at the track.

MAY 22, 1957   CAPTURED IN INDIANAPOLIS

Sgt. George McAllister and Patrolman Melvin Jordan arrested Kelly Petillo at a drugstore at Illinois and Ohio streets at 5:10 p.m. Earlier in the day Petillo had spoken with Indianapolis Star sports editor Jep Cadau to see if he could help him line up a ride to race in the Indianapolis 500. He told Jep, "I know I can do it. I want to prove to the public that it's all the car." Parole officer Robert Todd sent a squad of police to the Speedway to apprehend Petillo. Todd had been chasing him throughout the midwest at county fair race tracks where Kelly was driving under an alias.

After his apprehension at the police station, Kelly claimed he was a victim of a misunderstanding. He said he witnessed his West Coast parole officer write a letter to the Indiana parole officials which authorized his trip. Todd claimed to have never received the letter. Petillo was returned to the correctional facility on May 24 for parole violation. Paul Myers, chairman of the state board of corrections, said Petillo had been delinquent in submitting his parole reports for nearly a year. Sarcastically, he said Kelly will be "home in prison for dinner." Soon after his return, it was announced that 11 months and 29 days more will be added to his sentence as a parole violator.

MARCH 23, 1959   RELEASED FROM STATE PRISON

As soon as Kelly Petillo got his long-sought release from prison (he would not have to report to a parole officer), he immediately boarded a bus headed to Indianapolis determined to drive in the 1959 Indianapolis 500. Kelly also planned to compete in the southern stock car circuit to make money to fund his pet project. Ten years in prison couldn't hide his exuberance over a new engine that he developed—a supercharged automatic valve two-cycle internal engine. He had hoped to install his motor in a car owned by veteran Indy car owner Pete Wales.

MAY 25, 1959   FILES SUIT AGAINST THE SPEEDWAY
                & USAC

United States Auto Club president Thomas Binford ruled against a Petillo attempted comeback at the

Indianapolis Motor Speedway. Kelly promptly filed a $50,000 damage suit against the Indianapolis Motor Speedway and the United States Auto Club (USAC) charging he was wrongfully barred from competing in the Indianapolis 500. In his suit, he charged that he was refused being able to attempt to qualify for the 500-Mile race because the AAA refused to let him drive in 1946. He also charged that USAC could not continue the ban that AAA imposed because it was no longer the sanctioning body.

A year later, Petillo asked the USAC board of directors to grant him a driver's license and, in return, he would be willing to drop his $50,000 lawsuit. He also said he would not attempt to drive the entire 500 miles.

KELLY PETILLO——"I would start the car, drive the first hour or so, then yield to a relief driver.

"Then I will get back in again for the finish."

Tom Binford would finally end any hope of the 57-year-old Petillo ever being allowed to drive in the 500-Mile Race.

TOM BINFORD——"All of your associates from your racing days have come to the conclusion that their reflexes are no longer quick enough to keep them in competition and out of trouble. I know Kelly Petillo realizes that time has passed him by and it will be a bitter pill to shoulder, but it's a pill we all have to swallow sooner or later."

66-year old Calvino "Kelly" Petillo's life of turmoil ended June 30, 1970, after a long illness. He was inducted into the National Sprint Car Hall of Fame in 2009.

1961

Here for the Golden Anniversary,
Eddie Rickenbacker, Tony Hulman and
Pole Position winner Eddie Sachs.
Sachs says, "Oh boy, the **former** owner
of the Indianapolis Motor Speedway, the
current owner of the Indianapolis Motor
Speedway, and the **future** owner of the
Indianapolis Motor Speedway!!!"

21-additional drivers, who raced at least one time in the "Eddie Rickenbacker Era," also competed in the Indianapolis 500 under Tony Hulman's ownership.

EMIL ANDRES   Born: Died:
                  February 22, 1911 July 20, 1999

Emil Andres drove in nine 500-Mile Races, four times under Hulman's reign. His best finish was fourth in 1946 and ninth in 1949 in addition to 13th in 1947 and 31st in 1948. Andres would fail to qualify in 1950. He drove 1006 laps but never led the race. Emil was part of the "Chicago Gang" that included Jimmy Snyder, Paul Russo and Tony Bettenhausen. He captured the 1939 Springfield 100 and was the 1949 AAA Sprint Car Champion. In the 1938 Indy 500, Emil was seriously injured. The tire came off his race car and it struck and killed a 33-year old man. Andres was forthright why he never won the Indianapolis 500. "It was my fault I never won at Indy. I wasn't very sociable, which is why I never had a car that could win. I was rough and tough. I think you had to be that way during the Depression. You had to fight for every buck you got." During World War II, Andres served in the Army Air Force inspecting airplane engines. Emil was inducted into the National Sprint Car Hall of Fame in 1996. He is also a member of the National Midget Hall of Fame.

HERB ARDINGER   Born: Died:
                 April, 25, 1910   June 6, 1973

Because Doc Williams failed to obey orders to not complete his qualifying run, Herb Ardinger was selected to replace him in the powerful #54 Novi in 1947. Herb's last start in the 500-Mile race was in 1939. He would drive the first 69 laps before being replaced by Cliff Bergere, who would drive the remaining 131 laps and finish fourth. Ardinger started third in 1937 and led the first two laps of the race. His car would finish sixth in 1938 with relief from Cliff Bergere for 78 laps and Russ Snowberger for ten laps. In 1934, Herb's rookie year, his car finished 10th with Danny Day driving 41 relief laps.

HENRY BANKS   Born: Died:
                June 14, 1913   December 18,
                                   1994

Henry Banks captured the AAA National Driving Championship in 1950 in a tight three-way battle for the title. Banks earned 1390 points despite finishing 25th in the Indianapolis 500, Walt Faulkner with 1317 was second, Johnnie Parsons 1313 third. In 1941 he won the East Coast midget championship. Sixth in the 1951 500-Mile Race was his highest finish in six attempts. He would appear in two racing movies "To Please a Lady" starring Clark Gable and Barbara Stanwyck and the 1953 film, "The Roar of the Crowd" with Howard Duff. On May 22, 1954, both Banks and George Connor announced their retirement from auto racing. Henry would comment, "It's no fun anymore. It's too business-like now, and they're going too fast." From 1959 to 1970 Banks served as Director of Competition for the United States Auto Club (USAC). 1985 Henry was inducted into the Indianapolis Motor Speedway Hall of Fame. He is also a member of the National Midget Hall of Fame.

CLIFF BERGERE   Born: Died:
                    December 6, 1896 June 18,
                                      1980

Few drivers lived a more colorful life than Cliff Bergere. A Hollywood stuntman for 19 years, he appeared in nearly 350 movies and performed over 400 car and plane crashes. Cliff joked, "I tried all the stunts at first, but fist fights were too rough so I specialized in air plane and auto crashes." He raced in 16 Indianapolis 500s, competing in three different decades. His rookie year at Indy was 1927 and he would finish 9th. In 1946, he would qualify on the Pole Position and become the oldest Pole winner at age 49. In 1947, he would start second in the Novi, which would be his last 500-Mile Race. His best finishes were third in 1932 and 1939. In 1941, Cliff became the first person to drive the entire 500 miles non-stop in a gasoline-powered race car. He served in the Army Air Force ascending to the rank of Major. He, along with Eddie Rickenbacker were members of the secretive club, "ye Anciente and Secret Order of Quiet Birdman" for noted airmen in America. Bergere would log 6,142 miles and lead the 500-Mile

Race 35 laps. He had great pride that in all the years he drove race cars, he never spent a night in a hospital. In 1976, Cliff was inducted into the Indianapolis Motor Speedway Hall of Fame.

JOIE CHITWOOD   Born: Died:
                 April 14, 1912 January 3,
                                 1988

Born George Rice Chitwood, Joie would race in seven Indianapolis 500s scoring three 5th place finishes in 1946, 1949 and 1950 while completing 1092 laps in competition. He started the Joie Chitwood Thrill Show in 1945. It grew in popularity to where he had five units performing throughout North America until 1998. His thrill show was featured in the movie classic, "To Please a Lady" when Clark Gable's character was banned from automobile racing because of a fatal accident he had been blamed for causing. Gable's character, Mike Brennan, would resort to driving as a 'Hell Driver" for Chitwood's Thrill Show. His son, Joie Chitwood II, started performing with his father at age 5. His grandson, Joie Chitwood, served as President of the Indianapolis Motor Speedway from 2000-2004. Joie claimed to have intentionally crashed over 3,000 vehicles. He was inducted into the National Sprint Car Hall of Fame in 1993 and the Motorsports Hall of Fame of America in 2010.

GEORGE CONNOR   Born: Died:
                    August 16, 1906   March 28,
                                      2001

Connor was considered an "automatic" qualifier at the Indianapolis Motor Speedway. He would qualify for 14 straight 500-Mile Races beginning in 1935. His best finish was third in 1949. Five times he would finish in the Top Ten. He completed 1,703 laps but never led the race. On May 22, 1954, at age 46, George would announce his retirement from auto racing. The same day Henry Banks also hung up his goggles. A photographer snapped a photo of both drivers holding their helmets as they stood side-by-side. After retiring, George took a position with the Ford Motor Company.

BILLY DEVORE   Born: Died:
                    September 12,   August 12,
                    1910   1985

The son of 1927 second place finisher Earl Devore, Billy would drive in seven Indianapolis 500s. His best finish was seventh in his rookie year in 1937. Four times he would finish in the Top Ten and would drive a total of 1,244 laps. He would never lead the 500. In his final race, Billy drove a six-wheeled car to a twelfth place finish. Before he was a race driver, he served as a riding mechanic with Wilbur Shaw in 1933, who would finish 2nd.

KEN FOWLER   Born: Died:
              March 15, 1907   April 28, 1982

Ken Fowler would compete in two 500s a decade apart. In 1937, he drove a car owned by famous stunt driver Lucky Teter and would finish 19th. Ten years later Fowler would finish 15th. Ken holds the distinction of winning the first race held at the Dayton Speedway on June 3, 1934. He would have a 30-year career with Frigidaire after retiring from driving race cars.

ROLAND FREE   Born: Died:
               November 18,   October 11,
               1900   1984

For 67 years, Roland Free and Cy Marshall shared the distinction of the great gap in appearances in the Indianapolis of 17 years—1930 to 1947. (Jacques Villeneuve, 1995 Indianapolis 500 winner, would not compete in the Indy 500 again until 2014.) Free was an acclaimed motorcycle racer who would break the American Motorcycle Land-Speed record on September 13, 1948. He laid head down with his legs outstretched. The record run was dubbed, the "Bathing Suit Bike". In an attempt to streamline himself to eliminate as much air resistance as possible, he removed his helmet, pants, gloves, and boots. Roland would average 150.313 mph on his record-setting run. Free would joke, "I stole the swimming trunks idea from Ed Kretz, who used to do the same on Southern California dry lakes. Incidentally, Ed looks much nicer in a swim suit than I do." He was an Indian Motorcycle dealer in Indianapolis in 1927. During World War II, he would serve in the Army Air Force as an aircraft mechanic. Free would finish 19th in 1930 and 17th in 1947. Roland would become one of the foremost authorities in motorcycle racing. In 1998, he was inducted into the Motorcycle Hall of Fame.

SAM HANKS   Born: July 13, 1914   Died: June 27, 1994

Sam Hanks didn't let the superstition about his 13th 500-Mile Race stop him from giving it one more try to win the Indianapolis 500. Hanks had finished second in the 1956 500-Mile Race and gave serious consideration to retiring from auto racing. George Salih had an idea of laying an engine on its side to lower the center of gravity and he tried persuaded Hanks to drive it for him in the 1957 race.

Revolutionary in its design, Sam like the concept and agreed to drive it. He would even start the race in 13th position and win in dominating fashion, leading the race three-times for a total of 136 laps. A tearful Hanks would announce his retirement in Victory Lane. Tony Hulman would name him the Indianapolis Motor Speedway's Director of Competition in 1958 and he would drive the Pace Car from 1958 to 1963. Hanks finished third twice in 1952 and 1953. He would capture the 1953 AAA National Driving Championship by a whopping margin of over 400 points over Jack McGrath. Sam was victorious in the Springfield 100 and DuQuoin 100 en route to the title. Ol' Sambo would be inducted into the Indianapolis Motor Speedway Hall of Fame in 1981, the National Sprint Car Hall of Fame in 1998, the National Midget Hall of Fame in 1984 and the Motorsports Hall of Fame of America 2000.

MEL HANSEN	Born: June 8, 1898	Died: June 25, 1963

Mel Hansen loved to throw a firecracker at any individual and thought it was funny as hell when he or she jumped (Hansen didn't discriminate whose feet he'd toss them at). He quickly got the moniker the "Firecracker Kid." Hansen was extremely talented when driving a midget race car. He won the 1939 Turkey Grand Prix at Gilmore Stadium in LA at the wheel of Rex Mays midget. In 1940, he captured an unbelievable 53 midget features. Mel would compete in the Indianapolis 500 six times with 1940's eighth place finish his high-water mark. He was victorious in the 1948 Atlanta 100 and in the 1949 Springfield 100. On September 9, 1949, the 38-year old Hansen's career would come to an abrupt end when he was paralyzed with a severed spinal cord in a midget race at Motor City Speedway in Detroit. Hansen lost control of his midget as he entered turn one, hit the concrete retaining wall, then flipped end-over-end two times. Mel would recover but he would be a paraplegic and wheelchair-bound the remaining 15 years of his life. Mel Hansen would be inducted into the National Midget Hall of Fame.

TOMMY	Born:	Died:
HINNERSHITZ	April 6, 1912	August 1, 1999

Some say Tommy Hinnershitz was one of the top-three drivers to ever race on dirt. Had the Indianapolis Motor Speedway been a two-and-one-half mile dirt track, the "Flying Dutchman" would have been a multi-500 winner. Over his 30-year racing career, he was victorious in 103 AAA and USAC features. He was a seven-time AAA East Coast Sprint Car champion—1949-1952, 1955-1956 and 1959. However, his results were mediocre in the three times he drove at the Speedway beginning in 1940. Tommy finished 10th in 1941 and 9th in his final drive in 1948. Tommy Hinnershitz was inducted into the National Sprint Car Hall of Fame in 1990 and the Motorsports Hall of Fame of America in 2003.

CY MARSHALL	Born:	Died:
	April 17, 1902	December 20, 1974

17 years after his brother Paul was killed serving as his riding mechanic, Cy Marshall would race again in the Indianapolis 500. Cy would tie Roland Free as being the driver who had the greatest gap of years racing at Indy from his first Indianapolis 500 and his next one—1930 to 1947. He lost his left ear in the accident that killed his brother. Marshall drove in relief of Earl Devore in 1928. Cy became a mechanic and ran a garage near the Speedway.

HARRY   Born: Died:
McQUINN   December 13, 1905 January 1, 1986

Harry McQuinn made ten appearances in the Indianapolis 500 with his highest finishes being 7th in 1938 and 1941. He was running in 5th place in the 1936 500-Mile Race but his car would run out of gas on lap 196 and would wind up 13th. His last race at Indy was in 1948. Harry would log 1084 laps but not lead a lap. McQuinn would serve as Chief Steward for the 500 from 1953-1957. He was outstanding as a midget driver winning the 1938, 1939 and 1940 track championship at the 124th Field Artillery Armory in Chicago. Harry would win 61 feature races in 1938. He holds the distinction as the only person to land an airplane on the Indianapolis Motor Speedway. During World War II he was a reserve pilot. Harry McQuinn was inducted into the National Midget Hall of Fame in 1986.

AL MILLER   Born: Died:
                 April 28, 1907   August 18, 1967

Al Miller was an eleven-time starter in the 500-Mile Race but he had only one Top Ten finish—6th in 1934. His last Indy 500 was in 1947 when he drove the Preston Tucker Special. Al lost a leg from a motorcycle racing accident. That didn't deter him and he raced with a prosthetic leg. Miller's brother Bruce was killed in a race on July 4, 1928, at Milwaukee. His car collided with a car that had skidded in his path. Bruce Miller was thrown onto the track and was struck by a trailing car as he tried to crawl clear of the wreckage.

DUKE NALON	Born:	Died:
	March 12, 1913	February 26, 2001

No one came closer to taming the powerful Novi than Dennis "Duke" Nalon. In 1948, Ralph Hepburn was killed practicing after a two-year hiatus. After Chet Miller officially stepped out of the sister car, Duke took over the car and was the fastest-overall qualifier even though he would have to start 11th. His team had wanted to run the entire race on just one pit stop. Stopping just past the half-way mark in the race, when the gasoline tank was refilled, a vapor lock prevented filling the tank to its capacity. On lap 186, while running second to Mauri Rose, Nalon had to make an unexpected pit stop to top off his tank to make it to the finish of the race. As he was ready to leave, he stalled his car costing him two additional minutes before he was able to rejoin the pursuit. Rose's teammate Bill Holland would pass Nalon for second and Duke finishing third.

In 1949, he would win the Pole Position and Rex Mays, Nalon's teammate, would qualify second. Duke would jump to the front and remain in the top spot until lap 23, when his rear axle would break as he entered into turn three. Nalon's Novi would slam hard into the outer retaining wall. A huge fire erupted and spread down the race track. It was remarkable that Duke survived but he suffered severe burns to his legs. Two years later, he would win the Pole Position a second time. "The Iron Duke" drove 1,284 laps of competition, leading 32 circuits in his ten years competing at Indy. He won the 1938 AAA East Coast Sprint Car Championship. Duke was inducted into the Indianapolis Motor Speedway Hall of Fame in 1983, 1991 National Sprint Car Hall of Fame, 2015 Motorsports Hall of Fame of America and the National Midget Hall of Fame.

MAURI ROSE   Born: Died:
                May 26, 1906   January 1, 1981

Mauri Rose drank the milk in Victory Lane on three occasions——1941 as a co-winner with Floyd Davis and in 1947 and 1948. Mauri qualified his Maserati on the Pole in 1941, but his car would break down early in the race. Dissatisfied with Floyd Davis's pace, car owner Lou Moore ordered Davis to the pits on lap 72 and he replaced him with Rose. Mauri would take the lead on lap 162 and go on to receive the checkered flag. Rose would drive in 15 consecutive Indianapolis 500s beginning in 1933. His first AAA race win was in the 1932 Detroit 100. At Indianapolis, Rose would finish 2nd in 1934 and 3rd in 1940 and 3rd in 1950 (rain stopped the race after 345 miles). In the 1951 500-Mile Race, while running among the leaders, the 45-year old Rose crashed and his car ended upside down in turn four. He would retire from racing after this accident. Rose had an outstanding work ethic working as an engineer for Lockheed Aircraft in Burbank, California; Studebaker

Corporation in South Bend, Indiana; Allison Engineering in Speedway; Hupmobile in Detroit; General Motors Tech Centers in Warren, Michigan and American General Corp., Division of American Motors. In 1967 Rose was inducted into the Indianapolis Motor Speedway Hall of Fame and in 1991 the Motorsports Hall of Fame of America.

PAUL RUSSO   Born: Died:
                  April 10, 1914   February 13, 1976

The younger brother of the late Joe Russo, who was killed at Langhorne in 1934, Paul drove in 14 Indianapolis 500s and co-drove with Tony Bettenhausen to a second place finish in 1955. Driving the Novi in 1956, now sporting a distinctive tail fin, he quickly moved from 8th to 1st and led 11 laps before blowing a tire and crashing in turn one. The following year, he was the fastest driver in the field in the Novi. Starting 10th he would lead the race a total of 21 laps and finish fourth. In 1961, Russo was struggling to get his race car up to speed on the Friday before the First Day of Qualifications. He asked his close friend Tony Bettenhausen if he could test-hop his car. Bettenhausen would be killed in Russo's car when a bolt fell out of the radius rod causing Tony to crash atop the main straightaway wall. Paul would capture the 1938 AAA Eastern Midget Championship as well as the 1950 Springfield 100 and 1951 Detroit 100 AAA Champ Car events. Russo was inducted into the National Midget Hall of Fame in 1992.

RUSS SNOWBERGER Born: October 8, 1901 Died: September 28, 1968

Russ Snowberger won the Pole Position for the 1931 500-Mile Race and would start 2nd in 1938. He would compete in 15 Indianapolis 500s beginning in 1928 and drive 1633 total laps. His car would drop out of the 1928 Race early but later he would relieve Jimmy Gleason and lead 13 laps. On several occasions, he drove a race car powered by a stock block Studebaker motor. Russ's best results was a pair of 5th place finishes in 1931 and 1932. Snowberger would win the first race held at Langhorne, Pennsylvania. After retiring as a race driver, he was Chief Mechanic on the Federal Engineering Special. In 1985, Russ was inducted into the Michigan Motor Sports Hall of Fame.

LOUIS TOMEI Born: February 17, 1910 Died: May 15, 1955

Like Cliff Bergere, Luiji "Louis" Tomei was a stuntman in Hollywood and a race car driver. Tomei specialized in fist fights and car crashes. His speciality wound up killing him. On April 20, 1955, while on location in San Francisco Bay, Tomei was appearing in a fight scene set in a motorboat. He hit his head on the speedboat's windshield while doubling for actor Edgar G. Robinson in the movie, "Hell on Frisco Bay." Louis left San Francisco and return to his home in North Hollywood where he would complain of dizziness. It was determined that he suffered a cerebral hemorrhage and underwent surgery. The 45-year old Tomei would remain in a coma until his death on May 15.

He would drive in the Indy 500s from 1935 through 1946. His best finish was 10th in 1937. After Ernie Triplett's funeral, several race drivers took offense of a Los Angeles Examiner reporter and photographer taking photos at the gravesite. Tomei and others roughed them up. Louis would be sentenced to six months in prison causing him to miss racing in the 1934 500-Mile Race. Tomei was involved in a front page scandal of a paternity suit with a war widow, who charged he fathered her daughter Willow. That case drug on for 17 months in the newspapers.

FRANK WEARNE	Born:	Died:
	May 27, 1913	February 21, 1985

Frank Wearne came to Indianapolis with the reputation as a young, talented race driver but he never was able to back up his reputation. Frank would race at the Speedway seven times beginning in 1937. Although never displaying a front runner status, he did have a run of five consecutive Top Ten results——1938, 10th—1939, 9th—1940, 7th—1941 & 1946, 8th.

DOC WILLIAMS   Born: Died:
                    October 20, 1912 April 28, 1982

Merrill "Doc" Williams made an appearance at the
Speedway from 1933 to 1949 but he would only start
four races—1936, 1940, 1941 and 1948. In 1947, Doc
experienced the ultimate of humiliation when he was
removed as driver of the Novi after he failed to abort his
qualifying run. It was a speed much lower than owner
Lew Welch had expected. His pit crew had frantically
gestured for him to not take the checkered flag but
he ignored their orders and finished the run. Herb
Ardinger was selected to replace him. Williams would
also drive hot rods. After retiring from driving, he ran
a motel in Richmond, Indiana.

※ ※ ※

Fifteen outstanding drivers drove in the International
500-Mile Sweepstakes when Eddie Rickenbacker owned
the Speedway, but would not compete in the 500 under
Tony Hulman's ownership following the conclusion of
World War II. They either won the Race, led the Race,
should have won the Race, won the Pole, was the Fastest
Qualifier, or who was tempted and almost came out of
retirement to drive the Brickyard one last time——Billy
Arnold, Frank Brisko, Floyd Davis, Peter De Paolo, Leon
Duray, Fred Frame, Tony Gulotta, Harry Hartz, Ronney
Householder, Louis Meyer, Tommy Milton, Lou Moore,
George Souders, Babe Stapp and Cliff Woodbury.

BILLY ARNOLD   Born: Died:
                December 16,   November 10,
                1905   1976

After retiring just before his 27th birthday, Bill Arnold would join Chrysler Corporation as an engineer. He would earn a B.S. degree in Mechanical Engineering at the University of Illinois and a Ph.D. from the Michigan Institute of Technology. A week after Pearl Harbor he would enlist in the Army Air Corps as an engineer and pilot. Arnold would serve under General Dwight Eisenhower as chief of maintenance for the 8th Air Force. Billy would leave the armed service in 1945 as a one-star general.

For five years he was an auto dealer in Oklahoma City before entering the lumber and construction business. Between 1950 and 1958 he develop Aqua King water skis which became the official water ski of Cypress Gardens in Florida. Billy would die of a cerebral hemorrhage in 1976 at the age of 66. Arnold was inducted into the Indianapolis Motor Speedway Hall of Fame in 1977.

FRANK BRISKO   Born: Died:
                August 24, 1900 November 26,
                                 1990

A 12-time starter in the Indianapolis 500, Frank qualified on the front row twice and his 69 laps led in the 1934 race topped his competitors. He was highly regarded as an engine designer having built three-quarters of Bill

Cumming's winning motor in the 1934 500-Mile Race. In 1936 he designed a six-cylinder engine with a double-overhead camshaft and would continue to refine this motor over the next five years. Frank oversaw a crew of mechanics who operated out of a Chicago garage at 5530 W. Irving Park Road.

His son, Gerald Brisko, was groomed as his right hand man. Gerald was a pilot of a P-61 night fighter and he earned four battle stars during 14 months of service in the Pacific. He was a decorated "Black Widow" pilot with the 548th Night Fighter Squadron. The younger Brisko was head mechanic for Emil Andres in the 1946 Indianapolis 500 and was prepared to serve as relief driver for Andres's Maserati if needed. On June 26, 1950, Gerald was one of three people killed in a two-car, head-on collision in heavy fog northwest of Chicago. Five other passengers were injured. After the death of his son, Frank founded Brisko Mille Saver Company, a parts manufacture, in Wisconsin. He also ran a dairy farm in Madison, Wisconsin. Frank would die at his home in Radisson, Wisconsin at age 90.

FLOYD DAVIS	Born:	Died:
	March 5, 1904	May 31, 1977

Floyd Davis always claimed he would have won the 1941 Indianapolis 500 had Lou Moore not made a driver change and replaced him with Mauri Rose on lap 72. Rose's Maserati, which started on the Pole, dropped out early in the race. Officially Floyd would be declared co-winner, even though he did not lead a lap in the race. It had been said that Floyd was so disgusted about being removed from the seat, he chose never to compete at Indianapolis again.

Floyd worked at Detroit Diesel Allison for nine years before becoming a salesman for Hall-Neal, Peerless Heating and Air Conditioning Company. Even into his retirement years, he was still semi-employed as a general contractor. Davis died at home the day after the 1977 Indianapolis 500. Earlier that month Floyd suffered a heart seizure just before a Borg-Warner reception honoring past 500-Miler winners. He had been scheduled to have open-heart surgery in June.

PETER DE PAOLO   Born: Died:
                  April 6, 1898 November 26,
                                 1980

After seeing his mother so excited that her brother won the 1915 Indianapolis, Pete De Paolo told his mom he was going to accomplish the same feat some day. Initially, he would serve as a riding mechanic for Uncle Ralph before embarking on his own racing career. However, when Pete first started driving, he did not demonstrate any particular talent behind the wheel. In fact, he crashed more than most of his fellow competitors, helping him earn the nickname "Little Wall Smacker". Ten years later, he fulfilled his promise, by winning the 1925 Indianapolis driving his yellow Duesenberg to victory—the first person to average above 100 m.p.h.

Pete called his car the "Banana Wagon." It was this race car that he tied a pair of his young son Tommy's baby shoes to the front axle for good luck. Pete would win the AAA National Driving Championship in 1927 and 1927.

De Paolo would retire after the 1930 Indianapolis 500 to take a position with Chrysler Corporation. However, the opportunity to race in Europe in the Grand Prix circuit was too tempting. In 1934, while practicing on the city streets of Barcelona, he would deliberately crash his Maserati race car when he saw a boy run across the road as he was rounding a corner. Pete swerved and the resulting crash left him in a coma for 11 days. He would announce his "permanent" retirement from his hospital bed. Pete lost a vast amount of his personal fortune with the stock market crash in 1929 and in the Great Depression. In 1935 DePaolo wrote his autobiography, "Wall Smacker." Racing people jokingly say that Pete personally autographed so many of his books that only non-signed books are valuable.

Later in life he picked up the moniker "Toastmaster of Racing" as he crisscrossed America lecturing on a variety of auto racing subjects. Pete became a team manager for the Ford Motor Company's entry into stock car racing. Later he was employed with the American Rubber and Plastic Company. In 1971, the 73-year old Pete DePaolo sang the traditional "Back Home Again in Indiana" before the start of the 500-Mile Race. Pete would lose his two-year battle with cancer, dying at his home in Laguna Hills, California on November 26, 1980 at age 82.

LEON DURAY   Born: Died:
                       April 4, 1894 May 12, 1956

Few people were as intimidating as the big, gruff Leon Duray. His birth name was George Stewart but track promoter Alex Sloan changed his name before a race in New Orleans to cover up that his race headliner, Frenchman Arthur Duray, was a no-show. After the race, Creole fans came by to meet Leon speaking in French, a language he could not speak. Leon was one of the most colorful daredevil-type drivers at the Speedway in the 1920's. He would capture the coveted Pole Position in 1925 and 1928 and would start in the front row five consecutive years. His one-lap track record of 124.018 mph stood for nine years. Almost always Duray would wear black racing coveralls and his race cars were often painted black.

His eyesight went bad and he became a car owner—sometimes having tragic consequences—as both his drivers Johnny Hannon and Clay Weatherly were killed in the same car—Hannon killed on his initial practice lap and Weatherly on lap 9 in the 1935 500-Mile Race. In his garage at the Speedway, he posted a sign that read—"Worry Dept. $1.25 an Hour." Leon had a stool in the front of his garage where he would sit and contemplate ways to develop an engine that would give him an advantage over the rest of the field.

Wilbur Shaw would finish second for him in 1933 and Mauri Rose was runner-up a year later. He would provide eventual 500 winner Sam Hanks his first ride at Indy in 1940. In the later stages of his life, Leon owned a realty business in Twentynine Palms, California. He suffered with a heart ailment for several years and would have a stroke in late April in 1956. On May 12, 1956 Leon suffered a second stroke and died at age 61.

FRED FRAME   Born: Died:
                June 3, 1894   April 25, 1962

On August 17, 1947 Fred Frame, winner of the 1932 Indianapolis 500 and runner-up the year before, learned the tragic news that his son Bob was killed in a racing crash at Owatonna, Minnesota, at the Steele County Fairgrounds. His car overturned twice and tore through the track fence. Bob was hurtled from his race car, landing 40 feet from his crashed racer. The younger Frame was driving with one arm in a cast. On August 10, the opening night of the All-Iowa fair at Cedar Rapids, Bob Frame was injured when his race car crashed into the tow truck during warm-ups. He suffered two cracked ribs and a broken wrist. Track officials tried to discourage him from racing. 66-year old Fred Frame would suffer a fatal heart attack at his home in Hayward, California on April 25, 1962. He was inducted into the Indianapolis Motor Speedway Hall of Fame in 1984.

TONY GULOTTA   Born: Died:
                             August 4, 1903   March 2,
                                                 1981

Like Babe Stapp and Harry Hartz, Tony Gulotta was one of the best race drivers who survived a career as a race driver, and not win the Indianapolis 500. Gulotta came gut-wrenchingly close to winning in both 1928 and 1931. Unlike Stapp and Hartz, he was never a seriously injured driving like the two of them. One thing Tony was noted for was to do physical training by lapping the Speedway on his bicycle. After retiring from racing, Gulotta worked for the Ford Motor Company at their test track in Dearborn, Michigan. The 78-year old Tony Gulotta lived in Canoga Park, California, at the time of his death.

HARRY HARTZ   Born: Died:
                             December 24,   September 26,
                             1896   1974

Harry Hartz was a rookie in the 500-Mile Race in 1922 and would begin five consecutive years of qualifying in the front row including 2nd four times. If Harry Hartz had less scruples, he would have been the co-winner of the 1930 Indianapolis 500. Not yet entirely recovered from the severe injuries to his leg, Hartz would miss the 1928 and 1929 Indianapolis 500s. However, with

Eddie Rickenbacker mandating the "junk formula" and the return to the riding mechanic for the 1930 500-Mile Race, Harry would build a car from various parts. He felt certain that his car would win the 500-Mile Race with the new regulations Rickenbacker had imposed.

The car wound up dominating the race with Billy Arnold leading the remaining 198 laps after Louis Meyer grabbed the top spot for the first two circuits. Hartz had actually posted a speed during his qualification run that would have earned the outside starting position in the front row. But Harry returned to the pits before completing the run and offered the car to Arnold, believing there was a lot more speed in the car than he was unable to get from the car. Arnold would take advantage of this opportunity and qualify on the Pole. In the late stages of the race he held a 10-lap lead over second place rookie, Shorty Cantlon. Hartz could have ordered Arnold into the pits and taken over the driving chores in the car.

Arnold was leading by a sizable margin in both the 1931 and 1932 races, only to crash over the retaining wall. Fred Frame, driving the team car to Arnold, would finish second in 1931 and would be the winner in 1932. Hartz would win permanent possession of the 7-1/2 foot, silver Wheeler-Schebler Trophy for leading at the 400-mile mark for three consecutive years. Also, Harry would appear as himself in the James Cagney racing movie, "The Crowd Roars". Ted Horn would also place second in a Harry Hartz car in 1936.

He was alleged to have driven a DeSoto backwards across the United States in 1933 and would serve as a stunt driver at the Chrysler Exhibit at the Chicago World's Fair in 1933. In 1934 Harry would set 72 new AAA stock car records at the Bonneville Salt Flats in Utah. Later he would serve as vice-chairman the technical committees for both the American Automobile Association then later with the United States Auto Club. The 77-year old Harry Hartz would die on September 26, 1974. He was inducted into the Indianapolis Motor Speedway Hall of Fame in 1963 and the National Sprint Car Hall of Fame in 1998.

RONNEY HOUSEHOLDER	Born: May 8, 1908	Died: November 11, 1972

Decades have passed but Ronney Householder still holds the track record for fastest qualifying speed of 125.769 mph set in 1938. It is a record that will most likely will never be broken because there was a ten-lap requirement for a qualification attempt. Householder raced in just two Indianapolis 500s in 1937 and 1938. The following year, he came close to drowning at the Speedway when his car crashed and landed upside-down in the creek that flowed through the infield side of the track in turn one. His shunt caused him to quit running Indy cars. Ronney, National Midget champion in

1934, would continue racing midgets and be regarded as one of the finest midget racers of all-time, finally retiring in 1947. Among his career highlights, he would capture the Detroit Coliseum championship in 1935 and score back-to-back victories in the prestigious Turkey Night Grand Prix at Gilmore Stadium in 1936 and 1937. During World War II, Householder would rise to the rank of lieutenant colonel. Following the war, Ronney would acquire several radio stations.

After retiring from driving, Householder, who graduated in engineering from the University of Southern California, went to work for Chrysler Corporation from 1955 thru 1972. He became the high performance director for their stock car program and would become one of the most powerful corporate executives in the automotive industry. Under his no-holds-barred leadership from 1964 through 1971, Chrysler dominated in stock car racing as Richard Petty would win multiple NASCAR Cup championships and Daytona 500s. On November 11, 1972, 64-year old Ronney Householder would succumb to lung cancer. Ronney was inducted into the National Midget Hall of Fame in 1984.

LOUIS MEYER   Born: Died:
                July 21, 1904 November 7,
                               1995

The first three-time winner of the Indianapolis 500 lived a full life centered around auto racing. Louis introduced the tradition of drinking milk in Victory Lane in 1936 when he was handed his favorite beverage, a cold bottle of buttermilk. The Dairy Association saw a photo of Louis drinking what they believed to be milk in the Winner's Circle and decided to offer a cash prize for future winners to drink "milk" in celebration of their win.

In 1939, Louis was in a strong position to win his fourth 500-Mile Race until he blew a tire late in the Race. After a pitstop for a new tire, he mounted a banzai charge after the new race leader Wilbur Shaw. Three laps before the finish the race he was be involved in a nasty-looking crash in his Bowes Seal Fast Special. Uninjured, he retired en route to the track infield hospital. The decision was made easier when Henry Ford said, "If you're sure you're done driving, I want you working at the Ford Motor Company." Meyer accepted.

He would serve as Rex Mays's pit manager on Race Day in 1940. It was Bob Bowes hope that Meyer could temper Mays's hard-charging manner and slow him down enough where his car would last the entire 500 Miles. They succeeded as Mays would finish second both in 1940 and 1941. In 1946 Louis Meyer and Dale Drake bought the engine plant from Fred Offenhauser and began building the Meyer-Drake racing engine which would win every Indianapolis 500 from 1947 through 1964. Later that year he sold his interest in the company to his partner, Dale Drake. Meyer became the distributor for the Ford Motor Company's racing engine.

Louis's wife June died in 1990. Louis Meyer would die on November 7, 1995 in a Las Vegas hospital at age 91.

TOMMY MILTON   Born: Died:
November 14,   July 10,
1893   1962

Known as the "Babe Ruth" of race drivers during the Roaring Twenties, Tommy Milton would win the Indianapolis 500 twice in 1921 and 1923, despite have eyesight in just one eye. During that time frame, he was embroiled in a much publicized feud with his former mechanic and now chief rival on the race track, Jimmy Murphy. It was a battle of one-upmanship between Milton and Murphy. Jimmy would capture the 1922 Indianapolis 500. However, the feud ended tragically on September 15, 1924, when Murphy was killed at Syracuse. A grief stricken Milton took responsibility for the return of Murphy's body to Los Angeles for burial.

Milton's only serious injury occurred at Uniontown, Pennsylvania, when his car caught fire. He was severely burned and spent several months in the hospital. After retiring from racing, Tommy became a service engineer for the Packard Motor Car Company. He gave to Louis Meyer, after his third win in 1936, the Packard Pace Car which began the tradition of the new winner getting the key to the car that paced the race. From 1949 to 1953 he was Chief Steward of the Indianapolis 500. He would serve as president and general manager of

Hercules Forging Company. Milton also started Milton Engineering Company.

The 68-year old Tommy Milton would commit suicide on July 10, 1962. He shot himself twice in the chest with a .22 caliber pistol. Tommy had been in poor health, having suffering several heart attacks in recent years, plus he had two bouts with pneumonia the past two months. His brother Milton told authorities he had made funeral arrangements for the following week. Tommy Milton was inducted into the Indianapolis Motor Speedway Hall of Fame in 1954, the National Sprint Car Hall of Fame in 1992 and the Motorsports Hall of Fame of America in 1998.

LOU MOORE   Born: Died:
                September 12, 1904 March 25,
                                   1956

For nearly forty years, Lou Moore was the winningest Indy 500 car owner—1938 Floyd Roberts, 1941 Floyd Davis/Mauri Rose, 1947 & 1948 Mauri Rose again, and Bill Holland in 1949. Had the 1950 Indianapolis 500 had gone the distance instead of 345 miles, Holland might well have caught race winner Johnnie Parsons. Prior to becoming a prominent car owner, he was successful as a race driver qualifying on the Pole in 1932, plus he would finish second in 1928 and third in 1933 and 1934.

Lou Moore would invest nearly all his money to build the two Blue Crown Specials for the 1947 Race with Mauri

Rose and rookie Bill Holland tapped as his drivers. 1947 would be the year when he displayed on a pit board to both drivers saying "E-Z." Holland slowed down, and believing he was a lap ahead, waved at Rose when Mauri passed him on lap 193. Moore would say later that Rose's victory cost him more money since he was driving for 10% more than the rookie Holland.

Lou quit racing when his good friend Chet Miller, out practicing at near record speeds, crash to his death in the Novi in May, 1953. Moore would then venture into the construction and real estate business in Fort Lauderdale in 1950. Three months before his death, Lou Moore took the position with Pontiac supervising the production of their stock cars. While in the pits at Lakewood Speedway near Atlanta, Lou suffered a massive brain hemorrhage and would die soon after arrival at Grady Memorial Hospital. Moore, who lived most of his life in southern California, had recently moved to 1101 Elmhurst in Indianapolis. He was survived by his wife Marian and two-small sons—Gary, age 4 and Thomas, age 3. Lou Moore was inducted into the Indianapolis Motor Speedway Hall of Fame in 1969.

GEORGE SOUDERS	Born:	Died:
	September 11, 1900	July 28, 1976

After winning as a rookie in 1927 and finishing third in 1928, George Souders was seriously injured in July at Detroit, ending his racing career. Souders, who had taken engineering classes at Purdue University, had prior to his near-fatal accident, purchased a tire business in Ohio. He would live most of his life in Lafayette, Indiana, his boyhood home. For many years he operated a filling station at 10th and Ferry streets. The trailer he was living in burned six days before Christmas in 1974. Most of his clothes and furniture were lost in the fire. The Indianapolis 500 Oldtimes Club helped find him a place to live in Indianapolis and replaced items lost in the fire. When he could no longer afford to pay his dues, he was given a lifetime membership in the Lafayette Elks Club. He would suffer a stroke and would return to his native Lafayette to undergo physical therapy. At age 75, he was found dead in his cluttered apartment strewn with old newspapers and lots of garbage throughout.

BABE STAPP	Born:	Died:
	February 26, 1904	September 17, 1980.

Egbert "Babe" Stapp, nicknamed the "Boy Wonder", was one of the finest, perhaps the best race car driver to compete during the Eddie Rickenbacker Era who survived a career in racing but never won the Indianapolis 500. He was seriously injured several times and his passion for the sport lured him back to the cockpit. It would take the birth of his son Steve to cause Babe to finally hang up the goggles. After his retirement from racing, he served as a racing promoter and official. Babe would start a successful air conditioning business in Hollywood, California. In 1973, he would move from Sherman Oaks, California to Brownsburg, Indiana, to be near his son Steve, who operated a very successful race team mainly chauffeured by Pancho Carter. Babe operated a car wash in Brownsburg until he suffered a stroke. After a long illness, 76-year old Babe Stapp would die at Methodist Hospital in Indianapolis. Babe was inducted into the National Sprint Car Hall of Fame in 1994 and son Steve joined him in their HOF in 1999.

CLIFF WOODBURY   Born: Died:
                  July 8, 1894 November 13,
                                1984

Early on in his racing career, he was a performer in Ruth Law's Flying Circus. Cliff, in his Duesenberg race car, would race around the track with Law's plane speeding overhead. The show would include wing-walkers and an act where a rope ladder was lowered from the airplane and join to Cliff's race car. Referred to as the "Dashing Windy City Demon", Cliff Woodbury was the unofficial champion for one-mile dirt tracks in 1923-24-25. His rookie year at Indianapolis he finished third even though he discovered the day before the race that his cylinder block was cracked. Woodbury added Stop Leak to the radiator several times throughout the race and, to his surprise, the motor held together for 500 miles. In 1927, he won the first AAA Dirt Track Champion.

Cliff Woodbury had the good fortune to get to pilot Iron Mike Boyle's race cars. The electrical union boss from Chicago made Cliff the captain of his Boyle AAA team. Woodbury got caught up in the fatal crash of Ray Keech on June 15, 1929, at Altoona. Originally medical rescue people thought the unconscious Woodbury was also killed and they left him in the ambulance instead of rushing him the local hospital. In the family produced book, "The Racing Career of Clifford Ray Woodbury", they tell of his wife Sadie being in labor at the time of his accident. She prayed to St. Theresa that if she would allow her husband to survive, she would name the baby after her. Cliff did recover from his injuries and the child was named Trixie. Cliff would spend five weeks in the hospital and upon his release announced he promised his wife that he was retiring from racing. It didn't take much persuasion for him to accept the chance to set a new one-mile speed record at Daytona Beach, Florida. He was timed at 180.90 mph in establishing the new mark.

Cliff had started second in the 1928 Indianapolis and was on the Pole for the start of the 1929 500-Mile race. He would crash his car on lap 4 but would return to the race as a relief driver in three different race cars. All would fail to go the distance. He and his brother, Elmer, ran a successful garage—WOODBURY BROTHERS GARAGE—located at 4918 Madison Street in Chicago.

OCTOBER 11, 1972   RICKENBACKER'S BEGINNING OF THE END

Eddie and Adelaide had flown down to their villa in Key Biscayne, Florida three days before his 82nd birthday on October 8. His life would experience a major medical change when he suffered a stroke and was rushed to Mercy Hospital in Miami in critical condition. Initially he was unable to speak and had no use of his left arm. His long-time personal physician, Dr. John Handwerker, remarked, "When you talk about him, he's a legend, and when you talk about him medically, he's legendary. The man seems to be working on the 10th of his nine lives." Rickenbacker would eventually be transferred to nearby Lutheran Medical Center for physical therapy. He would be released to return home on January 18, 1973.

Adelaide's eyesight had been deteriorating so Eddie decided to take her for treatment by an eye specialist in Zurich, Switzerland. On July 5, four days after he and his wife had arrived in Zurich, Eddie would be hospitalized in Neumenster Hospital in Zurich for a heart condition.

JULY 23, 1973   RICKENBACKER DIES IN SWITZERLAND

Captain Edward V. Rickenbacker would suffer a fatal heart attack on July 23, 1973. Eddie held the belief, "The easiest thing in the world is to die—the hardest is to live." He would proudly boast, "I've cheated the old Grim Reaper seven times that I know of." (Eight after his stroke in 1972). In addition to all his military awards he earned, Rickenbacker was inducted into the Indianapolis Motor Speedway Hall of Fame in 1954, the National Sprint Car Hall of Fame in 1992 and the Motorsports Hall of Fame of America in 1994.

The body of Eddie Rickenbacker was cremated and flown back to the United States. Services were held on July 27, 1973, at the Key Biscayne Presbyterian Church in Miami, Florida. The following Tuesday, July 31, a second service was held at Marble Collegiate Church on Fifth Avenue, New York. On August 10, The Rev. Richard C. Reynolds, associate minister of North Broadway United Methodist Church in Columbus, Ohio, officiated at the final memorial service in the marble chapel of Green Lawn cemetery. In his eulogy Rev. Reynolds would state, "Eddie Rickenbacker not only witnessed but took part in the most astounding changes of life on this planet. He has come home to the city of his origin." 100 mourners attended his final services.

At the conclusion of the service four Air Force F-4 Phantom jet fighters roared overhead performing the "missing buddy" formation as the Air Force saluted Col. Rickenbacker one last time.

FEBRUARY 2, 1977   ADELAIDE COMMITS SUCIDE

Despondent having lost her eyesight and for being in failing health the past five years, Adelaide took a pistol and shot herself in the head in her Key Biscayne villa's upstairs bedroom on February 2, 1977. Her niece Nedra Swasey was downstairs the dining room when the shot was fired at 9:05 p.m. She telephoned Ed Yarnell, director for governmental affairs for Eastern Airlines and a close family friend, for help. He came immediately and discovered Mrs. Rickenbacker lying on her bed mortally wounded. A fire rescue unit came and transported her to Mercy Hospital in Miami where she died at 11:30 p.m. Surviving immediate family members included adopted sons William and David Rickenbacker.

Acknowledgments

A special thank you to these individuals who helped contribute to the completion of "The Eddie Rickenbacker Era" book. Without your help, this could not have been accomplished.

Nancy dela Roca, Corinna Miller, Hector Cademartori, Gary Irvin, Corey Coulson, Bill Shaw, Johnny Pappas, Tom Malloy, Bob Schilling, Rex Mays Jr., Mauri & Mickie Rose Jr., John Snowberger, Sonnie Turner, Bob Gates, Tim Considine, Doug Sholty, Jeff Sholty, Sam Mudd, Suzanne Stapp, Steve Stapp, Rick Hammer, Lindell Lummer, Lynn Paxton, Stephen Budd, Beth Wishard, Gary Schroeder, Harry Whitman, Bob Baker, Bill Wright, Larry Ball, Tom Skaggs, Sonny & Sue Meyer, Scott Balch, Bill & Louise Barringer, Robert Baumann, Buzz Rose, Fred Chaparro, Pat & Barbara Culligan, Mark Dill, David Story, Sage Miller, Grayson Miller, Buddy Urbanski, Mike Flaherty, Dave Ondo, Jeanette Lopp, Brenda Smith, Eve Ardell, Melanie Lear, Joe Scaggs & the staff at Author House.

And a most special thanks to my good buddy Kobe Miller!!! (11/11/2001— 3/3/2020)

CPSIA information can be obtained
at www.ICGtesting.com
Printed in the USA
LVHW110051301220
675349LV00014B/140/J